Crony Comprador Capitalism

Jianyong Yue

Crony Comprador Capitalism

The Institutional Origins of China's Rise and Decline

palgrave
macmillan

Jianyong Yue
London School of Economics
and Political Science
London, UK

ISBN 978-3-031-53153-8 ISBN 978-3-031-53154-5 (eBook)
https://doi.org/10.1007/978-3-031-53154-5

This Palgrave Macmillan imprint is published by the registered company Springer Nature Switzerland AG
The registered company address is: Gewerbestrasse 11, 6330 Cham, Switzerland

Preface

In the past two decades, various terms such as the Beijing Consensus, market authoritarianism, and state capitalism have been used to describe the Chinese model of development. These concepts have often attributed China's economic success to effective market-oriented reforms under the auspices of a strong and autonomous state. However, this book offers a different perspective. While acknowledging the introduction of market capitalism within China's Communist system, it refrains from prematurely concluding that China's economic success is inevitable and raises doubts about the "rise of China" thesis.

This skepticism arises from a global oversight in international scholarship—a phenomenon known as China's "comprador capitalism." Surprisingly, this concept has either intentionally or unintentionally been overlooked. The oversight can be attributed to the impressive growth miracle and a tendency to equate growth with development. Additionally, it is influenced by pragmatic considerations, as proponents of the new Cold War narrative, both in China and the West, remain reticent to classify China as an adherent of comprador capitalism.

In my prior work, published in 2018 by Palgrave Macmillan under the title *China's Rise in the Age of Globalization: Myth or Reality?*, I introduced the concept of "crony comprador capitalism." It emerges as a result of the convergence between China's market Leninism and global capitalism. In a recent article published in *Global Policy* in January 2022, entitled "The Limits to China's Peaceful Rise—Deep Integration and a New Cold War," I underscored the critical role of crony comprador capitalism as an internal factor impeding China's ascent. This concept generated significant interest among reviewers, who expressed a desire for a more comprehensive exploration.

However, it is essential to underscore that this concept did not occupy the central focus of that earlier article. Toward the end of the same year, a distinguished scholar specializing in Chinese studies in North America, who had been invited by an SSCI-indexed journal to curate a series on China's transition to capitalism, approached me. I contributed an article that delved into the intricacies of China's crony comprador capitalism. Regrettably, despite the organizer's acknowledgment of its scholarly caliber, this article faced outright rejection by the journal owing to its perceived "high political sensitivity." Both the organizer and I subsequently unearthed the concealed affiliations of the journal. This compelled me to seek publication elsewhere. Even *Foreign Affairs* declined, stating that "it is not for us."

Given the profound intricacies surrounding this issue, I resolved to expand this research into a comprehensive book. This book aims to undertake an exhaustive inquiry into the nature of the China model and its implications. It also seeks to shed light on a possible *liberal* alternative pathway of development within the existing liberal international order.

This book posits that China's crony capitalism, which emerged and evolved over the years, owes its roots to Deng Xiaoping's market-socialist reforms of the 1980s, primarily driven by influential princelings and their New Class patrons, notably Chen Yun. The foundations of this embryonic system began to take hold with the advent of market Leninism, a pivotal moment occurring after Deng's historic southern tour in early 1992. Concurrently, Mao's self-reliant socialist policies, facing faltering progress, compelled the post-Mao leadership to pivot their economic focus outward, a shift that commenced in the mid-1980s.

Following the landmark year of 1992, comprador capitalism gained rapid ascendancy as comprador elites, in exchange for the promises of export-driven economic growth, departed from economic nationalism in favor of adopting Western liberal economic doctrines. They championed reforms reminiscent of the Washington Consensus, akin to "shock therapy," and embraced an anti-nationalist development strategy.

The fusion of China's unique brand of market Leninism with global capitalism ultimately gave rise to a distinctive form of capitalism: crony comprador capitalism. This system's institutionalization became evident following China's accession to the World Trade Organization (WTO) in December 2001. This system, inherently at odds with both Marxism and democracy, propelled the Communist regime through robust economic growth while simultaneously setting the nation on a trajectory of dependency, increasing vulnerability to the precarious "middle-income trap." The entrenched grip of crony comprador capitalism triggered what can aptly be termed a Chinese "Tocquevillian Moment," rendering the nominally Communist system resistant to substantive reform. Given China's monumental scale, its emergence as an input-driven economic powerhouse within the semi-peripheral sphere has amplified global tensions rather than fostering international harmony.

In this complex context, Xi Jinping's tenure since assuming power in 2012 holds little promise of success, given his aversion to both socialism and liberal democracy. For Western policymakers, in stark contrast to decades of engagement that inadvertently nurtured a "Frankenstein," the imperative now lies in decoupling. This strategy is vital to facilitate China's transition toward democracy and its transformation into a democratic developmental state, all within a reformed global economic framework that prioritizes development and stability. Such a transition would make the world safer for democracy, rather than autocracy.

London, UK Jianyong Yue

Acknowledgements

Throughout the process of researching and writing this book, I have had the privilege of sharing my ideas with numerous scholars, whose invaluable feedback enriched and inspired my perspective on Chinese politics, the nature of the regime, and global politics. I extend my sincere gratitude to Professor MacGregor Knox, Professor Michael Cox of the London School of Economics and Political Science, Professor Yinghong Cheng of Delaware State University, and Professor Guoguang Wu of the Stanford Center on China's Economy and Institutions, Stanford University for dedicating their time to read my manuscript and provide constructive feedback. To my friends in academia and other institutions currently residing in China, whose names I must regrettably withhold for understandable reasons, I offer my heartfelt thanks for their selfless and generous assistance in the production of this book. Their insights have served as an additional wellspring of inspiration, deepening my understanding of the character of the party state and the China model.

I also wish to express my profound appreciation to my publishers, Ellie Duncan, Aishwarya Balachandar, and the copy editor. My deepest gratitude is reserved for my wife, Diana, with all my love.

Contents

About the Author

Jianyong Yue holds a Ph.D. in Political Science from the London School of Economics and Political Science (LSE). His most recent publication is *China's Rise in the Age of Globalization: Myth or Reality?* (Palgrave Macmillan, 2018). He formerly taught Chinese politics and development at King's College London and at the LSE. He is currently conducting research as a visiting fellow at the LSE.

Abbreviations

AI	Artificial Intelligence
AML	Anti-Monopoly Law
AUKUS	Trilateral Security Pact between Australia, the United Kingdom, and the United States
BIT	Bilateral Investment Treaty
CAI	Comprehensive Agreement on Investment
CAS	Chinese Academy of Sciences
CASS	Chinese Academy of Social Sciences
CCP	Chinese Communist Party
CDIC	Central Disciplinary Inspection Committee
CER	China Eastern Railway
CFIUS	Committee on Foreign Investment in the United States
CFR	Council on Foreign Relations
CIGA	Centre for International Governance Innovation
CNC	Computerized Numerical Control
CoCom	Coordinating Committee for Multilateral Export Controls
Comintern	Communist International
CPSU	Communist Party of the Soviet Union
CPTPP	Comprehensive and Progressive Agreement for Trans-Pacific Partnership
CSIS	Center for Strategic and International Studies
DPRK	Democratic People's Republic of Korea
DRC	Development Research Centre of the State Council
EMAT	Exchange Market Access for Technology
EOI	Export-Oriented Industrialization
EPA	Economic Partnership Agreement

FDI	Foreign Direct Investment
FIEs	Foreign-Invested Enterprises
GATS	General Agreement on Trade in Services
GATT	General Agreement on Tariffs and Trade
GPA	Agreement on Government Procurement
IEA	International Energy Agency
IEEPA	International Economic Emergency Power Act
IISS	International Institute of Strategic Studies
IPE	International Political Economy
ISI	Import-Substituting Industrialization
JCCT	Joint Commission on Commerce and Trade
KMT	Kuomintang, the Nationalist Party of China
M&A	Mergers and Acquisition
MDG	Millennium Development Goals
MIIT	Ministry of Industry and Information Technology
MITI	Ministry of International Trade and Industry (Japan)
MNCs	Multinational Corporations
MOFCOM	Ministry of Commerce
MOFTEC	Ministry of Foreign Trade and Economic Cooperation
NDAA	National Defense Authorization Act
NDCs	Now-Developed Countries
NDRC	National Development and Reform Commission
NIEs	Newly Industrialized Economies
NPC	National People's Congress
NRGs	New Red Guards
NSI	National System of Innovation
NSS	National Security Strategy
ODA	Official Development Assistance
ONDI	Office of the Director of National Intelligence
ORGs	Old Red Guards
PBOC	People's Bank of China
PCAOB	Public Company Accounting Oversight Board
PCT	Patent Cooperation Treaty
PLA	People's Liberation Army
PLAN	People's Liberation Army Navy
PTT	Power Transition Theory
QFII	Qualified Foreign Institutional Investors
PRC	People's Republic of China
ROK	Republic of Korea
SAIC	State Administration of Industry and Commerce
SBS	State Bureau of Statistics
SEC	U.S. Securities and Exchange Commission
SOEs	State-Owned Enterprises

S&ED	U.S.-China Strategic and Economic Dialogue
TNCs	Transnational Corporations
TPP	Trans-Pacific Partnership
Triad	The United States, the EU, and Japan
TRIMs	Trade-Related Investment Measures
TRIPs	Trade-Related Aspects of Intellectual Property Rights
TTC	Technology and Trade Council
USCC	U.S.-China Economic and Security Review Commission
USTR	United States Trade Representative
WIPO	World Intellectual Property Organization
WOFE	Wholly-Owned Foreign Enterprises
WTO	World Trade Organization

List of Figures

List of Tables

CHAPTER 1

Introduction

Virtually no country in the world views today's China as a socialist state.[1] Although some far-right Western parties and politicians may insist that they are engaging in a life-or-death struggle with "Chinese Communism," serious and pragmatic politicians in the West, such as Joe Biden, would prefer to use neutral terms such as "autocracy" to describe the Chinese party state.[2] It is indeed the case that today's China is anything but Communist. Since the mid-1990s, international scholarship, especially that of the New Leftists, has recognized China's swift transition to capitalism after Deng Xiaoping's famous southern tour in early 1992, and has attempted to theorize it in a variety of ways. For instance, Gerard Greenfield and Apo Leong coined the term "Communist capitalism" to describe "market socialism with Chinese characteristics," which they view as a socialist project that adopts a state-capitalist approach similar to

[1] For example, H. R. McMaster, former U.S. National Security Advisor 2017–2018, wrote in his memoire, "Deng Xiaoping's reforms generated prosperity, but they also caused ideological incoherence... Authoritarian capitalism created ample opportunities for corruption and produced a bourgeois class larger than any other self-proclaimed Communist country has ever seen." McMaster, H. R. (2020): *Battlegrounds: The Fight to Defend the Free World*. London: William Collins, p. 101.

[2] "Biden Defines His Underlying Challenge with China: 'Prove Democracy Works'." *The New York Times*, 26/03/2021. https://www.nytimes.com/2021/03/26/us/politics/biden-china-democracy.html.

J. Yue, *Crony Comprador Capitalism*,
https://doi.org/10.1007/978-3-031-53154-5_1

Lenin's New Economic Policy in the 1920s, but with more exploitative and repressive features during socialist primitive accumulation.[3] Others, such as Maurice Meisner and Au Loon Yu, have used the term "bureaucratic capitalism" to describe the phenomenon of "the use of political power for private pecuniary gain through capitalistic or quasi-capitalistic methods of economic activity."[4]

When characterizing Chinese capitalism, the modifier "crony" stands out as the preferred choice over "Communist" or "bureaucratic" for several compelling reasons. Firstly, the Chinese Communist Party (CCP) underwent a significant transformation, abandoning its previous hostility toward capitalism and imperialism by the turn of the millennium.[5] Since then, it has steadfastly adhered to the principles of market Leninism. Thus, using "Communist" to describe Chinese capitalism would be misleading, as it fails to account for this pivotal shift in ideology.

Secondly, the term "bureaucratic capitalism" emphasizes the bureaucracy's enrichment through rent-seeking, which shares certain connotations with crony capitalism. However, it is crucial to recognize that the Chinese bureaucracy is not a monolithic or meritocratic entity. It is susceptible to state capture by various institutional interests, both private and public. In contrast, "crony capitalism" more accurately describes the intricate power dynamics between Party officials, their relatives, and their proxies, who often wield more influence than the bureaucratic institutions themselves. For instance, in 2015, Alibaba Group's chairman and co-founder, Jack Ma, managed to compel the State Administration for Industry and Commerce to withdraw its "white paper," which had charged Alibaba with a series of irregularities. Ma's ability to exert such influence stemmed from his powerful backers, including figures like former General Secretary Jiang Zemin's grandson, Jiang Zhicheng, and

[3] Greenfield, G and Leong, A (1997): "China's Communist Capitalism: The Real World of Market Socialism." *Socialist Register*, Mar 18. https://socialistregister.com/index.php/srv/article/view/5684.

[4] Meisner, M (1996): *The Deng Xiaoping Era: An Inquiry into the Fate of Chinese Socialism, 1978–1994*. New York: Hill & Wang; "*China: Bureaucratic Capitalist?*" An interview by Terry Conway with Yu, A. L., 07/11/2012. https://socialistresistance.org/china-bureaucratic-capitalist/4188.

[5] Yu, A. L. (2014): "What Is the Nature of Capitalism in China? On the Rise of China and Its Inherent Contradictions," in Yu, A. L. et al., *China's Rise: Strength and Fragility*. Merlin: Resistance Book, p. 8.

former Premier Wen Jiabao's son, Winston Wen.[6] This power imbalance allows certain crony capitalists to pursue their economic interests, often compelling the bureaucracy to collaborate with them.

Therefore, "crony capitalism" more accurately encapsulates the essence of Chinese capitalism within China's contemporary landscape, marked by prevalent rent-seeking behavior, and its relations to robust economic growth.

Similarly, this book avoids using the term "state capitalism" to describe China's economic system because it fails to fully capture its complex and dynamic nature. While the state does play a significant role in China's economy, it is not the dominant player in all sectors. In the absence of state sponsorship, private enterprises and entrepreneurs have become increasingly important, particularly in high-tech industries. Moreover, the state's interventions in the economy are often motivated by political considerations, such as maintaining social stability and political control. Thus, despite the prominent role of the state in China's economy, the term "state capitalism" is not entirely accurate.

Furthermore, while the central role of the state characterizes state capitalism, it is a vague term that is subject to differing definitions.[7] Throughout modern economic history, state capitalism has been a common phenomenon that runs counter to the myth of laissez-faire. Many countries have relied on a strong state to achieve modernization and development, particularly in the early stages of capitalist development. Interestingly, countries such as the United States, Germany, and Japan,[8] which have had prominent state involvement in their economies, are seldom labeled as state capitalists. Therefore, labeling China as state

[6] "Alibaba's I.P.O. Could Be a Bonanza for the Scions of Chinese Leaders." *The New York Times*, 21/07/2014. https://archive.nytimes.com/dealbook.nytimes.com/2014/07/20/alibabas-i-p-o-could-be-a-bonanza-for-the-scions-of-chinese-leaders/.

[7] For instance, Joshua Kurlantzick identifies "state capitalists as countries whose government has an ownership stake in or significant influence over more than one-third of the five-hundred largest companies, by revenue, in that country, a situation that gives these governments far greater control over the corporate sector than a government in a more free-market oriented nation like the United States or the United Kingdom, Generally, in these state-capitalists countries the government sees itself as having a direct role to play in managing the economy and guiding the corporate sector." Kurlantzick, J (2016): *State Capitalism—How the Return of Statism Is Transforming the World*. Oxford: Oxford University Press, p. 9.

[8] Olson, M (1982): *The Rise and Decline of Nations: Economic Growth, Stagflation, and Social Rigidities*. New Haven: Yale University Press; Wade, R (2003): *Governing the*

capitalist does not differentiate it from other late-developing countries at similar stages of development.

It is important to acknowledge that state capitalism is not limited to developing countries and has been a long-term phenomenon, contrary to the views of some scholars who regard it as a mere temporary solution for crises in developed nations.[9] For example, industrial economies in Western Europe after World War II underwent state-capitalist development that lasted for over two decades, during which the proportion of public sector ownership rose from 25% before the war to 50% in the 1970s, leading to impressive economic outcomes.[10] Similarly, most of the successful East Asian economies had large state sectors, with few exceptions.[11] Grabas and Nutzenadel pointed out that "by using state intervention, state ownership, and macroeconomic planning, Asia and Western Europe experienced a real economic miracle."[12]

It is also worth noting that the United States, which is often viewed as a model of free-market capitalism, was strongly drawn to a "Singapore-type" state-capitalist approach following the 2007–2009 financial crisis, as evidenced by the repeated endorsements made by Barack Obama.[13] Moreover, it is often misunderstood that the role of the federal government has been continuously strengthened since the Civil War rather than weakened. Michael Lind has argued that "government in America has never been limited to enforcing property rights, educating workers, and acting as an impartial umpire in competitive markets."[14] Furthermore, industrial policy, which is often associated with state capitalism today, is actually deeply ingrained in the American tradition, as Lind notes, and

Market—Economic Theory and the Role of Government in East Asian Industrialization (2nd ed.). NJ: Princeton University Press, Intro: xlviii.

[9] Kurlantzick, J (2016), p. 10.

[10] Grabas, C & Nutzenadel, A (2014): *Industrial Policy in Europe After 1945—Wealth, Power and Economic Development in the Cold War*. London: Palgrave Macmillan, pp. 38–9, 74, 127, 144–8,153, 155–6, 284.

[11] Chang, H. J. & Grabel, I (2004): *Reclaiming Development—An Alternative Economic Policy Manual*. London: Zed Book, p. 87.

[12] Grabas, C & Nutzenadel (2014), p. 285.

[13] Kurlantzick, J (2016), p. 200.

[14] Lind, M (2012): *Land of Promise: An Economic History of the United States*. New York: Harper Collins, p. 465.

not a foreign concept.[15] In addition, in industries requiring economies of scale, state sponsorship is critical in terms of gaining a competitive advantage.

Recent developments in global capitalism have confirmed Guoguang Wu's observation that state power and market forces have converged in the era of liberal globalization, resulting in the widespread manifestation of "economic state" as a form of state capitalism.[16]

Moreover, it is essential to highlight that there is limited evidence suggesting that state-owned enterprises (SOEs) underperform compared to privately owned companies in terms of profitability, efficiency, productivity, and employment.[17] While the high proportion of SOEs in China's gross domestic product (GDP) has been cited as indicative of a state capitalist system, this assessment requires a nuanced perspective, especially when juxtaposed with the post-war economies of Western Europe.

The unique characteristic of China's SOEs lies in their historical management practices. They have not consistently operated with professionalism or meritocracy, often subject to the regime's "Party controls talents" (*dangguanrencai*, 党管人才) mechanism. Many of them operate inefficiently, heavily reliant on state-sanctioned monopolies or oligopolies. Consequently, there is a growing consensus that restructuring or even complete privatization may be necessary to facilitate the desired structural transformation.

Therefore, it is arguable that the Chinese-style state capitalism does not inherently guarantee economic success, which challenges the assertion made by Joshua Kurlantzick that China's "most efficient state capitalism ... can be maintained for a long time, even decades."

It should be noted that the Chinese development model is not without its flaws, prompting questions about its suitability as an economic system and development strategy. While the Chinese government has achieved remarkable economic growth and poverty reduction, it has faced criticism for its shortcomings in safeguarding social justice, enforcing property rights, and realizing specific national objectives—fundamental characteristics of a strong state. These inadequacies are often attributed to the

[15] Ibid.

[16] Wu, G (2017): *Globalization against Democracy—A Political Economy of Capitalism After Its Global Triumph*. Cambridge: Cambridge University Press, p. 297.

[17] Kurlantzick (2016), p. 177.

phenomenon of "state capture," raising the possibility that the Chinese state, in broader socio-economic terms, may be considered a "soft state" or even a "failed state."[18]

Ironically, despite the state capitalism framework appearing to clash with neoliberal policies, the Chinese party state effectively implemented these policies throughout much of the 1990s and beyond. In its recent stated efforts to establish a rule of law, beginning in 2010, China has, in some aspects, experienced a "great leap backward,"[19] regressing in terms of legal reforms and protections.

In essence, the authoritarian Leninist party-state system in China distinguishes itself from the strong states of both the now-developed countries and the East Asian developmental states in its approach to modernization. Consequently, there is a pressing need for a more comprehensive analysis of the Chinese development model that goes beyond the confines of the state capitalism framework.

Minxin Pei's book, *China's Crony Capitalism—Dynamics of Regime Decay*,[20] provides a comprehensive examination of the various forms and institutional mechanisms of crony capitalism in China. However, the first part of the book takes a distinct approach by delving into the broader context in which China's crony capitalism emerged and thrived. This approach seeks to unravel the intricate political-economic underpinnings of crony capitalism in China.

By tracing the origins of China's crony capitalism back to the Communist Revolution itself, the book explores how the Revolution inadvertently fostered a New Class after 1949. The tumultuous Cultural Revolution further heightened the awareness of the offspring of this upper-New Class, known as the "princelings," who began to perceive themselves as natural rulers entitled to possess all national resources, both political and economic, in perpetuity. This evolving self-perception transformed them

[18] In her article "30 Years of Reform: The Abnormal Development of State Capacity and Its Consequences," He Qinglian issued a warning that the Chinese state could potentially descend into the category of "failed states" in broader socio-economic terms. *Modern China Studies*, No.4, 2008.

[19] "Jiang Ping: China's Rule of Law Is in a Period of Great Retrogression," VOA (Chinese), 03/03/2010. https://www.voachinese.com/a/article-20100303-chinarulelawullretreat-86185087/462920.html; Also Jiang Ping: "Ten Years of Reflection on the Rule of Law in China." 16/11/2010. https://www.sinoss.net/c/2010-11-16/533485.shtml.

[20] Pei, M (2016): *China's Crony Capitalism—The Dynamics of Regime Decay*. Cambridge: Harvard University Press.

into crony capitalists, solidified their interests during the reform era, and ultimately contributed to the Party's transformation into a plutocracy, alongside the rent-seeking bureaucracy.

This book introduces a distinct perspective on Chinese economic reform, challenging the prevailing view that sees it as a gradual transformation of Chinese socialism. Instead, it underscores the sharp distinction between two stages of economic reform in the 1980s and 1990s. The first stage, marked by market socialism, retained fundamental features of a socialist economy while permitting limited market forces under state planning. The second stage, characterized as market Leninism, witnessed the emergence of a capitalist economy co-existing with a Communist state. In this phase, the state retained control by maintaining dominance over the "commanding heights" of the economy. Under market Leninism, socialism existed in name only. With the decline of socialism, a crony capitalist system took root, marked by an extensive money-power nexus that incentivized the bureaucracy to pursue high growth through radical marketizing reforms.

It is important to note that characterizing the Chinese model as crony capitalism is less contentious than *simultaneously* labeling it as comprador capitalism, which faces challenges due to prevailing political correctness that assumes China's rise as a given, both in China and the West. Many economists and development experts suggest that China's success is largely due to a strong commitment to economic nationalism, as reflected in its approach of "taking advantage of globalization without being taken advantage of by globalization."[21] However, this view is not entirely accurate. Evidence indicates that China's deep integration into the capitalist world economy has been a reality since the late 1990s. Although this integration has resulted in remarkable export-led growth, it has not led to structural transformation, leaving the country vulnerable to falling into the "middle-income trap." This developmental pitfall, which does not replicate the East Asian model, as argued by Yasheng Huang,[22] has affected many semi-peripheral states at similar stages of economic development.

[21] Stiglitz, J (2003): *Making Globalization Work: The Next Step to Global Justice*. London: Penguin Books, p. 31.

[22] Huang, Y (2008): *Capitalism with Chinese Characteristics—Entrepreneurship and the State*. NY: Cambridge University Press, pp. 43, 280–1.

Comprador capitalism refers to a situation in which a domestic economy relies on foreign capital, and the ruling class collaborates with foreign capitalists to exploit their own country's resources and labor. A defining feature of comprador capitalism is the existence of a comprador class that acts as an agent for foreign capital. The terms "comprador" and "comprador class" are key concepts in the field of dependency theory, which argues that certain countries are underdeveloped because they are integrated into the global capitalist system as subordinate producers of raw materials and cheap labor, reliant on foreign technology. According to Vincent Ferraro, the elites who were trained in the West "voluntarily" maintained a dependency relationship not necessarily because they "consciously" betrayed national interests or the interests of the poor, but because they sincerely believed that "the key to economic development lies in following the prescriptions of liberal economic doctrine."[23] Nicholas Jepson noted that these elites "jumped on the neoliberal bandwagon"[24] partly out of willingness and partly due to a lack of choice.

By aligning with global capitalists and manipulating foreign economic policy, China's comprador class has captured the state to a large extent, serving the interests of both global capital and domestic elites. The comprador elites believed that forming an "unholy alliance" with Western capital would bolster the Communist regime, bring lasting peace, and move the country away from its periphery status. However, this developmental journey has resulted in a pitfall conceptualized by Peter Evans as "dependent development,"[25] where China has made some progress but still struggles to become a metropolitan core in the global economy.

The relationship between China's crony capitalism and comprador capitalism is intricate and interdependent. The rise of crony capitalism, characterized by rent-seeking, led to acute underconsumption toward the end of the 1990s, forcing China to rely more on exports and foreign investment, and giving the comprador class a strong *raison d'être*. Comprador capitalism, in turn, created more economic opportunities for crony capitalists, further strengthening China's crony capitalism and

[23] Ferraro, V (2008): "Dependency Theory: An Introduction," in Secondi, G. (ed.), *The Development Economics Reader*. London: Routledge, p. 64.

[24] Jepson, N (2019): *In China's Wake—How the Commodity Boom Transformed Development Strategies in the Global South*. New York: Columbia University Press, p. 241.

[25] Evans, P (1979): *Dependent Development: The Alliance of Multinational, State, and Local Capital in Brazil*. NJ: Princeton University Press.

inclining them toward economic internationalism. The two forms of capitalism mutually reinforced and justified each other, resulting in the institutionalization of a Chinese-style crony comprador capitalism that was solidified by China's accession to the WTO. As China grapples with sustaining economic growth and development amid increasing external pressures and internal tensions, understanding the relationship between these two forms of capitalism will remain critical for policymakers, scholars, and the general public.

The dearth of attention directed toward Chinese comprador capitalism by international scholars and policymakers can be attributed to two primary factors. Firstly, proponents of market liberalism, who often conflate economic growth with economic development, have adhered to neoliberal doctrine. This ideological stance has led them to disregard the "comprador" phenomenon in China, aligning themselves with Chinese "Chicago boys." The implicit yet erroneous assumption that economic growth inevitably leads to catch-up has fostered a lack of critical examination of this issue.

Secondly, those skeptical of market forces have held the belief that the ostensibly "strong" Chinese state maintains substantial autonomy from both domestic and foreign institutional interests. This viewpoint has further perpetuated the misconception that China has always been steadfastly committed to economic nationalism. Consequently, efforts to comprehend China's economic landscape have been fraught with risks, both for those advocating increased liberalization of global finance, trade, and investment and those advocating a new Cold War.

The concept of "dependency reversed"[26] has compounded this complexity, blurring the reality that China is, in fact, more economically and technologically reliant on the United States than the reverse. This inherent vulnerability has prevented China from disengaging fully from the capitalist world system, underscoring the existence of an entrenched comprador class that has remained well-nigh invulnerable.

Indeed, an interdisciplinary approach is imperative for a comprehensive grasp of the intricacies inherent in China's crony comprador capitalism. By delving into its historical origins and dissecting the interplay of political and economic factors that have contributed to its emergence and persistence, we can cultivate a holistic understanding of its dynamics and

[26] Wu, G (2017), p. 16.

potential trajectory. Such a multifaceted analysis equips policymakers and scholars with invaluable insights into both the strengths and vulnerabilities of this system, as well as its long-term ramifications for China's economic development and its role in the global political economy. In the face of the complex challenges posed by this phenomenon, only a multidisciplinary approach can provide the nuanced understanding required for effective engagement and resolution.

Overview of the Book

The introductory chapter of this book offers an overview of the concepts of crony capitalism and comprador capitalism in China. The first part of the book comprises Chapters 2 and 3, which delve into the emergence of crony capitalism in China. Chapter 2 scrutinizes the initial economic reforms of the 1980s, implemented under the banner of "reform and opening up," aimed at resolving the crisis that had followed the Cultural Revolution. While these reforms were not inherently capitalist, they drew inspiration from market-socialist experiments in countries like Hungary and Poland, and Lenin's New Economic Policy. The princelings, the offspring of senior Communist Party cadres, played a vital role in advancing China's crony capitalist development during this era. It is critical to examine their impact and conduct in the wider context of China's post-totalitarian transformation following Mao's death.

Chapter 3 explores the critical shift that occurred after Deng Xiaoping's southern tour in 1992, which marked China's institutional move toward capitalism. This transition saw the shift from market socialism to what is referred to as market Leninism. Under immense pressure to achieve rapid economic growth to legitimize the regime, the New Class, which broadly refers to the political bureaucracy of the Communist state, had a strong incentive to pursue growth at any cost and quickly embraced crony capitalism, linking rent-seeking and economic growth to benefit themselves. The princelings, while still playing a significant role, were eclipsed by the bureaucracy that had taken over the reins of power. The link between crony capitalism and economic growth became fully institutionalized when the Chinese Communist Party completed its transition from a "left-wing dictatorship" to a "right-wing dictatorship" at the turn of the millennium.

Part II of the book includes Chapters 4 and 5, which analyze the emergence of China's comprador capitalism. Chapter 4 explores the roots of this system, tracing it back to the late 1980s. It begins by examining Zhang Chunqiao's warning about China's inevitable transformation into a comprador capitalist system in the post-Mao era. It identifies the loss of national pride resulting from extreme poverty and underdevelopment as a key factor that contributed to the rise of a comprador mentality not only among the elites but also among various social classes. People from all walks of life were inclined to idolize foreign goods and ideas, perpetuating a cultural narrative that prioritized foreign products over domestic ones.

During the 1990s, and particularly after 1992, China underwent extensive trade and investment liberalization, with the aid of the "Chicago boys," even during its early stages of economic development. Rather than adopting an economic nationalist stance, the Chinese state sought to attain a Ricardian growth miracle by integrating with global capitalism. As a result of China's accession to the World Trade Organization (WTO) in 2001, the institutionalization of comprador capitalism was further cemented. Despite being a product of independent development, comprador capitalism in China is closely intertwined with crony capitalism, a relationship that this book will explore in greater depth.

Chapter 5 exposes the CCP's nationalist facade and critically evaluates China's global integration approach, which has resulted in "growth without development." It posits that China's crony comprador capitalism has steered the country toward a path of dependent development rather than transforming it into the economic superpower that it is often perceived to be. The "empire-sized" country's entrapment in semi-peripheral development presents its peaceful rise as illusory.

Part III of the book comprises Chapters 6 and 7, which delve into the dynamics of U.S.-China great power competition and analyze Xi Jinping's strategies for addressing domestic and international challenges, evolving from a trade war into a new Cold War.

Chapter 6 explores the progression of Sino-U.S. conflict, tracing its evolution from the initial trade war to the emergence of a new Cold War. It highlights intervening variables such as the North Korean denuclearization issue and China's alternative "diplomatic diplomacy" approach, which could have potentially averted both "wars."

Chapter 7 examines Xi Jinping's "reverse course" in response to the inherent tensions arising from crony comprador capitalism. These tensions have impeded China's progress toward achieving a fully modernized economy and have led to conflicts with the international system of global capitalism. Drawing parallels with the economic reorganization of the Third Reich during a period of crisis, this book provides valuable insights into China's political and economic development and explores how the new Cold War may shape its future. This chapter seeks to determine whether China will pursue a traditional path of external expansion or turn inward, potentially adopting more repressive measures and confronting even more severe crises in an uncertain future.

Chapter 8, the concluding chapter, examines how democracies worldwide should respond to China's ascent in the context of the emergence of "Capitalism 3.0" and the anticipated "self-revolution" within global capitalism. Its aim is to lay the groundwork for a world that safeguards the enduring stability of democratic values.

PART I

The Making of China's Crony Capitalism

CHAPTER 2

Market Socialism and the Emergence of China's Crony Capitalism: The Role of the Princelings

In 2000, Wang Lixiong, a prominent Chinese dissident scholar, observed a fundamental difference in the goals of Mao Zedong's socialist revolution after 1949 and Deng Xiaoping's reforms in the post-Mao era. Mao aimed to "turn private property into public property" or "abolish private property" (*huasiweigong*, 化私为公), while Deng sought to do the opposite by "turning public property into private property" (*huagongweisi*, 化公为私).[1]

In *The Communist Manifesto* (1848), Marx and Engels used the term "bourgeois property" to describe private property,[2] and this terminology is relevant to the discussion of Mao and Deng's differing policies on private and public property. Mao took the *huasiweigong* policy to the extreme during the Great Proletarian Cultural Revolution (1966–1976), linking it to his goal of preventing the Communist bureaucracy's embourgeoisment and the emergence of a privileged class. However, Deng's reversal of Mao's policies after his death, albeit not entirely intentionally, led to the entrenchment of privileged class interests and hastened China's

[1] Wang, L (2000): "The 'Mao Zedong Complex' at the Bottom of Chinese Society and Undercurrents." *Modern China Studies*, issue 3. https://www.modernchinastudies.org/us/issues/past-issues/70-mcs-2000-issue-3/543-2012-01-03-12-11-40.html.

[2] https://www.marxists.org/archive/marx/works/1848/communist-manifesto/ch02.htm.

J. Yue, *Crony Comprador Capitalism*,
https://doi.org/10.1007/978-3-031-53154-5_2

transition to capitalism. Both policy designs have benefited the Communist party state, consolidating its rule, yet creating an unprecedented socio-economic crisis.

The New Class: From Privileged Class to New Bourgeoisie

In 1963, the World Affairs Publishing House (世界知识出版社), an influential publisher affiliated with the Chinese Ministry of Foreign Affairs, translated a sensitive political science book into Chinese. The book, entitled *The New Class—An Analysis of the Communist System*, was written by Milovan Djilas, a veteran Yugoslav Communist, and had been published in the United States in 1957. However, due to its critical nature, the book was classified as a "grey book" by the CCP's cultural censor and was only allowed to circulate among senior Chinese Communist cadres.

During the Cultural Revolution, especially after the Lin Biao incident in September 1971, many "educated youth" who had been sent to the countryside by Mao's regime stole the book from local libraries and read it among themselves. These young people were inspired and enlightened by the book's critical analysis of the Communist system and it played a crucial role in shaping the thinking of a generation of Chinese youth well into the first decade of the reform era in the 1980s.

Milovan Djilas identified the power-holders in the senior ranks of the Communist Party, after its seizure of power, as the "New Class." He also used the term to refer to the entire political bureaucracy. According to Djilas, the New Class exercised control over nationalized property, using and disposing of it at will, which gave them an exclusive right, as a party monopoly, to distribute national income, set wages, direct economic development, and dispose of nationalized and other property. Djilas argued that the New Class obtained its power, privileges, ideology, and customs from one specific form of ownership: collective ownership.[3] He believed that this "ownership privilege" made the New Class highly repressive "owners and exploiters" who enjoyed privileges that were unimaginable in other societies. Djilas further suggested that the New Class established a monopoly of power over the working class, which

[3] Djilas, M (1957): *The New Class—An Analysis of the Communist System*. Orlando: Harcourt Brace Jovanovich Publishers, pp. 43–44.

allowed them to exercise complete control over all political-economic resources.[4] This notion of a privileged class within Communist societies was later echoed by other dissident scholars, who argued that the Communist Party had become a new bourgeoisie.

Mao Zedong established the People's Republic of China, or the "New China," in 1949. He was quick to recognize the dangers of an increasingly bureaucratic state apparatus, which Leon Trotsky had described as the "degeneration of workers' state" and the resulting "dictatorship of the bureaucracy over the proletariat." Mao used various terms, such as "aristocracy," "vested interest groups," and "new bourgeoisie," to describe the potential emergence of a privileged class in China. He feared that this class could lead to a restoration of capitalism, even in the absence of the necessary material foundations.

To address this potential threat, Mao formulated the theory of "continuous revolution" in the mid-1960s, with the primary objective of constraining the bureaucratic apparatus. He categorized individuals he perceived as advocating capitalist restoration as "intra-party bourgeoisie." Mao maintained that a top-down social revolution was imperative to thwart their ascendancy to power.[5] In parallel with Djilas' conceptualization of the New Class, Mao and his adherents held a similar perspective. However, they diverged from Djilas in terms of the underlying causes for its emergence and his advocacy for a return to a multi-party democratic system. Instead, Mao advocated a variant of totalitarian democracy as a mechanism to rein in the bureaucracy.[6] Qi Benyu, a steadfast disciple of Mao and favored by Jiang Qing, underscored the indispensability of the Cultural Revolution for preventing the rise and consolidation of a privileged class.[7] Notably, Mao's theory regarding the Cultural Revolution was underpinned by political determinism, a departure from the classical Marxist theory grounded in economic determinism.

[4] Ibid., p. 42.

[5] 生活读书新知三联书店香港分店《走资派就是党内的资产阶级》,1976年(92页)。

[6] Mao was viewed by some radical leftists as a de facto "Revisionist and Anti-marxist Leninist." See "Mao Apologised to Yugoslavian Delegates, told Stalin Blocked Our Revolution." *Other Aspect*, posted on 11/08/2015. https://otheraspect.org/category/revisionism-of-mao/.

[7] Qi, B (2016): *A Memoir of Qi Benyu*. Hong Kong: 中国文革历史出版社, pp. 669–670.

Mao's final attempt at revolution ultimately ended in a catastrophic failure. Despite his endeavors to institute a system of totalitarian democracy with the aim of mobilizing "revolutionary rebels" to periodically cleanse the bureaucracy and combat the "dictatorship of the bureaucracy over the proletariat," he found himself unable to rival the formidable Leninist behemoth he had emulated after the Soviet Union. The Cultural Revolution, which Mao had utilized as a tool to disrupt the bureaucracy and assert his authority, had the unintended consequence of inciting open defiance from the very bureaucrats it was intended to target. This, in turn, led to the marginalization of the emerging "New Class"—new power-holders originating from the Rebels in most Chinese regions except Shanghai.

Mao's reliance on the fervent support of the "Rebels" proved to be a double-edged sword, as those bureaucrats who remained unpurged successfully derailed Mao's efforts to establish a new order. Despite the brutal purging of the bureaucracy, Mao could not prevent its resurgence, which had already gained momentum following the demise of Lin Biao in September 1971. Until Mao's passing five years later, the bureaucracy's "counteroffensive" became an unstoppable force, sealing the failure of Mao's final revolution.

Mao's tragedy lay in his resentment of the New Class, yet he was forced to govern through them. His determination to preserve the totalitarian state instead of dismantling it doomed his continuous revolution from the start. In the end, the bureaucracy emerged as the victor, and Mao suffered a fatal defeat.[8] With collective leadership reasserted to prevent the trauma of an omnipotent dictator, the New Class would grow even more potent than before.

Despite Mao's passing, the post-Mao era in China was not without its challenges. The new leadership faced two significant issues that required immediate attention: widespread poverty that had severely undermined the CCP's legitimacy, and the regime's inability to regain the harsh totalitarian rule that had been weakened by Mao's final revolution. Although some progress was made toward greater freedom of speech and reduced social control, the New Class remained determined to protect the CCP's monopoly on power. While Deng Xiaoping initially sympathized with the Democracy Wall Movement, also known as Beijing Spring, which

[8] Yang, J (2016): *The World Turned Upside Down?* Hong Kong: Cosmos Books, p. 1127.

emerged in September 1978, he quickly recognized the danger of spontaneous political liberalization that could lead to a regime change, as exemplified by the uprisings in Hungary in 1956 and Czechoslovakia in 1968. His crackdown on the Beijing Spring movement in 1979 revealed the limits of de-Maoification. Deng's ultimate goal was to maintain the Party's unchallenged monopoly of power. His unfolding market-oriented reforms were intended to rescue the Party from deep crisis rather than undermine its rule.

In the early post-Mao years, the CCP reasserted "the dictatorship of the bureaucracy over the proletariat" to restore law and order. This was evident in the removal of the "four great freedoms"—the freedom to speak, air views, write big-character posters, and hold debates—and workers' rights to strike—which were Mao's legacy from the Cultural Revolution, from the 1980 and 1982 Constitution amendments. The CCP's response was partly motivated by the Polish crisis of 1981, which saw the rise of the Solidarity Union and unnerved China's rulers. Chen Yun, a veteran Communist leader and Deng Xiaoping's political counterweight, was particularly alert to the situation in Poland, emphasizing the importance of economics and propaganda. This helped to strengthen his position in economic policymaking and reinforced the CCP's commitment to the "Four Modernizations" project, which aimed to modernize industry, agriculture, defense, and science and technology. This reorientation was politically necessary and established a "social contract" of exchanging material gains for citizens' political obedience.

In the aftermath of Mao's backward socialism, the ongoing Sino-Soviet split since the late 1950s, and China's intimate relationship with the West since Nixon's visit in 1972, the post-Mao leadership reached an implicit consensus of "using capitalism to develop socialism." This was similar to Lenin's New Economic Policy in the 1920s, which aimed to improve the economy while maintaining the socialist ideology. Deng's reform and opening-up did not aim to discard socialism, but rather to perfect it and consolidate the legitimacy of the Communist regime, which had been severely damaged by Mao's continuous revolution. This rationale became an integral part of China's market-socialist reforms throughout the 1980s.

However, Deng lacked the theoretical interest and prowess of Mao, who was a brilliant Communist thinker. As a result, Deng resorted to opportunistic pragmatism, known as the "Cat Theory," to navigate the ideological orthodoxy. Sensing the worldwide decline of socialism since the late 1970s, Deng increasingly lost faith in socialism as a belief system, in a similar manner to how Leonid Brezhnev lost faith in the Soviet Union's "advanced socialism." In 1984, Deng gave blunt advice to an African leader, saying, "I suggest you not practice socialism right now. As long as you have a strong economy, you can call your system whatever-ism you like."[9]

While Deng held undisputed political authority, his absence of a clearly defined ideological framework rendered him susceptible to criticism from both ideologues and conservative central planning reformers led by Chen Yun. Paradoxically, it was Chen Yun who initially introduced the concept of a "market economy," albeit one that underscored the preeminent role of state planning. Chen Yun's "bird-cage theory" diverged significantly from the concept of a "regulated market economy" put forward by Soviet reformers in the late 1980s.

Even though Deng also advocated the development of a market economy, beginning in 1984, he and Chen Yun increasingly found themselves at odds regarding the pace of market-oriented reforms, notwithstanding Deng's general endorsement of Chen Yun's "bird-cage" theory. Given China's historical stigmatization of capitalism, both Deng and Chen Yun refrained from making their internal discussions on "developing a market economy," however constrained, which had been publicly known for over a decade.

Being the de facto paramount leader, Deng had the responsibility of providing socialism with a definition, albeit a vague one. He associated socialism with "common prosperity" and declared in 1985 that: "The objective of socialism is to guarantee that the entire nation prospers together and does not become polarized. If our policies result in *polarization*, we will have failed. If a *new bourgeoisie* arises, we will have truly gone astray."[10]

Deng's "socialist promise" was fundamentally flawed both in theory and practice. Firstly, the criteria of "common prosperity" without polarization proved inadequate in terms of distinguishing socialism from other economic systems. This deficiency led to situations where numerous

[9] "A Dialogue with Du Daozheng: on New Democracy." *Southern People Weekly*, 04/11/2011. http://news.sohu.com/20111104/n324552378.shtml.

[10] *Selected Works of Deng Xiaoping*, vol 3. Beijing: renmin chubanshe, 1993, pp. 110–111.

countries, including Organisation for Economic Co-operation and Development (OECD) member states and nations like the United Arab Emirates, could technically qualify as socialist.[11]

Secondly, the vision of achieving common prosperity was a long-term aspiration. Deng acknowledged the necessity and feasibility of allowing certain individuals to accumulate wealth first, particularly during China's "preliminary stage of socialism," a euphemism for adopting capitalist methods. However, it remained unclear which segment of the population would benefit from this policy and under what conditions. Deng envisaged that the superstructure of socialism would remain intact, with capitalism—in the form of private enterprises or joint ventures—developing to a limited extent and being subject to controls to prevent social polarization and the emergence of a new bourgeoisie. Nevertheless, Deng underestimated the potential adverse consequences of unleashing market forces and their interaction with unchecked state power, which ultimately resulted in institutional corruption and a transformation in the character of the Communist Party—an outcome Deng had sought to avoid.

Despite Deng's strong preference for radical marketizing reforms in the 1980s, particularly from the second half of the decade onwards, in order to justify his approach of "perestroika without glasnost," these reforms were not fully implemented due to the power structure of the Deng-Chen condominium and the continued influence of socialist ideology. Consequently, SOEs continued to dominate the Chinese economy, obscuring the emergence of polarization and small-scale capitalism in rural areas. Given the relatively weak market forces, it was difficult for party-state bureaucrats to "legitimately" profit from rent-seeking, making it unlikely that they would become a new bourgeoisie during this period. This also explains why many civil servants joined the pro-democracy movement in 1989. In contrast, Deng's "socialist promise" was ultimately eroded by the princelings, the children of senior Communist Party leaders, who became part of the upper-New Class after the Cultural Revolution. They were the new bourgeoisie who fostered China's crony capitalism, protected by their New Class parents, which effectively nullified Deng's vision of a market-socialist economy that would benefit the entire Chinese society.

[11] OECD Data: Income Inequality. https://data.oecd.org/inequality/income-inequality.htm; Gini Coefficient by Country 2021: https://worldpopulationreview.com/country-rankings/gini-coefficient-by-country.

The Role of the Princelings

While Djilas acknowledged the emergence of a new ruling class in his critiques of socialism, Mao initially failed to recognize the connection between the totalitarian state he had created and the emergence of a similar class in China. However, by the late 1950s, Mao grew increasingly alarmed by revisionist tendencies within the CCP, which he believed had been influenced by the tactics of U.S. Secretary of State John Foster Dulles. Dulles had advocated "peaceful evolution towards democracy" in a series of speeches made in 1958–1959, which Mao interpreted as an attempt to subvert socialism from within.[12] Mao perceived revisionist tendencies in Khrushchev's Soviet Union, which he believed had emerged earlier than those in China and were also influenced by Dulles's tactics. In 1964, Mao proposed the idea of "fostering revolutionary successors." He further launched the Cultural Revolution in 1966 as a means of ensuring revolutionary immortality among the Party elites and the people.

Mao established five conditions for becoming a revolutionary successor. Firstly, candidates must be true Marxist-Leninists and opposed to revisionist ideas. Secondly, they should serve the interests of the majority, and oppose imperialist and reactionary forces at home and abroad. Thirdly, they must be proletarian politicians who could unite people, even those who had made mistakes or opposed them. Fourthly, they should adhere to the Party's democratic centralism and adopt the leadership method of "from the masses, to the masses." Finally, they must be modest, critical, and courageous in correcting their own mistakes.[13] The emphasis on these conditions was designed to ensure that the next generation of Chinese leaders would continue to uphold the revolutionary spirit and principles of the CCP rather than succumbing to revisionism or bourgeois tendencies.

However, Mao's selection of revolutionary successors was limited to individuals from the "five red categories," which included revolutionary soldiers, cadres, workers, poor and hired peasants, and lower-middle peasants. Mao's anti-intellectual beliefs and his preference for individuals from

[12] Saussy, H (2001): *Great Walls of Discourse and Other Adventures in Cultural China*. 1st ed., vol. 212, Harvard University Asia Center, p. 237.

[13] Song Yijun: "Revealing the secret: Mao Zedong talked about training successors in 1964." 09/06/2013, *People's Daily* Online: news network of the Chinese Communist Party. http://dangshi.people.com.cn/n/2013/0609/c85037-21804526.html.

these categories effectively excluded those from the "five black categories" (landlords, rich peasants, counter-revolutionaries, bad elements, and Rightists) from consideration. This institutionalized a caste system that hindered the advancement of individuals in these excluded categories. Even within the "five red categories," revolutionary cadres were often prioritized for advancement, leading to what was dubbed the "dictatorship of the bureaucracy over the proletariat." Consequently, the children of these revolutionary cadres, known as the princelings, interpreted Mao's "revolutionary successor" thesis as an exclusive designation of their future leadership roles.

One complex legacy of Mao's last revolution is the entrenchment of ruling-class consciousness among the princelings, who formed the core of the Old Red Guards (ORGs). These groups responded to Mao's call for rebellion, with the ORGs believing they were the rightful successors to the revolution, entitled to inherit power because their fathers had seized it. They viewed themselves as controlling the state machinery, committed to "bloodline theory," which held that social status was predetermined by family class position, and believed that political status should be hereditary.[14]

In contrast, the New Red Guards (NRGs) were predominantly made up of young people from humble backgrounds who saw the Cultural Revolution as a means to redress the inequalities and injustices that had arisen in the "New Society" after 1949. They were more ideologically committed to Mao's vision of the Cultural Revolution and viewed themselves as the true vanguard of the revolution, responsible for purging capitalist-roaders and counter-revolutionaries.

It is noteworthy that at the beginning of the Cultural Revolution, the ORGs took the initiative to purge the "black five categories" instead of targeting the "capitalist-roaders," as Mao had expected. Mao's inner circle, including Jiang Qing and Chen Boda, dismissed the bloodline theory as "reactionary." Mao did not share this view either. He saw through their subterfuge of protecting their capitalist-roader parents and purged them. However, they were swiftly pardoned. Despite Mao's opposition to the bloodline theory, the rebellion against it was quickly suppressed, with the greatest victim being Yu Luoke (遇罗克). Yu was

[14] Wu, Y (2014): *The Cultural Revolution at the Margins: Chinese Socialism in Crisis*. Cambridge: Harvard University Press, p. 58, 60.

a young worker from a "black five categories" family in a Beijing state-run factory. His article "On Class Origins" (《出身论》), which circulated in the second half of 1966, was hugely influential and gained him the title of "China's Human Rights Pioneer" after the Cultural Revolution.[15] He called for equal treatment of all revolutionary young people, regardless of their class origins, and highlighted how the Communist system created inequalities between elite and ordinary people, particularly those from unfavorable classes.[16]

Although the Mao Group accommodated Yu's view for a short while, he was arrested on the orders of Premier Zhou Enlai[17] and executed shortly after, as his article served to delegitimize the CCP's right to justify itself as the new ruling class. His execution marked the end of the "dissenting tendency" within Mao's Cultural Revolution.[18] There have been rumors that Mao directly ordered Yu Luoke's execution, but there is no evidence to support this claim. However, such rumors at the time emboldened the ORGs, who were excited and said: "Ultimately, the Chairman is the defender of our class's interests."

There is substantial evidence to indicate that the initial rebellion of the ORGs was covertly supported and incited by their imperiled "capitalist-roader" parents. Paradoxically, as previously mentioned, the Cultural Revolution acted as a catalyst for the princelings' own development of class consciousness. They held the belief that they represented the natural ruling class of the nation and were entitled to inherit power and privileges in the post-Cultural Revolution era based on the bloodline theory. Although their suffering was considerably less pronounced than that experienced by individuals from lower classes, including the working class, they remained highly motivated to seek retribution for the losses they had endured during Mao's Cultural Revolution.

[15] "The Meteor That Cuts Through the Night—Record of Yu Luoke, the Pioneer of Emancipation of Thought." *Guangming Daily*, 21–22/07/1980; Jin Zhong (ed.) (2010): *Yu Luoke: China's Human Rights Pioneer*. Hong Kong: Open Press.

[16] Yu, Luoke: "On Class Origins." 18/01/1967. https://www.marxists.org/chinese/reference-books/minjian-1966-1976/05.htm.

[17] Hu Ping: "Interpretation of Zhou Enlai in his later years." 27/07/2017. https://www.chinesepen.org/blog/archives/83833.

[18] Charles Reeve's Review on Yiching Wu's The Cultural Revolution at the Margins: Chinese Socialism in Crisis, published on H-Socialisms (October 2015). https://www.h-net.org/reviews/showrev.php?id=43036.

During the early years of the reform era, the princelings were remunerated in various forms, such as obtaining top jobs in state-owned companies, receiving state funding for overseas studies, and rapidly advancing within the bureaucracy. Chen Yuan, the son of Chen Yun, openly stated within his "red aristocracy" inner circle that "as the ruling class, we must have the ruling consciousness!"[19] This implies that, like dynastic rulers throughout Chinese history, the princelings regarded the whole nation as their private property. They saw themselves as the rightful rulers, entitled to power and privilege by virtue of their bloodline, rather than their abilities or achievements. In their view, the princelings were the guardians of the Communist Revolution and its legacy, and it was their duty to ensure that it remained intact. They saw the post-Mao era as an opportunity to reassert their rightful place at the top of the social and political hierarchy.

The princelings' ruling-class mentality and desire for revenge against their families' past humiliations led to their abuse of privileges, which fueled public discontent. However, they were able to withstand efforts by General Secretary Hu Yaobang to curb their excesses in 1984 with the help of their New Class parents who had returned to power.[20] Moreover, due to the significant damage caused by the Cultural Revolution to the Communist Party's organization,[21] Chen Yun played a critical role in shielding the ORGs, who had proved loyal and reliable in defending the interests of the New Class during the Cultural Revolution, from state retaliation and penalties. Meanwhile, the New Red Guards were barred from upward mobility in the *nomenklatura* system. Under the purview of the Central Organization Department, a powerful CCP body overseen by Chen Yun, the princelings were rapidly promoted and appointed to key bureaucratic posts, as part of the post-Mao *nomenklatura* system known as "cultivating the 'third echelon' (successor candidates)."

The nepotistic ties among senior leaders granted the princelings not only political power but also economic advantages. Deng Xiaoping and Chen Yun's opposition to the overcentralization of power, which had stifled economic dynamism, created room for the princelings to generate wealth. The creation of four monopolistic state trading companies

[19] Yan, H (2017): *In and Out of the Central Organization Department*. New York: Mirror, p. 253.

[20] Ibid., pp. 204–205.

[21] Dikötter, F (2022): *China after Mao—The Rise of a Superpower*. London: Bloomsbury, p. 43.

between 1979 and 1984, known as the "official-profiteering companies" (*guandao gongsi*, 官倒公司), exemplified the nexus of money and power. The princelings utilized political nepotism to gain exclusive access to national resources and the state apparatus to create wealth.[22] The peak of princeling wealth accumulation came with the introduction of the "dual-pricing" regime in March 1985, which allowed the princelings to amass enormous wealth overnight by capitalizing on the price differences set by the state and the market. This regime was part of Premier Zhao Ziyang's reform drive to expand the corporate autonomy of SOEs. Several senior leaders, including Hu Yaobang and Zhao Ziyang, who were otherwise considered to be progressive figures, were implicated in the "getting rich first" scandals that followed. For instance, most of the profitable businesses of the People's Liberation Army (PLA), including the monopolistic munition trading (Poly Group), were controlled by the "three sons-in-law" of Deng Xiaoping, Yang Shangkun (State President), and Zhao Ziyang.[23]

Despite their professed commitment to socialist ideals, the senior leaders of the Party, whether they were for or against Deng's market-oriented reforms, turned a blind eye to their family members' abuse of power for personal financial gain. Deng Xiaoping's eldest son, Deng Pufang, candidly told Chen Yizi, Zhao Ziyang's senior economic advisor, that "anyone who is capable of grabbing a piece of the pie [from the state], just let it be." Deng Pufang readily agreed when Chen asked if the "anyone" referred to people with close ties to political power who were capable of enriching themselves at the expense of ordinary citizens.[24] Exiled political activist Wang Xizhe argued that this approach of turning political privilege into personal wealth was the "entire secret of Deng Xiaoping's 'reform and opening'," or, more precisely, the "fundamental

[22] Ho, W. C. (2013): "The New 'Comprador Class': The Re-emergence of Bureaucratic Capitalists in Post-Deng China." *Journal of Contemporary China*, 22:83, pp. 812–827. The four infamous companies are: China International Trust and Investment Corporation (CITIC, 1979), China Poly Group Corporation (Poly Group, 1983), China Everbright Group (Everbright, 1983), and Kanghua Development Corporation (Kanghua, 1984).

[23] Luo, Y (2015): *Bidding Farewell to the General Staff*. Hong Kong: Open Books, p. 242.

[24] Chen, Y (2013): *A Memoire*. Hong Kong: New Century Publisher, pp. 294–295.

secret of 'letting some people become rich first.'"[25] This marked the birth of China's crony capitalism, which was promoted by senior leaders of the New Class under the guise of promoting "reform and opening" along *socialist* lines.

The working class, who were politically marginalized, had lost their ability to challenge the "dictatorship of the bureaucracy," which had supported the princelings and enabled them to become a new bourgeoisie. By the end of 1988, economic reforms had reached a deadlock, due in part to the failed price reform of six months earlier. The rapidly widening income gap and the hardships faced by ordinary Chinese people exposed the hypocrisy of the official slogan of "enabling some people to become rich through their honest labor and legal business operations." As a result, widespread disillusionment with Deng Xiaoping's "socialism with Chinese characteristics" led to broad resentment against the regime. This resentment directly fueled the pro-democracy movement in the summer of 1989. The movement was, in large part, a public protest against the emerging crony capitalism that had been fostered by Deng's economic liberalization reform under a relatively benign post-totalitarian regime.

Following the Tiananmen Square crackdown in June 1989, the Communist leaders were taken aback by the level of public outrage. Initially, they contemplated implementing a ban on the children of CCP officials at all levels from participating in business activities as a way of appeasing the public. However, this regulation was swiftly abandoned, as it was their own children who had proven their loyalty to the Communist regime in a time of crisis. As Chen Yun stated: "Only our kids are reliable. After all, they will never dig our own graves [in the future]."[26] Soon after, an unwritten rule was established within the Party, requiring that at least one child from each "Red Family" be promoted to a ministerial position within the central government. This system of collective inheritance of political power was designed to ensure that the New Class maintained a tight grip on power, safeguarding their interests, and preventing the emergence of Gorbachev-like figures from within the Communist bureaucracy.

[25] Wang, Xizhe: "China's Bureaucratic Bourgeoisie and the Insights of Chen Yun—An Interview with Yan Huai." *Mingjing News*, 07/07/2018. https://www.mingjingnews.com/article/91551-80.

[26] Ching Cheong: "How the CCP's Crony Capitalism Came into Being?" *HK: ejinsight*, 29/05/2014. http://forum.hkej.com/nodel/113277.

The ambitious princelings were driven by their awareness of belonging to the "ruling class" and motivated by the failed coup in the Soviet Union on August 19, 1991. Led by Chen Yuan, they completed a special report on September 9, just three weeks after the coup, which they delivered to the highest authority and which received serious attention. In the report, the princelings petitioned the top leadership to discard the "social contract" and abandon the policy of "appeasing the people" (*jiaomin zhengce*, 骄民政策) that had been implemented in the first decade of reform. Instead, they suggested imposing discipline and order heavy-handedly without hesitation. They recommended holding tightly to the "barrel of the gun" and suggested that the CCP draw lessons from the fall of the Communist Party of the Soviet Union (CPSU) by directly assigning state assets to party-state officials, making them stockholders rather than mere managers of SOEs as before in order to ensure their absolute loyalty. In addition, they suggested that small and medium-sized SOEs that were insignificant and loss-making could be privatized for the sake of efficiency.[27]

The recommendations put forward by the princelings were largely in alignment with the political and economic transformations that China underwent in the subsequent decades, with only minor disparities in terms of how to dispose of state assets. However, their disdain for the Chinese populace and their disregard for socialist principles and state property demonstrated an extreme self-centeredness and a readiness to treat the nation as their personal domain.

While the Communist leadership initially hesitated to allocate state assets directly to officials due to ideological reservations, they tolerated the privatization of SOEs by local elites at minimal or no cost during the mid-1990s. The report by the princelings laid bare the harsh reality that Communism had lost its appeal not only among ordinary citizens but also among the elites. Their apprehension about the possibility of the CCP losing its grip on power fueled their insatiable greed. Deng Xiaoping's youngest son, Deng Zhifang, confided in a friend shortly after the

27 The report titled "China's Realistic Response and Strategic Choice after the Dramatic Change in the USSR" was drawn up by a group of princelings in the name of the Theory and Ideology Group of the official *China Youth Daily*, one of the key mouthpieces of the CCP affiliated with the Communist Youth League. The full text of this report was cited by *China Spring*, No. 1, 1992. http://non-violentes.blogspot.co.uk/2014/06/blog-post.html.

events at Tiananmen Square that "prioritizing personal wealth was not a consideration before, but now it must be taken seriously."[28] A few years later, Deng Xiaoping's elder daughter, Deng Lin, was taken aback by the democratization in Taiwan, where the ruling Kuomintang lost both political control and economic wealth. She proposed the idea of "converting state-owned enterprise assets into Party-owned assets" to bolster Party finances.[29] This raised questions about whether the true purpose of the Party was to serve the interests of the offspring of its founding revolutionaries, as a crony capitalist succinctly summarized.[30]

The report presented by the princelings, along with their relentless pursuit of personal wealth, served as early indicators of the Chinese Communist Party's shift from left-wing to right-wing politics. Despite the tragic events at Tiananmen Square and the conservative backlash against Deng Xiaoping's "reform and opening" policies, the CCP's transition toward capitalism was further solidified following Deng's southern tour, which garnered support from the People's Liberation Army.[31]

Chen Yun, who had ceased to oppose Deng's capitalist agenda, insisted on placing princelings from all the "Red Families" in key positions within the central government and the upper management of large SOEs to safeguard against any potential regime change. This agreement was brokered between the princelings (with covert support from Chen Yun) and General Secretary Jiang Zemin, who assumed leadership after Zhao Ziyang's removal in June 1989.[32] These institutional arrangements paved the way for the expansion of Chinese crony capitalism, particularly in the wake of the radical marketizing reforms initiated from 1992 onward.

Mao's Communist revolution inadvertently gave rise to a New Class, even though he refrained from explicitly acknowledging this term. He hoped that his final revolution—the Cultural Revolution—would prevent

[28] Luo, Xiaopeng: "The Premier's Dilemma under the Party's Heaven." *China-in-Perspective*, 24/08/2012. https://chinainperspective.com/default.php?id=16432.

[29] Shum, D (2021): *Red Roulette—An Insider's Story of Wealth, Power, Corruption and Vengeance in Today's China*. London: Simon & Schuster, p. 171.

[30] Ibid., p. 283.

[31] Yue, J (2018): *China's Rise in the Age of Globalization: Myth or Reality?* London: Palgrave MacMillan. Chp. 4: From Tiananmen to Shenzhen: Transition to Capitalism, pp. 187–207.

[32] Wang, Xizhe (2018): 07/07/2018. https://www.mingjingnews.com/article/915 51-80.

the emerging privileged class from evolving into a new bourgeoisie. However, Mao's unwavering commitment to Communist totalitarianism left him susceptible to a resurgence of bureaucracy even before his passing. Deng Xiaoping, who held contrasting views on capitalism compared to Mao, pursued a process of economic de-Maoification by implementing a market-socialist approach to modernize the nation during the 1980s.

Initially, the limited market forces of the 1980s did not offer significant opportunities for the political bureaucracy to extract rents. However, it was the upper echelons of the New Class, specifically the princelings who staunchly believed in the bloodline theory, who exploited these emerging market forces to amass wealth. In doing so, they unwittingly fostered the growth of China's crony capitalism, paradoxically becoming the new bourgeoisie that Mao had vowed to eliminate.

Like Mao, Deng was unwavering in his commitment to preserving the Party's monopoly on power. His approach of "perestroika without glasnost" eventually reached an impasse in the late 1980s. However, following the tragedy at Tiananmen Square, an even more radical wave of marketizing reforms was initiated. These reforms unleashed colossal market forces that intertwined with state power, benefiting the entire bureaucracy in a vast nexus of power and money. This trajectory marked the shift from market socialism to market Leninism in the 1990s, ultimately leading to the flourishing and institutionalization of crony capitalism.

CHAPTER 3

The Institutionalization of Crony Capitalism in Market Leninism (1990s–2002)

Frank Dikötter's influential work *China After Mao—The Rise of a Superpower*, published in 2022, sheds light on the unwavering belief of Chinese Communist leaders in the superiority of the socialist system.[1] However, it is crucial to delve deeper into these statements and examine the disparity between their rhetoric and actions. China's belief system has undergone significant changes both before and after the tragic events of Tiananmen square.

One might question why Party veterans persist in their commitment to Communism when even Leonid Brezhnev lost faith in the "advanced socialism" of the USSR. Mao's "last revolution" and the subsequent disastrous state of the economy had almost delegitimized Communist rule, resulting in a widespread "belief crisis" throughout the 1980s. Deng Xiaoping, a prominent figure, exemplified this departure from staunch Communism. Although he found certain fundamental concepts of socialism intriguing, Deng Xiaoping ultimately embraced an opportunistic pragmatism.

During the initial decade of reforms in the 1980s, the erosion of socialism became apparent with the rise of crony capitalism championed by the princelings. Market socialism, a reform approach within socialist boundaries, faced significant obstacles by the late 1980s. Further progress

[1] Dikötter, F (2022): Preface, p. xii.

J. Yue, *Crony Comprador Capitalism*,
https://doi.org/10.1007/978-3-031-53154-5_3

necessitated a more comprehensive dismantling of socialism, as envisioned by reformers associated with Zhao Ziyang. While conservative reformers attempted to regain control after the Tiananmen square incident, they were not entirely opposed to the market. Crony capitalism was curbed, but not completely eradicated.

In 1992, Deng Xiaoping seized upon the global changes of 1989 to introduce a comprehensive agenda of radical market-led reforms, known as market Leninism. This agenda aimed to replace market socialism with a system characterized by profound marketization and an emphasis on efficiency, all under tighter authoritarian rule. The goal was to salvage the notion of "socialism," not due to its perceived superiority, but rather as a means to preserve the Party's unchallenged grip on power.

The fusion of market forces with unchecked state power created the institutional conditions for the thriving of crony capitalism, leading to widespread corruption within the nomenklatura throughout the 1990s. Over time, this phenomenon became institutionalized, ultimately culminating in the demise of socialism by 2002. The Party's Sixteenth National Congress solidified the transformation from a "major left-wing dictatorship" to a "major right-wing dictatorship."

By examining the evolution of China's socialist system and the entanglement of market forces with state power, this chapter explores the institutionalization of crony capitalism within the framework of market Leninism from the 1990s to 2002.

Market Leninism: Deng Xiaoping's Post-Tiananmen Quest for Legitimacy

Deng Xiaoping's reforms in the first decade brought significant benefits to Chinese society as a whole, particularly when compared to the Mao era. Instead of solely focusing on identifying winners and losers, it is important to consider the distribution of gains from these reforms. While the general public anticipated higher income as a result of Deng's departure from Maoist policies, they also wished to preserve certain advantages of the Mao era, such as job security, minimal income disparity, and low inflation. However, reconciling these dual sets of benefits proved to be a formidable challenge for any regime, regardless of its nature.

On the other hand, intellectual elites driven by a strong desire for greater political freedom sought more than just economic improvements. The widening income gap among different social strata generated a sense of victimization among intellectuals within the new wealth distribution, which appeared to disproportionately favor certain manual laborers, particularly self-employed peddlers and merchants involved in illicit activities. Consequently, discontentment with the regime grew. Liberal intellectuals, who initially supported Deng's reforms in the early 1980s, voiced their dissent against his "perestroika without glasnost" approach. They advocated radical market-oriented reforms and political liberalization, finding support from segments within the bureaucracy who also resented the expanding income gap, as they derived fewer benefits from it. Despite their differing demands and motivations behind the scenes, these collective forces played a crucial role in fueling the pro-democracy movement of 1989.

The use of armed forces by Deng Xiaoping to suppress the demonstrators significantly undermined the legitimacy of the Communist regime, despite the continued support he received from the Party's hardliners and a considerable number of peasants who experienced improved living conditions. The collapse of Communist regimes in Central and Eastern Europe between 1989 and 1991, commonly referred to as the *Global 1989*, including the fall of the Soviet Union, created unease among Chinese rulers and led to widespread questioning of the regime's viability during this unprecedented crisis.

However, following the Tiananmen square crackdown, Deng Xiaoping's primary concern was not focused on the perceived external threat posed by the so-called "international hostile forces," as suggested by the Party's statements aiming to incite regime change. His foremost preoccupation lay in the impending backlash from staunch ideologues and conservative reformers, led by Chen Yun, who vehemently opposed his agenda of "reform and opening." Deng's main apprehension was the potential abandonment of his reform legacy rather than an immediate collapse of the regime. The likelihood of the latter diminished as stringent control was established, social order was swiftly restored, and disunity among Western nations imposing sanctions became evident. Notably, the United States and Japan took the lead in opposing China's isolation, fearing that pushing China into pariah status would prove counterproductive in strategic terms. This stance played a role in alleviating some of the pressures faced by the Chinese regime.

Overall, the impact of the *Global 1989* was significant, and Deng Xiaoping was keenly aware of the discrediting effect it had on Communism worldwide. He held a clear-headed perspective that Mikhail

Gorbachev's policies of glasnost and democratization were a path toward political suicide. In fact, as early as May 1989, Deng referred to Gorbachev as "an idiot!"[2] However, reverting to Maoist policies in China was not a politically viable option either. Such a move would have undermined Deng's reform and opening policies and disqualified him as the paramount leader.

Deng Xiaoping recognized that even returning to Maoist principles would not guarantee the Communist Party's long-term dominance, as demonstrated by the regime changes in East Germany under Erich Honecker and Romania under Nicolae Ceausescu. These events convinced Deng that clinging to the old socialist economic model was not a viable solution. He understood the imperative of forging a unique path for China's future, one that would enable the Communist Party to retain power while adapting to the changing global landscape and the discrediting of traditional socialist ideologies. Consequently, in the aftermath of the Tiananmen square incident, Deng embarked on a quest for legitimacy, seeking a solution that would shape China's future trajectory. This endeavor laid the foundations for the subsequent Chinese economic reforms and market-oriented policies. Deng's understanding of the need to adapt and evolve while maintaining Party control had a lasting impact on China's trajectory, paving the way for the country's remarkable economic growth and transformation in the ensuing years.

To many observers, it seemed that Deng Xiaoping's reform and opening policies encountered substantial challenges, marked by opposition from left-wing factions within the Party and economic sanctions imposed by the United States and its allies. Despite the hurdles confronting Deng Xiaoping's initiatives, it is crucial to emphasize that the central planners, who now wielded economic control, generally leaned toward conservatism in their economic thinking compared to Deng. Nevertheless, they demonstrated pragmatism and were not entirely averse to incorporating market mechanisms. Notably, certain regions in

[2] Sergey Radchenko (a renowned Cold War historian) twittered on 10 March 2022. https://twitter.com/DrRadchenko/status/1501795798178217988; The original source was from the memory of Zhang Weiwei, who interpreted for Deng Xiaoping in the 1980s. He recalled Deng's comment on Gorbachev after their summit meeting in May 1989: "This man may look smart but in fact is stupid." "Zhang Weiwei: My Personal Memories as Deng Xiaoping's Interpreter: From Oriana Fallaci to Kim Il-sung to Gorbachev," 25 Aug 2014 (updated on 6 Dec 2017). https://www.huffpost.com/entry/deng-xiaoping-remembered_b_5706143.

China persisted in undertaking pilot reform experiments with distinct "(neo)liberal orientations."[3]

Moreover, China's commitment to opening up to the outside world remained strong, and its import and export activities continued to experience significant growth. This can be partly attributed to the decision of the George H. W. Bush administration to retain China's most-favored-nation trading status, thereby ensuring normal trade relations between China and the United States. Concurrently, the Chinese regime, under the control of central planners, made efforts to liberalize inbound foreign investment. In April 1990, amendments were made to the Joint Venture Law, which allowed for greater participation of foreign investors in joint ventures. These amendments ensured that joint ventures would not be subject to nationalization or expropriation, providing a more secure environment for foreign businesses. Additionally, foreign residents were permitted to be appointed by the board of directors as the chairman, further promoting foreign involvement in Chinese enterprises.

These policy changes had tangible effects on China's foreign economic activities, encompassing foreign borrowing, foreign trade, and foreign direct investment (FDI). Table 3.1 illustrates some of the notable shifts in these areas. By avoiding the domino effect of Communist collapse experienced in Central and Eastern European countries, China demonstrated its resilience and commitment to the reform and opening-up process. While it is true that there were occasional policy reversals and efforts by central planners to tighten control over the economy, such measures should not be viewed as signaling the end of China's reform and opening. Instead, they represented temporary adjustments aimed at maintaining stability and addressing specific concerns. China remained determined to pursue its path of economic reform and opening to the world.

Following the Tiananmen square incident, the once temporary alliance between Deng Xiaoping and Chen Yun swiftly dissolved as their differing reform policies became more pronounced and intensified. Chen Yun, who had already acted as a counterbalance to Deng Xiaoping during the 1980s, emerged as a formidable rival, gaining consolidated control over economic matters. This solidified his position as a prominent figure in economic decision-making, challenging Deng's political and military

[3] Yue, J (2018), p. 193.

Table 3.1 Foreign trade and investment statistics (1988–1991) (US$ billions)

Year	*Exports*	*Imports*	*FDI*
1988	47.52	55.27	10.22
1989	52.54	59.14	10.06
1990	62.09	53.35	10.29
1991	71.91	63.79	11.56

Sources Chinese government website:
(1) Exports and imports: http://www.gov.cn/test/2005-06/27/content_10116.htm
(2) Foreign investment (including foreign borrowing and FDI): http://www.gov.cn/govweb/test/2005-06/27/content_10109.htm

dominance. Nevertheless, Deng Xiaoping's firm control over the military ensured his enduring position within the Party.

The delicate balance of power between Deng Xiaoping and Chen Yun formed the basis for a potential compromise, with the goal of establishing a regulated market economy within a vibrant one-party system, akin to the model observed in Singapore. However, the influence of Leninist principles, which discouraged open factionalism, the enduring impact of Mao's philosophy of struggle, and the setbacks faced by Deng, particularly with the fall of Zhao Ziyang, contributed to the radicalization of each faction. The intense rivalry between Deng and Chen resulted in a mutually exclusive and dichotomous perception of their opponents, significantly constraining the available options for Deng Xiaoping and the Party as they sought to shape a new political and economic system following the events of the *Global 1989*.

During the "improvement and rectification" period spanning from 1989 to 1991, Deng Xiaoping faced a challenging situation as his "reformist camp" weakened. With limited options available, he had to adopt a defensive stance and wait for the right moment to advance his agenda. Meanwhile, the central planners, under the leadership of Chen Yun, struggled to present an alternative approach to ensure China's long-term prosperity by recentralizing the economy. Despite their achievements in controlling inflation and achieving substantial economic growth in 1991 (as shown in Table 3.2), they were unable to propose a comprehensive strategy that addressed the evolving needs of the country.

While the Chinese economy exhibited relative stability during this period, the seismic events of the *Global 1989*, including the failed coup

Table 3.2 China's economic growth: 1988–1991

Year	1989	1990	1991
%	4.2	3.9	9.3

Source World Bank data: GDP growth (annual %)—China, https://data.worldbank.org/indicator/NY.GDP.MKTP.KD.ZG?locations=CN

in the Soviet Union, the collapse of the CPSU, and the dissolution of the Soviet Union itself, had a profound impact on Deng Xiaoping's perspective. These global developments cast doubt on the viability of the socialist model as an alternative for China, presenting Deng with an opportunity to assert his influence and advocate for more radical, market-oriented reforms. He believed that unleashing greater market forces was imperative for driving China's long-term economic growth. With a clear vision in mind, Deng directly confronted his opponents, implementing an audacious agenda of marketization without further negotiations or compromise. He recognized the necessity of a decisive shift and remained resolute in advancing his reform agenda.

During his highly acclaimed southern tour in the spring of 1992, Deng Xiaoping diverged significantly from the Communist Party's customary rhetoric. Notably, he refrained from mentioning Communism, while firmly maintaining his belief that only socialism could save and develop China. The omission of Communism while staunchly "upholding" socialism underscored Deng's rejection of ideological constraints, recognizing that socialism could be more flexibly defined in ideological language. Deng even candidly acknowledged the challenge of providing a definitive definition of "socialism, Marxism, and capitalism," which included himself and Mao in this assessment.[4] Instead, Deng introduced his own interpretation of socialism by presenting three criteria. According to him, as long as a system promoted the growth of productive forces, improved people's living standards, and enhanced China's overall national strength, it could be considered socialist.[5] This discrepancy between his ideological rhetoric and pragmatic approach grew more pronounced, echoing his earlier unannounced conversations in 1984 when he advised

[4] "Deng Xiaoping's Southern Tour Remarks" [Original]. *zhongwaiguanli* (《中外管理》), 20/07/2016. https://k.sina.cn/article_1790671321_6abb79d9022001lah.html.

[5] *Selected Works of Deng Xiaoping*, Vol. 3, p. 372, Beijing: Renmin Chubanshe, 1993.

visiting African leaders to prioritize economic development over fixating solely on the label of socialism.

Deng Xiaoping's resolute advocacy for radical marketizing reforms in early 1992 was deeply influenced by three pivotal lessons he drew from the Tiananmen incident and the subsequent events that occurred between 1989 and 1991. These lessons stemmed from the imperative to avoid political reform, the perception of the futility of appeasing the populace, and the recognition of the need to appease Western powers.[6] The collapse of Communism in Central and Eastern Europe and the dissolution of the Soviet Union played a profound role in Deng's thought process, reinforcing his rejection of democratic reforms and his determination to preserve the Leninist party state.

Deng was acutely aware that, despite the significant improvements in living standards that many had experienced under his leadership compared to the Mao era, he harbored a sense of dissatisfaction with what he perceived as an insufficient level of gratitude from a segment of the population. This discontent fueled his resolve to push forward with unwavering marketizing reforms, irrespective of potential public reactions. The report presented by the princelings lent support to Deng's convictions, further strengthening the perceived need for resolute and decisive action.

Moreover, Deng demonstrated a keen awareness of the prevailing reality, marked by the "institutional triumph of global capitalism" in the wake of the *Global 1989*. He understood that this trend was both widespread and resistant to opposition. Like other developing and transition economies, China found itself with limited alternatives other than to embrace global capitalism. This entailed advancing economic liberalization and immersing deeply into the global economy.

Deng placed immense importance on nurturing a stable and mutually beneficial relationship with the West. Such a relationship would grant China access to export markets, capital inflows, technological advance, and managerial expertise. These elements were crucial for the country's ongoing development and modernization.

Therefore, Deng astutely recognized the political imperative of accommodating Western powers, driven by his far-sighted strategic vision. His goals extended beyond mere economic benefits, encompassing the ambition of elevating China's international standing. By actively engaging

[6] Yue, J (2016): "China, Global Capitalism, and the Quest for Legitimacy," *International Politics*, 53:6, pp. 752–774.

China with the capitalist world, he aimed to strengthen its global influence and legitimacy as a prominent player on the world stage. Deng understood that aligning with the forces of global economic powers would eventually yield substantial political and diplomatic advantages. This, in turn, would consolidate China's position in the international arena, contingent upon the maintenance of domestic political stability.[7]

Deng's ultimate goal was unquestionably the preservation of the CCP's monopoly on power. At the core of his ideology lay an unwavering belief that robust economic growth was an absolute political imperative.[8] He argued that this growth could only be achieved through the implementation of more extensive marketizing reforms, effectively unleashing market forces. Within this framework, he anchored the CCP's legitimacy on its economic achievements, firmly convinced that sustained economic growth and improved living standards were fundamental in maintaining the Party's authority and securing continued support from the Chinese populace.

Deng's rhetoric introduced a paradoxical logic: it was no longer the case that socialism could rescue China. Instead, socialism as an economic system had to be discarded to facilitate the operation of a market economy. The success of this market economy, in turn, would ensure the CCP's monopoly on power, thereby preserving Chinese "socialism" as a political and ideological symbol. By aligning the CCP's legitimacy with its economic performance and utilizing marketizing reforms as a means to drive robust GDP growth, Deng adeptly navigated the intricate political terrain of the era. This distinctive approach allowed him to simultaneously address both internal and external pressures, safeguarding the party's firm grip on power.

The year 1992 marked a pivotal turning point in China's trajectory, signifying its transition to capitalism. During this period, the prior pursuit of market socialism in the 1980s gave way to a governance model known as market Leninism. This approach allowed for unrestricted capitalist development within the framework of a tightly controlled authoritarian regime. Deng, distancing himself from both Marxist principles and liberal democracy, established a strong connection between radical marketizing

[7] *Deng Xiaoping Nianpu* (1975–1997) (II), zhongyang wenxian yanjiushi (Beijing), 2004, p. 1289. http://news.china.com/history/all/11025807/20120301/17066016.html.

[8] *Selected Works of Deng Xiaoping*, Vol. 3, p. 375, Beijing: Renmin Chubanshe, 1993.

reforms, rapid economic growth, and the legitimacy of the ruling regime. To ensure the enduring impact of his reforms, Deng spearheaded nationwide efficiency-focused reform initiatives, with sustained high growth as the foremost priority.

However, Deng soon came to recognize the negative consequences of his strategy. By 1993, he acknowledged the widening income gap resulting from the exclusive nature of economic growth. His failure to fully appreciate the importance of inclusive growth became evident, as the model of exclusive economic growth posed more challenges than solutions for overall development.[9]

It is worth noting that, despite his adherence to socialist principles, Deng was unable to prevent the institutional changes brought about by his unfolding market-Leninist reforms. These reforms inadvertently facilitated the rise and expansion of crony capitalism throughout much of the 1990s and beyond.

The Bureaucracy: Emerging Crony-Capitalist Bourgeoisie

One of the enduring economic legacies of Mao's China is characterized by crude planning and provincial autarky, which sharply contrasted with the computer-based centralized planning system implemented in the Soviet Union's "advanced socialism." Between 1958 and 1970, Mao initiated a series of decentralization efforts aimed at addressing the rigidity of central planning. By granting local governments the authority to allocate resources, manage state-owned enterprises, collect taxes, and formulate economic plans, Mao sought to infuse the economy with local dynamism. However, this administrative approach to revitalizing the economy resulted in macroeconomic management chaos.

In 1970, Mao's strategy of preparing for a potential surprise attack from the Soviet Union transformed administrative decentralization into provincial autarky, signifying a significant institutional change. This military strategy reinforced the concept of self-sufficiency at the provincial level, urging provinces to strive for economic independence and reduce

[9] *Deng Xiaoping Nianpu* (1975–1997) (II), zhongyang wenxian yanjiushi (Beijing), 2004, p. 1364.

reliance on external resources. The practice of administrative decentralization persisted into the 1980s and, combined with institutionalized provincial autarky, resulted in economic balkanization (federalism). This fragmentation, rather than unification, of China's domestic market has had far-reaching consequences that continue to be felt even today.

Under the system of economic federalism, local administrations assumed the role of de facto economic planners and resource allocators, which naturally inclined them to compete for control over resources. This competition often undermined the effectiveness of central planning.[10] Moreover, excessive competition between provinces emerged, resulting in diseconomies of scale and diminishing macroeconomic efficiency as a whole.

From a political standpoint, despite the increasing power of local authorities during the Mao era, the central authority remained robust. In the post-Mao era, the subsequent leadership inherited Mao's legacy of administrative decentralization and further expanded it in the 1980s. Local governors gained even greater power and access to resources from the central state, challenging Deng Xiaoping's strong leadership. Unlike Mao, Deng adopted a style of collective leadership, sharing power with other Party veterans known as the "eight immortals," which fragmented political influence at the local level. Premier Zhao Ziyang, who oversaw fiscal-administrative decentralization in the 1980s, grew concerned about the defiance of local forces, which weakened the central state's leadership.[11]

As the paramount leader, Deng exercised unparalleled control over the local states, surpassing the other "immortals" who were unable to resist his encroachment into their fiefdoms, which served as their power bases in the localities, once he made up his mind. In early 1992, during Deng's southern tour, he embarked on a significant visit to Wuhan, the capital city of Hubei Province and a major industrial hub in central China. This visit held immense significance as it provided Deng with a direct opportunity to address the pressing issues of slow economic growth in Hubei province and assert his authority over the local bureaucracy. Deng's

[10] Wu, J & Ma, G (2012): *Twenty Topics on China's Economic Reform*. Beijing: Sanlian Bookstore, p. 42.

[11] "*Zhang Aimei Talks About Zhao Ziyang's Last Words and Prophecy*," in Commemorating the Hu-Zhao Foundation "China's Constitutional Reform" Symposium No. 13, posted on YouTube, 08/10/2012. https://www.youtube.com/watch?v=9t6_yTVEl10.

visit to Wuhan served as a platform for him to express his concerns and criticisms regarding the resistance posed by conservative forces, with a particular focus on Wang Renzhong, a conservative Party veteran and influential mentor to the bureaucracy of Hubei. Deng utilized this occasion to urge Wang to cease opposing his reform and opening policies,[12] thereby signaling his unwavering determination to forge ahead with his agenda despite the resistance encountered from entrenched conservative elements.

In the 1980s, during the early phase of reforms in China, the appointment of local provincial governors, including party bosses and provincial governors, was influenced by factional alignments, despite their ultimate appointment by the central government. Various factions within the Communist Party held different levels of influence over the appointment process, resulting in the selection of local leaders aligned with specific factions. For example, influential figures like Chen Yun wielded significant authority in appointing local leaders in Shanghai, while others like Ye Jianying held greater sway over selecting officials in their respective power bases such as Guangdong province. The attitudes and stances of local bureaucrats often mirrored those of their mentors in Beijing, displaying loyalty to the factional interests and political inclinations of their influential supporters. This intricate network of factional alignments in the appointment process had implications for governance and the implementation of policies at the local level.

Deng strategically adopted an approach to build his support base in the coastal provinces of China, recognizing their faster economic growth (such as Guangdong) and greater developmental possibilities (such as Shanghai) once market forces were unleashed. He actively cultivated a network of supporters who would champion his reform agenda and drive economic progress in these crucial regions. Even after Zhao Ziyang was removed from power in 1989, attempting to purge all of Zhao's clients in the localities proved impractical due to the implicit backing given to them by Deng. This implicit support granted them a significant advantage and prevented their complete removal from positions of influence. Deng, understanding the necessity of collaboration, recognized that he could not achieve his goals alone and relied on the emerging vested interests that had developed during the initial decade of reforms in the 1980s.

[12] Interview with an informed source in Beijing, 20/12/2015.

In 1992, Deng took a significant and definitive step by explicitly endorsing the market economy, thereby aligning himself with the emerging vested interests, particularly the bureaucrats in coastal regions. This endorsement marked a crucial turning point as it enabled Deng and the vested interests to overcome the resistance of conservative reformers who opposed the transition to radical marketizing reforms. The alliance between Deng and the emerging vested interests played a pivotal role in solidifying the dominance of market Leninism, serving as both a political instrument to legitimize the regime and as a foundation for the new economic system.

As the broader transformation took place, Chen Yun's composed response to Deng's push for China's transition to capitalism had a significant impact. Local states associated with conservative forces found themselves compelled to align with Deng's directives, as their mentors were also obliged to accept Deng's authority. With Deng's reshuffling of the top authority, particularly the Politburo's Standing Committee, to consist entirely of "reformers," local states had to adapt to his new course of market Leninism.

However, the legacy of provincial autarky and decentralized planning persisted. Efforts to institutionally overhaul these legacies and construct a unified national market were avoided due to both myopic perspectives and political expediency of the third-generation leadership, particularly First Deputy Premier Zhu Rongji, who became the de facto economic tsar from 1992 onward.[13] The continuation of these legacies was seen as playing a positive role in facilitating high economic growth. Local states retained their crucial role as resource allocators at the local level, further reinforcing their significance. The top-down systemic pressure for "forced growth" from the central government also strengthened the resolve of local states to reinforce regional autarky instead of dismantling it. These local states recognized that by expanding their local economies, they could enhance their relative position in relation to the central government. Additionally, by contributing to the expansion of the overall economic pie, they could secure a greater share of it for their own benefit.

[13] Yue, J (2018), p. 219.

The concept of "forced growth," as convincingly put by Janos Kornai, characterized the classic socialist system, aiming to demonstrate its superiority over capitalism and thereby legitimizing the regime's monopoly of power.[14] However, it is important to note that forced growth did not necessarily entail consistently maintaining high growth rates. During the 1980s, there were varying attitudes among the elites, even within the same factions. For instance, Deng Xiaoping and Hu Yaobang favored a high growth rate, while Deng's protégé, Premier Zhao Ziyang, shared Chen Yun's preference for moderate growth. These divergent perspectives reflected different understandings of modern economics and strategies for achieving modernization.

A profound transformation took place from 1992 onward when Deng established a connection between high growth and regime legitimacy. This led to the further amplification and institutionalization of "forced growth" as "forced high growth." The prevailing reality of the "institutional triumph of global capitalism" in the post-Cold War and post-Communist context made it challenging for the Chinese leadership to resist adopting radical marketizing reforms aligned with neoliberal principles. However, the stability of the regime relied heavily on economic stability. During Deng's southern tour, economic disorder emerged, providing Zhu Rongji with a valid justification to reintroduce state control, implicitly endorsed by Deng. Zhu recognized that China's "socialist market" lacked a strong foundation in the rule of law. The establishment of a genuine market economy contradicted the Party's absolute monopoly of power, thereby necessitating the continued reliance on administrative means to regulate the economy.

Furthermore, international experience indicated that marketization alone could not ensure high growth. Consequently, the government's intervention through a "visible hand" became indispensable for addressing market failures, ensuring macroeconomic stability, and achieving the predetermined targets of high growth. This approach involved extensive state-led investments in infrastructure and support for SOEs. While certain aspects of "neoliberalism with Chinese characteristics" were implemented following Deng's southern tour, such as price deregulation, privatization of SOEs, and significant trade and investment liberalization, which aligned with the core policy prescriptions of

[14] Kornai, J (1992): *The Socialist System: The Political Economy of Communism*. Oxford: Clarendon Press, pp. 197–198.

the Washington Consensus,[15] the government's interventionism persisted instead of full deregulation. As a result, the CCP retained and even expanded its substantial administrative power at all levels of governance.

The concepts of "forced high growth" and state interventionism are closely intertwined, highlighting the critical role of the bureaucracy in post-1992 market-based development. In contrast to the enduring meritocratic tradition of imperial China, Mao's New China witnessed prolonged anti-intellectualism after 1949, which excluded well-educated intellectual elites from the nomenklatura system. Although the emphasis on professionalism in the appointment of officials and managers of SOEs during the post-Mao era has gradually mitigated the negative effects of Mao's anti-intellectualism, political considerations such as candidate reliability and nepotism have remained predominant. Even two decades after the initiation of Chinese reform, as noted by Henry Paulson, who has had decades of experience dealing with China, "political patronage, not meritocracy, remains one of the main factors in senior appointments for SOEs."[16] The nomenklatura appointment mechanism, controlled by the Party's Organization Department at various levels of governance, has persisted to this day, keeping China far from being a technocratic government in institutional terms.

Similar to Deng Xiaoping's perspective, it is evident that many leaders in the country lack a fundamental understanding of economics, leading to a fixation on a single metric: growth.[17] Despite economic development being identified as the central task of the Party, the Party's organization department struggles to employ economic experts. Instead, the evaluation and promotion of party-state officials rely solely on their ability to achieve a top-down, pre-set target of economic growth rate. Due to inadequate knowledge stemming from China's flawed educational system, only a few party-state bureaucrats can distinguish between economic growth and economic development. In fact, influenced by misguided imported neoliberal ideas, they often confuse the two concepts, assuming that

[15] See Chap. 5: "Neoliberalism with Chinese Characteristics" (pp. 120–151) in David Harvey (2007): *A History of Neoliberalism*. New York: Oxford University Press; Also, Yue, J (2018): Chap. 5: "The 1990s: Washington Consensus in China?" (pp. 209–233).

[16] Paulson, H. M. (2015): *Dealing with China—An Insider Unmasks the New Economic Superpower*. New York: Headline, p. 322.

[17] Dikötter, F (2022): Preface, p. xiii.

economic growth automatically leads to structural change. This mechanism, which links GDP with officials' chances of promotion, has given rise to the prevalence of "GDP-ism"—a mindset that prioritizes achieving the economic growth rate at any cost, even at the expense of development. This stands in contrast to the bureaucrats of South Korea and Taiwan, who demonstrate true professionalism and a sense of mission in achieving development through inclusive growth and economic nationalism. The sense of mission in these late-developing economies has also prompted their top leaders to address corruption with a heavy-handed approach.

After 1992, following the embrace of the market economy, Deng successfully steered China away from its market-socialist path, instead establishing a market-Leninist approach to economic reform. During China's transition to capitalism, the bureaucracy was infused with what scholars have termed "an ideology of no ideology,"[18] indicating the absence of idealistic goals and a sole focus on materialistic GDP-ism within the framework of market Leninism. The third-generation leadership, led by Jiang Zemin, demonstrated even greater opportunism than Deng in implementing marketizing reforms and combating corruption, with the latter being utilized as a means to exert control over Party officials. Jiang and his close aides recognized that rejecting democracy would better serve the interests and privileges of the New Class.[19]

Those who portrayed Jiang Zemin as "a staunch Marxist-Leninist"[20] misunderstood the evolving political landscape of 1990s China. In reality, with Communism losing its appeal, the motivation behind the nomenklatura's fervor for radical economic reforms no longer derived from a dysfunctional official ideology, but rather from unprecedented opportunities for a power-money nexus. As Pei observed, the absence of checks and balances allowed the bureaucratic elites, who wielded unchecked power, to succumb to the temptation of enriching themselves through the exploitation of the wealth generated by economic growth. In other words, these elites now had every incentive to maximize their gains by expanding the economic pie.

[18] Lin, C (2008): "China: Changing the Rules of the Game." *Soundings*, 39:1, pp. 7–19; Nolan, P (2001): *China and Global Economy*. New York: Palgrave, p. 14.

[19] Zong, F (2007): *Zhao Ziyang: Captive Conversation*. Hong Kong: Open Press, p. 116.

[20] Dikötter, F (2022), p. 151.

Therefore, a connection between rent-seeking and economic growth was established, defining the notion of "capitalism with Chinese characteristics." As early as 1993, in the immediate aftermath of Deng's southern tour, crony capitalism began to experience explosive growth, primarily driven by the families of the New Class. According to some estimates, "the relatives of 1,700 party leaders controlled 3,100 of the country's top jobs. Another 900 family members ran the country's major trading companies."[21] While the princelings naturally viewed public assets as their private property, the bureaucratic elites took a different approach. They privatized the state by fragmenting state power into rent-seeking domains, either within specific sectors or at the local level. This fragmentation provided them with privileged access to scarce resources under their control, effectively transforming themselves into a de facto bourgeoisie.

The new bourgeoisie, as the dominant player of crony capitalism, operated through their own companies or through cronies, while also cultivating "white gloves"—proxies who profited from monopoly businesses on their behalf. These proxies served as intermediaries and were provided political cover by the elites, allowing the elites themselves to accumulate a larger share of wealth. Another significant aspect of crony capitalism involved the systematic plundering of state-owned assets by the elites, facilitated by "deliberate policy choices"[22] in the sophisticated nomenklatura privatization of SOEs. One such "reform" strategy, known as "grasp the big, let go of the small," was first propounded in 1993. This involved continuing support for larger SOEs, which were considered the lifeline of the Communist regime, while privatizing politically insignificant small and medium-sized loss-making SOEs.

The control over SOE privatization became a protracted tug of war between the central and local governments. On the one hand, the central government expressed concerns about the ideological and political implications of privatization, as Deputy Premier Zhu Rongji reiterated throughout the 1990s.[23] On the other hand, the central government refrained from intervening in privatization efforts at the local level, as this helped alleviate the fiscal burden of the central state. Eventually, the latter

[21] Dikötter, F (2022), p. 189.

[22] Pei, M (2016), p. 19.

[23] *A Record of Zhu Rongji's Remarks* (2011). Beijing: Renmin Chubanshe, vol. 2, p. 375; vol. 3, p. 184.

aspect took precedence, leading to the abolition of the State Administration of State-Owned Assets in 1995, which further facilitated the local states' spontaneous privatization endeavors.[24] The declining performance of the SOEs provided justifications for China's accelerated privatization from the mid-1990s onward. The collusion between the central and local states greatly fostered China's crony capitalist development.[25]

As noted by Yasheng Huang, China's political system underwent a significant transformation in the 1990s, characterized by its "increasingly self-serving nature."[26] However, the market-Leninist reforms pursued by the regime were not aimed at preserving socialism, but rather at dismantling it.[27] This shift marked a profound change in both ideology and institutions, propelling China into a "Great Leap Forward" toward capitalism in the social and economic realms. The Chinese Communist Party, which had previously been hostile to capitalism and imperialism, ceased to be a Marxist party and rapidly evolved into "a political party of capital and bureaucratic capitalists."[28]

While the princelings had played a notable role in the emergence of crony capitalism during the 1980s under the framework of market socialism, it was the bureaucratic elites of the 1990s who assumed a central role in advancing the development of crony capitalism. Their convergence with the princelings led to the cultivation of a shared consciousness akin to a "ruling class," as they sought to exert control over all available resources through their pervasive and omnipotent power. In 2001, Jiang Zemin introduced the "Three Represents" theory, which aimed to expand the Party's ruling base by including private capitalists into its ranks. This approach focused on forming an elite coalition rather than tightening control over private capitalists. The majority of private capitalists, in turn, demonstrated limited political engagement and

[24] Yue, J (2018), p. 218.

[25] Pei, M (2016), pp. 66–67; Yue, J (2018), pp. 225–226.

[26] Huang, Y (2008), p. 282.

[27] In his previous book, Yasheng Huang asserted that "in China, the goal [of the SOEs' reform] has been to preserve socialism, not to dismantle it." See Huang, Y (2003): *Selling China—Foreign Direct Investment during the Reform Era*. New York: Cambridge University Press, pp. 336, 345.

[28] Yu, A. L. (2014): "What Is the Nature of Capitalism in China? On the Rise of China and Its Inherent Contradictions," in Au Loon-Yu et al (ed.): *China's Rise: Strength and Fragility*. Merlin: Resistance Books, pp. 27–28.

readily aligned with the Party's emphasis on generating "wealth without freedom." They understood that political connections, or *guanxi*, were key to success in China, as revealed by Demond Shum in his influential book *Red Roulette*.[29] Shum exposed their role as "white gloves" for the Wen Jiabao family, whose amassed wealth of $2.7 billion shocked the world.[30] It became evident that making oneself a crony capitalist was the path to making a fortune in China.

In September 2002, Jiang Zemin declared the "building [of] a Chinese-style socialism" (中国特色社会主义) at the CCP's Sixteenth National Congress, which was attended by crony capitalists, as astutely observed by the *New York Times*. This declaration marked a departure from Deng Xiaoping's concept of "building a socialism *with* Chinese characteristics" (有中国特色的社会主义) and carried profound significance for China's political trajectory. While it may appear as a minor semantic alteration in Chinese-language version, it symbolized a significant shift in China's political direction. It signified the official departure from Deng's trial-and-error approach, which allowed for theoretical reversibility when deviating from the principles of "socialism." Instead, it solidified the institutionalization of crony capitalism within the framework of "socialism," now redefined as "Chinese-style socialism" to obfuscate the substantial erosion of socialist ideals. This formalized entrenchment represented a discernible transformation in the character of the Communist Party, transitioning from "the world's last major left-wing dictatorship" to "the world's last major right-wing dictatorship."[31]

Corruption: Regime Consolidation and Deconstruction

Fritz Bartel argues that the end of the Cold War can be attributed to the adeptness of the capitalist camp in reconfiguring the social contract, which promised economic well-being and security. This strategic approach was

[29] Shum, D (2021), pp. 74, 215.

[30] "Billions in Hidden Riches for Family of Chinese Leader." *The New York Times*, 25/10/2012. https://www.nytimes.com/2012/10/26/business/global/family-of-wen-jiabao-holds-a-hidden-fortune-in-china.html.

[31] "The Nation: Party of the Rich; China's Congress of Crony Capitalists." *The New York Times*, 10/11/2002. https://www.nytimes.com/2002/11/10/weekinreview/the-nation-party-of-the-rich-china-s-congress-of-crony-capitalists.html.

also pursued on the other side of the Iron Curtain in response to the crisis of the oil shock and the need for improved economic efficiency. The aim of these revisions was to diminish societal well-being without triggering significant social upheaval, aligning with the inherent goal of democratic capitalism to avoid destabilizing consequences. In contrast, Communism's failure to embrace economic discipline ultimately led to its peaceful demise in Central and Eastern Europe, with the exception of Romania. The Communist rulers in these countries recognized the need for a democratic transition as the solution to the challenges they faced.[32]

In China, however, Deng Xiaoping took a different approach by forcefully suppressing any social opposition to his vision of "perestroika without glasnost." This was evident in his decision to use force to suppress the Tiananmen demonstrators, effectively preventing a potential social backlash. Instead of fundamentally altering the political system, Deng introduced market Leninism, which imposed economic discipline along neoliberal lines. He achieved the dismantling of socialist welfare in favor of economic efficiency through the "shock and awe" effect of the Tiananmen square crackdown, which served as a catalyst for change. The lessons learned from Tiananmen and the events of the *Global 1989* further reinforced Deng's unwavering commitment to advancing market-Leninist reforms without appeasing the people. As a result, Deng successfully revised the social contract by promising *efficiency-oriented* prosperity in exchange for individuals' political obedience.

However, the success achieved by Deng came at a price: the exacerbation of corruption, which was facilitated by the thriving of crony capitalism. A group of China's liberal economists staunchly defended the flawed process of marketizing reform, arguing that corruption was an inevitable cost of achieving economic liberalization. They viewed corruption as a lubricant for reform, claiming that it propelled China's economic growth in a more institutionally stable manner.[33] This perspective had already emerged in the mid-1980s, with neoliberal economists like Steven N. S. Cheung (Zhang Wuchang, 张五常) advocating market fundamentalism. Their influence grew significantly, particularly after brokering a meeting between Milton Friedman and General Secretary Zhao Ziyang

[32] Bartel, F (2022): *The Triumph of Broken Promises—The End of the Cold War and the Rise of Neoliberalism*. Cambridge: Harvard University Press, pp. 13; 18–19.

[33] Zhang, W (1997): "Corruption: The Second Best if not the First Best," in: *China's Economic Debate*. Beijing: Jingji Guanli Chubanshe.

in 1988. Against this tide, in-depth theoretical critiques of corruption were rare both before and after the Tiananmen square crackdown, and remained relatively unknown outside of economic circles until a decade later.[34]

Ironically, the issue of corruption, which had been a central concern of pro-democracy demonstrators in the summer of 1989, gradually faded into the background with Deng Xiaoping's relaunch of marketizing reforms in 1992. This move resonated with numerous Chinese intellectuals who had longed for both economic and political freedoms throughout the 1980s. Driven by a personal incentive to restore his tarnished reputation following his fateful decision in 1989, Deng sought to please these intellectuals and reignite their support for his vision. The renewed focus on economic liberalization overshadowed the calls for political reform and accountability, allowing corruption to persist and even flourish in the subsequent years. Deng's prioritization of economic growth and stability over democratic principles further reinforced the dominance of crony capitalism and limited avenues for combating corruption within the system.

Following the tragedy of Tiananmen Square, many Chinese intellectuals experienced a loss of enthusiasm for politics. Economic hardships resulting from the J-curve effect during the market transformation in transition economies of Central and Eastern Europe, the tumultuous democratic transition under Gorbachev leading to the disintegration of the Soviet Union, and the perceived act of malign hegemony in the U.S.-led Western invasion of Iraq all contributed to a reduction in their hostility toward the regime.

These intellectuals, who had been shaped by decades of CCP's ideological indoctrination, were driven to refrain from outright rejecting cooperation with the regime. The resumption and expansion of economic freedom after 1992 played a significant role in enhancing their respect for Deng Xiaoping, who they viewed as a figure fighting against conservative forces. The focus on economic development and stability appealed

[34] For instance: Wu, Jinglian, et al. (1989): *Corruption: An Exchange Between Currency and Power*. Beijing: China Outlook Publishing House. The second edition of this book was renamed *Corruption: An Exchange between Power and Money*, published by Chinese Economics Publishing House in 1993. The third edition was published by the same publisher in 1999 and renamed *In Search of Roots for Corruption: Will China Become a Rent-Seeking Society?*

to their aspirations for prosperity and improved living standards, which overshadowed their concerns about political freedoms and human rights. This shift in attitude allowed for a degree of intellectual accommodation with the regime, as they saw economic progress as a necessary step toward potential future political reforms.

The complexity arises from the fact that, like the bureaucratic elites, a significant portion of Chinese intellectuals also shifted their focus from idealistic objectives to material gains. In response, the regime initiated a strategy of co-opting intellectuals after 1992, aligning with the country's market-Leninist reforms and transforming them into vested interests. A significant milestone was the implementation of Premier Zhu Rongji's "education, housing, and medicare" reforms in 1998, which directly benefited intellectuals and solidified their collaboration with the regime. In addition to appeasing business elites, particularly influential private entrepreneurs, Jiang Zemin's "Three Represents" further integrated intellectual elites into the CCP-led elite coalition. This formation of an unholy alliance significantly bolstered the Communist regime by providing it with intellectual support and a veneer of legitimacy. The regime's ability to co-opt and appease intellectuals played a crucial role in maintaining social stability and countering potential challenges to its authority.

He Qinglian, an independent-minded sociologist, stood apart from the co-option of intellectuals and emerged as a prominent figure among the few liberal intellectuals who challenged the prevailing view advocated by Chinese neoliberal economists in defense of corruption. Through extensive research that encompassed both second-hand and first-hand case studies of "asset stripping," a term used to describe the privatization of SOEs, He delved into the startling truth of collusive corruption. She uncovered how local officials and insiders within the SOEs colluded to loot state-owned assets during the manipulative process of nomenklatura privatization, disguised as "strategic corporate restructuring" and the establishment of a "modern corporate system."[35] In her analysis, He refuted the argument that corruption effectively lowered the costs of Chinese marketizing reforms, enabling China's market-led high growth. Instead, she shed light on the substantial socio-economic and moral costs that corruption imposed on Chinese society, which, in the long run, far outweighed any perceived benefits. He's research and dissenting voice

[35] He, Q (1998): *The Pitfalls of Modernization*. Beijing: Jingji Zhongguo Chubanshe, Chap. 3, pp. 78–116.

provided valuable insights into the detrimental effects of corruption and its impact on Chinese society's well-being.

Further studies conducted by researchers and scholars within the system on a more professional basis have provided additional insights into the relationship between rent-seeking and growing income inequality (Table 3.3). These studies have highlighted the widening income gap in Chinese society. For example, a survey conducted by the Renmin University of China in 1995 revealed that the income disparity between the top 20% (the richest families) and the bottom 20% (the poorest families) was 11.6 times, surpassing the income gap observed in the United States. Subsequently, a survey conducted by the Institute of Sociology of the Chinese Academy of Social Sciences in 2008 indicated that this income disparity had further widened to 17.1 times.[36] By the late 1990s, China had become one of the most unequal societies in the world, as measured by various indicators. These findings shed light on the detrimental consequences of rent-seeking and its contribution to the exacerbation of income inequality in China.

Alice Amsden presented a counter-argument to the prevailing notion that portrayed the government as inherently corrupt and solely focused on rent-seeking behavior. She emphasized that corruption exists in various forms and is not solely determined by government intervention in markets.[37] Amsden cautioned against oversimplifying the role of the state in relation to corruption, citing successful late-developing economies in East Asia, such as Singapore, Taiwan, and South Korea, where effective government control of corruption has been observed. Her point

Table 3.3 Rents as a percentage of GNP and Gini coefficient (1988 vs. 1995)

Year	*Rents ratio (%)*	*Gini coefficient*
1988	20	0.38
1995	32.3	0.45

Source Wu, J (1999): *Studies on China's Economic Development*. Shanghai: Far East Publishing House, p. 418

[36] Wu, J & Ma, G (2012): *Twenty Issue on China's Economic Reform*. Beijing: Sanlian Bookstore, p. 247.

[37] Amsden, A. H. (2007): *Escape from Empire—The Developing World's Journey Through Heaven and Hell*. Cambridge: MIT Press, p. 131.

was that corruption can manifest itself in diverse ways beyond rent-seeking. Amsden's perspective is illuminating when reflecting on China. It is important to consider other factors, such as state predation, which can also contribute to rising inequality. Taking a broader perspective on corruption reveals that addressing this issue requires comprehensive measures that go beyond simply blaming government intervention.

In the years after 1992, China experienced a significant rise in extravagant government expenditure that went largely unchecked. By 2011, administrative outlays accounted for approximately 40–50% of fiscal expenditure.[38] However, it is important to note that state predation is not unique to China and has been observed in other late-developing economies as well. What sets China apart from successful late industrializers is the underlying purpose of state predation. Chalmers Johnson, who introduced the concept of the "developmental state," argues that while the state has the capacity to shape market incentives to achieve developmental goals, it can also manipulate them for self-enrichment.[39] In China, the expansion of state power since the mid-1990s has resulted in the emergence of a highly predatory state with a strong focus on extracting resources for self-enrichment rather than prioritizing national objectives.

As a prominent development economist, Amsden boldly emphasized that: "A strong state is as dysfunctional as a weak one if it uses its power only to enrich itself."[40] In the Chinese context, the party state does not possess the imagined strength associated with centralized authority capable of effectively controlling the powerful provinces that directly control economic resources. However, it is not so weak as to be unable to maintain social order. The party state demonstrates significant strength in terms of its extractive and repressive capacity, but it notably lacks in enforcing the law, upholding social justice, and combating corruption—characteristics more commonly associated with pre-modern institutions.

[38] Hu Xingdou (2011): "How Away Is the Public Budget from Us?" *Southern People Weekly*, No. 5; Also Zhou Tianyong: "The New Dynamism of Economic Growth Originates from Reform and Innovation." *China Economic Daily*, 17/09/2013.

[39] Johnson, C (1999): "The Developmental State: Odyssey of a Concept," in Meredith Woo-Cuming (ed.): *The Developmental State*. Ithaca and London: Cornell University Press, p. 48.

[40] Amsden, A. H. (1989): *Asia's Next Giant—South Korea and Late Industrialization*. New York: Oxford University Press, p. 148.

Thus, it can be considered a strong state only to a limited extent. Moreover, its susceptibility to capture by vested interests, resulting from extensive rent-seeking practices, has further undermined its overall capacity, rendering it akin to what Gunnar Myrdal described as a "soft state" in his political science book *Asian Drama—An Inquiry into the Poverty of Nation*.[41]

For the top rulers in Beijing, corruption poses a complex dilemma. On the one hand, it has the potential to undermine regime legitimacy, but on the other, it can facilitate control over the nomenklatura. This suggests that corruption has been intentionally tolerated to a significant extent in the interest of maintaining regime stability. The prevalence of state predation exemplifies this phenomenon. Both central and local officials understand that the central authority would never risk implementing a genuine anti-corruption campaign, as doing so would damage the Party's reputation and undermine its rule. Hence, an unspoken agreement exists between the central government and local authorities, allowing corruption to persist within certain boundaries. As depicted by the author of the political novel *The Wrath of Heaven* (*Tiannu*, 天怒), quoting a fictional corrupt senior official, "corruption makes our [regime's] rule more solid!" This highlights the understanding that corruption, to some extent, helps solidify the regime's grip on power.[42]

The solidification of the regime's rule through crony capitalism persisted until the early 2000s. However, challenges began to emerge during this period. One significant issue was the persistent increase in economic costs driven by corruption. As a result, the regime artificially kept wages low to sustain rapid economic growth under an extensive industrialization model. This deliberate suppression of wages disrupted the traditional alliance between the Party and the working class, leading to notable political costs, including the emergence of labor movements in the new millennium. Furthermore, it contributed to a longstanding problem of underconsumption, leaving China susceptible to systemic pressures from global capitalism. Meeting the demands of global capitalism, which required greater market access, became a prerequisite for achieving export-led growth in line with Ricardian economics. To

[41] Myrdal, G (1968): *Asian Drama—An Inquiry into the Poverty of Nations*. London: Allen Lane; The Penguin Press, p. 208.

[42] Chen, F (1997): *The Wrath of Heaven*. Hohhot: Yuanfang Chubanshe, Chap. 17, p. 283.

fulfill these demands, China had to abandon economic nationalism and promote the development of comprador capitalism, a concept that will be further explored in the subsequent chapters.

In contrast to the "authoritarian resilience" thesis put forward by Andrew Nathan in 2003,[43] there were growing indications of institutional sclerosis in China, characterized by a resistance to political change and a trend of Brezhnevization when Hu Jintao succeeded Jiang Zemin in 2002 and rejected democratic transformation more firmly. Faced with increasing inequality and social unrest that posed a significant threat to social stability, the Communist regime adopted an uncompromising stance of "no appeasing the people." This approach involved escalating internal security expenditures to suppress dissent, surpassing defense expenditure for the first time in 2011 and remaining higher ever since. By 2020, internal security spending had more than doubled, reaching $210 billion, which was 7% higher than national defense spending.[44] This trend highlights the influence of vested interests that have captured the state, prioritizing their own agenda over addressing the failures of crony capitalism and avoiding the "middle-income trap" through proactive institutional transition.[45]

The strong inertia of bureaucratic self-enrichment within the context of political Brezhnevization would inevitably lead to what Minxin Pei referred to as "pervasive institutional decay" and "deteriorating governance," both of which are long-term indicators of "regime decay."[46] As will be discussed in the upcoming chapters, China has experienced significant economic development since 1992, particularly after its accession

[43] Nathan, A. J. (2003): "China's Changing of the Guard: Authoritarian Resilience." *Journal of Democracy*, 14:1, pp. 6–17.

[44] "China Spends More on Controlling Its 1.4bn People Than on Defense—Silencing Dissent Also Nips Innovation in the Bud." *Nikkei-Asia*, 29/08/2022. https://asia.nikkei.com/static/vdata/infographics/china-spends-more-on-controlling-its-1-dot-4bn-people-than-on-defense/.

[45] On 9 Jan 2012, the official *China Youth Daily* reported the 2011 "Social Progress Series Research Report" issued by the Institute of Social Progress of Tsinghua University's Kaifeng Development Research Academy and the Social Development Research Group of the Department of Sociology of Tsinghua University. The online version of the report was quickly deleted by the Internet supervision department. See news report "Tsinghua University Report Calls for Mass Consensus to Restart Political Reform," *Radio France International*, 09/01/2012.

[46] Pei, M (2016), p. 264.

to the WTO in 2001. However, this economic growth has been accompanied by the increasing risk of falling into the "middle-income trap," a path of semi-peripheral development that contributes to growing social instability and political conservatism in China. This situation further exacerbates elite disunity within the regime, which goes beyond a struggle for power distribution and encompasses a clash of ideas on how to address the unprecedented crisis resulting from China's crony comprador capitalist development. Xi Jinping's rise to power in 2012 occurred during a critical period marked by the consequences of Deng Xiaoping's market Leninism and the manifestation of crony capitalism. Addressing these challenges is imperative and should not be delayed any further.

In 1992, Deng Xiaoping's intervention marked a crucial turning point in China's path of market-oriented reforms, ushering in the era of crony capitalism. This transition, often referred to as "market Leninism," represented a shift away from the previous model of market socialism that had guided China's economic policies. The combination of a predatory state and market forces not only fueled economic growth and strengthened the Communist regime's legitimacy, but also solidified the emergence of Chinese crony capitalism, which had already been taking shape during the preceding period of market socialism.

However, the successful consolidation of the CCP's rule through exclusive growth inadvertently sowed the seeds of opposition. This was evident in the resurgence of Maoism and its appeal to segments of the underprivileged population in different regions of China, particularly from the late 1990s onward. This opposition movement reflected discontent with the growing wealth disparities and perceived injustices perpetuated by the crony capitalist system. The resurgence of Maoism served as a critique of the prevailing socio-economic order and an alternative vision for addressing the challenges facing Chinese society.

The formation of an elite coalition within the CCP had far-reaching consequences, not only leading to an unequal distribution of wealth that disadvantaged the working class but also impeding social mobility and perpetuating a closed political system resistant to change. This development compromised and obscured the original principles of socialism within the nominally Marxist party. The nomenklatura elite effectively captured the state, solidifying a deeply rooted crony capitalist system. This distinct form of state capitalism thrived not only due to the strengthening of authoritarianism following the Tiananmen square crackdown, but, more significantly, through its alignment with global capitalism. However, the ironic alliance between the Chinese crony capitalist system and global capitalism came at the expense of China's pursuit of autonomous development. The integration into the global capitalist system constrained China's ability to chart an independent course and fully realize its socialist aspirations.

Deng Xiaoping, despite his socialist background, displayed a keen awareness of the potential dangers posed by China's crony capitalist development as early as 1993. He recognized the growing wealth disparities and the problems that could arise from such an imbalanced distribution of resources. Deng acknowledged that while development had been prioritized in the past, the challenges resulting from its consequences were equally important.[47]

Unfortunately, Deng's influence was limited in terms of mitigating the profound institutional transformations that had taken place. He could not foresee the eventual decay of the regime and the complexities it would face. These complexities left the regime vulnerable and grappling with numerous internal and external challenges. Despite Deng's initial recognition of the risks, the deep-rooted nature of the crony capitalist system proved difficult to counteract, leading to significant repercussions for China's socio-economic fabric and the stability of its political system.

[47] On September 16, 1993, Deng Xiaoping expressed the following sentiment to his younger brother, Deng Ken: "A small number of individuals have amassed significant wealth, while the majority have not. If this trend continues, it will inevitably lead to future issues. Unequal distribution will result in polarization, and problems will eventually arise. This issue must be resolved. In the past, our focus was primarily on development, but upon reflection, the challenges that arise after development are no less significant than those faced in the absence of development." *Deng Xiaoping Nianpu* (1975–1997) II, zhongyang wenxian yanjiushi (Beijing), 2004, p. 1364.

PART II

China's Semi-peripheral and Comprador Capitalism

CHAPTER 4

Zhang Chunqiao's Curse and the Transition to Comprador Capitalism (Late 1980s to 2002)

Comprador or compradorism has historically carried a derogatory connotation within China's official ideology, particularly during the pre-reform era. While the term originally held a neutral meaning, its connotation underwent significant changes over time, eventually transforming into a fully negative term with the rise of Chinese nationalism in the 1920s. As Jung-fang Tsai aptly stated, "the meaning of the word comprador was gradually expanded beyond its original commercial sense to include any Chinese who collaborated with foreigners in one way or another, serving the interests of the imperialists and thereby acting as a traitor."[1]

Through meticulous examination of the historical facts, Tsai suggested in his 1982 essay that compradorism and patriotism are not necessarily mutually exclusive. In other words, one can engage in comprador activities while still maintaining a sense of loyalty to their country. In fact, with China's entry into the post-Mao era, there has been a notable shift in attitudes toward historical compradorism.[2] This shift became particularly evident in the late 1990s when China embarked on radical trade

[1] Tsai, J. F. (1981): "The Predicament of the Comprador Ideologists: He Qi (Ho Kai, 1859–1914) and Hu Liyuan (1847–1916)." *Modern China*, 7:2, pp. 191–225.

[2] Huang Yifeng, et al. (1982): *The Comprador Class in Old China*. Shanghai People's Press. Huang altered his comments 15 years (1997) after the book's publication which he deemed had oversimplified the issue of compradorism in Old China. Some "big-name

J. Yue, *Crony Comprador Capitalism*,
https://doi.org/10.1007/978-3-031-53154-5_4

and investment liberalization, leading to the pronounced emergence of a comprador class.

Dependency theorists shared similar perspectives, positing that the existence of a dominant comprador class posed a significant obstacle to the developmental aspirations of (semi-)peripheral states. However, many of these theorists maintained a balanced approach, suggesting that the actions of the comprador class in Global South countries were not necessarily deliberate betrayals of national interests. Instead, these elites placed their faith in the "free market logic" as a means to achieve modernity. This mindset was often influenced by their Western education, which frequently instilled a deep commitment to the principles of the Chicago school of economics.[3]

Many academics and policymakers worldwide may find it challenging to associate China's remarkable economic growth with compradorism. Three major reasons can be given for this. Firstly, since the establishment of the People's Republic in 1949, the Chinese Communist Party (CCP) has consistently portrayed the regime as patriotic and committed to revitalizing China. Through official propaganda, the narrative of ending the "hundred-year humiliation" has effectively forged a strong connection with nationalism and patriotism, contrasting with preceding regimes that embraced compradorism.

Secondly, China's widely recognized economic success has often been interpreted as a deliberate rejection of the neoliberal Washington Consensus in favor of an active pursuit of economic nationalism. This interpretation gained momentum following the global financial and economic crisis of 2007–2009, coinciding with the "power shift" thesis. Consequently, a consensus emerged within Western policy and academic circles that acknowledged China's ascent as an established reality.[4] Even among experts well-versed in China's structural economic weaknesses and its deep integration into the global capitalist system, such as Nicholas Lardy, there has been reluctance to directly link these shortcomings with

compradors" were delisted. https://baike.baidu.com/item/%E6%97%A7%E4%B8%AD%E5%9B%BD%E7%9A%84%E4%B9%B0%E5%8A%9E%E9%98%B6%E7%BA%A7/12518072.

[3] Chwieroth, J (2007): "Neoliberal Economists and Capital Account Liberalization in Emerging Markets." *International Organization*, 61:2, pp. 443–463; Jepson, N (2019), p. 41.

[4] Buzan, B (2010): "China in International Society: Is 'Peaceful Rise' Possible?" *The Chinese Journal of International Politics*, 3:1, pp. 5–36.

compradorism.[5] Consequently, academic literature has seldom explored the concept of compradorism and has allocated limited attention to its theoretical development.[6]

Thirdly, the United States and various Western nations have consistently leveled accusations against China, alleging its involvement in market-distorting practices, most notably trade protectionism and techno-nationalism. These allegations are often linked to an alternative model of state capitalism, portraying China as actively fostering a robust and diversified economy. Concurrently, political statements and media coverage have further solidified the perception of China's evolution into an industrial powerhouse driven by economic nationalism.

However, these perceptions were not consistently grounded in reality. Within China's tightly controlled official economic ideology, economic nationalism has been marginalized, with proponents of economic liberalism overwhelmingly dominating academic and policy circles. Chinese scholars and policymakers have shown a stronger inclination toward the ideas of Adam Smith rather than Friedrich List. While elements of statism have been present, their primary role has paradoxically been to facilitate economic regulation, particularly in enforcing trade, investment, and financial liberalization.

As this chapter will elucidate, Chinese nationalism often appears as vacuous propagandist rhetoric. Politically, it has been selective and opportunistic, while economically, the ruling elites, the majority of whom are economic internationalists, have reluctantly embraced economic nationalism on occasion, primarily out of necessity rather than genuine conviction. This reluctance can be likened to Britain's post-World War II era, which faced significant balance of payment crises, resulting in temporary suspensions of unilateral free trade policies and the imposition of trade barriers. Nevertheless, these measures did not signify a departure from economic liberalism.

[5] Lardy, N (1995): "The Role of Foreign Trade and Investment in China's Economic Transformation." *The China Quarterly*, Dec, 144, pp. 1065–1082; Lardy, N (2002): *Integrating China into the Global Economy*. Washington: Brookings Institution Press, p. 21.

[6] Articles covering China's comprador capitalism have been seldom observed in academic literature over the past three decades. One distinguished piece cane be seen in Ho, W. C. (2013): "The New 'Comprador Class': The Re-emergence of Bureaucratic Capitalists in Post-Deng China." *Journal of Contemporary China*, 22:83, pp. 812–827.

What is particularly noteworthy is that China's often-lauded economic progress has been marked more by semi-peripheral development than by complete economic modernization. Related to this, the undeniable presence and growing influence of an entrenched comprador class challenge the expectation of an imminent and assured escape from the so-called "middle-income trap" after four decades of reform and opening. This underscores the need for a critical evaluation of China's development as a comprador capitalist entity over the past few decades.

This chapter is divided into three main sections. The first section delves into the nature of the CCP, aiming to determine whether it can be characterized as a political party dedicated to nationalism. The second section investigates the origins of compradorism in the reform era, with a primary focus on its emergence in the 1980s and its initial confinement to the intellectual sphere. Finally, the third section examines the factors that compelled China's transition to comprador capitalism in the 1990s and its institutionalization at the turn of the millennium.

Unveiling the Nationalist Facade: A Historical Overview of the CCP

In Western academic circles, the CCP is frequently perceived as a party characterized by persistent nationalist inclinations, rooted in its century-old quest for national rejuvenation.[7] Many of these scholars tend to dismiss the idea that the CCP was merely a puppet of Moscow. They argue that its success was primarily an indigenous achievement, independent of Soviet support.[8] However, this perspective may overlook the CCP's underlying commitment to Communist internationalism, to which the leaders' nationalist fervor is subservient. Additionally, it fails to consider recent revelations from declassified archives of the former Soviet Union and the Communist International (Comintern). These revelations highlight the CCP's profound dependence on Moscow's sponsorship throughout its formation, expansion, and eventual ascent to power in

[7] Dosh, R: "The Chinese Communist Party Has Always Been Nationalist—China's Quest for Rejuvenation Dates Back More Than a Century." *Foreign Policy*, 01/07/2021. https://foreignpolicy.com/2021/07/01/chinese-communist-party-nationalist-centennial/.

[8] Brown, A (2020): *The Human Factor—Gorbachev, Reagan, and Thatcher, and the End of the Cold War*. Oxford: Oxford University Press, p. 18.

1949. This challenges the assertion that the CCP's motivations are solely rooted in nationalism.

The rise of the CCP in the 1920s was a consequence of Soviet ideological expansionism following the Bolshevik Revolution in 1917. Its emergence was intricately linked to Lenin's strategy of world revolution, aimed at undermining British imperialism in the Far East. Both the Kuomintang (KMT or Nationalist Party) and the CCP served as proxies in this endeavor. The CCP's eventual attainment of state power relied heavily on substantial Soviet financial and military assistance between 1921 and 1949, which played a decisive role. Notably, the military support offered to the CCP by Stalin far surpassed the aid received by the KMT from the United States between 1945 and 1949. According to Xu Zerong's estimates, the Soviet Union supplied the CCP with enough ammunition to equip 150–200 infantry divisions, while the United States provided the KMT with only the equivalent of 45 divisions before October 1949.[9] This political indebtedness shaped the CCP's internationalist agenda, compelling the CCP to align with Moscow's foreign policy objectives, leaving little room for independent initiatives by Mao Zedong, which would have been unsustainable and subject to Stalin's coercion.

An illustrative example of the CCP's transition toward internationalism can be discerned through the actions of Li Dazhao, one of the Party's founders in 1920. In 1922, Li expressed his dissent to Wellington Koo, the Foreign Minister of the Republic of China government, advocating the unconditional establishment of diplomatic relations with Soviet Russia. This incident occurred shortly after the Soviet Red Army occupied Outer Mongolia in July 1921. This occupation displaced Chinese forces and civilians who had returned to reclaim Chinese sovereignty following the Bolshevik Revolution. The Soviet installation of a pro-Soviet regime in Outer Mongolia primarily aimed to create a buffer zone against Japan rather than liberate the Outer Mongolian people. While the Soviet intentions remained unclear, Li did not oppose the encroachment on Chinese sovereignty. Instead, he engaged in an ideological debate with Koo. Li asserted that "people in Outer Mongolia would enjoy better living conditions under Soviet Russia's control and domination," even if it meant

[9] David Tsui (Zerong Xu) (2015): *China's Military Intervention in Korea: Its Origins and Objectives*. Bloomington: Trafford Publishing, pp. xlv, xlviii.

compromising Chinese sovereignty. Koo, a staunch Chinese nationalist, vehemently rejected Li's perspective.[10]

In the historical narrative of the CCP, the 1924 Sino-Soviet Treaty is often portrayed as the first equal treaty signed by pre-1949 Chinese governments with foreign powers. However, this treaty actually contained unequal clauses that violated previous commitments made by Lenin's Soviet Russia in the three "Manifestos toward China" from 1919 to 1923. These Manifestos, significant for their promises, had assured the return of the China Eastern Railway (CER) to Chinese sovereignty without any compensation demanded from China. Contrary to these promises, the Soviets, through secretive means, effectively gained control over the CER by persuading the local warlord Zhang Xueliang to sign a confidential agreement. This agreement granted the Soviet Union majority control of the railway.

In July–August 1929, the Chinese Nationalist government's revolutionary diplomacy translated into radical actions in an attempt to compel the Soviets to return control of the CER to China. This resulted in an armed conflict between Zhang Xueliang's Manchurian army and Soviet armed forces in the border area. Zhang was ultimately defeated and forced to accept a protocol that reinstated the status outlined in the 1924 Sino-Soviet Treaty. However, this protocol was declined by the central government in Nanjing.

In the midst of the conflict, the CCP found itself engaged in civil wars with the KMT government, operating from its base in Jiangxi Province. During this time, the Comintern instructed the CCP to prioritize the defense of the Soviet Union. In response, the CCP actively dispatched guerrilla troops to the Soviet Far East, where they fought alongside the Red Army against Zhang Xueliang's forces. Additionally, the CCP organized a general strike in Shanghai to demonstrate their support for the Soviet Union.

However, these actions, including the CCP's public appeal for "defending the Soviet Union with armed forces," not only discredited the CCP as a patriotic organization but also created internal divisions within the Party. Chen Duxiu, one of the CCP's co-founders and the former General Secretary, an idealist Communist inclined toward Trotskyism, opposed this appeal, viewing it as detrimental to China's interests.

[10] *Wellington Koo Memoirs* (Chinese version), vol. 2. Beijing: Chunghwa Book, pp. 339–340.

Consequently, Chen was expelled from the Party. The consequences of this conflict had far-reaching implications for China. The Soviet Union took advantage of the situation and occupied two specific Chinese territorial areas, returning only a portion of them to Chinese sovereignty 75 years later, as late as 2004. This prolonged occupation further complicated China's territorial integrity and sovereignty, a fact that the CCP intentionally dismissed in Chinese middle-school history textbooks from 1949 until today.

The Chinese Communists were initially inspired by Lenin's Manifestos, which pledged to eliminate secret treaties and address historical injustices concerning China. Embracing Communist internationalism, the CCP's active alignment with Comintern directives turned them into a tool of Soviet foreign policy, primarily advancing the national interests of the Soviet Union rather than those of China.

In April 1941, a neutrality pact was established between the Soviet Union and Japan during the Second Sino-Japanese War. In this pact, both powers recognized Manchuria and Outer Mongolia as each other's spheres of influence. This pact directly undermined China's territorial integrity as it disregarded China's sovereignty over these regions. As it did in 1929, the CCP celebrated the neutrality pact, defending Soviet international behavior and presenting it as a "great victory of Soviet foreign policy" that favored peace-loving people and oppressed nations. The CCP believed that, despite the pact, the Soviet Union would continue to support China's independent and just war against Japanese imperialism.[11]

To the CCP's surprise, just half a year later, in October 1941, the Soviet government abruptly announced the termination of aid to China. This decision was clearly influenced by Operation Barbarossa, which was Germany's invasion of the Soviet Union. The neutrality pact severely undermined China's resistance efforts during a period when China heavily relied on arms supplies from the Soviet Union. The CCP's initial optimism regarding the implications of the pact turned out to be misplaced,

[11] "Chinese Communist Party Expresses Opinion on Soviet-Japanese Neutrality Treaty." *Xinhua Online*, 22/05/2007. http://www.ce.cn/xwzx/gnsz/szyw/200705/22/t20070522_11452445.shtml.

and China had to bear the consequences of the Soviet foreign policy change.[12]

Labeling the Chinese Communists as nationalists becomes more complex when considering their emphasis on expanding their strength by exploiting Japan's aggression, even at the expense of the KMT, their wartime ally and the legitimate leader in the United Front against Japan. Mao's influential role in shaping consensus within the Party was exemplified in the so-called "7.2.1 policy." This policy suggested allocating 70% of efforts for self-expansion, 20% for propaganda, and 10% for combating the Japanese aggressors. The existence of the "7.2.1 policy" has been the subject of academic dispute, but subsequent developments have substantiated the CCP's de facto implementation of such a strategy.[13]

Another indirect piece of evidence was the account of Li Rui, Mao's secretary, who quoted Mao's words during the Lushan Conference held in 1959, summarizing this self-expansion strategy. On July 31, during that conference, Mao bluntly stated: "Some comrades believed that the less land occupied by Japan, the better. Later, they reached a unified understanding: Let Japan occupy more land to be patriotic. Otherwise, we will become a country that supports Chiang Kai-shek. There will be a country within the country, Chiang, Japan, and me, and (this repeats) the history of the Three Kingdoms."[14]

Some contemporary academic literature in the PRC tends to exaggerate the CCP's deviation from the principle of "defending the Soviet Union" during the Sino-Japanese War. These accounts portray the CCP as defenders of national interests by resisting the launch of a premature war in southern Manchuria, as called for by Stalin in the name of the Comintern in 1942. According to these narratives, the Comintern-ordered second front offensive, which aimed to tie down the imperial

[12] Li, Jiagu (1998): "On the Signing of 'Soviet-Japanese Neutrality Treaty' and Its Actual Influence on China's War of Resistance." *The Journal of Studies of China's Resistance War against Japan*, No. 1, pp. 56–75.

[13] Lyman P. Van Slyke (ed.) (1968): *The Chinese Communist Movement—A Report to US War Department*. Redwood: Stanford University Press, pp. 101–102.

[14] Li Rui (1989): *A True Record of Lushan Conference*. Beijing: chunqiu chubanshe, p. 223.

Japanese army, would allow the Soviet Union to concentrate on the war with Nazi Germany, which was a significant strategic concern.[15]

In fact, unlike Tito of Yugoslavia, Mao's resistance to Stalin's orders was not primarily motivated by China's national interests. His decision was influenced by his own political calculations and the perceived imminent collapse of Stalin's regime in the first half of 1942 following the military debacle faced by the Soviet Union during Operation Barbarossa. Consequently, Mao calmly declined Moscow's requests and began exploring closer relations with the United States, distancing himself from the Soviet Union. This marked a significant shift in his foreign policy approach.[16]

Mao's primary objective during the Second World War was to expand the armed forces and political influence of the CCP. In pursuit of this goal, he went to the extent of establishing clandestine contacts and engaging in direct negotiations with Japan, the arch-enemy of the Chinese nation.

Operating under extreme secrecy, Mao, along with other senior CCP leaders such as Liu Shaoqi, Zhou Enlai, Ren Bishi, and Kang Sheng, attempted to broker a truce between the CCP-led New Fourth Army and the imperial Japanese army.[17] Mao's intention was clear: to advance the interests of the CCP by sharing intelligence on the Nationalist regime, even if it meant compromising China's national interests, in order to undermine the KMT.[18] To facilitate this covert collaboration, a secret communication channel was established between Yan'an, the CCP's headquarters, and Nanjing, where Japan's occupation forces were headquartered.

This covert collusion persisted even after the war's conclusion, which was regarded as a disgraceful act by Petr Parfenovich Vladimirov, Stalin's representative in Yan'an. Such collusion had the potential to blemish the

[15] Jintang Zou (2015): "The Debate on the Issue of 'Armed to Defend the Soviet Union' Between the Communist International and the Communist Party of China." *Advances in Social Sciences*, 4:4, pp. 225–229.

[16] Xu, Z (2015), p. 47.

[17] Ding Dong: "The Archive Incident Concerning Zeng Shan During the Cultural Revolution." http://www.hybsl.cn/beijingcankao/beijingfenxi/2013-05-15/37151.html.

[18] Endo, H (2015): *Mao Zedong—The Man Who Conspired with the Japanese Army*. The Chinese version of this book was published by Mirror Books based in New York.

image of the CCP as the vanguard of Chinese national interest and delegitimize the Communist revolution from its very origins. Nevertheless, it facilitated the swift expansion of the CCP into a formidable political force, ultimately clearing the way for its seizure of power in 1949. This significant factor helps elucidate why, in the post-World War II period after 1949, Mao Zedong displayed minimal concern for the Nanjing massacre during his rule. He prohibited publications of relevant historical investigations[19] and even expressed gratitude for Japan's aggression, which greatly benefited the CCP. Furthermore, he renounced all war indemnities from post-war Japan.

Mao's attempt at greater autonomy from Moscow through even approaching the United States and Japan during the closing stages of World War II had consequences as it backfired in Moscow, leading to a series of retaliatory actions that reminded Mao and the CCP of their absolute subordination to the Soviet Union. With the war coming to an end, the KMT's nationalist pursuit of recovering sovereignty in Manchuria rather than staying neutral between the United States and the USSR enraged Stalin. His resentment toward the pro-American KMT regime, rather than any empathy for the CCP, led him to sponsor the latter's entry into Manchuria, making a Civil War in China inevitable.

The CCP's collaboration with the Soviet Union to consolidate control of Manchuria after World War II triggered massive anti-Soviet student demonstrations in February 1946. These demonstrations denounced the CCP in Manchuria as an illegal "separatist power" and questioned the CCP's patriotism. The CCP, however, dismissed the student movement as "xenophobic."[20] In a retaliatory move, the CCP mobilized popular support to oppose the conclusion of the Sino-American Treaty of Friendship, Commerce, and Navigation by the KMT later in the year. The *Liberation Daily*, one of the CCP's key propaganda outlets, wrote in its editorial: "This is the most shameful traitorous treaty in history, and it is one of the major signs that the Chiang government regards China as a

[19] Research on the Nanjing Massacre has been a political taboo since 1949. Gao Xingzu, a historian at Nanjing University, completed a book manuscript in 1962 titled "The Massacre of Japanese Imperialism in Nanjing" after two years of on-site investigation. However, no institution dared to publish it at the time. It was not until 17 years later, in 1979, that the book was finally published, albeit with limited internal distribution.

[20] *Xinhua Daily*, 23/02/1946.

vassal state of the United States. It is another new national humiliation for the Chinese nation."[21]

As the Civil War drew to a close, the CCP's dependence on the Soviet Union was reinforced by the urgent need to modernize China after the establishment of the PRC in October 1949. The Soviet Union became the only model of industrialization for China to emulate. Consequently, Mao announced a "leaning to one side" foreign policy on the eve of the founding of the PRC, anticipating massive Soviet sponsorship.

Emulating the Soviet Union entailed instilling Communism in China. However, Mao recognized that there were diverse opinions among the Chinese population regarding the suitability of Communism and the Soviet system for China. Many were influenced by Sun Yat-sen's perspective, which emphasized the need for a distinct Chinese path and criticized the shortcomings of Soviet Communism in the Chinese context. To mitigate resistance and alleviate fears of Communism, the CCP skillfully employed nationalist rhetoric, portraying itself as the liberator of the country and the leader in ending the era of foreign oppression and humiliation. Mao's famous declaration from the Tiananmen rostrum, where key political events often take place, "The Chinese people have stood up" aimed to reinforce this narrative and evoke a sense of national pride.

As part of its efforts to legitimize its own rule, the CCP engaged in a comprehensive demonization of previous regimes, particularly the KMT, portraying them as reactionary, corrupt, and a comprador regime serving the interests of Western imperialism. While the CCP highlighted its role in eliminating imperialist privileges and unequal treaties granted by the previous regimes, it selectively addressed the issue of past treaties and did not openly confront the detrimental unequal treaties imposed by czarist Russia on China since 1858, which resulted in significant territorial losses.

Although Mao did raise the issue of returning Outer Mongolia to Chinese sovereignty on two occasions, once with Stalin through Molotov in 1949 and later with Khrushchev in 1956, he eventually gave up when meeting with firm Soviet rejection. Mao was highly sensitive to domestic public reaction to the alliance treaty he concluded with Stalin in February 1950. Although securing concessions from Stalin on a number of issues,

[21] *The Liberation Daily*, 26/11/1946. http://dangshi.people.com.cn/n/2012/1213/c85037-19881537-4.html.

the Treaty did contain clauses that some may view as unequal, especially among liberal intellectuals and college students, whose nationalist sentiment aroused Mao's deep concern.[22]

Mao's private expression of discontent, suggesting that China still looked like a colony due to the Soviet presence in Manchuria and Xinjiang,[23] also reveals his reservations about the extent of Soviet influence in China. The regime's double standard in approaching historical treaties implies the limits of the CCP's nationalism, demonstrating a complex balance between pursuing China's own national interests and depending on Soviet support for its quest for rapid industrialization.

China's involvement in the Korean War (1950–1953) solidified Sino-Soviet ties and convinced Stalin of Mao's loyalty, leading to substantial assistance. Leveraging the Korean War as a catalyst, Mao implemented a comprehensive process of Stalinization in China, which involved the introduction of a centrally planned economy and the enforcement of forced collectivization. To assure the Soviets of China's commitment to suppressing anti-Soviet sentiments, particularly prevalent among liberal intellectuals and college students, Mao personally introduced an additional criterion for labeling these individuals as "Rightists" during the "anti-Rightist" campaign of 1956.

The regime's move to suppress nationalism was not merely to please the Soviets, but can be understood within the framework of Marxist ideology. Mao and the CCP aimed to establish a unified ideological framework centered around Communism and class struggle rather than nationalism. By suppressing nationalist sentiments and labeling them as bourgeois ideology, the CCP sought to consolidate its control over the intellectual and ideological spheres. This allowed the Party to shape the narrative of the revolution and maintain ideological coherence.

Despite denying nationalism and using patriotism as a replacement, the boundary between the two is blurred. As Mao clarified at the Lushan Conference in 1959, being in power or not makes a big difference in the CCP's attitudes toward nationalism. Mao himself underwent a significant

[22] Yang, Kuisong (2000): "The Initial Collision of National Interests and Emotions Between China and the Soviet Union—with the Signing of the 'Sino-Soviet Treaty of Friendship, Alliance and Mutual Assistance' as the Background." *Journal of Historical Research*, No. 6. https://xinguancha.net/?p=4214.

[23] Conversation in Beijing with a prominent Chinese Cold War historian who joined the CCP in the late 1940s, dated 20/01/2000.

role change, transitioning from being a secessionist in his youth to a unification defender after 1949. Once deeply resigned to the Leninist principle of "national self-determination," the CCP adopted diametrically different attitudes regarding China's unification and intra-China ethnic nationalist movements, depending on the circumstances.

For instance, from 1928 to 1943, the CCP consistently recognized the Taiwanese as a distinct "nation" or "nationality." However, after 1943, following the Teheran Conference where the return of Taiwan to Chinese sovereignty was confirmed, the CCP reversed its stance and voiced opposition to Taiwan's independence.[24]

Similarly, the CCP supported the Second East Turkistan Independence Movement (1944–1949), also known as the "Three-Region Revolution" of Ili, Tarbaghatai, and Altai, which was secretly sponsored by the Soviet Union in an attempt to separate from China. Mao depicted it as "a part of the entire Chinese people's democratic revolutionary movement" to oppose the reactionary rule of the KMT. The CCP turned a blind eye to the separatist nature of the movement and the Soviet sponsorship behind it. It was not until the events of September 11, 2001 that the Chinese regime underwent a delicate change in attitude, cautiously acknowledging the role Chiang Kai-shek and the KMT regime had played in "safeguarding China's territorial integrity."[25]

Except for Outer Mongolia, which had been a highly sensitive issue in Chinese politics, particularly against the backdrop of the KMT regime retreating to Taiwan and rescinding its previous recognition of Outer Mongolia's independence, Mao's anti-nationalist patriotism did not entail irredentism, as typical nationalist politicians did in many parts of the world. The PRC's border negotiations with the Soviet Union, which began in 1964, did not involve demands for the return of lost territories previously occupied by the Russian Empire and Soviet Russia in the past century. Instead, the focus was on the recognition of the "unequal" nature of treaties imposed on China, where "unequal" refers to treaties

[24] Hsiao, F & Sullivan, L. R. (1979): "The Chinese Communist Party and the Status of Taiwan, 1928–1943." *Public Affairs*, 52:3, pp. 446–467.

[25] Kang, See-Way (2008): "The Root Cause of East-Turkistan Issue: A Study of Xinjiang's 'Three Regions' Revolution'." *Prospect & Exploration* (Taiwan), 6:10, p. 59; Also: "The Truth of East Turkistan Republic." 16/08/2019. https://www.facebook.com/kitabxumar/posts/2667013239998241/.

that favored one party over the other, a request that the Soviet negotiators flatly rejected.

In fact, during the 1950s, the Chinese government adopted a policy of "avoidance and tolerance" when dealing with specific border conflicts, driven by ideological considerations. For example, in the early 1950s, the Soviet Union supplied the Chinese government with a complete set of modern large-scale topographic maps, which included border lines that deviated from the treaty line and extended into Chinese territory. Surprisingly, China did not immediately raise objections to these "Soviet-map lines." Instead, Chinese atlases continued to delineate the border line in accordance with the Sino-Russian historical border treaty. This evasive approach persisted until the late 1950s, when China finally communicated through low-level diplomatic channels with the Soviet side about the significant conflict between the Soviet map line and the treaty line. According to the former, the Soviet Union had invaded and occupied a substantial portion of Chinese territory.

Yet despite this conflict, the Chinese side remained reticent regarding Soviet encroachment and acquiesced to the border line marked on the Soviet maps. As a result, many young people in China knew little about the history of Soviet Russia's annexation of Chinese territories in modern times. The "border consciousness" of residents in the border areas was largely indifferent, and some residents in special border areas lacked a strong sense of national consciousness.[26] Mao's rejection of nationalism rendered China's nation building problematic, resembling the post-1949 New China more as a traditional Chinese empire than a Westphalian modern nation-state.

Those who perceive Mao as a committed nationalist have overlooked the significant concessions made by China to neighboring countries regarding land disputes after 1949. These concessions resulted in a total loss of approximately 200,000 square kilometers of land.[27] One prominent example is the 1962 border treaty with North Korea, in which

[26] Chen, X: "Lessons from Sino-Soviet Territorial Negotiations in the Mao Zedong Era." *Mirror-History*, 05/07/2012. http://www.mingjinglishi.com/2012/07/blog-post_2890.html.

[27] Territorial Changes of the People's Republic of China: calculating from data suggested in notes 1 & 2. https://zh.wikipedia.org/wiki/%E4%B8%AD%E5%8D%8E%E4%BA%BA%E6%B0%91%E5%85%B1%E5%92%8C%E5%9B%BD%E9%A2%86%E5%9C%9F%E5%8F%98%E5%8C%96.

China ceded 54.5% of Tianchi (Cheonji in Korean), an area of about 500 km^2. This concession surpassed even the expectations of North Korea. In January 1968, the PRC's State Council issued an internal notice prohibiting the sale of all maps published in previous years. This action may have caught the unaware North Koreans off guard. Fifteen months later, the North Koreans pleaded with the Chinese side to update their national map in accordance with the revised standard of the new North Korean map.[28]

Mao's decision to cede territory was motivated by the need to gain North Korea's support in China's ideological dispute with the CPSU, which enjoyed significant backing from its socialist allies. To secure stronger support from Kim Il Sung, Mao chose to offer additional concessions. From 1963 to 1964, Mao made repeated promises to Kim that he would hand over Manchuria, China's three northeastern provinces, for North Korea's administration. Zhou Enlai and Deng Xiaoping played pivotal roles as active implementors of Mao's plan to establish Manchuria as North Korea's strategic rear logistic base.[29]

Mao's disregard for regaining sovereignty over disputed territories was bolstered by the belief that as long as those lands were governed by regimes led by Communists or socialist-oriented leaders, it did not matter that they were ceded in exchange for the friendship and respect of the neighbors in question. This prioritization of ideology over national interest reflected the mindset of Chinese imperial sovereigns, who believed that all land belonged to the ruler and those who governed the land were subjects of the ruler. Shen Zhihua, a Cold War historian in China, argues that Mao's "celestial power" mentality aligned perfectly with his pursuit of Communist internationalism, which can be seen as a "regression of history" within the framework of modern international relations.[30]

The same mindset influenced China's approach to the territorial dispute with India, specifically concerning the Tibetan region. Despite India's gradual encroachment on the portion of Tibetan land south of the McMahon Line, starting in 1951, China maintained a deliberate silence

[28] Shen Zhihua (2017): *The Last "Celestial Empire"—Mao Zedong, Kim Il-Sung and Sino-North Korean Relations (1945–76)*. Hong Kong: The Chinese University Press, pp. 543, 545.

[29] Shen, Z (2017), pp. 551–555.

[30] Ibid., p. 550.

for almost a decade to foster a favorable relationship with India, an important non-aligned ally in the Third World. Mao displayed minimal concern about ceding the Tibetan territory south of the McMahon Line, known as Zangnan (藏南, meaning "southern Tibet" in Chinese), as long as India remained under Communist Party leadership.[31]

Another crucial factor contributing to China's indifference toward Zangnan was its prioritization of securing the return of the Dalai Lama, who had been forced into de facto exile in India in 1956, during a tumultuous period of rebellion in Tibet stemming from the radical CCP's reform campaign. This unforeseen factor took precedence over other considerations when Premier Zhou Enlai discussed territorial issues with Nehru's bourgeois-nationalist government. During secret talks held in India, Zhou acknowledged the PRC's *recent* awareness of the McMahon Line. He promised Nehru that China was prepared to relinquish its claims over Zangnan in exchange for India's assistance in persuading the exiled Dalai Lama to return to Tibet. Zhou also committed to "promoting the acceptance of the McMahon Line among the Tibetan people," a pledge that met with a surprisingly positive response from Indian leaders.[32] In April 1960, during Zhou Enlai's official visit to India, he formally proposed a trade: Zangnan, encompassing approximately 90,000 km^2, in exchange for India's acceptance of the smaller western portion of the disputed territory, roughly 33,000 km^2.[33] However, India's persistent intransigence toward the disputed land, especially the continuous advances of its forces in Zangnan, brought the border conflict to the brink of war.

In October 1962, Mao ordered the PLA to launch a "self-defense counterattack" along the Sino-Indian border. The objective of this war was not to reclaim the lost land in Zangnan, but rather to send a message to India. In a swift campaign, China emerged victorious in just over a month. However, to the surprise of the world, instead of capitalizing on the victory and expanding its territorial gains, China announced an unprecedented and surprising move—an unconditional and unilateral

[31] Song, Yongyi (ed.) (2018): *Newly Discovered Talks of Mao Zedong in Confidential Archives*. New York: guoshi chubanshe, pp. 172–173.

[32] Ding Yifu: "The Question of Tibet and Sino-Indian Border Issue." 21/12/2010. https://xizang-zhiye.org/2010-12-21-07-09-49/.

[33] Yang, Degang: "The Ultimate Investigation on the Sino-Indian Border Issue." 19/04/2019. https://www.aisixiang.com/data/74079.html.

troop withdrawal. China returned to the original line of control and even pulled back an additional 20 km. This decision left the international community stunned, as it had no parallel in the history of world wars: the victor unconditionally and unilaterally withdrew its troops without seeking any commitments or concessions from the defeated side. This move, as highlighted by Neville Maxwell in his book *India's China War*, effectively nullified the hard-won fruits of victory, which had been achieved at a significant cost.[34]

According to the known facts, Mao's decision to unconditionally withdraw from the border conflict with India was not influenced by "international pressure, domestic economic difficulties, or logistical obstacles."[35] The withdrawal was a strategic choice made by Mao himself. The motivation behind this decision remains a subject of dispute to this day. However, this fatal decision proved to be futile as it failed to deter India from resuming its annexation of Zangnan shortly after the war had ended. Mao's mishandling of the conflict highlighted the CCP's lack of nationalist tendencies and their ineffective approach to managing international affairs, which was to be further substantiated by China's reluctance to challenge Sikkim's annexation by India in 1975 that provided India with a geopolitical advantage.

Following Mao's death in 1976, the bitter legacies of the border conflict continued to breed resentment among many PLA strategists and intellectuals. Their discontent toward India fueled a growing nationalist sentiment. This sentiment was particularly strong within the PLA in 1987, especially when the Indian Parliament elevated the reoccupied disputed area of Zangnan to Arunachal Pradesh, making it challenging for China to contest India's sovereignty over the region.[36] In 2003, China and India exchanged recognition of India's sovereignty over Sikkim and China's sovereignty over Tibet, even though India had previously accepted Tibet as part of China in 1954. This outcome clearly demonstrated India's diplomatic victory in the matter.

During Mao's era, ideology played a dominant role in shaping China's foreign policy. Mao placed a strong emphasis on exporting revolution to

[34] Maxell, N (1970): *India's China War*. London: Pelican, p. 459.

[35] An Interview with Former Chinese Ambassador to India Pei Yuanying. *Nanfengchuang*, No. 21, 2009.

[36] Wang, L (1998): *Sky Burial: The Fate of Tibet*. New York: Mirror Books, p. 75.

Third World countries, even at the expense of China's national interests. This led to China's isolation on the international stage, particularly during the climax of the Cultural Revolution in 1966–1968.

However, there was a demonstrable shift toward pragmatism in Mao's foreign policy, especially after the rapprochement with the United States in 1972. This change became evident in Mao's withdrawal of support in 1975 for Kim Il Sung's conception of a military takeover of South Korea, as he sought a more practical approach to maintain stability on the Korean Peninsula. Mao's decision arose from a willingness to seek stability rather than reunification of the Peninsula through great-power cooperation between China and the United States. This new approach, eventually aligning with China's national interests, showcased Mao's pragmatism in addressing various foreign policy challenges, as he recognized China's lack of power to achieve his "world-revolution" vision and the limitations of Chinese revolutionary foreign policy.

After Mao's death, Deng Xiaoping implemented significant changes in China's foreign policy, moving away from Mao's strategy of "world revolution" and instead focusing on modernizing China through closer ties with the capitalist First World. Deng believed that engaging with the global capitalist system would benefit China's modernization efforts, leading to a reduced emphasis on providing assistance to Third World countries.

Deng's post-Mao state-rebuilding efforts aimed to transform China into a modern nation-state, which required filling the ideological void left by Mao's revolutionary ideology. Nationalism became an integral part of Deng's approach as he recognized its role in uniting the country and promoting China's national interests. Unlike Mao's "celestial empire" approach to state-to-state relations, Deng adopted a pragmatic stance that prioritized national interest over ideological considerations.

While Deng had previously been involved in transferring northeastern provinces to North Korean administration during Mao's era, he distanced himself from Mao's approach and ceased to appease North Korea economically and diplomatically. In a notable move, he even risked offending Kim Il Sung by establishing diplomatic relations with South Korea in 1992. Deng's actions were driven by a *raison d'état* rationale, emphasizing the pursuit of national interests over idealistic utopianism.

In essence, Deng strategically harnessed nationalism as a controlled and deliberate tool, fully cognizant of China's economic and military vulnerabilities. He embraced a defensive realist perspective, prioritizing the safeguarding of China's national interests and approaching foreign policy cautiously, taking into consideration China's capabilities within the broader international system. Deng's pragmatic nationalism marked a significant departure from Mao's revolutionary fervor and underscored his strategic considerations for China's development and security.

In the 1980s, Chinese nationalism experienced a resurgence orchestrated by the Chinese state in response to a "belief crisis" stemming from Mao's radical revolutionary policies. The most severe consequence of these policies was extreme poverty and economic hardship, which not only eroded national pride but also led to an intriguing phenomenon. Chinese society began to display a strong admiration for foreign cultures and products, even those from Global South countries that were less advanced than China.

Simultaneously, the lingering trauma of the Cultural Revolution created a complex perspective among many intellectuals regarding the CCP's official patriotic ideology. Their resentment toward Mao's artificially manufactured nationalism resulted in a broader disdain for all forms of nationalism, associating them with Maoism.

Paradoxically, these perspectives, exemplified by works like "River Elegy" (*Heshang*, 河殇), a renowned documentary from the late 1980s, carried strong elements of Chinese racialism.[37] While rejecting nationalism, this racist narrative advocated complete Westernization as the path to modernity and the restoration of China's national greatness. In their emphasis on "Chineseness," like the CCP's frequent discourse in the 1980s, they unconsciously employed Communist rhetoric, mimicking the very Communist regime they sought to reject.

Another example can be found in the anti-Japanese demonstrations held by college students in several Chinese cities in 1985, marking the fortieth anniversary of the end of World War II. These demonstrators' slogans and perception of the Sino-Japanese War were heavily influenced by decades of official patriotic education, serving the purpose of historical legitimization for the CCP. Ironically, the spontaneous nationalist movement among students was precisely what the regime was eager to suppress, as it feared that it might affect Japan's extension of Official Development Assistance (ODA) to China.

[37] Cheng, Y (2011): "From Campus Racism to Cyber Racism: Discourse of Race and Chinese Nationalism." *The China Quarterly*, 201, pp. 561–579.

The 1980s are widely regarded as the most liberal period in the history of the PRC since 1949. This was not primarily due to the CCP reinventing itself institutionally from a revolutionary party to a ruling party under a legal framework. Rather, it was driven by Deng Xiaoping's strong self-confidence in his ability to govern and his belief that the interests of the regime were aligned with the national interest. Initially, this confidence even led to the permission of sensitive publications, such as *The Vladimirov Diaries*, albeit restricted to internal circulation to professional researchers, published in 1980. However, as Deng and the CCP swiftly realized that the publication inadvertently revealed information detrimental to the Party's image as the defender of national interests, their confidence waned, leading to a natural instinct for tighter control. Consequently, the initial liberal atmosphere gradually soured when nationalism became a double-edged sword, sandwiching the Party between nationalist backlash and anti-nationalist mockery.

As mentioned earlier, the primary objective of Chinese reforms was to strengthen, rather than undermine, the CCP's monopoly on power. This implies that the concern for regime interests consistently takes precedence over national interests. The leaders' commitment to nationalism remains selective and inconsistent unless their nationalist pursuits align with regime interests. A clear example of this can be seen in the reclaiming of Hong Kong, where both regime and national interests converged under the "one country, two-system" scenarios. However, this approach sharply contrasts with the CCP's nationalist pursuit in the case of Taiwan's unification. In the 1990s, when Lee Teng-hui insisted on terms of unification based on democratic principles, he was demonized as a separatist and traitor to the Chinese nation, without Mainland Chinese people being aware of the preconditions Lee had raised, which actually served China's long-term national interests. But for the CCP, such a scenario of unification would jeopardize the life of the Party, prompting it to prioritize its own survival over China's national interest.

After the events of Tiananmen, the worldwide collapse of Communism unsettled the Communist rulers in China, leaving them with no choice but to resort to nationalism in a more forceful manner. However, this does not indicate a sincere commitment to nationalism in any genuine sense. Unlike the revolutionary Deng Xiaoping, the technocratic politicians who succeeded him were neither dedicated Communists nor committed nationalists. They acted even more opportunistically when confronted with the unprecedented institutional failure of Communism following the Tiananmen crackdown, which had severely damaged the Party's legitimacy. Their embrace of global capitalism after Deng Xiaoping's southern tour created internal tensions within their nationalist narrative. Deep, rather than shallow, integration into the global economy meant abandoning economic nationalism, while maintaining a one-party dictatorship required fostering nationalist fervor among the people under the guise of opposing American hegemony. This approach proved effective, particularly with the arrival of the unipolar moment characterized by the decline of post-Communist Russia, the U.S.-led invasion of Iraq, the reinforcement of the U.S.-Japan alliance, and Taiwan's increasing independent tendencies perceived as encouraged by the United States. These factors further fueled Chinese people's nationalist sentiments. The best-selling book *China Can Say No*, published in 1996, emerged in this context.

Nevertheless, the prevailing ideological current within Chinese society remained one of liberalism, which the authorities closely monitored but also exploited to legitimize themselves, particularly in light of their emphasis on economic liberalism. Guided yet vexed by "an ideology of no ideology," this party state did not hesitate to capitalize on various "New Thinking" movements emanating from industrial democracies, whether leaning toward liberalism, the New Left, or nationalism. This flexibility stemmed from the regime's opportunistic nature, exemplifying what is often termed "authoritarian resilience." It enabled the government to adapt and adopt different ideological currents. *China Can Say No* perfectly illustrated the regime's adaptability. This spontaneous nationalist outburst invited an immediate crusade from liberal intellectuals and saw its influence constrained. It was not until the bombing of the Chinese embassy in Belgrade by U.S. bombers in May 1999 that the non-official version of nationalism experienced a substantial surge in influence, under the state's acquiescence, eventually surpassing the influence of the liberal camp.

But the authorities' tolerance of spontaneous nationalism had its limits, even in the face of significant events like the embassy bombing in 1999 and the subsequent Hainan Island incident in April 2001. Radical activists received warnings from the authorities, who were concerned about a nationalist backlash against the regime itself. In fact, the regime had proactively obstructed non-governmental movements in the 1990s that aimed to defend the Diaoyu Islands (known as Senkaku in Japanese) and seek war indemnities from the government of Japan. These efforts had become particularly challenging due to Mao's decision to renounce all war reparations from Japan.

In contrast to the extremist nationalist bestseller *China Can Say No*, which the regime actively exploited to bolster itself, scholarly publications with nationalist inclinations, such as *China's Road under the Shadow of Globalization*, written by left-leaning scholars Wang Xiaodong and Fang Ning, were more alarming to the regime. Moderate in tone, this book critically examined the concept of "American post-colonialism," which was perceived as a renewed means for the West to exert dominance over the world through military control, political influence, and economic supremacy. In an era of liberal globalization characterized by prevalent cosmopolitanism, this book advocated a realist approach to handling China's foreign relations within the framework of global capitalism. Interestingly, *China's Road under the Shadow of Globalization*, despite its nationalist undertones and skepticism toward globalization and U.S. hegemony, faced reprimands not only from liberal intellectuals but also from the Communist regime itself.[38]

The true face of Chinese nationalism was most evident in its handling of border disputes with neighboring countries. The eagerness of the third-generation leadership, led by Jiang Zemin, to end China's diplomatic isolation after the Tiananmen incident in 1989 prompted decision-makers to compromise China's territorial integrity in exchange for improving and stabilizing its relations in the periphery. The importance of these relations ranked second in China's foreign policy architecture, with relations with the U.S. being the highest priority, and relations with developing nations ranking third in importance. In this context, the Chinese leadership continued Mao's policy of appeasing neighboring countries by making concessions in border negotiations since 1991, adopting a Chinese-style "land for peace" approach. This approach may seem inconceivable to the rest of the world, given China's relative strength compared to its weaker neighbors.

As highlighted in the November/December 2003 issue of *Foreign Affairs* by Medeiros and Fravel, China actively pursued the resolution of territorial disputes that historically caused tensions with its neighbors. Between 1991 and the 2000s, China successfully settled border conflicts

[38] While residing in Beijing in early 2000, I received information from one of the authors of this book that, during an internal meeting, the deputy Party leader of the Beijing Municipality referred to this publication as "a poorly regarded work." 6/3/2000.

with Kazakhstan, Kyrgyzstan, Laos, Russia, Tajikistan, and Vietnam through peaceful negotiations. However, in many of these agreements, China accepted less than 50% of the disputed territory, demonstrating its willingness to compromise. For example, in the resolution of a long-standing dispute over the Pamir Mountains, which Tajikistan inherited from the Soviet Union, China only acquired 1,000 km^2 out of the contested 28,000 km^2 to its neighbors.[39] These territorial losses, suffered by China as a rising potential regional hegemonic power, were intentionally kept hidden from the Chinese citizens, as the authorities feared that it might trigger a nationalist backlash if revealed.

The border settlement with Russia served as a significant test of the CCP's commitment to nationalism. With the ideological constraints of the Mao era lifted, the post-Mao leadership, particularly the third-to-fifth-generation leadership following Deng Xiaoping, who refrained from intervening in Chinese politics after 1992, had the opportunity to demonstrate genuine nationalism. They could have done so by adopting a non-recognition stance regarding border disputes with Russia, given Russia's decline and China's rise in the post-Cold War era. This can be contrasted with Japan's longstanding approach to the Northern Territories occupied by the Soviet Union in 1945, where the Japanese government has consistently maintained its position based on international law.

However, the Chinese government appeared to lack skill in navigating international law. While it demanded that the U.K. return Hong Kong to China based on its rejection of unequal treaties, it downplayed similar unequal treaties regarding larger lost territories and was willing to accept them. In 1991, 1994, and 1999, China concluded three protocols with Russia, which settled 98 percent of the border demarcation between the two countries. These protocols confirmed Russia's sovereignty over the "lost territories," including Tannu Uriankhai (known as Tannu Tuva in Russia), an enclave unilaterally occupied by Soviet Russia in 1921 and annexed into the Soviet Union in 1944, which had never been recognized by China before. This confirmation was achieved through legally binding international treaties, resulting in China permanently losing approximately 1.6 million square kilometers of territory. In 2004, the remaining two percent of land disputes were resolved with the signing of the last border protocol during Hu Jintao's first term as President.

[39] Medeiros, Evan S. & Taylor Fravel, M (2003): "China's New Diplomacy." *Foreign Affairs*, Nov/Dec, 82:6, pp. 22–35.

The Sino-Russian Joint Communiqué announced on March 21, 2006 declared "the complete settlement of the border issue between the two countries."[40] On April 12, 2022, Chinese Foreign Ministry spokesman Zhao Lijian reaffirmed that both countries had thoroughly resolved the historical boundary issues, and there were no territorial claims against each other.[41]

High-politics calculations by Chinese decision-makers, seeking an improved relationship with Russia to serve as a counterweight to the U.S.-Japan strategic alliance in the Far East, may account for China's compromises. However, the payoff might be asymmetrical when compared to China permanently losing its vast "lost territories," which remain underdeveloped yet rich in natural resources that China was eager to access. Interestingly, leaders who succeeded Jiang Zemin, including Hu Jintao and especially the fifth-generation leader Xi Jinping, known for his "wolf warrior" diplomacy, were often perceived as more nationalistic compared to Jiang, who was considered "pro-American." Yet behind the regime's nationalist facade, all post-Deng leaders did not act differently when it came to dealing with the border issue with Russia.

Repeating the conduct of old reactionary regimes in selling China's "sacred territories"—a label that could now be applied to the Communist regime itself—necessitates the blocking of people's access to relevant information, often classified as top state secrets. Individuals attempting to disclose China's concessions risked state penalties. Taking a cue from Russian media, Ching Cheong (程翔), a Hong Kong-born journalist based in Singapore and a renowned pro-Beijing left-winger, was infuriated by Jiang Zemin's perceived "traitorous deeds" during negotiations with Russia. In September 2004, he revealed details in *Ming Pao* about China's permanent loss of a significant portion of territory to Russia and criticized Jiang's attempt to "use new 'equal treaties' to legalize old

[40] Joint Statement between the People's Republic of China and the Russian Federation, signed by Chinese President Hu Jintao and Russian President Vladimir Putin in Beijing on March 21, 2006. https://www.gov.cn/gongbao/content/2006/content_283963.htm.

[41] Radio Free Asia, 12/04/2022. https://www.rfa.org/mandarin/Xinwen/wul0412a-04122022061015.html.

'unequal treaties.'" Ching Cheong presented three points to emphasize his criticism[42]:

Firstly, the CCP is even worse than the Kuomintang regime, which has been ridiculed by the CCP as a traitor and ousted from power for allegedly selling the country. The KMT regime's struggle against the Soviet Union on territorial issues continued until the early 1950s. Even after retreating to Taiwan, it lodged a complaint with the United Nations against the Soviet Union's aggression towards China in 1952. Despite the CCP's initial proclamation that it would not recognize the "unequal treaties" imposed on China by imperialist powers, it remained silent about the land occupied by the Soviet Union. Ironically, the CCP never took the return of the land promised to China by Lenin's Manifestos seriously and argued fervently for territorial claims against the Soviet Union.

Secondly, Jiang Zemin's approach to this issue falls short compared to other Communist Party leaders. During Mao Zedong's administration, he and his colleagues consistently raised the issue of Soviet Union's occupation of Chinese territory. Under Deng Xiaoping's leadership, although he was willing to use the border's status quo as a starting point for negotiations with the Soviet Union regarding territorial restoration (accepting the existing border), it was premised on the Soviet Union publicly acknowledging that it had plundered part of its territory from China during the Tsarist Russia era. Only after this admission would the two sides discuss the way forward. In Jiang Zemin's era, this insistence on Deng Xiaoping's premise was not evident, at least not to journalists like myself. The entire negotiating process remained shrouded in secrecy.

Third, this treaty, which signifies China's formal renunciation of a significant piece of territory, has remained undisclosed from the negotiation process to its final signing. Even after the formal signing, the map indicating the direction of the border is still unavailable. As far as the author knows, even the National People's Congress, the highest authority in the country, only reviews it when ratifying a treaty, and the discussions of the Standing Committee of the National People's Congress are confidential. In other words, ordinary Chinese people have no right to be informed about how the CCP has permanently relinquished our claim to the lost Chinese territories on our behalf. Therefore, the author

42 "Ching Cheong was sentenced to 5 years in prison by the CCP for angering Jiang Zemin with this article." *bannedbook.org*, 24/07/2021. https://www.bannedbook.org/bnews/lifebaike/20210724/1593076.html.

believes that both Jiang Zemin and the CCP owe an explanation to the Chinese people. National territory is not the private property of one party, and since they have made this decision, they have the obligation and responsibility to provide detailed reasons to the Chinese people.

Ching Cheong faced retaliation from the party state shortly after his disclosures. He was arrested in Guangzhou in April 2005 and subsequently sentenced to five years in prison on spying charges. However, spontaneous nationalist activists continued their activities bravely in this context.

On August 17, 2017, Yu Minhong (俞敏洪), an independent history researcher and retired PLA serviceman, submitted a request to the Chinese Foreign Ministry demanding the release of documents relating to the territorial ownership of Tannu Uriankhai, a former Chinese enclave located to the north and west of Outer Mongolia. The Foreign Ministry responded by stating that the requested information fell within the scope of confidential documents and did not fall under the category of government information disclosure, as outlined in Articles 14 and 21 of the Regulations on the Openness of Government Information of the PRC. In March 2018, Yu appealed to the Beijing No. 3 Intermediate People's Court and later to the Beijing Municipal High People's Court, but unfortunately his efforts were unsuccessful.[43]

To the disappointment of many nationalistically inclined Chinese citizens, territorial ownership has always been treated as a closely guarded state secret since Mao's era. It is worth noting that neither the PRC nor Taiwan has ever made a clear public statement on the sovereignty of this land,[44] despite the Chinese government's position of "non-recognition" regarding Russia's illegal occupation. Even in August 1964, when Chinese negotiators raised the issue of Tannu Uriankhai for the first and last time, they only claimed the right to recover it as long as the Soviets refused to acknowledge the *unequal* nature of the treaties imposed on China.[45] In a similar vein to his stance on the lost territories spanning nearly 1.6

[43] BBC (Chinese), 07/11/2018. https://www.bbc.com/zhongwen/simp/chinese-news-46120157.

[44] Elleman, B. A. (2021): *International Rivalry and Secret Diplomacy in East Asia, 1896–1950*. London: Routledge. Preface.

[45] Li Danhui: "The Truth of the Zhenbao (Damansky) Island—An Investigation into Sino-Soviet Border Relations." 10/04/2010. https://www.aisixiang.com/data/36173.html.

million square kilometers, Mao told visiting high-ranking officials from North Korea and Albania in October 1964 that his intention in raising the issue of Tannu Uriankhai was not to reclaim it, but rather to prompt Soviet recognition of the unequal nature of the treaties, thereby gaining the moral high ground.[46]

Interestingly, the official publication of *The Atlas of Post-World War II International Politics* in January 1999 briefly mentioned on page 28 that "Tannu Uriankhai is Chinese territory" (Fig. 4.1). However, this mention seemed to be accidental, considering past instances where maps containing sensitive content failed to pass censorship by the Chinese Foreign Ministry. The approval of the map's inclusion in the publication was likely due to an oversight rather than a change of mind by the censors. Consequently, it cannot be equated to an official public statement by China claiming sovereignty over this land.

China's compromise with Vietnam regarding Bạch Long Vĩ Island (known as Nightingale Island in Chinese) in the South China Sea serves as another example of the regime deviating from nationalism rather than upholding it. Bạch Long Vĩ Island holds significant importance not only for security and defense purposes but also for oil and gas exploration, marine economic development, and environmental conservation in the region. Additionally, it plays a crucial role in the fishing industry, with substantial potential for seafood processing, fishing logistic services, and maritime preservation.[47]

Despite having stronger historical evidence to claim sovereignty over Nightingale Island compared to Vietnam, China, in response to Ho Chi Minh's request, agreed to "lend" the island to Vietnam in 1957 as a radar base against potential American airstrikes and to facilitate material aid transfers from China. Vietnam promptly renamed it Bạch Long Vĩ after assuming control.

On December 25, 2000, China and Vietnam finalized two agreements: one on the delimitation of the territorial sea, exclusive economic zone, and continental shelf; and another on fishery cooperation in the Gulf

[46] Sergey N. Goncharov and Li Danhui (2002): "'Territorial Claims' and 'Unequal Treaties' in Russia-China Relations." *Twenty-First Century*, Issue No. 85 (October), pp. 110–117.

[47] Zhen-Gang Ji: "The South China Sea Island China Gave Away—Bach Long Vi Island and Its Secret Transfer from China to Vietnam." *The Diplomat*, 14/08/2019. https://thediplomat.com/2019/08/the-south-china-sea-island-china-gave-away/.

Fig. 4.1 *The Atlas of Post-World War II International Politics* (p. 28): Tannu Uriankhai. Published by SinoMaps Press (Beijing), January 1999. The illustration on page 28 contains a sentence (underlined in red): "Tannu Uriankhai is an integral part of Chinese territory"

of Tonkin (referred to as the Northern Bay in Chinese). These agreements confirmed the transfer of Bạch Long Vĩ Island to Vietnamese sovereignty. The immediate consequences were twofold. Firstly, China lost significant areas of continental shelf and fishery resources, impacting the lives of hundreds of thousands of Chinese residents in the region. Secondly, the old 11-dash line, originally demarcated by the Nationalist Government in 1947, was reduced to a 9-dash line. The strategic implications were even more significant. Retired Vietnamese navy Rear Admiral Lê Kế Lâm argued that if the Cam Ranh Bay port was combined with the Subic seaport in the Philippines and the U.S. military base in Singapore, it would enable control over the entire South China Sea and its crucial passages. Lê Kế Lâm speculated that had Mao Zedong been aware of these consequences, he would likely have regretted his decision to gift Nightingale Island to Vietnam at that time.[48] On the same day of the conclusion of the Agreements, the Chinese Foreign Ministry's website posted an "Introduction to the China-Vietnam Agreement on the Delimitation of the Northern Bay." It appears that the webpage in question has been removed for approximately two years now, but its contents can still be found in archived mirrors of the original weblink (see Fig. 4.2): https://www.fmprc.gov.cn/web/ziliao_674904/tytj_674911/tyfg_674913/t145558.shtml.

News of China's concession of Nightingale Island spread rapidly on China's internet, giving rise to considerable skepticism and resentment toward China's foreign policy. Deputy Foreign Minister Li Zhaoxing addressed a leading university in northern China, where he explained the reasons behind China's decision to cede the island to Vietnam. He revealed two main factors that influenced Chinese policymakers: firstly, the late Premier Zhou Enlai had already promised to give the island to Vietnam; and, secondly, the current Prime Minister of Vietnam, Phan Văn Khải, had shown great friendliness toward China. Naturally, skepticism emerged: should China's current regime be bound by the former Premier's words, which were clearly detrimental to China's national interests? Moreover, if future Vietnamese prime ministers become unfriendly toward China, would China have the right to revoke the agreement and reclaim the island by any means necessary? Li, however, did not face these sharp questions from the audience, who were requested by him at the beginning of his speech not to take notes, record, or post the content on the website.[49]

Li's explanation, when viewed from a technocratic perspective, implies that despite decades of reform and opening, China has not made significant progress toward becoming an advanced modern state governed by meritocratic elites. This observation does not negate the fact that in the PRC, foreign policies have always been shaped by politicians rather than career diplomats. These politicians are motivated not necessarily by the pursuit of national interest, but rather by the need to maintain regime stability.

[48] "Historical Truth: The Story of Mao Zedong Gifting China's Nightingale Island to Vietnam." *VOA (Chinese)*, 06/10/2016. https://www.voachinese.com/a/news-how-mao-handed-over-bach-long-vi-island-to-vietnam-as-a-gift-20161005/3538216.html.

[49] Li Zhaoxing on Chinese foreign policy (late 2001), according to a well-informed source.

Fig. 4.2 Internet Screenshots of the Chinese Foreign Ministry Webpage (now and December 25, 2000). Screenshots of Chinese Foreign Ministry website carrying the "Introduction" article. *Left*: current website showing the page has been removed; *right*: archived page

As discussed in the previous chapter, the process of market-Leninist reforms in the post-Deng era has resulted in the institutionalization of state capture by vested interests. This has made national interests increasingly irrelevant, as even the interests of the state or the regime have become fragmented into sectoral or local concerns. Consequently, the authoritarian regime is inherently unstable, and the rulers' apprehension of a Western-instigated color revolution from the mid-2000s onward has only heightened their concerns about regime change.

Dai Bingguo, the State Councillor in charge of foreign affairs, candidly conveyed China's "core interest" to American counterparts during the first Strategic and Economic Dialogue in July 2009. According to Dai, China's core interest encompasses: (1) safeguarding the basic system and national security; (2) safeguarding national sovereignty and territorial integrity; and (3) promoting sustained and stable economic and social development. Ostensibly, the true "core interest" for Chinese rulers is the viability of the regime itself, which is what "national security" ultimately signifies.

Dai's call for the United States to respect China's core interest served as a reminder that official nationalism in China is more symbolic than substantive. Overestimating the nationalist rhetoric of Communist leaders can lead to a misunderstanding of the true essence of Chinese nationalism. It primarily serves as a mobilizing tool used to bolster regime legitimacy rather than representing a meaningful and functional state ideology.

It is not uncommon to be misled by the Chinese regime's nationalistic rhetoric and misinterpret its various anti-nationalist actions as pursuing a hidden nationalist agenda aimed at making the country great again, with such actions seen as a necessary sacrifice for the greater good of national interests. Such misconceptions have been prevalent among Western academics and the policymaking community. Therefore, gaining a deeper understanding of Chinese nationalism is crucial to dispel common misconceptions about the supposed inherently nationalist character of the regime.

To be fair, the only period during which the regime's actions aligned with nationalism was the 1980s, during the era of Deng Xiaoping when regime interests coincided with national interests. However, even during that time, elements of comprador capitalism began to emerge.

It is important to emphasize that despite Mao's utopian internationalism, economic nationalism was both a genuine belief and a practical approach necessitated by economic autarky. From the mid-1980s onward, China began to move away from economic autarky with the assistance of the United States, which believed that integrating China into the global economy would serve fundamental U.S. national interests.

Following China's institutional transition to capitalism from 1992 onward, economic nationalism gradually faded due to the regime's close embrace of global capitalism, which led to the flourishing of comprador capitalism. Throughout the 1990s, crony capitalism and comprador capitalism co-existed, with each reinforcing the other in a mutually causal relationship.

In summary, the amalgamation of China's market Leninism with global capitalism gave rise to a distinct form of state capitalism, one that prioritized economic growth over social justice and self-reliance. This transformation led the country toward crony comprador capitalism as the new millennium approached.

Treading the Path of Compradorism: Unravelling the 1980s

Zhang Chunqiao, one of the members of the "Gang of Four" and Mao's favored theorist, expressed his views in an article titled "Why Must the Chinese People Oppose the Slavish Comprador Philosophy (*yangnu zhexue*, 洋奴哲学)?" published in *Red Flag* (No. 4), one of the CCP's prominent publications in 1976. In his article, he wrote: "If we do not prioritize self-reliance and instead rely on the importation of everything, even disregarding the socialist principles of economic development primarily based on the domestic market, we will only become an economic vassal of Western imperialism." He cautioned against following the path of capitalist-roaders, stating: "Those countries that depend on others for economic development may achieve temporary growth, but their prosperity is illusory due to their extremely fragile foundations, rendering them incapable of determining their own destiny."[50]

Zhang's critique followed a well-known debate in 1974 between the Gang of Four, the radical faction aligned with Mao, and the pragmatist faction led by Deng Xiaoping's technocrats. This debate centered on the dominant approach to development: the decision between buying a ship from abroad (*maichuan*, 买船) or building a ship on its own (*zaochuan*, 造船), or adopting a dependent approach based on importing technology versus a self-reliant approach based on import substitution. The issue that the Gang of Four sought to turn into a new line struggle was not a new one but had emerged a decade earlier when Premier Zhou Enlai proposed giving equal importance to both "buying" and "building."

[50] Zhang, Chunqiao (1976): "Why Must the Chinese People Oppose the Slavish Comprador Philosophy?" *Red Flag*, No. 4.

Zhou believed that these approaches were not mutually exclusive, but could reinforce each other. He emphasized import substitution to nurture domestic productive capabilities while importing what China temporarily could not produce, but was urgently needed in the national economy.

There is no evidence to suggest that Deng Xiaoping held a different view from Zhou Enlai in terms of a pragmatic approach that did not deviate from self-reliance. Ultimately, Deng was shielded by Mao from the censure of the Gang of Four for political reasons. Mao intended to cultivate Deng as a counterweight to balance Premier Zhou Enlai. Following Mao's death, the new leadership led by Hua Guofeng, whether benefiting from or suffering the consequences of the Cultural Revolution, recognized the necessity of changing Mao's policies.

In 1978, Chinese delegations sent by Hua Guofeng to five Western European countries significantly raised the awareness of the elites regarding China's considerable economic backwardness, notably the significant technological gap. This sparked their interest in learning from the West, just as previous regimes had done in the past century. The leadership, taken aback by the disparity compared to advanced capitalist nations, gradually established a link between China's economic backwardness and Mao's autarkic import substitution strategy.

During the Twelfth National Congress of the CCP in 1982, Deng Xiaoping, previously branded as the No. 2 "capitalist-roader" within the party by Mao, issued a warning: "The West should not anticipate China becoming a subservient state and enduring the harsh consequences of compromising our national interests."[51] However, Deng's concern primarily revolved around the political threat posed by Western ideological infiltration rather than economic dependency. Both Deng Xiaoping and Chen Yun possessed limited knowledge of the modern market economy. Their perspectives, especially Deng's, on global capitalism were initially influenced by Lenin's classical theory of imperialism. They had less familiarity with the post-World War Two era of "imperialism," characterized by democratic industrial capitalism. Furthermore, their comprehension of the post-war Western rules-based liberal order was restricted, making them uncertain about how China's gradual integration

[51] *Selected Works of Deng Xiaoping* (Vol. 3), 1993, Beijing: renmin chubanshe, p. 3.

into the global economy might lead to potential economic dominance by Western powers.[52]

Despite Chen Yun's greater vigilance than Deng regarding Western capitalism, the vestiges of backward socialism left by Mao compelled both leaders to adopt a pragmatic and proactive approach when engaging with global capitalism, particularly through the introduction of FDI. Chen Yun's support for this approach was primarily driven by practical considerations, notably a shortage of hard currency. This situation necessitated his departure from his preferred strategy of exclusively purchasing technology in favor of embracing foreign collaboration through joint ventures.

Deng Xiaoping strongly advocated the early development of high technology. In 1986, he communicated to Dr. Tsung-Dao (T. D.) Lee (李政道), a Chinese-American physicist and Nobel Laureate, the necessity and significance of initiating China's high-technology sector while the country's economy was still in its early stages of development. He argued that delaying such development until later stages might hinder China's catch-up process and prove to be more financially burdensome.[53] Deng threw his full support behind the State High-Tech Development Plan, also known as "The 863 Program." This program, sponsored by the PRC government, aimed to promote the advances of cutting-edge technologies across various fields. Its objective was to reduce China's reliance on foreign technologies and the associated financial obligations. The program drew inspiration from the Strategic Defense Initiative (SDI) proposed by U.S. President Ronald Reagan in 1983. In 1988, Deng emphasized China's past accomplishments in developing "atomic bombs, hydrogen bombs, and satellites" (*liangdan yixing*, 两弹一星) to underscore the importance of possessing robust scientific and technological capabilities, which had established China as an influential great power.[54]

Was Deng's attitude coherent? How was China's high-tech development implemented? Similar to the Soviet economic system, which had a bias toward heavy and defense industries, China's high-tech sector was primarily concentrated in defense-related areas. This concentration was further exacerbated by the construction of the "Third Front" during

[52] Discussion with a senior diplomat in June 1989, Beijing.

[53] *Selected Works of Deng Xiaoping*, vol. 3, Beijing: renmin chubanshe, pp. 183–184.

[54] Ibid., p. 280.

Mao's era, a secretive military-industrial complex located in the mountainous regions of inland China. This initiative resulted in significant waste and had a negative impact on the national economy, despite limited positive aspects in promoting local economies.

In 1985, Deng made the decision to reduce the size of the PLA by one million and expedite the "military-to-civilian diversion" (*junzhuanmin*, 军转民) process. This process entailed converting a significant number of defense industries into producers of consumer goods. While this diversion initially yielded immediate results and led to a prosperous boom driven by consumption in the 1980s, it also resulted in a significant outflow of high-tech talent, thus having a detrimental impact on China's technological development in critical ways.[55]

Deng was a leader who prioritized achieving rapid success and did not pay significant attention to the potential drawbacks of his decisions. He firmly believed that any adverse consequences could be resolved once the nation attained prosperity. In pursuit of this objective, he insisted that the PLA accept military spending reductions and permitted the PLA to participate in business activities. Regrettably, this choice had immediate and severe repercussions, resulting in widespread corruption within the army.

Deng's decision faced opposition from Deputy Premier Zhang Aiping, a seasoned party veteran and an idealistic Communist general. Zhang openly criticized Deng's authorization of the military's involvement in business activities, expressing concerns that it would undermine and erode the army's morale. Furthermore, Zhang challenged Deng's support for the Daya Bay nuclear plant construction, which relied on French technology and was situated near Hong Kong. During the State Council meeting's discussion on the Daya Bay project, Zhang strongly advocated the preservation of the domestically produced nuclear plant in Qinshan, Zhejiang Province, emphasizing its positive impact on upstream industries, despite its lower power output of 300,000 kilowatts compared to the French-sponsored plant's 900,000 kilowatts.[56] Zhang's position centered on nurturing China's own technological capabilities in the long term.

[55] Yue, J (2018), p. 159.

[56] Zhang, Sheng (2008): *Coming Out of the War—A Dialogue Between Two Generations of Soldiers*. Beijing: China Youth Press, pp. 422–427.

However, Premier Zhao Ziyang, Deng's protégé, displayed impatience with Zhang, despite Zhang not opposing the Daya Bay project. In response to Zhang's insistence, the Qinshan plant was ultimately retained as the sole facility utilizing indigenous technology. Unfortunately, subsequent nuclear plants relied exclusively on imported foreign technologies from Canada, Russia, and the United States.[57]

In the 1980s, Deng Xiaoping and Zhao Ziyang made similar decisions regarding the development of China's automobile and aircraft industries. One notable project was the Y-10, aimed at creating China's own commercial aircraft. Despite making significant progress in indigenous technological advances, the Y-10 project was eventually discontinued due to a preference for technology imports and its association with the Gang of Four. Instead of prioritizing the cultivation of indigenous capabilities, the leaders chose to establish joint ventures with Boeing and Airbus, with the hope of building China's manufacturing capacity through these partnerships. However, this approach missed an opportunity to secure cutting-edge technology transfer from their European and American partners, which could have been highly feasible given China's substantial purchasing power.[58]

Rather than actively assimilating imported technologies, indigenizing them, and building a strong technological-industrial base, there was a noticeable shift toward a strong preference for sustainable technology acquisitions from advanced countries. This shift in thinking is exemplified by a State Council document drafted at the end of 1984, which addressed the restructuring of China's defense industrial system. The initial version of the document included a statement that emphasized "as long as we become prosperous in the future, we will have the ability to purchase 10,000 aircraft." However, due to its sensitive nature, this phrase was subsequently omitted from the final official document.[59]

Zhang Aiping considered such thinking as absurd since he staunchly believed that accumulating wealth did not necessarily translate into national strength. He vehemently opposed the abandonment of the previous principle of self-reliance and cast doubts on the feasibility of depending solely on the purchase of weapons (and related technologies)

[57] Luo Yu (2015), p. 118.

[58] Ibid., 450.

[59] Zhang, S (2008), p. 450.

to defend a vast country like China. With the fundamental guiding principle undermined, he began to question the value of further expressing his concerns, recognizing the erosion of the principles he held dear.

Zhao Ziyang's eagerness to pursue instantly visible economic progress led to his oversight of China's scientific and technological development. He sidelined the prescient endeavors of Lu Jiaxi in May 1981, a prestigious scientist and the President of the Chinese Academy of Sciences (CAS), by scolding him for his insubordination of CAS scientific research to the "main battlefield of the national economy." Zhao's veto of Lu's innovative reform initiatives in promoting scientific development, particularly basic research, resulted in Lu's removal and the abandonment of the "1978–1985 National Science and Technology Development Plan Outline," passed at the National Science Conference on March 18, 1978. Zhao's dismissal of Lu Jiaxi exposed the post-1949 Chinese top leadership's "sheer ignorance of what is science and their disrespect of science and scientists," a fact extending until today, as revealed by a senior CAS insider.[60]

Starting from the mid-1980s, Chinese leaders progressively adopted the concept of "external orientation" (*waixiangxing*, 外向型) as a strategy to drive China's industrial development. This marked a departure from the previous approach of autarkic import-substituting industrialization (ISI) that had been pursued in the preceding decades. The notion of external orientation focused on export-led growth and increased access to FDI.

The shift in thinking was largely influenced by Deng Xiaoping's "New Thinking" in 1984. In this new approach, Deng identified "peace and development" as the two primary issues confronting the world. Deng recognized that the pursuit of hegemony by superpowers posed a potential threat to global peace. However, he also observed the remarkable growth of global forces that were actively working to prevent the outbreak of a world war. These forces included countries such as China, Japan, Western Europe, and the Third World, which generally prioritized peace and stability.

Deng put forward the argument that the growing trend toward peace created a favorable environment for China's economic development, and

[60] A private corresponce between two distinguished scholars discussing what has institutionally impeded China's scientific development was made public on Chinese social media, on March 15, 2023.

he held the belief that China's progress would also contribute to global peace.[61] Deng's perspective effectively challenged Maoist theories on war and peace. Mao had asserted in 1969 that a world war would lead to either revolution or the cessation of war through revolution.[62] However, Deng's viewpoint diverged from that of Mao. He believed that it was not revolution that would halt war, but rather the development of China. Deng saw development as the key to eradicating poverty and paving the way for lasting peace.

Deng was a pragmatic and realistic politician who believed that a richer and stronger China would be better equipped to participate in the global power dynamics of the future. However, he was not an economic nationalist in any sense. Like Shigeru Yoshida in post-war Japan, Deng saw proactive alignment with the liberal international order under American sponsorship as a viable shortcut toward achieving long-term goals of "a rich nation and a strong army." Nevertheless, Deng's approach differed from Yoshida's mercantilist realism, aligning more closely with a Smithian philosophy than a Listian one. This was evident in his significant decision regarding the "military-to-civilian diversion" in the mid-1980s, his preference for "buying" rather than "building," as exemplified by his decision on Y-10, and his unwavering support for Zhao Ziyang's neoliberal-oriented Coastal Development Strategy in late 1987.[63]

Deng ostensibly pursued a strategy of employing liberal means to achieve realist ends, placing his bet on fostering a positive and enduring relationship with the United States as the cornerstone of China's modernization. China's successful collaboration with the United States in jointly containing the Soviet Union paid off economically and technologically throughout the 1980s, bolstering the confidence of Chinese elites in aligning with the U.S.-led international system of global capitalism. With sincere expectations of a prolonged peaceful environment to support China's economic development, the Chinese ruling elites reached the conclusion that "Peace and Development is the prevailing theme of the contemporary world" at the Thirteenth National Party Congress held

[61] Deng's Works, Vol. 3, pp. 104–106.

[62] *Mao Zedong's Manuscripts Since the Founding of the People's Republic of China*. Beijing: zhongyang wenxian chubanshe, 1998, vol. 13, p. 32.

[63] Yue, J (2018), pp. 160, 255.

in the Fall of 1987. While there were some reservations about this "two-theme" thesis, Deng wholeheartedly endorsed the judgment.

Nevertheless, Deng appeared to have overlooked a critical reality: despite allying with the United States to oppose the USSR, China, as a politically independent Communist power, was denied the privilege of "development by invitation" that the United States extended to the "lucky chosen few" anti-Communist allies in East Asia during the Cold War. This oversight, coupled with Mao's past failure of *autarkic* self-reliance, influenced the mindset of Chinese leadership. They viewed autarkism as the root cause of China's underdevelopment and associated it with the concept of self-reliance, motivating their decision to shift the country away from the path of *non-autarkic* self-reliance—a different approach to autonomous national development.

What adds complexity to this situation is that Deng, along with the entire Chinese Communist leadership, possessed limited knowledge of the nuances of "low politics" in international relations, including the distinction between growth and development. They remained unaware of the potential consequences of the failure of the "Southern Challenge," which became evident in the mid-1980s, along with the commencement of the Uruguay Round of Multilateral Trade Negotiations under the General Agreement on Tariffs and Trade (GATT) in 1986. These developments had significant implications for countries in the Global South, including China, whose elites at the time lacked both the knowledge and insights into the sea change in the global political economy resulting from the neoliberal counter-revolution.[64]

Throughout the 1980s, China experienced a growing openness to the prevailing neoliberal paradigm, resulting in a broader opening of its doors. This shift was accompanied by a pervasive sense of national inferiority across all sectors of society. The notion of "worshipping foreign things and fawning on foreign powers" (*chongyangmeiwai*, 崇洋媚外), or idolizing anything foreign, became dominant, not only among the general population but also among the ruling elites and intellectual circles. This

[64] According to a senior research fellow at the Chinese Academy of Social Sciences (CASS), "The Chinese Leadership' Understanding of GATT Is Rather Vague and Naive. For Instance, Premier Li Peng Once Said That the GATT Shouldn't Oppose Our Accession. He Has No Idea of What GATT and Its Whole Set of Rules Mean for China." 07/05/1992, Beijing.

shift paved the way not for economic nationalism, but for a widespread belief in free trade.

In contrast to the situation in "Asia's Next Giant" (South Korea) during a similar stage of economic development in the 1960s and 1970s, where Friedrich List's ideas held sway, the prevailing ideology in 1980s China embraced Adam Smith's doctrine of free trade. This ideology permeated Chinese university campuses and government think tanks. The shift in ideology was encapsulated in the influential political documentary "River Elegy" (1988), which advocated the development of an outward-oriented economy in China. The documentary criticized the notion of attempting to penetrate other countries' markets while keeping China's own market relatively closed.[65] Ignoring China's late development yet calling for reciprocal market openness, "River Elegy" adhered to the belief that free trade was the solution for China to modernize.

These free trade proponents, often referred to as "avant-garde enlighteners," staunchly believed that economic liberalism was the only correct path to development. However, their understanding of the economic history and international politics surrounding the rise of great powers was flawed. They misinterpreted the history of post-war Japan's emergence as an economic superpower, largely achieved through mercantilist strategies with substantial American sponsorship. Moreover, they may have been unaware of the nuanced views of classical liberals such as David Hume, Adam Smith, and David Ricardo. These thinkers supported free trade, but they also recognized the importance of protecting and nurturing domestic industries through the selective use of tariffs. They advocated free trade only under specific conditions to safeguard the domestic market and employment.[66]

Influenced by the myth of free trade, Zhao Ziyang, then the CCP's General Secretary, sought to break the reform deadlock in late 1987 by advocating a deepening of China's integration into the global economy, albeit with a parochial focus. This new approach, known as the Coastal Development Strategy, faced little opposition from party veterans, including Chen Yun. Deng Xiaoping fully endorsed Zhao's vision of

[65] The fourth episode of *River Elegy*: New Era, 1988.

[66] Sally, R (1998): *Classical Liberalism and International Economic Order—Studies in Theory and Intellectual History*. London: Routledge, pp. 38–39; Kiely, R (2006): *New Political Economy of Development: Globalization, Imperialism, Hegemony*. Oxon: Palgrave, p. 14.

deep integration. By late 1988, Zhao Ziyang had become firmly captivated by the neoliberal market-fundamentalist ideas propagated by Milton Friedman,[67] a prominent intellectual leader of the Chicago school of economics.

However, in the aftermath of the Tiananmen incident, Deng displayed mixed attitudes regarding China's future relationship with the global capitalist system. On June 16, 1989, Deng expressed his thoughts to two influential members of the Politburo Standing Committee, Premier Li Peng and First Deputy Premier Yao Yilin, who were closely aligned with the Chen Yun faction. Deng stated: "The whole imperialist Western world has been attempting to force all socialist countries to abandon the socialist path and *integrate them into the orbit of international capitalism*. We must resist this adverse trend ... If we do not uphold socialism, China will be nothing but a dependent state, especially considering that development is not easy due to *the saturation of the world market, making it challenging for us to find a place in it*."[68]

Deng's expression of pessimism should not be misconstrued as a desire to return to the old policy of autarkic self-reliance. Instead, he emphasized the imperative of bold reform and continued openness, urging conservative practitioners to take specific actions. These actions included attracting foreign investment and establishing more development zones, intended to showcase to the world that China remained steadfast in its commitment to "reform and opening," which would further evolve.[69]

To ensure the execution of his directives, Deng resorted to great-power diplomacy. During his meeting with a confidential envoy dispatched by President George H. W. Bush on December 10, 1989, Deng conveyed goodwill toward the United States. This gesture signaled his intention to foster amicable relations with the United States and the broader Western world. Its aim was to secure their acceptance of China's continued alignment with the U.S.-led liberal international order, thereby facilitating China's sustained, externally oriented economic growth.[70]

[67] Gewirtz, J (2017): "The Little-Known Story of Milton Friedman in Chin." Policy Report of CATO Institute, September/October. https://www.cato.org/policy-report/september/october-2017/little-known-story-milton-friedman-china.

[68] Deng's Works, Vol. 3, p. 311.

[69] Ibid., p. 313.

[70] Yue, J (2018), p. 192.

Deng's approach resonated with Americans, as they recognized the significance of a powerful and stable China that maintained a friendly stance toward the United States, particularly in countering the influence of Japan and the Soviet Union in the Far East. This sentiment was articulated by former President Richard Nixon, who had visited Beijing and met with Deng Xiaoping on October 31, 1989. He expressed these views in an article published in *Time* magazine on November 20.[71]

During the latter half of 1989, amid secret diplomatic exchanges between China and the United States, Ambassador Winston Lord astutely perceived the imminent changes in China's political economy following the end of the Cold War and the inevitable ascendancy of global capitalism. Lord strongly advocated maintaining ties with China, believing that the United States could influence China's behavior and guide it in a direction that aligned with U.S. national interests. He contended that China's pressing need for foreign markets, capital, technology, and managerial expertise left it with little alternative but to embrace global capitalism. To facilitate China's benefits from this integration, Lord implied that China should reciprocate by liberalizing trade and investment, and suggested streamlining its bureaucracy to ensure the "consistent implementation of agreements."[72]

Lord's assertion that China had "no alternatives" but to pursue deep *external* integration might have appeared theoretically implausible, considering China's existing strengths, such as a diversified economy and a large scientific community capable of furthering import substitution through deep *internal* integration.[73] However, in practical terms, Lord's perspective held merit due to intellectual limitations within the Chinese leadership and the country's backward educational system.

Despite a conservative resurgence following the Tiananmen incident, China's exposure to foreign influence continued to expand. This growing connection between "reform" and "opening" became evident when China resumed talks with GATT in April 1991. The mounting pressure from GATT for economic liberalization and market access compelled

[71] Nixon, Richard (1989): "Crisis in Sino-American Relations." *Times*, Nov. 20, pp. 45–49.

[72] Lord, W (1989): "China and America: Beyond the Big Chill," *Foreign Affairs*, 68:4, Fall, pp. 1–26.

[73] Yue, J (2016): "China, Global Capitalism, and the Quest for Legitimacy." *International Politics*, 53:6, pp. 752–774.

China to embrace radical marketization and renounce economic nationalism, a transition observed in many post-Communist economies "moving away from central planning and autarky."[74]

In pursuit of access to the markets of now-developed countries (NDCs), China sought institutional guarantees. Deng Xiaoping's southern tour in early 1992 marked a significant milestone in China's journey toward a market economy. This transition coincided with the gradual lifting of economic sanctions imposed by the West after Tiananmen. This interaction between internal and external factors provided a compelling incentive for China to deepen its external integration, aligning with the United States' consistent grand strategy of "drawing China out," which had been in place since Nixon's era.

In contrast to the elites in Meiji and post-war Japan, Chinese elites, both within the bureaucracy and intellectual circles, most enthusiastically embraced the intellectual influence of economic liberalism, particularly the neoliberal paradigm imported from the West. This highlights their myopia in charting China's own pathway of development. These intellectual defects, exacerbated by the triumphant rise of global capitalism at the juncture of the *Global 1989*, contributed to an ideological shift that firmly set China on an anti-nationalist path of development, which, at the time, appeared to be irreversible.

Thus, the Tiananmen incident did not push Deng to seek an alternative path; instead, it reinforced his belief that, given the prevailing institutional dominance of global capitalism, there were no viable alternatives. Unknowingly, Deng was inadvertently following the path of compradorism—a path cautioned against by Zhang Chunqiao more than a decade earlier.

From Ideals to Interests: China's Institutional Transition to Comprador Capitalism in the 1990s

Following Deng Xiaoping's influential southern tour in 1992, the justification for a market economy gained prominence in China. The regime established a direct link between GDP growth and its own legitimacy, considering high economic growth as politically essential and a matter

[74] Cox, M (2022): *Agonies of Empire—American Power from Clinton to Biden*. Bristol: Bristol University Press, p. 40.

of political correctness. With no other viable alternatives in sight, this perception led to the adoption of major policy prescriptions aligned with the Washington Consensus, including the radical privatization of the SOEs and extensive liberalization of trade and investment.

Nevertheless, government intervention continued to play a significant and even bigger role, which diverged from the neoliberal agenda. Rather than aiming to correct market failures and establish a market-based socialist developmental state, the intervention of the Chinese state deliberately created rents, enabling the New Class to profit from it. During the 1990s, the involvement of the United States in China's transition to capitalism was substantial, driven by strategic and economic motives. China's departure from economic nationalism became increasingly evident and rapid, resulting in the emergence of comprador capitalism. This transformation entailed closer integration with global capitalism throughout the decade, culminating in its institutionalization around the turn of the millennium.

Concomitant with the sea change in the Chinese political landscape around 1992, profound changes were also taking place in the United States, which found itself in an unprecedented unipolar moment. Its foreign policy focus shifted "from geopolitics to geoeconomics." The influence of Fukuyama's "end of history" thesis heavily impacted American foreign policy thinking, leading to a belief in "democratic peace" and a push for democracy promotion during the Clinton years.[75] However, the realist tradition did not retreat, but instead developed further, as demonstrated in the Defense Planning Guideline, a top confidential document of the Department of Defense that was leaked to the media in March 1992 during Bush's last year in office. Its central tenet was that U.S. foreign policy after the Cold War would prioritize "precluding the emergence of any future global competitor."[76]

These changes imply that U.S. foreign policy became subject to two seemingly contradictory principles: realism and democracy promotion. The former disregarded regime type, while the latter ignored power politics. The fall of the Soviet Union strengthened the belief within the

[75] Søndergaard, R. S. (2015): "Bill Clinton's 'Democratic Enlargement' and the Securitisation of Democracy Promotion." *Diplomacy & Statecraft*, 26:3, pp. 534–551.

[76] "Excerpts from Pentagon's Plan: 'Prevent the Re-Emergence of a New Rival.'" *The New York Times*, 08/03/1992. https://www.nytimes.com/1992/03/08/world/excerpts-from-pentagon-s-plan-prevent-the-re-emergence-of-a-new-rival.html.

Bush and Clinton administrations that the U.S. could change China.[77] This belief led to the policy of "comprehensive engagement" in 1993, designed by former U.S. ambassador to China Winston Lord. Given the "neither rigidly Wilsonian nor classically realist" character of Clinton's foreign policy,[78] the changes in U.S. foreign policy had two long-term implications for China. Firstly, China would only be tolerated as an emerging market rather than an emerging power or a global competitor. Secondly, as long as China remained undemocratic, it would be subjected to containment and the possibility of a new Cold War.

In other words, U.S. engagement policy, as convincingly described by Mastanduno, aimed to make China a "status quo power."[79] To facilitate China's transformation in this direction, integrating China into the global economy was an integral part of U.S. engagement policy. In practical terms, this meant encouraging China to relinquish economic nationalism in exchange for a growth miracle based on Ricardo's theory of comparative advantage. This approach of "growth by invitation," not limited to China but applicable to all developing and transition economies in the post-Cold War, post-Communist global context, stood in stark contrast to the far superior American gift of "development by invitation" granted to Japan and the newly industrialized economies (NIEs) in East Asia during the Cold War.[80]

China's transition to comprador capitalism was kickstarted against such a grand backdrop. On October 10, 1992, China concluded a memorandum of understanding on market access with the United States. In it, China agreed to remove most trade restrictions in the next few years. Additionally, at the "request" of the U.S., China committed that it "*would not subject any products to import substitution measures* in the future," while stating that it had eliminated all import substitution regulations, guidance, and policies.[81]

[77] McMaster, H. R. (2020), p. 128.

[78] Cox, M (2022), p. 32.

[79] Mastanduno, M (1997): "Preserving the Unipolar Moment: Realist Theories and US Grand Strategy After the Cold War." *International Security*, 21:4, pp. 49–88.

[80] Yue, J (2022): "The Limits to China's Rise—Deep Integration and a New Cold War." *Global Policy*, 13:1, pp. 91–106.

[81] Internal seminar this author joined in Shenzhen, 12–13/12/1992.

Chinese economic policymakers, led by Zhu Rongji, took their commitments seriously as they developed a new industrialization strategy known as the "exchange market access for technology" (EMAT). The roots of this strategy can be traced back to 1984 in China's auto industry. They recognized that previous investments in the 1980s by diaspora Chinese, primarily from areas like Hong Kong, Macau, and Taiwan, were focused on low-tech processing trade. In this type of trade, materials were imported for assembly into final products for re-export, resulting in limited positive effects on the Chinese economy. On the other hand, multinational companies (MNCs) were technologically more advanced. Chinese policymakers placed high hopes on the voluntary transfer of advanced technologies by MNCs, with the condition that China granted them access to the domestic market. Since import substitution was crucial for national industrialization, the enforcement of EMAT indicated that the Chinese regime, constrained by the 1992 deal with the United States, relied on achieving import substitution indirectly through technology transfer from MNCs. However, this approach inadequately prioritized two other strategies whose significance had been severely overlooked: firstly, cultivating indigenous assimilative and absorptive capacity; and, secondly, building an effective national system of innovation (NSI) to enable import substitution on a refreshingly non-autarkic self-reliant basis.

Contrary to the expectations of Chinese policymakers, the majority of the MNCs that experienced significant growth since 1992 primarily focused on tapping into the Chinese market rather than assisting China in increasing its exports. These market-seeking MNCs consistently recorded trade deficits until 1998 when their mission of market domination was largely achieved.[82] Despite the costs associated with market concessions, the spillover effect on China was relatively limited, especially considering that wholly foreign-owned enterprises (WFOEs) quickly surpassed joint ventures in terms of both numbers and investment sums by 1997 and 2001, respectively. This internalization of technology transfer between MNCs' headquarters and their subsidiaries effectively hindered deeper learning processes and spillovers into the local economy.[83]

[82] Yue, J (2004): "A Bleak Prospect of China's Industrialization." *Dushu* (Beijing), July.

[83] Chen, M (2001): "A Cost-Effect Analysis of FDI in China." *Strategy and Management*, No. 3, pp. 93–103.

Furthermore, Chinese policymakers seemed to have misconstrued MNCs' utilization of advanced technologies as China possessing those technologies in their entirety. They failed to recognize that MNCs, unwilling to transfer their most advanced technologies and cultivate their own competitors, had little incentive to share their comprehensive "know-how" and every intention of preventing technology leakage. Consequently, even if Chinese firms acquired manufacturing techniques, they lacked access to the necessary "know-how" and were unable to "catch up and get even" with their foreign partners. This situation further reinforced their dependence on continued technology imports from advanced countries.[84]

One of the most challenging issues often overlooked in the world development studies community, from an international political economy perspective, is the departure demonstrated by EMAT from the typical export-oriented industrialization (EOI) strategy implemented by East Asian developmental states from the 1960s through the 1980s. China's version of EMAT-based EOI, unlike the traditional approach that combined import substitution with export promotion, involved a peculiar blend of export promotion with radical trade and investment liberalization. EMAT, with its emphasis on investment liberalization, aligned well with the market-seeking motivations of advanced countries' MNCs, posing tremendous pressure for the survival of SOEs.

It is worth noting that under rigid top-down systemic pressure for "forced growth," local governments at all administrative levels actively engaged in competition to attract FDI to meet predetermined economic growth targets. This competition inevitably led to competitive concessions of tax preferences and land-use rights to foreign investors, further amplifying the existing competitive advantage of MNCs possessing a "global market, global brand, and global procurement system" compared to China's domestic firms. This overt discrimination against its own indigenous enterprises, including the SOEs, stood in sharp contrast to the economic nationalism exhibited by East Asian developmental states during the Cold War era, which spared no effort to sponsor domestic firms to become competitive global players.

The Chinese policymakers' obsession with EMAT highlighted the "no alternative" neoliberal solution to China's industrialization strategy.

[84] Yue, J (2018), p. 80.

Zhu Rongji's favored deep external integration approach was inherited from his successful management of the economy in Shanghai, where he served as the mayor and Party boss from 1987 to 1991. Shanghai, being an old treaty port with extensive external links and susceptible to foreign influence, shaped Zhu's perspective. When put in charge of economic affairs after 1992, he applied his experience of the external-oriented Shanghai nationwide and neglected institutional reform to dismantle inter-provincial barriers to national economic reintegration. While creating a level playing field for MNCs, he made little effort to overcome economic balkanization within China, thus allowing diseconomies of scale to persist in the domestic market.[85] Robert Wade has argued that development is essentially about internal rather than external integration.[86] Zhu and the Chinese regime's reluctance or inability to pursue deep internal integration left the country vulnerable to mounting pressures from the United States and the Bretton Woods institutions for greater market access. This vulnerability persisted as China sought to achieve sustained Ricardian growth in the face of a shrinking policy space following the establishment of the WTO in 1995.

China's adoption of comprador capitalism represents a complex blend of forced and voluntary decisions resulting from intellectual and institutional barriers to internal integration at home and systemic pressure for greater openness from global capitalism abroad. Paradoxically, among those who recognized the potential harm resulting from an excessive influx of FDI and its impact on Chinese enterprises sheltered by local governments, Zhu Rongji stood out. Throughout the mid-1990s, he consistently cautioned provincial governors about the adverse consequences of competing to attract foreign firms—a rational strategy aligned with the Party's "forced growth" mechanism. This competition often led to the closure of several SOEs in various provinces, resulting in widespread economic inefficiency at the national level.[87]

Despite his awareness of these issues, Zhu lacked the authority to curb the influence of the "local lords," whose unbridled pursuit of high GDP

[85] Yue, J (2018), pp. 215–220.

[86] Wade, R (2003): *Governing the Market—Economic Theory and the Role of Government in East Asian Industrialization* (2nd ed.). NJ: Princeton University Press, introduction: p. xlviii.

[87] *A Record of Zhu Rongji Remarks*. Beijing: renmin chubanshe, vol. 2, p. 375; vol. 3, p. 184.

figures served the interests of both the CCP and themselves. Averse to the alternative option of internal integration, Zhu's solution to sustaining economic growth could only be achieved through further trade and investment liberalization. This culminated in China's deeper external integration, even while considering the potential displacement effect of FDI on SOEs.

Zhu was more of an economic statist than an economic nationalist. Ironically, under his guidance, deliberate pro-FDI policies took precedence over support for private firms in Shanghai. This demonstrated China's departure from autarky and positioned Shanghai as a symbol of "external-oriented development." This fact, often overlooked by some Western development economists who characterized Shanghai as a typical "local developmental state" due to significant state intervention in the economy,[88] highlights a stark reality. By the end of 2022, foreign-invested enterprises (FIEs) accounted for 65% and 55% of total imports and exports in Shanghai, respectively.[89] Due to data restrictions in recent years, high-tech exports data were only available until the first half of 2014, during which FIEs accounted for 92.5% of total high-tech exports, while SOEs and private firms accounted for only 4.4% and 2.7%, respectively.[90] These figures reveal, in Yasheng Huang's words, "substantial structural weaknesses" in the Chinese economy, with Shanghai serving as a microcosm. As Huang shrewdly discerned in his 2008 book titled *Capitalism with Chinese Characteristics*, this path did not transform Shanghai or China into another East Asian Tiger, but brought them closer to a model resembling Latin American capitalism.[91]

Nevertheless, it became evident that a certain indifference and lack of resistance pervaded China as the economy and society gradually succumbed to creeping compradorization, allowing foreign interests and

[88] Thun, E (2006): *Changing Lanes in China: Foreign Direct Investment, Local Governments, and Auto Sector Development*. New York: Cambridge University Press, pp. 100–135.

[89] Statistics of Total Imports and Exports of Shanghai Municipality in 2022: data released on 20/01/2023. https://tjj.sh.gov.cn/ydsj54/20230119/12339ac027814ad7ba8e0513de277833.html.

[90] Shanghai statistics of high-tech imports and exports by ownership (Jan–June 2014): http://www.ststs-sh.gov.cn/fxbg/201103/88414.htm.

[91] Huang, Y (2008): *Capitalism with Chinese Characteristics—Entrepreneurship and the State*. NY: Cambridge University Press, pp. 230, 278–281.

influence to steadily gain control. Unbeknownst to many, including the elites, an important academic debate unfolded in the immediate aftermath of 1992 among prominent figures within the Chinese system. This debate centered on determining the most suitable development strategy for China.

Justin Yifu Lin, an economics professor at Peking University educated in the United States, opposed the catch-up strategy and instead advocated a "comparative advantage strategy," which he argued had previously proven successful in the East Asian Tigers. Conversely, Wang Xiaodong, who later became known as China's nationalist godfather and taught at a prestigious university associated with the Ministry of Foreign Trade and Economic Cooperation (MOFTEC), voiced his dissent regarding Lin's approach of pushing the logic of comparative advantage to the extreme. He argued that Lin's perspective disregarded the element of national security and insisted that pursuing catch-up was imperative for a country's long-term survival and prosperity, even at a considerable cost. Wang rejected the belief held by many Chinese liberal intellectual elite in a global village in the post-Cold War era, instead asserting that the world was entering a period of significant disorder.

In his defense of Latin America's catch-up strategy (ISI), Wang Xiaodong argued against dismissing this approach as an outright failure. He challenged Lin's perception that the East Asian miracle was solely driven by the logic of comparative advantage, suggesting that the success of East Asian Tigers was not a static but a dynamic process. Wang emphasized that their achievements were not solely dependent on comparative advantage, but involved proactive strategies for industrial deepening. To support his argument, Wang cited examples from history, such as the United States and Germany in the late nineteenth century, both of which pursued a catch-up strategy to successfully industrialize. These examples illustrated that a proactive approach to catch-up and industrial development could yield positive outcomes.[92] In the end, Lin emerged as the victor, with his ideas gaining state endorsement and being implemented by the government. Meanwhile, Wang found himself marginalized both intellectually and in terms of career advancement.[93]

[92] Shi Zhong (penname of Wang Xiaodong) (1995): "We Should Not Push the Logic of Comparative Advantage to the Extreme." *Strategy and Management*, No. 3, pp. 11–15.

[93] Wang Xiaodong revealed this inside story when addressing the audience in a public lecture at the London School of Economics, titled "Chinese Nationalism under the

In the years following 1992, throughout the 1990s, there was a notable influx of "Chicago boys"—members of the elite educated in the West, most notably in U.S. and U.K. universities—returning to China who occupied key positions in Chinese universities, state-controlled research institutions, and certain key bureaucratic posts. The influence of the Washington Consensus swiftly became overwhelming within the central government bureaucracy. Even if some initial skepticism arose among a few bureaucrats, the prevailing attitude eventually became "what other alternatives do we have?"[94] Just as Wang Xiaodong deeply expressed concern, the concept of comparative advantage was widely accepted without question on Chinese university campuses.[95] In contrast, the statist approach of interventionism, advocated by a small number of Listian economists, was largely disregarded and often criticized as synonymous with rent-seeking and crony capitalism. Students pursuing MBA and economics degrees were indoctrinated with the belief that "maximizing shareholders' value" was the sacred norm. From the mid-1990s onward, in leading management schools collaborating with Western counterparts, the curriculum design primarily aimed to train future middle or senior-ranking executives rather than nurturing business leaders. The top choice for students was securing positions in MNCs' subsidiaries, particularly in marketing, as their role was seen as facilitating these corporations' penetration of China's vast market rather than developing into globally minded business leaders with a comprehensive understanding of international politics and a genuinely global perspective.

On another level, state media relentlessly propagated the supposed advantages of trade and investment liberalization, touting the imported concept of "win-win" to reinforce the Party's permanent infallibility. They focused solely on the benefits of expanding market access while deliberately ignoring its potential drawbacks. Even isolated cases of corruption would prompt the *People's Daily* to issue editorials, emphasizing that the state actions of combating corruption would not hinder the Party's unwavering pursuit of greater marketization and openness. Simultaneously, censored TV dramas diligently portrayed higher salaries, superior working

Shadow of Globalization," dated 07/02/2005. https://digital.library.lse.ac.uk/objects/lse:mih335foy.

[94] Interviews and discussions with a number of bureaucratic and intellectual elites from the early 2000s to the present day.

[95] This has become an open secret since the late 1980s.

conditions, and extravagant lifestyles of Chinese employees working in Western multinational corporations. These depictions heavily influenced the mindset of young job seekers, who placed utmost priority on securing employment with foreign firms. Consequently, a significant brain drain occurred from the mid-1990s onward, with a large number of talented individuals leaving the state sector to work for foreign entities, which they considered prestigious and more desirable than Chinese companies. Chinese factories, in their television advertisements, made deliberate efforts to emphasize the superior quality of their products by highlighting the inclusion of "imported materials."

The involvement of princelings and individuals from non-Red senior-cadre families played a significant role in promoting China's comprador capitalism. These individuals were among the first to assume positions as compradors, acting as agents in senior executive ranks when Western MNCs entered China during the early stages of reform and opening in the 1980s and 1990s. Leveraging nepotism, they facilitated access to China's vast market, which greatly appealed to MNCs, leading to their recruitment in large numbers.

Many sons and daughters of senior leaders, including Jiang Zemin and Zhu Rongji, obtained degrees from Western universities and effortlessly secured jobs or internships in the headquarters of Western multinational firms. Upon their return to China, they occupied crucial positions within the bureaucracy or large SOEs. Alternatively, some ventured to establish their own monopolistic business conglomerates, with or without foreign involvement. Consequently, they became influential figures as either crony capitalists or comprador capitalists, or both. However, it was China's national interest that ultimately suffered.

Bureaucratic elites also acted as political compradors for Western capital. An illuminating example is a secret deal disclosed by the *Wall Street Journal* on February 6, 2015. The report revealed a conversation between the PRC's Minister of Commerce (MOFCOM) and a senior executive from J.P. Morgan, in which the minister pledged to "go the extra mile to help JPM in whatever way we think he can," on the condition that his underperforming son's job would be protected.[96] The report highlighted that MOFCOM did not have a direct client relationship with J. P. Morgan and was not involved in banking regulation. However,

[96] "J.P. Morgan Emails Illuminate Hiring of China Official's Son." *The Wall Street Journal*, 06/02/2015.

it possessed the authority to impact mergers and acquisitions (M&A) involving MNCs operating in China. Importantly, the report did not provide further insights into the fact that promoting M&A of SOEs by MNCs had become a new policy for investment liberalization in China since the leadership transition in 2003 when Hu Jintao's four-generation leadership succeeded Jiang Zemin.

Citing the 2015 example does not negate the prevalence of comprador capitalism in the 1990s, but it emphasizes the increasing exposure of foreign corruption by Western media after 2005. This revelation shattered the expectations of many liberal Chinese intellectuals in the 1990s who believed that MNCs would act as catalysts for the rule of law and the promotion of liberal democratic values, aiding China's gradual transition toward democracy. However, the reality turned out to be different. Once established in China, MNCs quickly adapted to the unique political-commercial culture of the country, often resorting to practices like "bribing Chinese officials for market access."[97]

Moreover, MNCs actively engaged in lobbying efforts with the Chinese government to safeguard their privileged status and dominance in the Chinese domestic market. A notable example of this was the legislation of the Anti-Monopoly Law (AML). Although initially drafted by MOFTEC (the precursor of MOFCOM from 2003) in 1994, it took 13 years for this significant law to be passed in the National People's Congress in August 2007.[98] Another case involved the Chinese government's attempt to equalize income tax rates between Chinese and foreign investors, which faced a boycott. The delayed enactment of the AML, which had discriminated against Chinese enterprises for nearly two decades, was only addressed in March 2007, with a five-year grace period. Both delays were primarily due to strong resistance from MNCs, who utilized their connections within the Chinese bureaucracy to postpone their implementation.[99]

The compradors within the nomenklatura and those working in foreign firms leveraged their influential positions to collaborate with MNCs, effectively facilitating the advance of the latter's interests in China. For MNCs,

[97] Gutmann, E (2005): *Losing the New China: A Story of American Commerce, Desire and Betrayal*. Ney York: Encounter Books.

[98] *China Economic Weekly*, 12/09/2005. http://business.sohu.com/20050912/n240371245.shtml.

[99] Yue, J (2018), p. 290.

lobbying was a two-way process. They actively lobbied with the Chinese government for greater market concessions, thereby reaping extraordinary profits that would have been challenging to attain elsewhere. The Chinese government secured the endorsement and support of these influential economic players, who became advocates for the political interests of the CCP, utilizing their influence to lobby their home-country governments to maintain stable relations with China.

This support proved vital for the Chinese regime, particularly in the post-Deng era when it prioritized its own viability, even if it meant compromising certain aspects of national interest. This grand bargain had been in place since 1993, when Zhu Rongji, often nicknamed the "economic tsar" and widely regarded as a pro-Western enlightened leader, reassured concerned cadres that "the CCP would not collapse like the USSR because it had the backing of Morgan Stanley and other Wall Street banks."[100]

This collaborative partnership worked to stabilize China-U.S. relations at the highest political levels. However, it also had a significant impact on the beliefs and actions of Chinese bureaucratic and intellectual elites, leading to their gradual compradorization in both psychological and practical terms. This trend became increasingly evident as China intensified its market access negotiations to secure membership in the WTO in the late 1990s. The dissemination of information against economic nationalism, orchestrated jointly by bureaucratic and pro-Western intellectual elites, indirectly reflected this shift. Statements such as "national industry is an anachronistic concept" or "there is no such thing as national industry in the age of globalization" gained prevalence in China. Additionally, a perception emerged that once foreign firms entered China, they "automatically" became Chinese national enterprises.

Economist Liu Shijin, a close aide to Zhu Rongji, played a crucial role in persuading the Premier, who took office in March 1998, that MNCs like Kodak and Fuji were not engaged in product dumping in the Chinese market and did not cause significant harm to their Chinese counterparts. Based on Liu Shijin's "findings," Zhu Rongji made the final decision to conclude the '98 Agreement (98协议) with Kodak, granting it a dominant position in the Chinese market while leaving the only national

[100] Ho-fung Hung on "irony of history," tweeted on 24/11/2021. https://twitter.com/hofunghung/status/1463536544430624769.

enterprise, Lekai (乐凯), in a difficult and disadvantaged position.[101] This decision further exemplified the growing influence of comprador elites and their willingness to prioritize MNCs over domestic companies.

Foreign involvement in China's compradorization extended well beyond trade and investment liberalization, encompassing a vigorous engagement in its domestic agenda. For instance, investment bankers from around the world played a pivotal role in educating Chinese elites about the imperative and methods of privatizing SOEs, which emerged as the central focus of reform efforts.[102] This influence, coupled with the impact of "Chicago boy" economists who had received Western training and had been returning to China in increasing numbers since the mid-1980s, contributed to a significant shift in Chinese policymaking. The history of unsuccessful SOE restructuring dating back to the 1980s solidified policymakers' conviction in the inherent inefficiency of SOEs, further strengthening their determination to adopt a neoliberal doctrine that promoted the privatization of the majority of SOEs as the singular solution.

Motivated by a deep personal disdain for inept leaders within SOEs, Zhu Rongji employed neoliberal strategies aimed at enhancing corporate governance. These strategies included the implementation of innovative incentive compensation structures inspired by Western global firms.[103] However, a significant challenge arose due to the prevailing mindset among Zhu Rongji's advisers, who adhered to a "Chicago boy" ideology.[104] This adherence limited the policymakers, with Zhu Rongji at the forefront, from gaining unbiased insights into the post-war economic histories of capitalist nations like Western Europe, Japan, and the successful experiences of the NIEs in East Asia, where SOEs had played substantial roles.[105] This oversight disregarded the critical fact that the efficiency of service provision under various ownership

[101] "China's Kodak Moment." *The Washington Post*, 07/06/2000. https://www.washingtonpost.com/archive/business/2000/06/07/chinas-kodak-moment/9c43eb9c-99c5-4db0-bffb-699dd5967800/; Yue, J (2018), Ch. 2: "Case Study: The'98 Agreement," pp. 87–89.

[102] Paulson, H. M., Jr. (2015): *Dealing with China—An Insider Unmasks the New Economic Superpower*. London: Headline, p. 39.

[103] Paulson, H. M. (2015), pp. 64, 78.

[104] Yue, J (2018), p. 211.

[105] Grabas, C & Nutzenadel, A (2014), pp. 16, 38; Chang, H (2004), pp. 85, 86, 87.

models (public, private, or mixed) hinges on factors such as competition, regulation, autonomy, and broader issues within the realm of international development.[106] Notwithstanding these complexities, Zhu Rongji's flawed interpretation of SOE mismanagement, which stemmed from the unmeritocratic "Party controls talent" regime rather than the inherent unreformability of the SOEs per se, heightened his determination to pursue their privatization during his tenure as the First Deputy Premier (1992–1998).

Indeed, Zhu Rong's intention of privatizing the SOEs aimed to make them more competitive by exposing them to competition through ownership restructuring. However, the privatization of large-sized SOEs could only be partial and remained state-dominated as they were deemed the economic lifeline of the Party. Small and medium-sized SOEs, especially those that were making losses, could be fully privatized without using the term "privatization" due to its political sensitivity. This is how the roadmap of the so-called "grasp the big and let go of the small" (*zhuadafangxiao*, 抓大放小) was unfolded as early as November 1993.

Ironically, China's wider market access following the Sino-U.S. deal in 1992, especially the implementation of EMAT, dealt a heavy blow to SOEs, accelerating their decline toward the end of the 1990s[107] and even causing the country's industrialization to falter.[108] The relative decline of the SOEs made their further privatization even more justifiable by the end of the 1990s when *zhuadafangxiao* was formalized as the Party's strategy to "reorganize the state economy." Consequently, China's privatization strategy inadvertently led to a situation where China's reform and opening-up efforts were not optimally aligned, benefiting crony capitalists domestically and global capitalists abroad who coveted China's vast domestic market. This situation undermined the country's potential to pursue autonomous national development.

Henry Paulson portrayed Zhu Rongji as a socialist, despite acknowledging that China's privatization under Zhu's leadership was driven by the absence of a well-funded nationwide pension and social safety net, which intensified the suffering of laid-off workers and was profoundly

[106] "*Is the Private Sector More Efficient? A Cautionary Tale*" 2015 by UNDP Global Center for Public Service Excellence (GCPSE).

[107] Yue, J (2016), pp. 752–774.

[108] Cheng, X (2003): "Reinterpreting China's Miracle: Dynamism and Consequences of Economic Growth." *Modern China Studies*, No. 1, pp. 25–46.

unjust.[109] Without the right to form their own Solidarity Union, which the CCP vehemently opposed, an estimated 40 million industrial workers lost their jobs between 1997 and 2001, as reported by the IMF in 2004, with inadequate compensation. This resulted in the near-complete disappearance of a modern urban working class and the de facto middle class that had emerged during Mao's era. The economic consequences were severe, contributing to a widening income gap and persistent underconsumption that persists to this day. This situation further reinforced China's reliance on exports and FDI, compelling the country to embrace economic internationalism more comprehensively during the subsequent WTO accession talks.

In other words, China's adoption of comprador capitalism exacerbated the challenges faced by SOEs, which in turn justified their crony capitalist privatization. These consequences, in a cyclical manner, further justified the continued embrace of comprador capitalism.

China's comprador capitalism reached a new height with its accession to the WTO in December 2001, a significant event that marked the point of no return for the country's deep institutional integration into the capitalist world economy. The WTO, established in 1995, was not about development, as argued by Robert Wade, given the shrinking "development space" (used interchangeably with "policy space").[110] Pascal Lamy, as the Director General of the WTO, sidelined development from the organization's agenda.[111] Ha-Joon Chang even claims that the WTO is "anti-developmental" due to its "anti-statist, anti-industrial policy" rules for deep integration.[112] By conflating growth with development and promoting an external (export) orientation, the WTO, with its faith in "market fundamentalism," advocates unrestricted market access through the three key agreements: TRIMs (Trade-Related Investment Measures),

[109] Paulson, H. M. (2015), pp. 76, 85.

[110] Wade, R (2003): "What Strategies Are Viable for Developing Countries Today? The World Trade Organization and the Shrinking of 'Development Space.'" *Review of International Political Economy*, 10: 4, pp. 621–644.

[111] Lamy, P (2013): *The Geneva Consensus—Making Trade Works for All*. Cambridge University Press, pp. 38, 44.

[112] Chang, H. J. (2010): "Hamlet Without the Prince of Denmark: How Development Has Disappeared from the 'Development' Discourse?" in Khan, S. R. and Christiansen (2011) (ed.): *Towards New Developmentalism—Markets as Means Rather Than Master*. London: Routledge, pp. 65–76.

TRIPs (Trade-Related Aspects of Intellectual Property Rights), and GATS (General Agreement on Trade in Services). This serves to "institutionalize protectionism of the strong at the expense of poor nations."[113] Andrew Walter convincingly argues that TRIMs and TRIPs were a result of techno-nationalism of Global North countries, which, through the enforced codification of their technological advantages, solidified the advanced countries' dominance in high-tech industries.[114]

There is abundant evidence suggesting that the Chinese elites, for the most part, had a limited understanding of this international economic organization and its various rules. In its pursuit of WTO membership, China made extensive concessions (including excessive ones) in terms of trade and investment liberalization that few other members had accepted. Peter Nolan drew a parallel between China's WTO agreement and the Treaty of Nanking (1842) following the First Opium War, highlighting the harsh and even humiliating terms that China was compelled to accept regarding market access.[115] Apart from willingly being classified as a "non-market economy" for 15 years, with uncertain justification thereafter, China was also subjected to three WTO-plus terms specifically designed to restrict the access of its labor-intensive products to the U.S. domestic market. These ad hoc discriminatory terms, as Nicholas Lardy expressed, "violated the most fundamental principles of the WTO."[116] It is worth noting the excessive commitment China made to relinquish its sovereign right to enforce "forced technology transfer" requirements on foreign investors—an entitlement that WTO members are still entitled to enjoy under TRIMs to this day.

Under the direct guidance of Premier Zhu Rongji and General Secretary Jiang Zemin, all the accession talks were conducted behind closed doors and intentionally kept secret not only from ordinary Chinese citizens but also from many senior officials within the central government and domestic industries. What is even more peculiar is the fact that the

[113] Nolan, P (2001): *China and Global Economy: National Champions, Industrial Policy, and the Big Business Revolution*. London: Palgrave, p. 152.

[114] Walter, A and Sen, G (2003): *Analyzing the Global Political Economy*. NJ: Princeton University Press, p. 53.

[115] Nolan, P (2001): "China, the US and the WTO: Battle of the Giants or Defeat of the Pygmies" (*manuscript*).

[116] "The WTO Accords Not Without Dangerous." *South China Morning Post* (SCMP), 22/05/2002.

final procedure of the National People's Congress authorizing MOFTEC to submit the Approval Text to the WTO was considered highly unconstitutional due to its violation of the Legislation Law, according to legal experts in China.[117] Despite these undemocratic proceedings, both the Chinese and Western media deliberately disregarded them. These explicitly "anti-developmental" actions serve as stark reminders of the existence of a comprador class, as cautioned by dependency theorists. Many Chinese elites, who had transformed into crony capitalists, consciously *betrayed* the interests of the poor, to say the least, while *sincerely* embracing the neoliberal dogma.

China's accession to the WTO is regarded by the United States as a significant foreign policy achievement. The United States actively supported China's bid for WTO membership based on three primary reasons. Firstly, with a strong belief in its overwhelming power as the "new Rome on the Potomac,"[118] the United States had little concern about China's relatively weaker power. Secondly, the United States was convinced that economic openness would have a liberalizing effect on Chinese society, ultimately leading to bottom-up pressure for political change.[119] Thirdly, the United States believed that opening China's vast market to American corporations and allowing China to benefit from the existing American-led international order would encourage China to act responsibly, curbing its revisionist tendencies and thus serving U.S. economic and strategic interests. A RAND Corporation report submitted to the U.S.-China Economic and Security Review Commission on May 19, 2005 expressed this optimism by stating that "China's turn to globalization has been one of the greatest foreign policy instruments in American history."[120]

Through inducement and coercion, the United States successfully enticed China's Communist leaders to take the risk of compromising the country's autonomous development in exchange for a Ricardian export-led growth miracle based on the principle of comparative advantage.

[117] Zhang, Niangen (2011): "On the Changes of Chinese Legal System for Implementing the WTO Laws." *The Legist* (faxuejia), Issue (1), pp. 9–18.

[118] Cox, M (2022), p. 154.

[119] Ikenberry, J (2020): *A World Safe for Democracy—Liberal Internationalism and the Crises of Global Order*. New Haven: Yale University Press, p. 263.

[120] Overholt, W (2005): China and Globalization—Testimony Before the U.S.-China economic and Security Commission, RAND, released on 19/05/2005.

The potential danger of "becoming an economic vassal of the West," as cautioned by Zhang Chunqiao almost two decades ago, was not unforeseeable to certain Chinese elites who provided advice to the top leadership. However, this did not deter the ruling party from confidently proclaiming the establishment of "a Chinese-style socialism" (*zhongguo tese de shehuizhuyi*, 中国特色的社会主义) as the new guiding ideology of the CCP, replacing the previous notion of "a socialism *with* Chinese characteristics" (*you zhongguo tese de shehuizhuyi*, 有中国特色的社会主义). The Party believed that it had identified a new and exclusive correct path for China to follow—the approach of liberal globalization in economic development.

This path, formed through the marriage of market-Leninism with global capitalism, was clearly aimed at aligning China's national crony capitalism with global capitalism, which would be favorable for regime consolidation. Such an implicit and unholy alliance was also seen as advantageous for China's national security, as the leadership believed in the peace-promoting role of economic interdependence with the U.S. The Chinese rulers, while still upholding Deng's "two-theme" thesis of peace and development, silently changed its theoretical foundation. It was no longer that a new world war was deemed *less likely*, as Deng Xiaoping had believed during his lifetime, but rather that a new world war was *entirely unlikely* in the age of globalization. With this "new thinking" in mind, the Chinese leadership decided to cease opposing capitalism and imperialism (with the term "hegemonism" used in the post-Mao era) in foreign policy, despite their avowed intent to promote a multipolar world through a soft-balancing approach against American hegemonic power.

It is highly misleading to portray the CCP as inherently nationalist. Historically, in political terms, the CCP has not been nationalistic. Economically, except for during the Mao era, it can hardly be characterized as nationalistic either. The emergence of the danger of comprador capitalism can be traced back to China's reforms and opening in the late 1970s, which took place against the backdrop of inheriting the complex legacies of developmental Maoism. These legacies involved crude planning, provincial autarky (liabilities), and a backward yet diverse economy (assets in some sense).

The trajectory toward comprador capitalism is not theoretically inevitable. The dichotomous thinking of the post-Mao leadership led to an excessive sublation of Mao's legacies, particularly in equating autarky with self-reliance. This resulted in the correct move to end autarky being transformed into a renunciation of economic nationalism. Initially, this process remained confined to the realm of ideas and began in the mid-1980s. However, it gained momentum in the late 1980s with the influence of neoliberal thinking from the United States.

The transition to comprador capitalism became increasingly difficult to resist after the global triumph of capitalism in the aftermath of the events of 1989. Chinese elites, including Deng Xiaoping, were myopic in their pursuit of performance-based legitimacy, on which the United States capitalized through tactics of coercion and inducement. China was prompted to abandon economic nationalism in exchange for an export-led growth miracle. The "Chicago boys" and Wall Street capitalists also played influential roles in guiding China's neoliberalization. Furthermore, the Tiananmen crackdown in 1989 had a "shock and awe" effect, which facilitated the implementation of near—"shock therapy" Washington Consensus reforms throughout the 1990s.[121]

The Sixteenth National Congress of the CCP, held in 2002, marked the institutionalization of Chinese crony comprador capitalism. This system was characterized by an unprecedented level of state capture by institutional interests that were not only self-serving but were also aligned with the interests of global capital.[122] The close alliance between CCP elites and global capitalists made it inherently incompatible with economic nationalism.[123] Consequently, criticism of globalization became a political taboo in China, a unique phenomenon not commonly observed in other parts of the world.

In summary, the CCP's radical right-wing shift brought about a significant change in the perspective of Chinese leaders regarding global capitalism and American hegemony. Instead of viewing the dependency relationship with the industrial West as a source of discontent, they grew

[121] Yue. J (2018), Chap. 5: "The 1990s: Washington Consensus in China?" (pp. 209–233), especially the section: "The Statecraft of Zhu Rongji," pp. 215–220.

[122] Yue, J (2018), pp. 271–331; Kwong, P (2006): "The Chinese Face of Neoliberalism," October 7. https://www.counterpunch.org/2006/10/07/the-chinese-face-of-neoliberalism/.

[123] As mentioned earlier, a notable illustration of this was the act of "naming and shaming" carried out by a deputy party secretary of the Beijing Municipality against the authors of a nationalist best-seller titled "*China's Road under the Shadow of Globalization*" in early 2000.

increasingly satisfied with it.[124] The practice of comprador capitalism by the Chinese Communist regime was seen as politically advantageous, reinforcing the alignment of interests between institutional elites and global capital. This transformation marked a departure from economic nationalism and entrenched China's integration into the global capitalist system, shaping the country's trajectory of semi-peripheral development in the contemporary era.

[124] The most representative example of such a change is the address delivered at the Fairbank East Asian Research Centre of Harvard University by Jiang Zemin's key advisor, Liu Ji on 27 May 1997, titled "Who Is the Marshall Today?—The Choice of Sino-U.S. Relations in the 21st Century," *Zaobao*, 23/10/1997.

CHAPTER 5

China's Rise in a Semi-peripheral Orbit (After WTO Entry)

Prior to China's accession to the WTO, the Chinese economy had experienced a significant downturn and faced an imminent recession. This was primarily attributed to the adverse effects of the Southeast Asian financial crisis, the devastating flood in 1998, and deflationary pressures resulting from underconsumption.[1] The international media captured this pessimistic economic outlook with headlines such as "China's Coming Recession" (*The Economist*, April 30, 1998) and "China: What's Going Wrong?" (*Business Weekly*, February 22, 1999). These headlines reflected the concerns surrounding China's economic performance during that period. Furthermore, Chinese policymakers grew increasingly worried as there was a noticeable decline of 11.3% in inbound FDI in 1999. However, what received less attention was the structural cause of China's economic downturn, namely the consequential displacement effect of the influx of FDI on SOEs, which had traditionally played a crucial role in China's manufacturing sectors. This development had led China's industrialization to flag at the turn of the millennium.[2]

Gerald Segal of the International Institute of Strategic Studies (IISS) offered a sober analysis of China's geopolitical power. In a highly influential article published in the September/October 1999 issue of *Foreign*

[1] Yue, J (2016), pp. 752–774.

[2] Cheng, X (2003), pp. 25–46.

J. Yue, *Crony Comprador Capitalism*,
https://doi.org/10.1007/978-3-031-53154-5_5

Affairs, Segal challenged China's status as a "second-rank middle power." He argued that China's perceived significance as "a market, a power, and a source of ideas" had been overestimated, suggesting its limited economic, military, and political relevance.[3]

Yet soon after China joined the WTO, profound changes took place. The massive influx of FDI resulted in a boom in export-led growth. This not only restored the lost economic momentum but also propelled China onto a fast track of industrial development. Contrary to Gerald Segal's pessimistic projection of Chinese power, the "rise of China" has increasingly gained global consensus from the late 2000s onward. This viewpoint is shared by numerous economists, international relations scholars, and politicians, including Danny Quah (2011),[4] Barry Buzan (2010),[5] and Tony Blair (2020).[6] China's overtaking of Germany in 2007 and Japan in 2010, becoming the second-largest economy, along with its economic size surpassing that of the United States in 2015 in terms of purchasing power parity (according to World Bank data), further solidified its significance on the global stage. China's ascent now holds significant importance in the global political economy, with its growth often attributed to the workings of globalization.

Currently, there is extensive discussion about China as the new world center of gravity, based on the implicit but flawed assumption that the country's ever-rising trend is irreversible. Leaving aside China's dubious statistics,[7] linear projections of Chinese power have largely

[3] Segal, G (1999): "Does China Matter?" *Foreign Affairs*, 78:5, pp. 24–36.

[4] Quah, D (2011): "The Global Economy's Shifting Centre of Gravity." *Global Policy*, 2:1, pp. 3–9.

[5] Buzan, B (2010): "China in International Society: Is 'Peaceful Rise' Possible?" *The Chinese Journal of International Politics*, 3:1, pp. 5–36.

[6] Tony Blair: "We are now dealing not with a rising China but a risen China and this rise is both inevitable and right." *Reuters*, 24/06/2020. https://www.reuters.com/article/U.S.-britain-blair-china-idUSKBN23V2OH.

[7] Chinese economist Xiang Songzuo revealed China's actual growth rate at just about 1.67%. He said: "according to the other calculation, the growth rate was negative," far below the official figure of 6.6% in 2018. "Outspoken China economist casts doubt on growth forecast—Professor says contradictions in government statistics do not add up." *Nikkei Asia*, 05/03/2019. https://asia.nikkei.com/Economy/Outspoken-China-economist-casts-doubt-on-growth-forecast; Eric Zhu and Tom Orlik wrote: "A study by economists at the Chinese University of Hong Kong and University of Chicago suggested that between 2010 and 2016, China's 'true' GDP growth was about 1.8 percentage points below what the official data suggested. If China is in fact already

ended the once-contentious "power shift" debate among IR scholars, and have rendered those "anti-(US) declinist" proponents anachronistic and marginalized in practical terms. Taking the power transition as a given, this debate, from a decade earlier, has been focused on whether this "risen" China will be a rule-taker or rule-breaker in the liberal international order, a benign or malign superpower in coming years or decades, and whether the power transition will make a new great power war inevitable.

Nevertheless, the validity of the "rise of China" thesis itself is open to questioning. Like the power-shift debate in which "prominent contributions rarely engage the question of what power is and how it might be measured,"[8] protagonists of the "rise of China" thesis, more often than not, overlook the more nuanced perspective of development—a concept in the field of international political economy (IPE) that is closely correlated with that of power. There is no denying that continuing rapid economic growth has characterized China's "rise." Yet GDP or growth rate alone are not the sole indices of economic success; development or "catch-up"—as Immanuel Wallerstein defined it[9]—is more crucial. Development carries different connotations than growth and involves two key notions: poverty reduction in humanitarian terms, which measures the result of economic growth, and catch-up in transformational (developmental) terms.

For late developers, to "catch up and get even" with the developed nations technologically through constant industrial upgrading is the only way to escape dependency and ensure national wealth and power. This is particularly true for countries like China, which have undergone large-scale late industrialization. Conventional wisdom has it that China is the greatest beneficiary of globalization, as evidenced by its strong export-led growth over recent decades. This growth-centered view is almost

on a slower growth path, overtaking the U.S. becomes harder." News features on Bloomberg—"When Will China Rule the World? Maybe Never—The Communist Party wants the world to see China's continued rise as inevitable. In reality, it's anything but." *Bloomberg*, 05/07/2021. https://www.bloomberg.com/news/features/2021-07-05/when-will-china-s-economy-beat-the-u-s-to-become-no-1-why-it-may-never-happen.

[8] Kitchen, N. & Cox, M. (2019): "Power, Structural Power, and American Decline." *Cambridge of International Affairs*, 32:6, pp. 734–752.

[9] Wallerstein, I, (1992): "The Concept of National Development." *The American Behavioral Scientist*, 35:4, pp. 517–529.

universally prevalent, but it conceals the assumption that technological advance is costless and that economic growth leads automatically to catch-up. The assumption implies that China would smoothly transition to high value-added activities, achieving industrialization at specific points through intensive growth rather than extensive growth.

China's persistent challenges in transitioning cast doubts upon the concept of an inexorable progression. China's compelled hesitations in adhering to the schedule for full industrialization, as evidenced by its two forced postponements of the industrialization timetable between 2015 and 2021,[10] along with the looming risk of falling into the "middle-income trap" over the past decade,[11] stand as compelling counterexamples to the prevailing doctrine.

[10] 2011 was the first time China set forth the timetable for industrialization at 2020. "Li calls for deeper trade ties with Germany." *The Financial Times*, 07/01/2011. http://www.ft.com/cms/s/0/d0244274-1a71-11e0-b003-00144feab49a.html#axzz1AXAIplJr; The State Council stated in the Notice on "Made in China 2025," that "by 2020, China will ***basically achieve industrialization*** ... By 2035, our country's manufacturing as a whole will reach the medium level of the world's manufacturing powers, and whereby to ***fully realize industrialization***." The State Council website, 08/05/2015. http://www.gov.cn/zhengce/content/2015-05/19/content_9784.htm); Oddly, then Minister Miao Wei of MIIT (Ministry of Industry and Information Technology) was quoted by Xinhua as saying that "By 2025, with comprehensive index approaching that of Germany and Japan when they realized industrialization, China will ***basically achieve industrialization*** of our own and whereby to enter the second echelon of global manufacturing business." *Xinhuanet*, 19/05/2015. http://www.xinhuanet.com//politics/2015-05/19/c_1115333559.htm; Miao Wei seemed to hint at a new timetable of ***achieving full industrialization*** at some three decades later (by 2050), far longer than the preset target of 2035. *China Daily*, 09/03/2021. (underlined and italics by the author).

[11] Lou Jiwei, former Minister of Finance, issued warning that there was 50% chance for China to fall into the middle-income trap "in the coming 5 to 10 years." *RFI*, 01/05/2015. https://www.rfi.fr/cn/%E4%B8%AD%E5%9B%BD/20150501-%E8%B4%A2%E9%95%BF%E6%A5%BC%E7%BB%A7%E4%BC%9F%E2%80%9C%E4%B8%AD%E7%AD%89%E6%94%B6%E5%85%A5%E9%99%B7%E9%98%B1%E2%80%9D%E9%A3%8E%E9%99%A9%E8%AE%BA%E5%BC%95%E7%88%86%E6%94%BF%E7%BB%8F%E7%95%8C%E8%AE%A8%E8%AE%BA; Economist Xu Xiaonian argued that China had fallen into the middle-income trap. See Xu Xiaonian's address delivered to the Shenzhen Institute of Innovation and Development dated 05/05/2017. https://xuxiaonian.blog.caixin.com/archives/162653; Both President Xi Jinping and Premier Li Keqiang expressed concern but optimism of transcending the "middle-income trap" by 2020, the symbol of which would be China's per capita GDP surpassing US$12,000 (According to Li). *China Economic Weekly*, 25/07/2017. http://www.chinanews.com/cj/2017/07-25/8286488.shtml. China's per capita GDP reached US$10,500 in 2020. https://data.worldbank.org/indicator/NY.GDP.PCAP.CD?locations=CN.

Some skeptics of the market and globalization, particularly proponents of "New Developmentalism" emerging in the wake of the global financial crisis of 2007–2009, may have downplayed China's deep integration into the global economy and the associated risks of falling into the "middle-income trap." They portray China as skillfully navigating global norms while enjoying the backing of a robust state apparatus, consciously avoiding scenarios dictated by the Washington Consensus.[12]

The objective of this chapter is to challenge the longstanding myth surrounding China's economic and technological ascent by dispelling the widely misunderstood notion of China's adoption of neomercantilism. The argument presented here contends that despite its deep global integration, China stands as a fragile great power rather than a stable superpower contender.

It is indeed ironic that China's trajectory has led to its entrapment in semi-peripheral development rather than the straightforward economic and technological rise that is often portrayed. This entrapment has, in turn, contributed significantly to the resurgence of great power rivalry on the global stage, thereby exacerbating the prospect of a new Cold War. This chapter serves as a critical examination of this paradox, shedding light on China's current position in the global order and its concept of a "peaceful rise."

A Semi-peripheral "Superpower": The Myth of China's Neomercantilism

Premier Zhu Rongji candidly told Stephen Roach, the chief economist of Morgan Stanley, in March 2002 that: "If China did not join the WTO, it would be impossible to restructure and sustain economic growth."[13] In fact, utilizing foreign pressure had gradually become a tactic employed by Chinese policymakers to drive domestic reforms since the late 1980s, although the strategy was initially unclear and only formalized after 1992. That year marked China's transition to comprador capitalism, characterized by its commitment to the United States for significant trade and

[12] Khan, S.R. & Christiansen, J (2011): *Towards New Developmentalism—Markets are Means rather than Master*. Routledge, pp. 177–202 & 257.

[13] Stephen Roach (during China Development Forum in Beijing): "China: Straight Talk from Zhu." 27/03/2002. www.morganstanley.com/GEFdata/digests/20020327-wed.html. This hyperlink no longer exists.

investment liberalization, and the renunciation of "import substitution of any product." This formalized the approach of "exchange market access for technology" (EMAT). However, the EMAT strategy, which relied on technology transfer from foreign investors as an indirect form of import substitution, did not yield satisfactory results. China granted market access, but fell short of achieving technological leapfrogging.[14]

This led to a significant policy debate in 2005, three years after China's accession to the WTO.[15] However, largely unknown to the contenders, China had already made a commitment to the United States in a bilateral agreement on market access on November 15, 1999, promising not to impose technology transfer requirements on foreign investors. This excessive commitment outside the WTO rules rendered EMAT ineffective. Nevertheless, influenced by a "highly respected foreigner" with neoliberal convictions, Zhu successfully convinced his Politburo comrades of the merits of the "anti-developmental" WTO deal.[16] Ostensibly, Chinese top leaders prioritized growth over development. It was not until 2011 that the failure of the EMAT strategy was widely acknowledged, particularly in the auto industry, where it had been first implemented and lasted for 27 years.[17]

It is worth noting that China's commitments were taken seriously within the country. Prior to and following China's entry to the WTO, numerous laws and regulations were re-examined, and those found to be in conflict with the WTO rules were either revised or repealed to ensure their full compliance. The Supreme Court ruled that in the event of conflicts between domestic laws and the WTO agreement, the latter would take precedence. The CCP's Propaganda Department issued directives, outlining how to leverage the benefits of WTO accession while downplaying or disregarding its potential drawbacks. These directives

[14] Chen, M and Yue, J (2002): "Exchange Market Share for Technology? An Analysis of China's Strategy in Absorbing FDI." *Modern China Studies*, No. 4, pp. 93–100.

[15] "EMAT Faces Challenge, Core Technology still Depends on Indigenous Innovation." *Economic Reference News* (jingji cankaobao), 30/11/2005; "Ten Big Debates in Economic Realms in 2005." *jingji cankao bao*, 31/12/2005; "Liu Yanhua (Deputy Minister of Science and Technology): The introduction of technology is not equal to the introduction of innovation ability." *The Workers' Daily*, 01/12/2005.

[16] Yue, J (2018), p. 86.

[17] Wei Jinqiao: "A Failed 'Market for Technology' Strategy." *The Financial Times* (Chinese version), 20/04/2011. http://www.ftchinese.com/story/001038180?full=y&archive.

were given to tightly controlled domestic media, which, ironically, were largely characterized by strong anti-economic nationalism.

In legal terms, extensive accession commitments made China the most open developing economy. Unprecedented market opening through massive trade and investment liberalization, coupled with an abundant supply of cheap labor, positioned China as the most vital segment of the global supply chain following its WTO accession. After effectively dominating China's market in 1998, MNCs expanded their presence beyond the growing Chinese domestic market. Leveraging their "3-globals" advantages (global market, global brand, and global procurement system), they shifted manufacturing operations to China, which emerged as their ideal production base due to its ultra-low-cost structure. This enabled large-scale exports to global markets. As a result, Western global firms attained greater economies of scale and an increased competitive advantage through their dominance of China's international trade and high-tech sectors.[18] Since 2001, foreign capital has maintained a strong grip on over half of China's foreign trade and its overall influence on the Chinese economy has remained uninterrupted. By the end of 2005, the import and export activities of foreign-invested enterprises (FIEs) constituted almost 60% of China's total import and export volume, with the export of high-tech products representing an even higher proportion, nearing 90%.

In the face of intense competition, Chinese manufacturing witnessed a significant decline, a fact extensively covered by China's domestic media. However, few in China were aware of the underlying cause and its connection to China's deep integration. Chinese leaders and academics appeared uncertain that, under WTO rules of deep integration, developing nations, for the first time, had to adhere to regulations that tightly restricted certain critical areas of industrial policy. Avoiding the trade regime's judicial rulings had now become virtually impossible, as noted by development economist Dani Rodrik.[19] Indigenous firms, situated at the lower end of the value chain, faced constant pressure to reduce costs. Even some "high-tech" local firms, despite importing state-of-the-art equipment for manufacturing new products, had limited options

[18] Yue, J (2008): "Peaceful Rise of China: Myth or Reality?" *International Politics*, 6:1, pp. 439–456.

[19] Rodrik, D (2011): *The Globalization Paradox: Why Global Markets, States and Democracy can't Coexist*. Oxford: Oxford University Press, p. 78.

other than to focus on commodity-focused production of undifferentiated and standardized goods. This commodification of production lowered entry barriers and significantly reduced profit margins for domestic firms as a whole. As a consequence, leading global competitors raced toward more sophisticated and challenging endeavors that were harder to replicate.[20] Consequently, domestic firms operating with narrow profit margins encountered tremendous difficulties in technological advance. This led to two outcomes: increased reliance on imports for "designs, critical components, and manufacturing equipment"[21] and the widespread prevalence of piracy, which lay at the core of China's economic boom.[22]

With significant foreign involvement in China's economic activities, the country's accession to the WTO transformed it into the "world's assembly plant" rather than the "world's factory" seen in 19th-century Britain during the First Industrial Revolution. The weakness of domestic industrial capacity was evident in its export performance, primarily characterized by the export of low-end and mid-end products. Even certain high-tech products were labor-intensive or processed using supplied materials, while high-tech products were predominantly imported. The official media agencies acknowledged that China's own manufacturing strength was shrinking in the face of strong foreign capital competition. In terms of equipment (capital goods) manufacturing, which formed the core of the manufacturing industry, China heavily relied on imports, with approximately 85% of IC manufacturing equipment, 70% of high-end Computerized Numerical Control (CNC) machine tools, and 100% of optoelectronic manufacturing equipment being sourced from abroad. In industries such as information technology, precision instruments, and biotechnology, China's involvement was limited to packaging and assembly processes, with around 90% of the value creation occurring outside China.[23]

In May 2004, the State Administration of Industry and Commerce (SAIC) issued warnings against the market monopoly by Western global firms, stating: "Their monopoly of the Chinese market has become very

[20] Steinfeld, E (2010): *Playing Our Game—Why China's Rise Doesn't Threaten the West*. NY: Oxford University Press, p. 105.

[21] Gilboy, G.J. (2004): "The Myth behind China's Miracle." *Foreign Affairs*, 83:4, July/Aug, pp. 33–48.

[22] Dikötter, F (2022), p. 239.

[23] *China Business News* (diyi caijing ribao, abbreviated as "*yicai*"), 28/11/2005.

conspicuous in recent years. The MNCs are using their advantages in technology, brand, and scale to expand their monopoly and have created high entry barriers."[24]

On January 26, 2005, the Ministry of Commerce (MOFCOM), following neoliberal-oriented policies, published the "Report on MNCs in China 2004." This report disclosed that MNCs had acquired more than one-third of the market share in sectors such as light industry, chemicals, pharmaceuticals, and mechanical electronics. However, it acknowledged that the anticipated technology transfer or spillover from MNCs to China's economic development had fallen significantly short. China's market concessions had not yielded the expected technological advances for domestic firms as a result of EMAT.[25] Interestingly, the dominance of MNCs in the market did not align with their contribution to China's capital formation, which displayed a declining trajectory. During the period 1990–1999, this contribution stood at 15.4%, but it declined to 10.6% during 2000–2003. Notably, this percentage was lower than the average of 25% for developed countries and 13% for developing countries as a whole.[26]

In August 2006, the Development Research Centre (DRC) of the State Council, the second-largest official think tank with a strong neoliberal orientation, released a more detailed report. The findings were even more remarkable, stating that in China's major industrial sectors opened up to FDI, the top five players in each sector were predominantly owned or controlled by MNCs. Out of the country's 28 major industrial sectors, 21 were de facto controlled by MNCs.[27]

MNCs' market dominance was seemingly reinforced by the new administration of Wen Jiabao, who took over the Premiership from Zhu Rongji in 2003. In that year, more radical FDI policies were introduced, actively encouraging mergers and acquisitions (M&A) of SOEs by MNCs as a new way of attracting FDI. MNCs specifically targeted China's

[24] *21st Century Business Herald*, 16/05/2004.

[25] "2005 Multinational Corporations in China Report," released by MOFCOM dated 26/01/2005.

[26] "Is foreign capital really that important to us?" *Shanghai Securities News*, 27/02/2006. https://business.sohu.com/20060227/n242031085.shtml

[27] Shi Weigan: "Re-examining the Role of FDI: of 28 Major Industries, 21 Controlled by the MNCs." *Nanfengchuang*, 28/08/2006.

leading capital goods producers, primarily large SOEs. Despite the declaration made by General Secretary Hu Jintao in January 2006 to build an "innovative state" by 2020, this policy remained unchanged. The declaration was closely tied to the increasing market domination by MNCs and China's continued dependence on technology imports from developed countries, which raised concerns among the Chinese leadership. Hu's goal aimed to increase China's research and development expenditure as a percentage of GDP from the current 1.35% to 2.5%, raise the contribution of science and technology to economic growth from 39% to over 60%, and reduce technology dependency on foreign countries from 50% to less than 30% by 2020.

This blueprint was widely touted by academics, business leaders, and political figures in the West as China's embrace of techno-nationalism, a Chinese version of neomercantilism. As a matter of fact, indigenous innovation, the core aspect of "building up an innovative state," focused on improving the absorptive capacity of domestic enterprises primarily through technology imports, rather than establishing a robust NSI. As a result, China's indigenous innovation scheme was never intended to reverse the trend of further liberalization of foreign investment, as exemplified by the 2003 policy encouraging M&A of Chinese enterprises by MNCs.

The argument that SOEs gained further protection after successful restructuring under the "grasp the big and let go of the small" policy since 1997, and that barriers against FDI increased in 2005,[28] overlooks the fact that some restrictions imposed by the Chinese central state against MNCs' takeover of leading SOE players were not voluntary. These restrictions were merely a forced response to the public outcry against "foreign economic aggression" in the form of M&A of prominent Chinese firms, many of which were national champions and symbols of national pride, such as the Xugong Mechanical Works.

An indisputable piece of evidence opposing China's shift toward economic nationalism was the government's response to the assertive expansion of MNCs into the Chinese market. In August 2006, DRC acknowledged this expansion. Nevertheless, in the same month, six central government ministries collaborated to develop regulations regarding M&A by foreign investors. The drafting of this so-called "most

[28] Dikötter, F (2022), pp. 254–255.

important law"—also known as "Document No. 10"—was overseen by Guo Jingyi, a senior official from MOFCOM responsible for treaties and laws. Guo was arrested two years later for accepting bribes from MNCs and acting as their agent. Despite this scandal, the number of M&A cases continued to increase rapidly. By the end of 2008, 300 domestic capital goods producers had become subsidiaries of MNCs. Guo's arrest and the public outcry against foreign takeovers of leading Chinese firms did not dissuade the PRC's central government from pursuing this policy.[29]

Pressures from China's major Western trading partners played a significant role in discrediting the industrial policies associated with indigenous innovation shortly after their implementation. China had the legal right to implement industrial policies, including the imposition of local content requirements, in unexploited areas such as high-end manufacturing, high-tech industries, new energy, and environmental sectors. These policies were entitled to greater policy space under WTO rules. During the period from 2009 to 2011, China and the United States held three Strategic and Economic Dialogues (S&ED), during which the United States exerted pressure on China and obtained several significant concessions regarding indigenous innovation and financial liberalization. As part of these concessions, China committed to joining the WTO's Agreement on Government Procurement (GPA) as soon as possible. Moreover, China pledged to separate its indigenous innovation policies from government procurement and ensure non-discrimination against foreign-funded enterprises in government procurement. Additionally, China promised to open up high-end manufacturing, allow for the trading of stock index futures, and increase the investment quota for Qualified Foreign Institutional Investors (QFII). These concessions were made in exchange for the United States refraining from taking strong measures to force China to revalue the RMB exchange rate.[30]

From 2007 (the year in which the global financial crisis began) until 2011, the United States was increasingly and widely perceived to be in a state of "real decline."[31] In contrast, China was seen as a successful

[29] Yue, J (2018), p. 290.

[30] Yue, J (2018), pp. 289–305.

[31] For instance, Rachman, M. (2011): "Think again—This Time, It's for Real." *Foreign Policy*, 03/01/2011. Available at: https://foreignpolicy.com/2011/01/03/think-again-american-decline/.

alternative state-capitalist model that appeared superior to America's free-market democracy. Wang Qishan, the Deputy Premier in charge of the S&ED talks, expressed this confidence to his American counterpart, Secretary of the Treasury Henry Paulson.[32] In the Western world, a heated debate was underway as to whether a fundamental power shift from the West to non-West, specifically from the United States to China, was occurring. However, these events did not seem to provide China with a strong bargaining chip in negotiations with the United States during both the S&ED and the Joint Commission on Commerce and Trade (JCCT) talks. China's further commitments on trade, investment, and financial liberalization, particularly the concessions on joining the GPA, which China was not obligated to do within the WTO's plurilateral framework, highlighted not China's increased national power relative to the United States, but rather the opposite.

Observers who touted China's "success" appeared to be blind to the country's economic difficulties, which were only masked by the global financial and economic crisis in the West, thanks to tight control over the media at home. They seemed to overlook the deep unease expressed by the top Chinese leadership during a Politburo meeting in February 2009, where it was acknowledged that the forthcoming year would be the most challenging since China's reform and opening up began in 1978. The economic reality was that numerous firms, especially small and medium-sized ones, were collapsing, and unemployment was skyrocketing, to a far more severe extent than in the United States.[33] Meanwhile, foreign dominance of the Chinese economy continued to grow.

According to the official "China Report 2009 on Industrial Control by FIEs," market control by FIEs had steadily increased since 1998, with the control ratio remaining above 30%, surpassing the alert level for China's industrial security. The report highlighted that the FIEs had the most effective control in the manufacturing sector, with the market control rate in the electronic information industry staying above 80% after 2004. Notably, foreign control of China's high-tech industry had reached approximately 70% in recent years.[34] On March 1, 2010, the *People's Daily* issued an editorial following the Politburo meeting, stating that

[32] Paulson, H. M. (2015), p. 240.

[33] Yue, J (2018), pp. 281–283.

[34] *Zhongguangwang*, Beijing, 30/11/2009.

the current development model characterized by "3-lows"—low price, low profits, and low value addition—was unsustainable and that industrial upgrading was necessary. This choice was deemed critical for China's modernization fate.[35]

Yu Yongding, an economist and prominent scholar at the Chinese Academy of Social Sciences (CASS), concluded by the end of 2010 that the China model itself, marked by "anaemic innovation, slow tech upgrades, and social tensions," had become unsustainable and required painful readjustments.[36] Henry Paulson was among the very few Western elites who recognized, amidst China's excessive export dependence during the global financial crisis, that the country's economic system was not superior, but rather exposed fatal structural weaknesses that necessitated economic rebalancing toward a consumption-driven economy.[37]

China's 4-trillion-yuan stimulus package, initiated in early 2009, was not aimed at rebalancing the economy, but instead worked to derail it. This package failed to mitigate China's excessive dependence on exports. This can be observed in China's decision to re-fix the RMB exchange rate with the U.S. dollar and implement measures to increase rates of taxation rebate in order to maintain labor-intensive exports and prevent the spread of unemployment. Given the pressures from both developed and developing countries to reduce trade surplus and address the unprecedented global imbalance, China was left with no choice but to increase imports. On December 12, 2010, the Central Economic Work Conference proposed "equal emphasis on import and export." Chinese leaders reiterated this statement during the "Two-Session" Conference in March 2011. The real focus, of course, was on increasing the import of "high-tech products, complete sets of equipment, and critical parts and components." In pursuit of this objective, China recognized the need to retreat from its assertive foreign policy, which had been in place from the end of 2008 until December 2010. This retreat stands as China's first grave misjudgment of American power and led to the reinstatement of

[35] *The People's Daily*, 01/03/2010.

[36] *The China Daily*, 30/12/2010.

[37] Paulson, H. M. (2015), p. 239.

Deng Xiaoping's "low-profile" approach by appeasing the West politically and diplomatically.[38]

Robert Wade has made a significant distinction between internal integration and external integration, associating them with development and dependency, respectively, in practical terms. He posited that development is primarily concerned with internal integration rather than external integration.[39] Wade defined development as a normative process of autonomous modernization, centered on domestic sectoral integration through backward-forward linkages and social cohesion, even under the auspices of regimes that may not necessarily be democratic. Through this definition, Wade established a connection between development and the concept of social democracy.

In other words, a statist-oriented approach to internal integration would not only lay the groundwork for autonomous national development but would also enhance the potential for peaceful democratic transformation in the future. Wade rejected the notion that external integration would strengthen internal integration, which he considered the most crucial prerequisite for development. On the contrary, he argued that "more external integration can erode more internal integration."[40] In the era of liberal globalization, according to him, the optimal strategy for developing nations would be to "combine the principle of comparative advantage and the principle of import replacement."[41]

Building on this perspective, the deepening of internal integration would involve the establishment of a unified and protected national market that would shield the country from the "anti-developmental" rules of deep integration imposed by the WTO. The creation of a highly integrated domestic market was intended to serve as the foundation for economic rebalancing. Nevertheless, China's institutionalization of deep (*external*) integration resulting from its WTO accession, its reluctance to address the impact of market Leninism and globalization—the institutional root causes of underconsumption and oversaving—and its aversion to national economic reintegration, especially regarding unifying the domestic market all indicate that Chinese rulers had no practical

[38] Yue, J (2018), pp. 303–304; Yue, J (2022), pp. 91–106.

[39] Wade, R (2003): Intro, p, xlviii.

[40] Ibid.

[41] Ibid., p. l.

choice but to persist in embracing economic internationalism. Therefore, their "staunchest support" for free trade was both sincere and imperative, as they had no other means to sustain export-led growth apart from wholeheartedly committing to comprador capitalism.

There is no need to delve into exhaustive detail on how China's industrial policies associated with indigenous innovation, implemented by both central and provincial administrations, were derailed or abandoned during their implementation. These industrial policies, which focused on unexplored areas, mostly operated within the legal boundaries of WTO rules or exploited the gray areas of international economic laws. Such utilization of "policy space" was a legitimate approach that any country could adopt. However, due to pressure from the United States, several instruments, including those promoting import substitution in equipment (capital goods) manufacturing, which were initiated as late as 2009, were swiftly abandoned. Furthermore, it is essential to note that the concerns raised by the United States and the EU regarding China's government procurement practices, which were viewed as significant industrial policy instruments, were often misplaced. Many discriminatory practices observed were not aimed at foreign firms, but rather at domestic enterprises.[42]

Nevertheless, solely attributing blame to anti-developmental globalization and the suppression of American hegemonic power, which is a typically biased structuralist dependency theory argument, does not sufficiently hold water. In January 2011, First Deputy Premier Li Keqiang, during his visit to Germany, introduced a timetable for achieving industrialization by 2020. Li emphasized the necessity of importing leading technologies, management expertise, high-skilled labor, and capital in a more open climate to facilitate China's industrialization. Li's acknowledgment of China's ongoing dependence on technology imports and even highly skilled labor served as a reminder of the significant "skill gap" between China and the West, despite more than three decades of reform and opening. This time span was sufficient for successful industrialization in East Asia's developmental states such as Taiwan, South Korea, and Singapore from the 1960s to the 1980s. China's inextricable reliance on technology imports from advanced countries raises serious questions about the effectiveness of the country's NSI.

[42] Yue, J (2014): "Has Globalization Led to China's Rise?" *Leaders*, No. 8, pp. 41–58.

The ineffectiveness of China's NSI can be attributed to several factors. Firstly, the country's increasingly closed society has stifled independent and critical thinking, while corruption has permeated the scientific community to an unprecedented extent. These factors have interacted with China's shrinking policy space, reinforcing its technological dependency and creating significant barriers to groundbreaking innovation. As a result, China has developed a deeply flawed innovation system that heavily relies on the global innovation ecosystem, making it highly parasitic.

To address this issue, the "Thousand-Talent Program" (*qianren jihua*, 千人计划) was initiated in 2008 with the aim of attracting educated elites from Western universities to bring back cutting-edge technologies and critical know-how to China. Additionally, industrial espionage activities have flourished. However, relying solely on these means without an effective NSI makes it highly unlikely for China to out-innovate the West, just as the notable contribution of the KGB in stealing advanced technologies did not ultimately succeed in elevating the science and technology capacity of the Soviet Union. China would face a similar challenge unless it developed a robust NSI of its own, in a similar manner to how Germany outpaced Britain during the Second Industrial Revolution in the late 19th and early twentieth centuries.

Indeed, by 2014, Chinese technocratic elites had come to realize that their prior approach of industrial upgrading through the importation of "used" technologies, while initially bridging the technology gap with advanced economies, had become increasingly unsustainable. This was primarily due to the mounting challenges in accessing more advanced, cutting-edge technologies that were actively "in use" by Western firms. This realization underscored, once again, the critical importance of developing indigenous innovation capabilities. The absence of such capabilities would risk impeding industrial upgrading, potentially resulting in the economic stagnation often associated with the phenomenon known as the "middle-income trap."[43]

By the year 2014, China's efforts to reduce technology dependency continued to underperform. The official *Blue Paper 2014*, issued by the Chinese Academy of Social Sciences, acknowledged that many high-end chains in Chinese industrial sectors heavily relied on imports. For instance,

[43] "Shao Ning: China's economy as a whole and manufacturing companies will face two major challenges." *Caixin*, 07/11/2014. https://opinion.caixin.com/m/2014-11-07/100748283.html.

90% of chips used in China were imported from foreign manufacturers, and the total costs of these imports exceeded that of oil. China still lagged behind in core technologies for crucial parts and components like engines, hydraulic devices, transmission devices, and control technologies, which were heavily dependent on imports. Additionally, 70–80% of expensive high-end medical equipment in China needed to be imported from abroad or sourced from MNCs operating within China.[44] As a result, China's technology dependency ratio did not experience even a slight decline below the 2006 level but remained above 50%, significantly higher than the technology dependency ratios of the United States and Japan, both of which remained below 5%.[45]

Nevertheless, a reluctance to engage in structural adjustments and the inability to establish a resilient NSI played a role in the short-lived effectiveness of the stimulus package in stabilizing the economy. Although there was a rapid recovery in 2010 and 2011, economic growth sharply declined in the following years (as illustrated in Table 5.1), exacerbating the issue of overcapacity. These challenges compelled the Chinese government to simultaneously pursue trade and investment liberalization while intensifying efforts in the realm of indigenous innovation under the banner of "Made in China 2025."

In the initial instance, China made substantial concessions to the United States during the fifth Strategic and Economic Dialogue (S&ED) held in July 2013. In these negotiations, China committed to the establishment of a high-standard Bilateral Investment Treaty (BIT), which the United States viewed as a priority and considered crucial for ensuring a level playing field for American workers and businesses. The BIT would encompass *all* stages of American investments across *all* economic sectors

Table 5.1 GDP Growth Rate (%): 2008–2016

Year	*2008*	*2009*	*2010*	*2011*	*2012*	*2013*	*2014*	*2015*	*2016*
GDP (%)	9.7	9.4	10.6	9.5	7.9	7.8	7.3	6.9	6.7

Source State Bureau of Statistics

44 *Xinhuanet*, Beijing, 10/12/2013.

45 "How to Forge an Upgrading of the Chinese Economy?" *Qiushi* (Seeking Truth, one of the CCP's key mouthpieces), 01/01/2014.

in China. As part of its commitments, China pledged to facilitate greater market access, eliminate investment barriers, refrain from imposing technology transfer requirements, and enhance transparency. Furthermore, China agreed to liberalize services, including electronic commerce and commercial factoring, and undertook to submit a revised offer to the Government Procurement Committee of the WTO by the end of that year.[46]

Following these liberalization commitments, on March 13, 2015, MOFCOM issued the "Catalogue Guiding Foreign Investment in Industries" (Guidance Catalogue). This directive lifted the ban that had been imposed in 2005 on FDI in the steel industry, which had previously held the status of a "strategic industry" in China. On September 17, 2015, the CCP Central Committee (the "Party Center") and the State Council jointly published an extensive document titled "Opinions on Constructing a New Open Economic System," which comprised 10,000 words and included 50 measures organized into 11 sections. Half a year later, in March 2016, MOFCOM went on to actively encourage mergers and acquisitions involving SOEs by global firms, with the intention of "elevating the overall level of economic openness"[47]:

- On December 29, 2016, during a meeting of the State Council, a momentous decision was made to encourage foreign investment in China's advanced manufacturing sector. It was emphasized that policy measures associated with "Made in China 2025" applied to MNCs operating within China.[48]
- On March 8, 2017, the influential *Wenhui Daily*, based in Shanghai, published an article titled "Assuming the Role of a Staunch Defender and Promoter of Globalization."[49]
- In June 2017, China continued its efforts to liberalize foreign investment through an updated "Guidance Catalogue" aimed at facilitating FDI.

[46] U.S. Fact Sheet—Economic Track Fifth Meeting of the U.S.-China Strategic and Economic Dialogue. 1/12/2013. https://home.treasury.gov/news/press-releases/jl2011.

[47] The Beijing News, 03/03/2016. https://finance.sina.cn/2016-03-03/detail-ifxqafrm6725036.d.html.

[48] Yicai, 29/12/2016. http://www.yicai.com/news/5194392.html.

[49] The *Wenhui Daily*, 08/03/2017. http://dzb.whb.cn/images/2017-03/08/5/50308.pdf.

- On November 10, 2017, the *People's Daily* published an extensive article authored by Deputy Premier Wang Yang, who had led four rounds of S&ED talks with the United States from 2013 to 2016. The article was titled "Promoting the Formation of a Comprehensive Open Economic Landscape."[50]
- From June to August 2018, Premier Li Keqiang, during meetings with visiting foreign dignitaries, consistently pledged to vigorously combat "forced technology transfer." He juxtaposed this prohibition with the imperative of safeguarding intellectual property, regarding both as an "inherent demand" in China's pursuit of economic rebalancing and the attainment of high-quality development.[51]

In 2015, paradoxically, just ten days after MOFCOM issued the "Guidance Catalogue" on March 13, which marked a significant step in FDI liberalization, on March 23, both the Party Center and the State Council jointly issued guidelines aimed at expediting the implementation of the "Innovation-Driven Development Strategy." This strategy had been introduced by Xi Jinping, the newly elected Party leader, during the Eighteenth National Party Congress in November 2012. The strategy's objective was to foster the development of "seven strategic new industries," comprising energy conservation and environmental protection, new-generation information technology, biology, high-end equipment manufacturing, new energy, new materials, and new energy vehicles.

In less than two months, on May 8, 2015, the Chinese government unveiled an ambitious initiative known as "Made in China 2025." This comprehensive plan aimed to achieve a "three-step" transformation: firstly, to turn China into a manufacturing powerhouse by 2025; secondly, to elevate the country to the status of a medium-level global industrial power by 2035; and, thirdly, to ensure that China's comprehensive strength would position it among the world's leading manufacturing powers by the 100th anniversary of the founding of the People's Republic of China in 2049.

This seemingly ambitious nationalist agenda in China, aimed at achieving technological autonomy, was later referred to in the West as

[50] The *People's Daily*, 10/11/2017. http://www.xinhuanet.com//politics/2017-11/10/c_1121933058.htm.

[51] The *People's Daily*, 22/06/2018; Xinhua, 28/08/2018.

"China's decoupling strategy."[52] However, this conceptualization can be somewhat misleading, as many NDCs have pursued similar strategies. Both the United States and the EU have heavily subsidized their strategic industries, such as Boeing and Airbus. Their opposition to "Made in China 2025" has at times been criticized as "kicking away the ladder."

Furthermore, arguments against China's perceived robust economic nationalism often overlook the country's simultaneous efforts to liberalize FDI, which serve to balance or counteract that perception. These arguments can also overstate China's unwavering commitment to achieving complete self-reliance in science and technology development.

Minister Miao Wei of the Ministry of Industry and Information Technology (MIIT), responded to a report issued by the European Union Chamber of Commerce in China titled "In China Manufacturing 2025: Putting Industrial Policy Ahead of Market Forces."[53] Miao clarified during a press conference on March 11, 2017 that the indicators mentioned in the report, such as domestic brand market share, were not deliberately pursued during the formulation process of "Made in China 2025." He explained that access conditions in fields like new energy vehicles require companies to possess the full set of development and manufacturing technologies. This requirement applies to all companies, not just foreign-funded enterprises. There is no mandatory transfer of technology to China for foreign-funded enterprises. The policy, formulated to prevent companies from exploiting loopholes by using government subsidies to profit from buying assembly parts and then leaving, was implemented to safeguard technological integrity. Miao emphasized that neither setting up a research and development center in China nor forcibly transferring technology to China was mandated. As long as the technology is being used, there is no need to force technology transfer.[54]

Miao's remarks make considerable sense as they were congruent with Li Keqiang's conception of achieving industrialization through greater

[52] Black, J.S. & Morrison, A.J. (2021): "The Strategic Challenges of Decoupling." *Harvard Business Review*, May–June, 99:3, pp. 49–54.

[53] This report was issued on March 7, 2017. https://www.europeanchamber.com.cn/en/china-manufacturing-2025.

[54] Miao Wei, Minister of Industry and Information Technology: 'Made in China 2025' treats domestic and foreign companies equally." *Xinhua*, 11 March 2017.

economic openness. This perspective challenges the prevailing international experience, as Ha-Joon Chang argued that "virtually all NDCs" have implemented "interventionist industrial, trade, and technology policies" to encourage industrialization during the critical stage of take-off.[55] Even with a stronger industrial foundation, post-war Japan, led by Shigeru Yoshida, pursued mercantilist realism to reindustrialize the country. So, why should China be an exception in achieving development within a strongly anti-developmental international economic system? It appears that Communist leaders saw no incompatibility between their ends and means. Instead, the tensions between the Party's nationalist rhetoric and the literal anti-nationalist economic practices underscored the elites' primary concern for regime legitimacy. They prioritized achieving assured growth at any cost rather than pursuing unpredictable technological catch-up on a self-reliant basis, which is crucial for achieving economic rebalancing and national prosperity.

Nevertheless, the Chinese elites' readiness to accept the correction of global imbalances, in which China had played a significant role, was primarily born out of necessity due to mounting pressures from its main trading partners in the Global North, pressures that were difficult to resist. This acceptance did not necessarily stem from the recognition that an export-oriented extensive industrialization model, at the expense of the rest of the world, was unsustainable and inevitably vulnerable to global backlashes. As a senior official from the People's Bank of China (PBOC) stated during a lecture at a leading Chinese university in 2010: "Since China has an advantage in manufacturing jobs, other countries needn't do it. Let us do it for you. We can lend money to you to facilitate your continued importation from us."[56] Such a view was not isolated, but rather was prevalent among many elites, indicating their naive understanding of global politics.

This remarkable ignorance was deeply ingrained in the elites' faith in economic globalism and the myth of free trade. Their perspective was not shaped by China's ascent through autonomous national development, but rather by its dependent development—a concept articulated by Peter Evans to describe previously underdeveloped nations that had managed

[55] Chang, H. J. (2003): *Kicking away the Ladder—Development Strategy in Historical Perspectives*. London: Anthem Press, pp. 17–18.

[56] Interview with an informed source in Beijing, 06/11/2010.

to find a "pathway from the periphery," but still grappled with becoming core players in the global arena.[57] China's persistent reliance on foreign technology, with only marginal reduction, combined with the leadership's unwavering commitment to liberalizing trade and investment, cast doubt on the prospects of "Made in China 2025," despite its stated objective of achieving self-sufficiency in high-tech industries and positioning China as an economic superpower. The notable ignorance and complacency of Chinese elites, particularly given their belief in the wholesale rejection of autarkism even among the minority of the *most* "statist-oriented" technocrats,[58] raise questions about China's active pursuit of decoupling from the global economy.

Minister Miao Wei of MIIT made it clear in mid-November 2015 when interpreting "Made in China 2025" that it was driven by the phenomenon of "double squeeze" (*shuangchong jiya*, 双重挤压): one from developed economies aiming to repatriate high-end manufacturing for reindustrialization purposes, and the other from emerging economies redirecting low-end manufacturing away from China.[59] This perspective aligns well with the insightful observations of certain Western scholars who aptly characterized China's approach as "an act of desperation" rather than "a plan to dominate."[60]

This "desperation" led to a significant academic debate between two leading mainstream economists at Peking University in November 2016. The debate between Zhang Weiying and Justin Yifu Lin even caught the interest of *The Economist*, in which it was nevertheless dismissed as "not quite Keynes-Hayek."[61] Both scholars received their training in Western universities and were ironically "Chicago boys," who wielded immense influence over Chinese policymakers for most of the reform decades since the late 1980s, particularly Zhang Weiying.

Zhang Weiying equated industrial policy with a planned economy, a viewpoint that other economists depicted as "not an academic point but

[57] Evans, P (1979): *Dependent Development*.

[58] This author's finding through conversations with within-system elites in recent years.

[59] CPPCC Daily, 17/11/2015, http://www.rmzxb.com.cn/2015-11-17/624116.shtml.

[60] NPF webinar: research fellow Alex Capri talked about Chinese techno-nationalism (12/06/2020): https://www.youtube.com/watch?v=-jCMovZUIkk.

[61] China's industrial policy: Plan v Market." *The Economist*, 05/11/2016. https://www.economist.com/finance-and-economics/2016/11/05/plan-v-market.

an ideology." The debate over industrial policy centered on the role of the state. Zhang argued against any form of government intervention, rejecting the notion of "market failure." He emphasized the "certain failure" of industrial policy and underscored the role of entrepreneurship in driving China's innovation. He suggested that the government's role should be strictly limited to "defining and protecting property rights." In contrast, Justin Yifu Lin focused on the indispensable role of the government, restricted to supporting basic research and the development of hard and soft infrastructure as a means to help fully exploit the country's comparative advantage. He advocated "a combination of an effective market with a proactive government."[62] However, he did not alter his previous position of opposing a "catch-up" strategy. His support for industrial policy was limited to aligning with China's existing comparative advantage.

As opposed to the overwhelming proponents of market liberalism, who advocated minimal government involvement in the development of an innovative national economy, true Listian economists like Jia Genliang, a professor of economics at the Renmin University of China, faced difficulties in expressing their views in top-tier professional academic journals, such as the *Economic Research Journal* (*jingji yanjiu*, 经济研究). However, they refrained from characterizing China's underdevelopment as a case of "dependent development," as the term "dependent" was significantly politically sensitive. Market liberals were reluctant to embrace this concept, attributing China's slow progress in catching up to government failure. They seemed to believe that the solution to China's catch-up lay in fully unleashing the "invisible hand" (the market) by rejecting any form of government intervention.

For unknown reasons, the renowned Chinese liberal economist Sheng Hong expressed considerable skepticism regarding the United States' apprehension of "Made in China 2025." During the "Economists 50 Forum" on December 11, 2018, he downplayed the significance of this grandiose plan, remarking candidly: "Americans have strong opinions on 'Made in China 2025,' which caught the Chinese by surprise. In reality, this document, although appearing impressive, is unlikely to see significant implementation. Even if some aspects are implemented, they are likely to yield little benefit, and in some cases, may lead to wastage and

[62] Sohu, 06/11/2016. https://www.sohu.com/a/118268159_468680.

even disaster. *Few take the plan seriously in China*, except for rent-seeking interest groups with vested interests."[63]

Arguing for China's dependent development, as this author did, does not negate the fact that China has made significant progress in enhancing its technological capabilities following the introduction of the "indigenous innovation" policy in 2006. However, it is imperative to carefully consider the connection between these advances and China's NSI. One notable achievement is the remarkable growth in international patent filings through the World Intellectual Property Organization (WIPO). In 2019, China surpassed the United States as the top filer of Patent Cooperation Treaty (PCT) applications, a position it has maintained for four consecutive years. In April 2020, WIPO Director General Francis Gurry highlighted China's rapid growth as the leading filer of international patent applications via WIPO and underscored "a long-term shift in the center of innovation towards the East."[64]

Nevertheless, this prevailing view among many Western observers has often overlooked a significant issue: the low quality of Chinese patents, despite their quantity. In fact, approximately 90% of these patents hold little market value, and their scope, grant ratio, rates of commercialization, and industrialization are remarkably low, rendering them ultimately useless or abandoned.

Comparisons with leading industrial nations, as noted by Alex He of the Centre for International Governance and Innovation (CIGA), reveal that the quality of Chinese patents falls below the global average and significantly lags behind that of other developed economies, including France, Germany, Italy, Japan, South Korea, the United Kingdom, and the United States. He identifies a series of institutional deficiencies contributing to this situation, arguing that the rapid increase in patent filings, including PCT applications, is primarily fueled by subsidies from governments at all levels.

Furthermore, the central government's emphasis on quantity-first and subsidy-driven instructions further promotes the increase in China's

[63] Sheng Hong: "From Chinese Manufacturing to Chinese Market." *Economists 50 Forum*, 11/12/2018. http://www.50forum.org.cn/home/article/detail/id/7502.html.

[64] "China Becomes Top Filer of International Patents in 2019 Amid Robust Growth for WIPO's IP Services, Treaties and Finances." WIPO, Geneva, April 2020. https://www.wipo.int/pressroom/en/articles/2020/article_0005.html.

patent output. Consequently, the majority of China's patent applications are motivated by factors other than innovation, such as seeking government subsidies, pursuing job promotions, building individual or institutional reputations, or obtaining certification as national high-tech enterprises.[65]

This further exacerbates China's existing parasitic national innovation system, hampering the country's ability to innovate despite its still-strong capability for reverse engineering. Therefore, even with the explosive growth of international patent filings and the acclaimed "breakthroughs" in science and technology development under the party-state's "all-nation system," Chinese manufacturing as a whole remains situated at the middle to lower end of the global value chain.

Zhou Ji, the former Director of the Chinese Academy of Engineering (CAE), stated at an Expert Forum held in Ningbo on November 15, 2019: "Core key technologies in some areas, such as lithography machines in the integrated circuit industry, high-end chips in the communication equipment industry, bearings and operation control systems in the rail transportation equipment industry, thermal equipment for gas turbines in the power equipment industry, as well as design and simulation software for aircraft, automobiles, and other industries, still need to be imported."[66]

According to the most authoritative accounts, out of China's 26 "representative manufacturing industries" compared with those of the NDCs, five have been identified as "world-leading," six as "advanced," ten lag behind by a "significant gap," and five by a "substantial gap." As a result, two types of industries are "highly dependent" and eight are "extremely dependent" on technology imports.[67] Among the *Top 100 Global Innovators of 2023*, only four state-sponsored high-tech firms from China were

[65] Alex He (CIGI senior fellow): "What Do China's High Patent Numbers Really Mean?" 20/04/2021. https://www.cigionline.org/articles/what-do-chinas-high-patent-numbers-really-mean/.

[66] Lian Ping: "Manufacturing Transformation under the New Development Pattern." *Sina Caijing*, 09/03/2021. https://finance.sina.cn/zl/2021-03-09/zl-ikknscsh9728236.d.html?vt=4&cid=79615&node_id=79615; Ful Report: https://pdf.dfcfw.com/pdf/H3_AP202103121471113543_1.pdf?1615537448000.pdf.

[67] 21st Century Economic Report, 16/10/2019. https://tech.ifeng.com/c/7qp0oL5yeXI.

ranked, in contrast to 11 private firms from Taiwan, 19 from the EU, 19 from the United States, and 38 from Japan.[68]

Of notable importance is the fact that "China is still far from achieving anything close to overall independence or even leadership in any specific segment of the sector," as concluded by Scott Kennedy of the Center for Strategic & International Studies (CSIS) in 2020 based on sector-by-sector industry analysis.[69] A prime example is the overhyped artificial intelligence (AI) technology that has seen successful commercialization in recent years. However, "the U.S. is still better at developing the tools, theories, and chips that power AI and the computers to make it work."[70] Another typical example is the machine tool industry, which has witnessed significant growth in terms of technology and market size, making China the world's largest machine tool producer, seller, and consumer. Nevertheless, this industry primarily engages in low-end production and faces a notable trade deficit due to critical reliance on importing high-end CNC machine tools. In 2021, an expert analysis remarked that China's machine tool industry has been "big (in size) but not strong (in competition)," and has failed to overcome the structural dilemma of "internecine infighting at the low-end, vicious competition at the medium-end, and losing market share to foreign competitors at the high-end" (*diduan hunzhan, zhongduan zhengduo, gaoduan shishou*, 低端混战、中端争夺、高端失守). This situation hampers the industry's ability to support the needs of China's industrial transformation and upgrading, posing significant risks to the country's national defense and industrial security.[71]

All of the aforementioned facts led Miao Wei, the former Minister of Industry and Information Technology, a knowledgeable and level-headed technocrat, to express his frank opinion during the annual national "Two-Session" Conference in March 2021. Despite significant progress

[68] Clarivate Top 100 Global Innovators 2023 report (released on 16/02/2023): https://clarivate.com/wp-content/uploads/dlm_uploads/2023/02/XBU975564118_Top-100-Innovators_Report_V7.2_singlepages.pdf.

[69] Kennedy, S: "China's Uneven High-Tech Drive: Implications for the United States." *CSIS*, 27/02/2020. https://www.csis.org/analysis/chinas-uneven-high-tech-drive-implications-united-states

[70] Schuman, M: "Don't Believe the China Hype." *The Atlantic*, 16/06/2020. https://www.theatlantic.com/international/archive/2020/06/united-states-china-power-influence/612961/.

[71] Su Nan (2021): "How to Break the 'Disadvantage of Backwardness' of China's Upgrading of Machine Tool Industry." *China's Science and Technology*, No. 4, pp. 1–4.

in recent years and the possession of the world's most complete industrial supply chains,[72] he candidly stated that "the situation of [China's manufacturing] being '*big but not strong, diversified but not superior* [in quality]' has not undergone fundamental change." Miao emphasized that basic capabilities were still weak, core technologies were in the hands of others, and the risks of vulnerability and setbacks had significantly increased.[73] He reiterated his earlier caveat that "in the four-tier structure of global manufacturing business, China is still in the third echelon" and stressed that "it will take at least *three decades* [for China] to achieve the goal of becoming a manufacturing powerhouse."[74]

Contrary to the prevailing complacency portrayed in "Amazing China" (《厉害了， 我的国》), literally translated as "An Unmatched China"),[75] a propagandistic movie under state sponsorship boasting China as No. 1 in many aspects, both Miao Wei and the incumbent MIIT Minister, Xiao Yaqing, warned against the dangers of premature deindustrialization that had befallen China in 2015. They argued that the "too early and too rapid" decline in the ratio of manufacturing output to GDP since 2015 not only weighed on economic growth and employment, but also posed security vulnerabilities to industries and weakened China's ability to withstand risks and maintain global competitiveness.[76] According to official accounts, China's deindustrialization process began as early as 2006. Former Minister Li Yizhong of MIIT stated at the Fifth China Manufacturing Forum in late December 2019 that the Second-Industry's share of GDP reached its peak of 42% in 2006 and has since

[72] Wu Haoyang and Li Ping (2021): "Analyzing China's Industrial Structure—Does China really Have 'All the Industrial Categories Listed in the United Nations Industry Classification System'?" *Ceibs Business Review*, No. 6, pp. 76–82.

[73] See report "China at Least 30 Years Away from Becoming Manufacturing 'Great Power': Former Minister." *BBC*, 07/03/2021.

[74] "Minister: Impetus for High-Quality Manufacturing." *China Daily*, 09/03/2021. http://epaper.chinadaily.com.cn/a/202103/09/WS6046b750a31099a2343547fe.html.

[75] In March 2018, a propagandistic movie titled "An Unmatched China" was screened in major theaters throughout the People's Republic of China. The film aimed to showcase the achievements of the CCP under the leadership of Xi Jinping since the 18th National Congress of the Communist Party of China in 2012, presenting China as an "unmatched power" in various areas of economic and social development. As part of the Party's "patriotic education" campaign, all state-sector work units were required to organize their staff to watch this movie.

[76] *China Daily*, 09/03/2021.

declined by one percentage point per year. It reached its lowest point of 33.3% in 2016 and stabilized at around 33.8% in 2018. Similarly, the manufacturing industry's share of GDP was 32.5% in 2006 and has continued to decline, stabilizing at around 29.5% in the past two years, which accounts for approximately 87% of the Second Industry. Li Yizhong cautioned: "China will not be able to achieve full industrialization until 2035, and we must be highly vigilant about the premature and rapid decline in the proportion of [Second] Industry."[77]

Ostensibly, the premature deindustrialization of a still-underdeveloped China could yield far-reaching socio-economic consequences, potentially surpassing the scale of Japan's "lost decade" (1991–2001)—a projection this author made prematurely in May 2012.[78] Eleven years later, this projection finds resonance in analyses by Paul Krugman and Martin Wolf, who contemplate China's likelihood of falling into the "Japan trap," albeit on somewhat similar yet diverging grounds.[79] In its video clip titled "2023 Year in Review: China in 2023: Is the Economy Okay?" dated December 26, 2023, Reuters, on Twitter, belatedly poses the question of whether China has started to resemble Japan.[80]

Asserting that China is the greatest beneficiary of globalization is thus untenable, considering both the process of China's crony comprador capitalist development fostered by globalization and the adverse consequences of premature deindustrialization it has caused. In fact, in addition to partially contributing to China's struggle to catch up, globalization, as in other parts of the world, has also widened income inequality. China's Gini coefficient continued to rise after it joined the WTO,

[77] *The 21st Century Business Herald*, 29/12/2019.

[78] Yue, J (2014), pp. 41–58. The earliest version of this work was presented as a guest speech at an Oxford University seminar in May 2012, titled "What does Globalisation Mean for China's Economic Development?" It was subsequently developed into a blog article on *Global Policy* Journal on May 24, 2012. You can access the article here: http://www.globalpolicyjournal.com/blog/24/05/2012/what-does-globalization-mean-china%E2%80%99s-economic-development.

[79] Paul Krugman: "What Happened to Japan?—What Japan's Economy Can Tell Us About China?" *The New York Times*, 25/07/2023. https://www.nytimes.com/2023/07/25/opinion/japan-china-economy.html; Martin Wolf: "How China can avoid the Japan trap?" *The Financial Times*, 26/09/2023. https://www.ft.com/content/156c092a-4313-48cc-8103-79bb26c0faaa.

[80] Refer to the Reuters tweet on 26/12/2023. https://twitter.com/i/status/1739773079742738482.

making China one of the world's most unequal societies.[81] Nevertheless, rising social tensions did not weaken the nominally Communist regime. Robust economic growth and the CCP's successful cooption strategy toward business and intellectual elites, culminating in an "elite coalition," tremendously strengthened the regime and reinforced its determination to resist change in its superstructure.

This Brezhnevization of the party state exacerbated nomenklatura corruption from the late years of Jiang Zemin's tenure through the Hu Jintao era (2002–2012), following the country's crony comprador capitalist development. Ever-growing social polarization has since thwarted upward mobility and exposed as a myth China's claim that it has created a thriving middle class. A clear illustration of this phenomenon is the decision made on October 1, 2018, when China increased the personal allowance from RMB ¥3,500 to RMB ¥5,000 per month, aligning it with a rough classification of the middle class as those with a monthly income of at least RMB ¥5,000. Consequently, this adjustment resulted in a reduction in the number of taxpayers to just 64 million, accounting for a mere 4.6% of the entire population.[82] The ratio may rise to no more than 7% if taxation-free pensioners with a monthly income of no less than RMB ¥5,000 are included.

This failure becomes evident when considering China's progress in meeting the United Nations' Millennium Development Goals (MDGs). Despite significant achievements, a substantial portion of the Chinese population remains in relative poverty, both by more reliable domestic estimates and World Bank standards. Since the late 1990s, social polarization in China has intensified, resulting in a pronounced income distribution characterized by a steeply inverted T-shape.

According to a stratified random survey conducted by Beijing Normal University (Figs. 5.1 and 5.2), approximately 600 million people, equivalent to 43% of the entire population, had a household per capita monthly income of less than RMB ¥1,090, or $163, roughly $5.42 per day per person (pdpp), considering China's average household size of 2.62 as of the end of 2020.[83] An additional 364 million individuals, constituting

[81] Jain-Chandra, S, et al. (2018): "Inequality in China—Trends, Drivers and Policy Remedies." *IMF Working Paper* (WP/18/127), June. https://www.imf.org/~/media/Files/Publications/WP/2018/wp18127.ashx.

[82] *Beijing News*, 01/01/2019.

[83] *ThePaper. CN*, 08/08/2021. http://m.thepaper.cn/baijiahao_13950085.

26%, fell within the income range of ¥1,090 to ¥2,000, while another 364 million (26%) had incomes within the range of ¥2,000 to ¥5,000. This implies that a total of 1,328 million people, or 95%, had a household per capita monthly income of no more than ¥5,000.[84]

Living on less than RMB ¥1,090 ($163) per month (approximately $5.42 per day), in comparison with the World Bank's newly established poverty line of $5.5 per day for upper-middle-income countries, equivalent to $7.2 per (Chinese) household per day per person (pdpp), indicates that certainly more than half of China's population still lives in relative

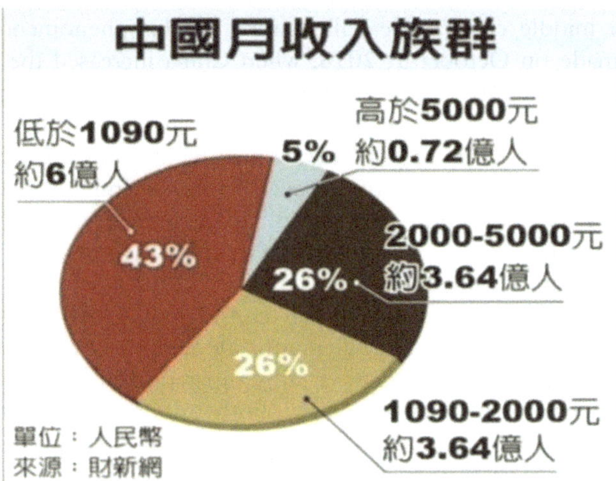

income range (Renminbi Yuan)	number of people (million)	% of entire population
<1,090 (red)	ca. 600	43%
1,090-2,000 (orange)	ca. 364	26%
2,000-5,000 (black)	ca. 364	26%
>5,000 (blue)	ca. 72	5%

Fig. 5.1 Percentage of people belonging to different income groups, based on household per person/per month (PPPM) basis

[84] *Caixin*, 03/06/2020. http://opinion.caixin.com/2020-06-03/101562409.html (content page deleted shorly). *Caixin*, 03/06/2020).

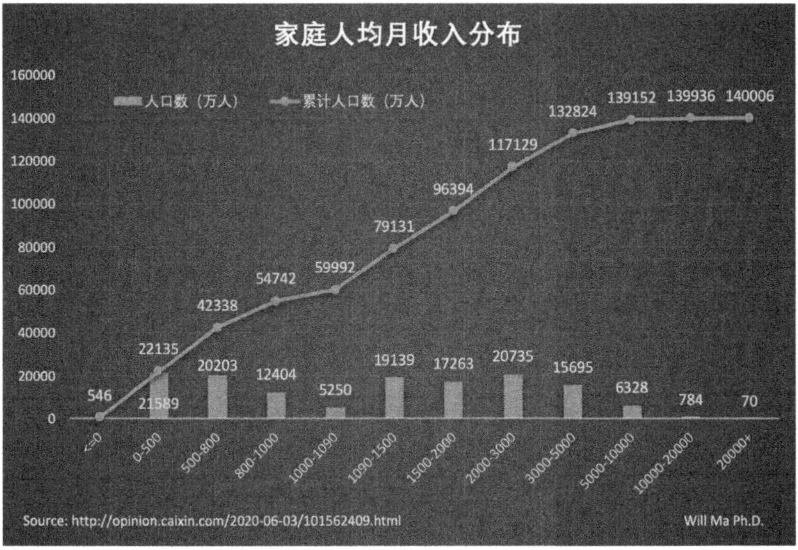

Fig. 5.2 Distribution of monthly household income per capita (scaled to units of per 10,000 individuals) (*Source Caixin* [one of the PRC's most influential weekly magazines on finance and business equivalent to the *Wall Street Journal*]: June 3, 2020 [the content page was swiftly removed due to sensitive political reasons]. The above revelations have been confirmed by *China Statistical Yearbook 2019* [p. 171] and *China Statistics Summary 2020* [p. 59]. *People's Daily* website [renminwang], Beijing, June 15, 2020: http://politics.people.com.cn/n1/2020/0615/c1001-31747507.html)

poverty. This fact is striking, especially considering that the World Bank categorized China as an upper-middle-income country as early as 2012.[85]

This pattern of income distribution underscores the enduring nature of China's status as a developing country, characterized by a significant low-income population. The proportion of this population segment is alarmingly high, exposing the illusion of China's transformation into an olive-shaped middle-class society.

[85] World Bank, 17/10/2018: https://www.worldbank.org/en/news/press-release/2018/10/17/nearly-half-the-world-lives-on-less-than-550-a-day. *World Development Report* 2012: https://elibrary.worldbank.org/doi/abs/10.1596/978-0-8213-8810-5.

In light of the aforementioned shortcomings, including insufficient innovation and acute inequality leading to underconsumption, it is challenging to regard China as a high-income industrial economy, let alone an economic superpower in the strictest sense. Therefore, it is safe to conclude that globalization has yielded a dual impact on China's economic development: on the one hand, it has promoted China's high export-led growth, but on the other hand, it has failed to promote its catching-up, as evidenced by the country's incomplete economic transformation, and has created an enduring import-dependence in key parts, major components, and sophisticated capital goods from the NDCs. "Still relying heavily on foreign technology"[86] did not make China qualitatively dissimilar to a handful of Global South countries that had experienced a "contradictory combination" of "some development happening" and being "still dependent on the Global North," a typical pathway of "dependent development."[87]

Accusations by the West over the past decade about China's intellectual property infringements, forced technology transfer (*legitimate* under TRIMs, but China had ignominiously committed not to impose such requirements upon WTO entry), and the numerous cases of industrial espionage inadvertently exposed the embarrassing reality that Jake Werner had described in 2018: the practical impossibility for "Third World countries to get on the path to development without 'cheating' the existing form of globalization."[88] Those "misbehaviors" as charged by the West are a clear manifestation of China's painstaking efforts to shake off the shackles of "anti-developmental" globalization, whose overall actual efficacy, as the facts have shown, has been considerably overstated.

China's dependent development, if properly examined, would presumably have contributed no less than the global financial and economic crisis

[86] A New Great Game—China, the U.S. and Technology—A Report By The China Senior Analyst Group, p. 11 (Published: 13/10/2020). https://www.spglobal.com/_division_assets/images/special-editorial/a-new-great-game-china-the-u.s.-and-technology/2019_05_csag_uschina.pdf.

[87] Kvangraven, I. H. (2017): "The Relevance of Dependent Development—Then and Now: Peter Evans," in Kvangraven, et al. (ed.): *Dialogues on Development Volume 1: Dependency* (eBook). NY: Institute for New Economic Thinking, p. 29.

[88] Werner, J: "China Is Cheating at a Rigged Game." *Foreign Policy*, 08/08/2018. Available at: https://foreignpolicy.com/2018/08/08/china-is-cheating-at-a-rigged-game/

in 2007–2009 to the subsequent revival of the once-disgraced dependency and developmental state theories. However, a considerable number of development economists across the globe genuinely believe in China's exceptionalism, even as they universally acknowledge the downsides of liberal globalization. Deliberately or not, they have grossly overestimated China's national autonomy and state capacity to leverage globalization to its benefit, while overlooking the country's deep integration into the global economy.[89] Empirically built upon the isolated case of China, which had been severely misread, the emerging paradigm of so-called "New Developmentalism" that arose from the ashes of the defunct neoliberalism has not only ignored the conspicuous stumbling block that globalization constituted for the country's externally oriented economy, but has also misconstrued the character of the Chinese state,[90] which has in reality been susceptible to both rent-seeking and neoliberal dogma.[91]

Extrapolating from notions of Robert Wade's "governing the market"[92] and Stephan Haggard's "democratic developmental state,"[93] this author argues that the "return of the developmental state" in the post-crisis global context requires a democratizing strong state committed to autonomous national development by dint of internal rather than external integration. Conceivably, a shortage of relevant institution-building in the age of the internet threatens to derail efforts to create a sound NSI. In the absence of an effective NSI, there is no way for China to out-innovate the West in the long run. Just think of the former Soviet Union![94] A total absence of a strong NSI suggests that the "risen" China remains unable to escape dependency in any meaningful way, and is by no means another post-1945 Germany or Japan. Its way of linking

[89] Yue, J (2018), pp. 17–18.

[90] Khan, S. R. & Christiansen, J (2011), pp. 177–202, 257.

[91] Yue. J (2014), pp. 41–58.

[92] Wade, R (2003).

[93] Haggard, S (2018): *Developmental States*. Cambridge: Cambridge University Press, p. 7.

[94] Sutton, A. C. (1972) *National Suicide: Military Aid to the Soviet Union*. LV: Dauphin Publications Inc.; Chan, C. L. (2015): "Fallen Behind: Science, Technology, and Soviet Statism." *Intersect*. 8:3, pp. 1-11; Farley, R: "How Does Industrial Espionage Affect Economic Growth?" *The Diplomat*, 15/1/2017. https://thediplomat.com/2017/01/how-does-industrial-espionage-affect-economic-growth/.

to the world has instead set the country on a path of dependent development that typically leads to the "middle-income trap" of semi-peripheral development.

The Limits to China's Peaceful Rise: Deep Integration as a Source of Conflict

China's declaration of a peaceful rise in 2003[95] exposes the nation's developmental quandary in the era of globalization, where continuous access to global markets is crucial for its dependent development. In contrast to the conventional belief that free trade is an ideology of the strong, China, as an underdeveloped nation caught in semi-peripheral development, fervently advocates free trade and wholeheartedly embraces globalization even more than many countries in the Global North. Guided by the myth of globalization, which often confuses growth with development, Chinese elites held lofty expectations of achieving lasting peace through an interdependent economic relationship, facilitated by China's deep integration into the global economy. These expectations endured until 2022, when the CCP was compelled to relinquish its longstanding idealistic perspective on "peace and development" since 1987, as well as the belief that China had been granted a "rare strategic opportunity for development" following the 9/11 attacks in 2001, which significantly improved Sino-U.S. relations. Chinese elites have long remained oblivious to the resolute pursuit of realism in U.S. foreign policy and have remained convinced of China's peaceful ascent within the prevailing liberal international order. They have steadfastly believed that China's trajectory would transcend the conventional path of rising great powers.[96]

The United States had a different agenda for integrating China into the global economy. In the early 1980s, American strategist Zbigniew Brzezinski and Senator Henry M. Jackson, one of the co-sponsors of the famous Jackson-Vanik Amendment of 1974, supported economic

[95] The term "peaceful rise" was first introduced in 2003. Due to its sensitive nature, it gradually fell out of use starting from 2004, and was replaced by more moderate terms such as "peaceful development" and "harmonious world.".

[96] Zheng, B (2005): "China's 'Peaceful Rise' to Great-Power Status." *Foreign Affairs*, September/October, 84:5, pp. 18–24.

cooperation with China, believing that "once the PRC had become developed economically, it would flourish into a democracy."[97] Even after the Tiananmen crackdown, the U.S. administrations under Bush and Clinton, influenced ostensibly by Fukuyama's overly optimistic vision of global democracy, deepened engagement with China, hoping that economic changes in China would bring about political change as well. However, as early as January 1994, three months before his death, Richard Nixon, who designed the "drawing out" strategy toward China, also known as "containment without isolation," expressed regret over his previous approach and the consequences of engaging with China, stating: "We may have created a Frankenstein."[98] Nixon's statement referred to mounting evidence that China was not democratizing, but was becoming more repressive, despite the expanding liberalization in economic and trade policies.

Following Liu Ji's address at Harvard University on fostering a cooperative Sino-U.S. relationship through interdependent core–peripheral economic interactions, in June 1997, Bill Clinton underscored the imperative of realigning the U.S. defense strategy toward Asia.[99] This shift ostensibly aimed to address perceived challenges posed by China. Pressured by U.S. Congressmen, particularly Republicans who distrusted the People's Republic due to its perceived lack of political change under Clinton's "comprehensive engagement" policy, a new form of engagement emerged in 2001, shortly after George W. Bush assumed office. This new approach, influenced by the neo-conservative "blue team" within the Bush administration, became known as "congagement," combining elements of engagement and containment, with a greater emphasis on the latter.[100] Despite China's relatively low-profile approach to foreign relations, it was not immune to being listed as one of the seven potential targets for pre-emptive nuclear strikes in the *Nuclear Posture Review*

[97] Dikötter, F (2022), p. 24.

[98] "The Biggest Vote." *The New York Times*, 18/05/2000. https://www.nytimes.com/2000/05/18/opinion/essay-the-biggest-vote.html.

[99] Sarotte, M. E. (2021): *Not One Inch—America, Russia and the Making of Post-Cold War Stalemate*. New Haven: Yale University Press, p. 283.

[100] Klare, M. T.: "'Congagement' with China?—GOP hawks want containment; others favor more trade and more toughness." *The Nation*, 12/04/2001. https://www.thenation.com/article/archive/congagement-china/.

Report 2002, submitted by the Bush administration to Congress on the final day of 2001.

Nevertheless, these unsettling developments did not deter the Chinese ruling elites from adhering to their belief in economic globalism in low politics and pacifist idealism in high politics. They had valid reasons for relief as the tumultuous Sino-U.S. relationship of the 1990s took a sudden turn for the better following the events of 9/11, when the United States swiftly shifted its strategic focus from geopolitics to the global war on terror. This shift in strategic focus led Chinese elites to conclude that a "rare strategic opportunity for development" had emerged for China. However, this assessment underscored their commitment to, rather than a deviation from, the pre-established path of crony comprador capitalism, which was institutionalized during the Sixteenth National Party Congress in September 2002.

The Chinese elites' preoccupation with liberal globalization led them to assume that traditional power politics had become obsolete and that aligning with the liberal international order in the era of globalization would incur no significant costs. In this context, they took China's sacrifice of substantial "development space" (used interchangeably with "policy space")—which encompasses the essential economic sovereignty required for autonomously enforcing industrial policies aimed at catching up with advanced nations—for granted. They held the belief that a closer embrace of global capitalism would suffice to curb America's realist inclinations and prevent interference with China's peaceful ascent.

This perspective, which appears flawed and myopic, overlooks an important question: had the events of 9/11 not occurred, would there still have been a genuine "strategic opportunity" for accommodating China's peaceful emergence, as the Chinese elites believed?

Chinese elites' overwhelming satisfaction with globalization prevented them from identifying the true origins of China's persistent underconsumption and excessive reliance on exports, particularly the adoption of crony comprador capitalism. This satisfaction hindered the implementation of effective measures to address the structural impediments to China's long-term economic rebalancing. Moreover, the mystification of globalization, promoted by both the Communist regime and domestic and international neoliberals, and the institutionalization of China's unique liberal globalization approach to economic development as "political correctness," led the ruling and intellectual elites to consciously avoid critical examination of the adverse aspects of globalization.

This consciousness can be discerned from the silent shift in attitude observed among the ruling elites, particularly when comparing the present time with the years before China's entry into the WTO. A notable example of this shift can be seen in the depiction of the Sino-American Treaty of Friendship, Commerce, and Navigation in November 1946, which was concluded between the Nationalist Government and the United States and is presented in officially sanctioned modern Chinese history books.

It wasn't until just a few years ago that the CCP portrayed this treaty as "a new national humiliation for China" because of its provision of near-complete market opening to the United States, which was reciprocated with the same extent of market access to China. However, this reciprocity was rendered meaningless, given the significant power disparity between the two countries, making the superficial reciprocal market opening a unilateral concession by China. The CCP launched an extensive propaganda campaign against the Kuomintang (KMT), denouncing the treaty as the "most shameless traitorous treaty" that would subject China to American imperialism's colonization.

Ironically, like Professor Peter Nolan's comparison of China's WTO deal with the 1842 Treaty of Nanking after the First Opium War, Communist China's entry into the WTO could also be portrayed as a treacherous act if the same standards were applied. Recognizing the difficulty in defending against such parallels, the CCP has in recent years refrained from emphasizing its patriotic image in the struggle against the KMT in 1946. The CCP's official webpage, which once contained reflections on the 1946 Treaty, has permanently removed the content, possibly in 2019 (Fig. 5.3).

The CCP's covert alignment with "old reactionaries" signifies a notable shift in its character, indicating a fundamental departure from the pursuit of autonomous national development. As a result, doubts arise regarding the external perception of China embracing techno-nationalism. This perception obscures the reality that China has been confronted with mounting challenges, including the potential risks of premature deindustrialization and falling into the "middle-income trap" since the late 2010s.

Influenced by an entrenched comprador mentality, Chinese elites have naturally viewed further globalization of the Chinese economy as the sole solution to the country's dependent development, paradoxically resulting from the "anti-developmental" aspects of globalization. This can

Fig. 5.3 Attitudinal Change of the CCP toward the 1946 Treaty (*Notes* **Left** snapshot of original CCP's webpage (by Baidu on 17:06:59, 04/18/2019: https://baike.baidu.com/reference/1915064/91feJO4Ew45V_24J-L1P31dkljhKC0bUPvERaxexJt5vpq4-oF_j6x03UvbuQ8QV8ixAwogDcYfTewjFsw9MzVTnHPn4lTS9Bdyklvwkk1d8Ic16KC8Udr13e6PW); **Right**: webpage shows "403 Forbidden": http://cpc.people.com.cn/GB/64162/64165/72301/72305/4956115.html)

be indirectly observed through the continued marginalization of Listian-type economic nationalism in academic scholarship, repeated government statements in defense of free trade and globalization, and consecutive reductions in the categories covered in the Negative List for market access issued by the State Council since 2016.

Further contributing to the elites' complacency is their perception of the underperforming U.S. economy, which suffered greatly during the financial crisis of 2007–2009. The collapse of neoliberalism, a consensus in advanced countries and most parts of the world except China,[101]

[101] Fahnbulleh, M (2020): "The Neoliberal Collapse—Markets Are Not the Answer." *Foreign Affairs*, January/February, 99:1, pp. 38–42.

compelled the Obama administration to employ statist and illiberal measures, similar to those used by China, to rescue its crisis-ridden enterprises. This role reversal reinforced the confidence of the Chinese ruling elites in the perceived superiority of their own economic system in handling crises. It highlighted a distinct state capacity that the liberal U.S. government appeared to lack.

However, the Chinese ruling elites failed to recognize that the structural challenges confronting China had not disappeared; instead, they had merely been postponed indefinitely due to the regime's ability to defer rather than resolve the crisis. This avoidance of painful structural adjustments, in contrast to Western countries, created an illusion of Chinese economic superiority. Nevertheless, astute Western elites familiar with China understood that the Chinese economy exhibited more pronounced structural vulnerabilities, such as an excessive reliance on exports and an urgent need for economic rebalancing, unlike the United States.[102]

This situation presents a marked contrast to the late 1970s and early 1980s when Western economies, grappling with stagflation, faced similar pressures for economic restructuring. This restructuring involved rewriting their post-war social contracts, much like their Soviet counterparts did under Gorbachev a few years later. It is crucial to emphasize that the Western economies did not consistently outperform their Soviet counterparts during this period; instead, it was the greater systemic flexibility inherent in open societies that allowed them to surpass Soviet Communism by "breaking promises." The Eastern Bloc countries, constrained by their political systems and ideological traditions, failed to address comparable crises despite the pressing need for structural reforms.[103]

In his seminal work titled *Globalization against Democracy—A Political Economy of Capitalism after its Global Triumph*, published in 2017, Professor Guoguang Wu introduced the concept of the "economic state." According to this concept, in the post-Cold War era of globalization, nations have found it increasingly challenging to resist the convergence of market forces and state intervention. The relationship between markets and the state is no longer mutually exclusive, but is now mutually reinforcing.[104] Practically all nations exhibit characteristics of state capitalism

[102] Paulson, H. M. (2015), p. 18.

[103] Bartel, F (2022), pp. 339–347.

[104] Wu, G (2017), p. 297.

in its broadest sense, recognizing the pivotal role of the state in advancing their countries' competitiveness.

Nevertheless, the perception of Western "economic states" as considerably ineffective in driving robust economic growth and swift crisis management notably misled Chinese elites. This misjudgment resulted in an underestimation of the gravity of the challenges facing China. Consequently, it has become even less likely for them to conduct a critical assessment of the impact of globalization on China's economic "success," let alone its connection to "The Neoliberal Collapse."[105] Moreover, this misjudgment by Chinese elites regarding American power, stemming from their underestimation, has influenced their foreign policy decisions, hastening "the return of great power rivalry" between China and the United States.

It is evident, as emphasized by John Mearsheimer on multiple occasions, that the United States does not envision tolerating China as a peer competitor. The U.S. grand strategy of transforming China into a "responsible stakeholder" within the international system concealed its true intention—to mold China into a "status quo power" instead of permitting it to ascend as an economic superpower like Germany or Japan, an outcome that would not align with America's national interests.

Contrary to the experiences of post-1945 Germany or Japan, China faces limitations within the liberal international economic system, particularly the "anti-developmental" rules of the WTO, which contribute to China's predicament of "growth without development." Instead of resisting mounting pressures for increased trade, investment, and financial liberalization, Chinese elites have chosen to adapt China's policies to align with greater economic globalism. When considering these factors collectively, China's "rise" appears increasingly formidable, if not altogether unattainable, whether achieved through peaceful means or otherwise.

Given the overwhelming military power possessed by the United States, the prospect of China achieving its rise through non-peaceful means is deemed unrealistic. The most practical and cost-effective approach for China to attain a peaceful ascent appears to be the establishment of a democratic developmental state, as advocated by Stephen Haggard. Such a transition would necessitate a significant shift in China's current development strategy.

[105] Fahnbulleh, M (2020): "The Neoliberal Collapse—Markets are not the Answer." *Foreign Affairs*, Jan/Feb, 99:1, pp. 38–43.

China's status as a great power, marked by its extensive population, vast geography, and the world's second-largest diversified economy, makes this shift both feasible and promising. This approach mirrors the import-substituting industrialization (ISI) strategies previously pursued by the United States, Germany, and Japan at comparable stages of economic development. Embracing a domestically focused strategy of this nature would substantially reduce China's reliance on exports and enhance its bargaining power in economic diplomacy.

By adopting this approach, China could negotiate more favorable terms for market access while retaining the policy flexibility required to facilitate technological catch-up. To construct an advanced economy rooted in internal integration, China would need to overhaul its NSI and promote economic reintegration by recentralizing state authority. This move would mitigate regional autarky, fostering the creation of a unified and protected national market.

China's primary national interest appears to revolve around the promotion of multipolarity rather than forging an "axis of convenience" with Russia, which may not align with its long-term objectives. A democratizing China, committed to diplomatic solutions rather than military force, could pursue an alliance with the post-modern EU, collectively challenging American hegemony through a soft-balancing approach. Achieving a historic accommodation with Japan holds significance in this context.

By discarding the "America First" approach in Chinese foreign policy and strategically aligning with both the EU and Japan, China could have reaped far greater economic benefits since the 1990s and could continue to do so in the twenty-first century. Such alignment, especially in terms of securing accommodation for China's state-centered strategic approach, would disrupt the Triad (the United States, the EU, and Japan) and counter their efforts to impose more stringent anti-developmental WTO reform agendas.

Equally crucial is the need to collaborate with India and Brazil in pursuing a pro-developmental, mild globalization approach as an alternative to the current trend of hyperglobalization within international economic organizations. Leveraging China's influence, an alliance with emerging economies in the Global South would rebalance multilateral negotiations. This would empower these nations to participate as rule-makers rather than passive rule-takers, thus shaping the global development agenda in the interests of China and the entire developing world.

Built on these strategic foundations, including partnerships with the EU, Japan, India, and Brazil, the concept of a peaceful rise for China appears both viable and attainable.

For a significant period following the initiation of reforms and opening up, China lacked a cohesive grand strategy to guide its peaceful ascent. Contrary to the notion that the CCP possessed a secretive century-long strategy to supplant the United States as a global superpower by 2049,[106] such thinking tends to conflate nationalist rhetoric with practical policies. It is worth noting that few post-Mao CCP leaders can be characterized as genuine economic nationalists, particularly during the initial two decades of reform and opening under Deng Xiaoping and Jiang Zemin.

During this era, a pervasive admiration for foreign elements, including among the elites, eroded national pride. Offspring of senior leaders competed to transfer wealth out of China and emigrate to Western nations, particularly the United States, underscoring the ruling elites' lack of confidence in China's future. Deng Xiaoping, a pragmatic leader, set the realistic goal of achieving parity with moderately advanced countries by the mid-twenty-first century and aiming to approach the most advanced nations by the century's end.[107]

Jiang Zemin, a technocrat with a technical background, recognized the challenges in narrowing the technological gap with advanced countries. His advisor, Liu Ji, delivered an address at Harvard University in May 1997, which illustrated Jiang's ambition to co-exist with the United States, assuming the role of a semi-peripheral economic power. This vision persisted, despite Jiang's emphasis on the importance of "reinvigorating China through science and education" (*kejiao xingguo*, 科教兴国).

Throughout much of Hu Jintao's leadership from 2002 to 2012, China's elites adhered to Deng Xiaoping's "low-profile" foreign policy directive. While they refrained from openly acknowledging the reality of China's dependent development, they exercised caution to prevent provoking the United States, especially given China's rapid GDP growth.

[106] Pilsbury, M (2015): *The Hundred-Year Marathon: China's Secret Strategy to Replace America as the Global Superpower*. NY: Henry Holt and Co.

[107] "Deng Xiaoping and the Formation of 'Three Steps' Development Strategy." *Guangming Daily*, 03/08/2011.

This caution stemmed from concerns that antagonizing the United States could jeopardize China's peaceful rise. Instead, Chinese leaders emphasized domestic challenges, portraying China as inwardly focused and committed to peaceful development on the global stage.

Maintaining stable relations with the United States was deemed essential for China's peaceful development and became the cornerstone of its "America First" foreign policy.[108] Deng Xiaoping initially embraced this policy in the late 1970s, driven by the belief that countries with amicable ties to the United States would prosper. Despite the waning of the decade-long honeymoon period during the 1980s, particularly in the post-Cold War era when America's intentions regarding China's economic integration and potential regime change became more evident, this belief continued to be unquestionably embraced by Chinese political and intellectual elites, persisting to the present day.

The deepening economic interdependence between China and the United States appeared to justify China's "America First" approach since the early 1990s, often overshadowing its concurrent partnerships with the EU, Japan, and Russia. However, China's rejection of democracy limited its strategic options, leading to significant political and military collaborations with an increasingly authoritarian Russia as a counterbalance to the perceived "unipolar moment" of the United States.

Nevertheless, the compelling need to prioritize "America First," driven by the far greater weight of Sino-U.S. trade compared to Sino-Russian trade and China's asymmetrical economic and technological dependence on the United States, resulted in China's relations with Russia being subordinated to maintaining stable ties with the United States. This pragmatic approach occasionally strained relations with Russia, which grew suspicious of China's intentions to hedge its connections with the PRC by fostering closer ties with China's historical adversaries, including India and Vietnam, particularly in China's southern sphere.

Unfortunately, China underestimated both the strength of the EU and its unwavering commitment to a multipolar world. China failed to recognize the strategic value of the EU in its pursuit of peaceful development. Occasionally, when apprehensive about direct confrontation with American hegemony, China played the "Europe card." This perspective

[108] Wang, J (2005): "China's Search for Stability with America." *Foreign Affairs*, September/October, 84:5, pp. 39–48.

erroneously magnified divisions between the EU and the United States, which China sought to leverage for its own benefit.

A notable example of this was the widespread belief among many Chinese ruling and intellectual elites that U.S. involvement in the Gulf Wars of 1991 and 2003, as well as the humanitarian intervention in Kosovo in 1999, aimed at destabilizing the European economy and the euro. Chinese elites also maintained a psychological readiness for a more turbulent world, hoping that regional tensions and conflicts would divert U.S. attention away from China and hinder its containment efforts. However, due to a limited understanding of global politics and a lack of sophisticated diplomatic skills, China's foreign policy achieved limited success in advancing a multipolar world conducive to its modernization agenda.

In comparison to Russia's decline in the post-Soviet era, China's apparent economic "success" can, to a considerable extent, be attributed to luck rather than predetermined outcomes. The United States' "drawing out" strategy, combined with China's increasing authoritarianism following the Tiananmen incident, created a situation that made it highly likely for China to pursue an extensive industrialization model, leveraging its comparative advantage in cheap labor. Furthermore, as the need for a shift in the U.S. grand strategy toward "congagement" became imperative at the turn of the century, the sudden occurrence of the 9/11 attacks saved China from a potential Cold War scenario that could have jeopardized its economic rise. At that time, China's significance in the global political economy was still relatively limited, and the outcome could have been less favorable for China had a Cold War materialized.

Compared to successful industrializers like Germany or Japan, China's nomenklatura system has made it improbable for great leaders like Otto von Bismarck, Ludwig Wilhelm Erhard, or Shigeru Yoshida to emerge from within the party-state bureaucracy. This is particularly evident due to the Party's longstanding tradition of anti-intellectualism. As a result, leaders who have come to power after Mao, without exception, lack far-reaching plans for the country's future, and their worldview has often been marred by fallacies. Even during the Deng Xiaoping era, discussions among senior revolutionary veterans who wielded actual power regarding China's international strategy were notably absent. Deng Xiaoping's "cat theory" reveals not only his pragmatism but also his short-sightedness in presenting a strategic vision for China's relations with the world accompanying the country's economic rise.

Deep in his heart, there may have been an underlying sense of "Après moi, le deluge" (After me, the flood) akin to King Louis XV of France in Deng Xiaoping's thinking, particularly heightened by the Tiananmen tragedy, which increased his insecurity about the regime's sustainability and his posthumous legacy. Subsequent leadership under Jiang Zemin and Hu Jintao was composed of technocrats whose economic and foreign policy insights were shaped by a flawed and biased educational system. They might have underestimated the element of luck. Nevertheless, this oversight, especially during Hu Jintao's tenure, whether deliberate or not, led the Chinese ruling elites to overestimate their strength while disregarding the urgent need for reform in the country's economic and political systems.

Ironically, their confidence was bolstered by the Western economic crises of 2007–2009. Consequently, they remained indifferent to China's dependent development and its association with globalization, incorrectly equating temporary economic hardships in the West with the West's overall decline.

China's initial misjudgment of the perceived decline of the United States marked a departure in its foreign policy approach, transitioning from a "low-profile" stance to a more assertive one. This shift commenced in late 2008, notably at the Copenhagen Climate Summit, and gained momentum with China's increasing assertiveness from 2009 onward. The expansion of the People's Liberation Army Navy (PLAN) played a pivotal role, prompting China to assert its territorial claims assertively against other claimant states.

The pursuit of substantial energy resources further fueled China's foreign policy re-alignment. Recognizing the growing significance of East Asia in geopolitics and geoeconomics, coupled with concerns about China challenging the post-war rules-based liberal international order through the use or threat of force to alter the status quo in East and Southeast Asia, the Obama administration swiftly adopted a diplomatic strategy termed "constrainment." This strategy aimed to re-engage Southeast Asian nations and apply pressure on China to either accept, moderate, or revise its assertive stance through a multilateral approach to addressing the South China Sea issue.[109]

Despite making some strides in countering the U.S. constrainment strategy, China felt the pressure from a seemingly robust U.S. response to its assertiveness. This was exemplified by China's isolation during the G-20 conference in February 2010, where all participants urged China to revalue its currency to address global imbalances.[110] Coupled with the United States' threats of a potential trade war and its mounting domestic economic challenges, China opted to reinstate its previous "low-profile" foreign policy.

On December 6, 2010, State Councillor Dai Bingguo published an article on the Foreign Ministry website titled "China Sticks to the Path of Peaceful Development." In the article, he emphasized that "it is a myth that China wants to replace the United States and dominate the world."[111] During his visit to the United States on May 18, 2011, Chen Bingde, PLA's chief of general staff, reiterated China's commitment to peaceful development. He clarified that China's military capabilities lagged behind the United States by approximately 20 years and emphasized China's defensive posture, asserting that China had neither the intention nor the capability to challenge U.S. superpower status. He stated: "Our greatest wish is to enhance China's development and improve the well-being of its 1.3 billion citizens. Central to Chinese traditional culture is the primacy of peace ... The development of our armed forces has, and will continue to uphold China's defensive defense policy. There is no need for the world to be concerned about China's development, let alone harbor fears."[112]

However, China's conciliatory approach did not prevent the implementation of Obama's "pivot to Asia" in November 2011, which signified a significant shift in U.S. strategy from Europe and the Middle East to China's periphery. Equally significant, the "rising" China was compelled

[109] Renato Cruz De Castro (2013): "The Obama Administration's Strategic Pivot to Asia: From a Diplomatic to a Strategic Constrainment of an Emergent China?" *The Korean Journal of Defense Analysis*, September, 25:3, pp. 331–349.

[110] "China Blinks on Yuan in late G-20 Deal." *The Wall Street Journal*, 21/02/2011.

[111] Dai Bingguo: "Stick to the Path of Peaceful Development." 06/12/2010. https://www.mfa.gov.cn/web/ziliao_674904/zt_674979/ywzt_675099/2011nzt_675363/jianchizouhepingfazhandaolu_675415/201012/t20101206_7956521.shtml.

[112] *The China Press*, 18/05/2011.

to make a series of significant concessions to the "declining" United States, including commitments to unilateral market access, furthering trade, investment, and financial liberalization during the Strategic and Economic Dialogues (S&ED) from 2009 to 2011.

During the 2010 S&ED negotiations, China, for the first time, proposed the idea of a "new-type great power relationship" between China and the United States. This concept was repeatedly raised in the years that followed. However, China's enthusiasm in calling for stability and equality in bilateral relations was met with cynicism from the United States, which viewed China's intentions as an attempt to reduce the United States to a declining established power in a "Thucydides trap," potentially undermining the U.S.-led alliance system in the Asia–Pacific region.[113] With growing apprehension about the influence of China's state capitalism, on February 18, 2015, Obama expressed his determination "to make sure the United States—and not countries like China—is the one writing this century's rules for the world's economy."[114] This principle formed the foundation of the U.S.-led Trans-Pacific Partnership (TPP) negotiations. On October 5, 2015, TPP members reached a landmark trade-liberalizing pact, which was hailed as "setting the rules for the twenty-first century for trade."[115] On the same day as the TPP's conclusion, Obama reiterated that "we can't let countries like China write the rules of the global economy."[116]

TPP, as the largest mega-free trade area in history encompassing 40% of global trade, was designed to "contain China in international

[113] Li, C and Xu, L: "Chinese Enthusiasm and American Cynicism over the 'New Concept of Great Power Relations.'" *Brookings Commentary*, 04/12/2014. https://www.brookings.edu/articles/chinese-enthusiasm-and-american-cynicism-over-the-new-type-of-great-power-relations/.

[114] President Obama: "Writing the Rules for 21st Century Trade." The White House, 15/02/2015. https://obamawhitehouse.archives.gov/blog/2015/02/18/president-obama-writing-rules-21st-century-trade.

[115] "TPP Deal: US and 11 Other Countries Reach Landmark Pacific Trade Pact." *The Guardian*, 05/10/2015. https://www.theguardian.com/business/2015/oct/05/trans-pacific-partnership-deal-reached-pacific-countries-international-trade.

[116] "Trans-Pacific Partnership Is Reached, but Faces Scrutiny in Congress." *The New York Times*, 06/10/2015. https://www.nytimes.com/2015/10/06/business/trans-pacific-partnership-trade-deal-is-reached.html.

trade."[117] It contained provisions targeting workers' rights, environmental obligations, and restrictions on China's support of SOEs, aiming to counter China's competitive advantages derived from low labor standards, oversight of environmental damages, and trade distorting practices allegedly benefiting Chinese SOEs at the expense of MNCs in China. The creation of the TPP would have placed China in an awkward position: joining it would neutralize China's cost advantages and inhibit its technological catch-up, while not joining would result in significant trade opportunities being missed by China's export-dependent economy. This U.S.-sponsored decoupling with China was not intended to deglobalize, but rather to reglobalize the global economy on more liberal terms. This posed significant challenges to China's semi-peripheral development and its ability to continue aligning with the existing liberal order to sustain export-led growth. Consequently, China became susceptible to the risk of being forced into some form of autarky. Surprisingly, Chinese elites appeared insensitive to the threat posed by TPP during its negotiation process until it was too late.[118]

After assuming power in late 2012, Xi Jinping became fully aware of the corruption and incompetence that had plagued the PLA. Unlike the U.S. military, which primarily focuses on external threats, as noted by David Frum, the "first and paramount mission [of the PLA] is preserving the power of the Chinese Communist Party against China's own people."[119] Like Obama, Xi recognized the importance of the economy, understanding that "it's still the economy, stupid!"[120] He was not blind to the fact that China was far more dependent on the United States than vice versa, that it still lacked effective alternatives to escaping from dependency and thus could ill-afford a complete decoupling, particularly in technological terms. Xi acknowledged that engaging in an all-out trade war or a military conflict with the United States, especially after the

[117] Chow, C. K. (2016): "How the United States Uses the Trans-Pacific Partnership to Contain China in International Trade." *Chicago Journal of International Law*, 17:2, pp. 370–402.

[118] As I knew from interaction with multiple sources from 2015 till 2022.

[119] Frum, D: China is a Paper Dragon. *The Atlantic*, 03/05/2021. https://www.theatlantic.com/ideas/archive/2021/05/china-paper-dragon/618778/.

[120] "It's Still the Economy, Stupid! Obama Goes on the Attack!" *The Guardian*, 20/09/2008. https://www.theguardian.com/world/2008/sep/20/uselections2008.barackobama.

populist President Donald Trump took office in January 2017, was not a viable option for China. He emphasized this point during his first meeting with Trump at Mar-a-Lago in April 2017, stating: "There are a thousand reasons to make the China-U.S. relationship work, and no reason to break it."[121] Thus, despite frequent saber-rattling and a cosmetic toughening of China's foreign policy aimed primarily at domestic opinion,[122] the Chinese Communist leadership has viewed continued bandwagoning on the liberal order as crucial to the country's economic dynamism and thus to the regime's own security "at the critical juncture of painful structural adjustment for fulfilling the desired economic transition."[123]

What relieved the Chinese leadership was their initial assessment of Trump, who, aside from his pro-autocratic remarks, was merely a mercenary businessman who it was easy to make a deal with. Such a figure lacked vision and was unlikely to drag his country into an unpredictable economic war with China, from which the United States would suffer enormously as well. One piece of evidence supporting this was his decision to withdraw from the TPP immediately after taking office. Despite the decelerating economy, which might become the "New Normal" in the long term, China's much faster rate of growth would sooner or later enable it to overtake the United States in the not-too-distant future. The political payoff of this shift would be immense, not only in consolidating the CCP's rule but also in enhancing China's international respectability.

As the Chinese elites envisioned, an internally divided United States might find itself increasingly powerless to check China's rise, eventually accepting it as a *fait accompli*. The revived confidence shortly after

[121] Xinhua, 07/04/2017. http://www.xinhuanet.com//2017-04/07/c_1120769372.htm; Also "'1,000 reasons' for enhancing ties." *China Daily*, 09/11/2017. http://usa.chinadaily.com.cn/world/2017-11/09/content_34333688.htm.

[122] Chinese IR scholar Chu Ying of the Institute of International Relations harshly criticized the CCP's expansive but ineffective foreign propaganda initiatives as ones that fell on deaf ears and focused instead on pleasing senior leaders and public opinion at home. He called such a failed attempt of extending Chinese "cultural soft power" as an "internalization of external propaganda" ("外宣内宣化": *waixuan neixuanhua*). *HK01*, 16/07/2021. https://www.hk01.com/%E4%B8%AD%E5%9C%8B%E8%A7%80%E5%AF%9F/650707/%E4%B8%AD%E5%9C%8B%E5%A4%96%E5%AE%A3%E8%A2%AB%E6%8C%87%E6%B0%91%E7%B2%B9%E5%8C%96%E8%88%87%E5%85%A7%E5%AE%A3%E5%8C%96-%E5%8C%97%E4%BA%AC%E5%AD%B8%E8%80%85-%E5%BF%99%E8%91%97%E6%88%B0%E9%AC%A5-%E6%98%AF%E6%9C%80%E5%A4%A7%E5%95%8F%E9%A1%8C.

[123] Yue, J (2018), p. 312.

Xi's takeover from Hu Jintao was largely prompted by the United States' faltering economy, which took until 2016 to fully recover from the 2007–2009 financial crisis. The rapidly narrowing GDP gap, accompanied by global fanfare over a power shift from the United States to China, fostered hubris among the entire Chinese leadership, not solely Xi Jinping. They chose to downplay the acute structural deficiencies of China's economic system.

This hubris was clearly reflected in the views of Premier Li Keqiang during his meeting with President Trump on the latter's state visit to China in November 2017. Seemingly oblivious to China's heavy dependence on imported high-tech inputs in its economic activities, Li claimed that China had already developed its industrial and technological base and no longer needed the United States. He dismissed U.S. concerns over unfair trade and economic practices, suggesting that the United States' role in the future global economy would be to provide China with raw materials, agricultural products, and energy to fuel its production of cutting-edge industrial and consumer goods. This statement enraged Trump and was considered by some U.S. elites as the trigger for the U.S.-initiated trade war against China the following year.[124]

Many elites in both China and the United States have exaggerated China's overall national strength, intentionally or unintentionally, for various purposes. However, there are notable exceptions that debunk the fallacy of a "power shift." Michael Beckley, who has measured power as the "function of net resources," compellingly argues that "the United States' economic and military lead over China is much larger than typically assumed—and that the trends are mostly in America's favor."[125] Taking inspiration from Susan Strange's inquiry into American structural power in international political economy, Sean Starrs empirically confirms that "American economic power has not declined—it has globalized,"[126] by considering the critical role of transnational corporations (TNCs) in the era of transnational modular production networks. A recent review conducted by LSE IDEAS, a foreign policy think tank, asserts that "China

[124] McMaster, H. R. (2020), p. 126.

[125] Beckley, M (2018): "The Power of Nations: Measuring What Matters." *International Security*, 43:2, pp. 7–44.

[126] Starrs, S (2013): "American Economic Power Hasn't Declined—It Globalized! Summoning the Data and Taking Globalization Seriously." *International Studies Quarterly*, No. 57, pp. 817–830.

is not yet a military challenge in the same way as Russia (or the Soviet Union) was during the Cold War."[127]

Peter Navarro, a staunch trade adviser to President Trump, asserted China's economic aggression by "quoting fictitious sources."[128] This paradoxical accusation inadvertently suggests China's status as a semi-peripheral state rather than a technological powerhouse. However, whether genuine or feigned, misperceptions like this, where China is perceived as a developed country, have practical implications. In response to the perceived "rise" of China, the U.S. administration, starting from Obama's second term, increasingly justified reinforcing containment measures to complement its engagement policy, and even began promoting decoupling from China through initiatives like the TPP, driven by mounting uncertainty about the regime's intentions and the security challenges posed by China's economic rise, increased military expenditure, and more aggressive international posture.

In Trump's National Security Strategy (NSS) of 2017, there was no reference to China's human rights abuses or ideological differences. Instead, it criticized the previous bipartisan policy of engaging China as a "false promise," emphasizing the need to acknowledge the fundamental reality of international relations: competition and great power rivalry are not accidental features but inherent aspects of the global system.[129] The 2018 NSS report explicitly stated that the resurgence of great power competition, particularly with Russia and China, posed the most significant threat to U.S. national security. However, privately, many U.S. defense officials view China as their "biggest concern."[130]

That scenario seems a good fit with "The Tragedy of Great Power Politics" paradigm advocated by John Mearsheimer, who draws parallels between the semi-peripheral China and the autarkic empires of industrial

[127] Watkins, P: "Introduction: A Three-Pillar Strategic Framework for Competing with China," in "*Protect, Constrain, Contest Approaches for coordinated transatlantic economic and technological competition with China.*" LSE IDEAS China Foresight Project (hereafter called "LSE-IDEAS Report 2021"), Jan, 2021. https://www.lse.ac.uk/ideas/Assets/Documents/reports/LSE-IDEAS-Protect-Constrain-Contest.pdf.

[128] "Peter Navarro, Trump's Trade Warrior, Has Not Made His Peace with China." *The New York Times*, 26/12/2019.

[129] Cox, M (2022), p. 143.

[130] Kroenig, M (2020): *The Return of Great Power Rivalry, Democracy Versus Autocracy from the Ancient World to the U.S. and China*. Oxford: Oxford University Press, p. 179.

Table 5.2 Number of Nobel Laureates in Natural Sciences by Country

Power transition from Britain to Germany (1901–1910)	*Britain: 5*	*Germany: 12*
Power transition from USA to China? (2011–2020)	United States: 44	China: 1

Source List of Nobel Laureates by country: https://en.wikipedia.org/wiki/List_of_Nobel_laureates_by_country

Germany or Japan before 1945. Comparisons of this kind are far less relevant to reality than they may appear. One notable difference is that the widely perceived power shift or "power transition" (2011–2020) from the United States to China was "occurring" at a time when the *rising or risen* China still significantly lagged behind the *declining* United States scientifically and technologically, and seemed destined to remain so into the far distant future. This stands in stark contrast to the power transition from Britain to Germany in the 1901–1910 decade, during which imperial Germany emerged as a superior scientific powerhouse (Table 5.2).

The fallacy of the power shift model is further confirmed by a series of significant concessions China was unilaterally *obliged* to make on market access to both the United States and the EU in 2020, a year when the alleged "power transition" to Chinese dominance was believed to be complete. The U.S.-China Economic and Trade Agreement, also known as the Phase One Agreement, signed on January 15th, extended the prohibition of forced technology transfer from the central government to sub-central governments. China was compelled to agree that there would be "no support or direction to Chinese companies to make outbound foreign direct investment to acquire foreign technology." The Agreement also included an exceedingly humiliating clause on "burden-shifting (to the accused party) in a civil proceeding" (Article 1.5), which violated the universally recognized principle of presumptive innocence. Furthermore, the Agreement established a strong dispute settlement mechanism, allowing the United States to vigilantly monitor China's progress in eliminating unfair trade practices and implementing these obligations. This enabled the Agreement to be fully enforceable in resolving structural issues.[131]

This Agreement, to be "orderly implemented" shortly,[132] was perceived as humiliating by many Chinese nationalists, who likened it to the 1842 Treaty of Nanking (Fig. 5.4). On the last day of the year, China signed the Comprehensive Agreement on Investment (CAI) with the EU, although it was later abandoned due to the European Parliament's boycott. The CAI included the EU securing China's commitment to renouncing forced technology transfer, a key issue of shared concern. This placed the EU on par with the United States' agreement in the Phase One deal. Ironically, the signing of the CAI was hailed by many Chinese international relations scholars, who were unaware of its implications for China's development, as a diplomatic victory. They viewed it as China's foreign policy success in creating divisions and driving a wedge in the seemingly unbreakable transatlantic relations.[133]

The imposition of harsher "anti-developmental" terms on semi-peripheral China suggests that the country's position of strength vis-à-vis the "declining" West has not significantly improved over the past two decades. This is reminiscent of the time when Jerald Segal asserted that "China does not matter" economically and technologically on the eve of its accession to the WTO, during which China was compelled to accept stringent terms for WTO membership. The continuing need to secure the U.S. market, as expressed by former MOFCOM minister Chen Deming, who stated "[we] must retain the U.S. market through all means," made eight months even after the signing of the U.S.-China deal,[134] indirectly underscores China's ongoing challenges. These developments align with Henry Paulson's astute observation, made half a decade ago, regarding

[131] USTR's 2021 National Trade Estimate Report on Foreign Trade Barriers (NTE), released on 31 March 2021. https://ustr.gov/sites/default/files/files/reports/2021/2021NTE.pdf; USTR: Rebalancing U.S.-China Trade: https://ustr.gov/phase-one.

[132] "China signals 'orderly' implementation of phase one deal with the US." *Global Times*, 25/04/2021. https://www.globaltimes.cn/page/202104/1222062.shtml.

[133] "Episode 148: The EU's new trade policy, with Sabine Weyand of DG Trade." Chad Bown, senior fellow at the Peterson Institute for International Economics, interviews Sabine Weyand, Director General for Trade of the European Commission. 17/01/2021. https://www.tradetalkspodcast.com/podcast/148-the-eU.S.-new-trade-policy-with-sabine-weyand-of-dg-trade/.

[134] Zaobao, 08/09/2020.

Fig. 5.4 Two ceremonies in comparison. **Upper part**: the signing ceremony of the Treaty of Nanking, August 29, 1842. **Lower part**: the signing ceremony of the Phase One Agreement, January 15, 2020)

the structural weaknesses and the difficulty of achieving economic rebalancing in the Chinese economy. His full quote is worth noting: "Despite its success and the fears of many in the U.S., China is not an unstoppable powerhouse that has invented a better economic model and will soon take over the world. Quite the contrary. Its economic system is sorely in need of a major overhaul and has few imitators. Its political system has none. Exaggerating China's strength is at least as big a risk as underestimating its potential. Either can lead to irrational responses and mistakes in the way we deal with China."[135]

[135] Paulson, H. M. (2015), p. 380.

However, the exaggeration of China's rise was widespread and often reinforced the "China's rise" thesis, which frequently aligns with the arbitrary assumption of the prevailing power transition theory (PTT). According to this theory, emerging powers are believed to be inherently dissatisfied with the existing international order and poised to overturn it. However, Odd Arne Westad has refuted this cliché, arguing that "there is little evidence that the regime is out to destroy the international system designed by and still dominated by Western power. Rather, it seems intent on getting more out of it."[136]

China's struggle to break free from dependency and its leadership's steadfast advocacy for free trade provide compelling evidence of its status as a fragile great power rather than a solid contender for superpower status. This notion is further underscored by China's perceived reckless concessions during market access negotiations with the United States and the EU in 2020, which effectively stripped it of its developing-country status.[137] This situation leaves China with no choice but to pursue continued alignment with the liberal order at all costs. China's eagerness to join the CPTPP (Comprehensive and Progressive Agreement for Trans-Pacific Partnership, formerly TPP) immediately after the formation of AUKUS (a military alliance targeting China between Australia, the United States, and the United Kingdom) on September 15, 2021, even though the body was created with the intention to exclude China, serves as a crowning example of China's inextricable dependence on the capitalist world system, particularly from an economic perspective.

An important aspect that is often overlooked but is worth noting is the intellectual background of the post-Mao leadership, including Deng, which has left them with insufficient knowledge and understanding of the current liberal order—how it emerged and the potential for its overturning.[138] Needless to say, as the Chinese economy continues to grow,

[136] Westad, O. A.: "Identity Politics with Chinese Characteristics—How the CCP's Quest to Define 'China' Shapes Beijing's Agenda." *Foreign Affairs*, 01/06/2021. https://www.foreignaffairs.com/reviews/review-essay/identity-politics-chinese-characteristics.

[137] On February 10, 2020, less than one month of the conclusion of the Phase One Agreement, USTR removed China from the list of developing countries. *China Daily*, 20/02/2020. "US removes China from list of developing countries." *China Daily*, 20/02/2020. http://epaper.chinadaily.com.cn/a/202002/20/WS5e4de0d1a310a2fabb7a24f4.html.

[138] Yue, J (2018), p.16.

it naturally desires to play a greater role in shaping global norms and governance rather than passively accepting rules drafted solely by Western nations, a legitimate right acknowledged by the latter. However, the lack of knowledge among the elites, stemming from the country's backward educational system, and the absence of necessary diplomatic skills based on proper knowledge hinder their ability to achieve this desire,[139] making it more rhetorical than substantive.

Related to this, China has taken many of the WTO's "anti-developmental" rules for granted, such as the issue of "forced technology transfer," which is still permitted under the TRIMs agreement of the WTO. Ironically, despite being a significant trading power and WTO member, the overwhelming majority of Chinese elites, including economists, have never heard of this issue or made in-depth studies of WTO rules. Instead, they have overwhelmingly accepted China's compliance with U.S. demands on technology transfer without serious questioning. Even the nomenklatura elites perceived U.S. and EU demands for China to refrain from imposing mandatory technology transfer as consistent with WTO rules, and eagerly emphasized the need to "plug loopholes" at the local level well before the signing of the Phase One Agreement.[140]

The new Foreign Investment Law, which explicitly banned forced technology transfer in Article 22, was enacted within just three months on March 15, 2019, after the draft law was submitted by the State Council to the National People's Congress, often referred to colloquially as the 'rubber stamp,' for final "review." It is thus no exaggeration to say that China, so tightly enmeshed intellectually and institutionally within the international system, lacks both the genuine will and the ability to challenge the United States through any sort of hard-balancing approach. Its lack of "potent soft-power sources" also leaves it no match for either the Third Reich or the USSR, which, as Joseph Nye noted, constituted competing alternatives in their respective eras in every sense.[141]

[139] Henry Paulson (2015, p. 393) tactfully wrote in his memoire that "the Chinese have not been very specific about what they want to change...".

[140] "Ex-PBOC chief says China must address 'loopholes' as part of WTO reform." *Reuters*, 19/09/2018. https://www.reuters.com/article/U.S.-china-economy-zhou-idUSKCN1LZ0XU.

[141] Nye, J (2015): *Is the American Century over?* Cambridge: Polity Press, p. 68.

For the United States, it serves vital American national interests to prevent emerging powers from seeking illiberal alternatives and challenging its leadership in the post-Cold War era. It is worth emphasizing that as one of the "enduring truths," the U.S. national interest has never been compromised by engaging with the nominally Communist power over the past decades.[142] Its "drawing out" strategy, at the very outset, was not designed to foster or tolerate China as a peer competitor,[143] but to "turn it into a status quo power,"[144] an economically and technologically dependent, pacific and responsible stakeholder in "the fundamental order of the existing international system."[145] Now that China is increasingly perceived as a strategic threat,[146] and with the "return of great power rivalry" that had begun in 2014,[147] "revising US grand strategy toward China" had ripened even before Trump's coming into office, into

[142] According to Nealer, "On Capitol Hill and with each successive administration, the focus was on advancing U.S. interests and creating incentives for China that resulted in improved U.S. economic and security options in Asia." Nealer, K. G.: "*Trading Iron Curtain for Chinese Walls: Is it different this time?*" in CSIS report: "China's Uneven High-tech Drive." 27/02/2020, pp. 47-50. https://www.csis.org/analysis/chinas-uneven-high-tech-drive-implications-united-states.

[143] "Mearsheimer: 'The US Won't Tolerate China as Peer Competitor.'" 23/09/2020. *Deutsche Welle*. https://www.dw.com/en/chinas-rise-and-conflict-with-us/a-55026173; Kitchen argued that "After all, no US leader seeks to encourage peer competitors." Kitchen, N (2020): "Why American Grand Strategy Has Changed." *Global Affairs*, 6:1, pp. 87–104.

[144] Mastanduno, M (1997), pp. 49-88.

[145] As the US Deputy Secretary of State, Robert Zoellick, remarked in 2005, "For fifty years, our policy was to *fence in* the Soviet Union while its own internal contradictions undermined it. For thirty years, our policy has been to *draw out* the People's Republic of China. As a result, the China of today is simply not the Soviet Union of the late 1940s… Chinese leaders have decided that their success depends on being networked with the modern world." "Wither China: From Membership to Responsibility?" R. Zoellick: Remarks to National Committee on U.S.-China Relations, 21/09/2005. https://2001-2009.state.gov/s/d/former/zoellick/rem/53682.htm.

[146] "U.S. 'Benign China' Policy Ending—CIA Analyst Declares China Now Waging Cold War on U.S." *The Washington Free Beacon*, 24/07/2018. https://freebeacon.com/national-security/u-s-benign-china-policy-ending/

[147] Kroenig, M (2020), p. 176.

a policy that "centers on balancing the rise of Chinese power rather than continuing to assist its ascendancy."[148]

Far from having achieved parity with the United States in terms of relational capabilities and a more accurate understanding of what it means to be powerful, China, according to Nicholas Kitchen and Michael Cox, will likely remain a "rule-taker" unless a new "world-making moment" occurs, providing China with the necessary structural power to wrest international leadership of the United States.[149] However, this is no easy feat, as the biggest challenge facing U.S. foreign policy is not its "lack of power," but rather the political polarization at home. This polarization has hindered Americans from forging a consensus and a coherent grand strategy.[150] A confrontation with China, on the other hand, could potentially foster a re-unity within the United States and bolster an even stronger American power that would be harder to challenge.

The paradox lies in the fact that even if China's problematic rise poses no real threat to the liberal international order, and the country simply aims to peacefully ascend within the existing international system, the country's "empire" size, both in physical and economic terms, raises the serious question of whether it can "fit" into the liberal order. The global impact of China's deep integration is twofold. Firstly, it leads to a global economic imbalance on an unprecedented scale that must be addressed sooner or later. Secondly, and perhaps even more significantly, it creates acute vulnerability to resource scarcity, prompting massive rearmament efforts by the PRC to address this vulnerability.

Unlike the United States, which has a self-sufficiency in natural resources, China is resource-poor, especially on a per capita basis, making it heavily dependent on importing various natural resources from the rest of the world. China's entrapment in semi-peripheral development implies that its extensive industrialization model may not be altered any time soon. Its past and ongoing input-driven growth inevitably leads to premature and perhaps accelerating depletion of domestic resources, exacerbating its import dependence on natural resources. This not only

[148] Blackwill, R. D. & Tellis, A. J. (2015): "Revising U.S. Grand Strategy toward China." *Council on Foreign Relations* Special Report released in April. https://www.cfr.org/report/revising-U.S.-grand-strategy-toward-china.

[149] Kitchen, N and Cox, M (2019): "Power, structural power, and American Decline." *Cambridge Review of International Affairs*, 32:6, pp. 734–752.

[150] Cox, M (2022), p. 158.

renders its high growth unsustainable but also places its economic security at stake (Fig. 5.5).

Take coal and oil as examples. In 2021, China consumed over 53% of global coal production, approximately 2.45 times the combined consumption of the rest of the world excluding India, the United States, and Japan (Table 5.3). In 2020, China's crude oil imports reached a record of 542 million tons, equivalent to 10.85 million barrels per day (bpd), with import dependency rising to 73.5%.[151] The International Energy Agency (IEA) predicted in November 2017 that "By 2040,

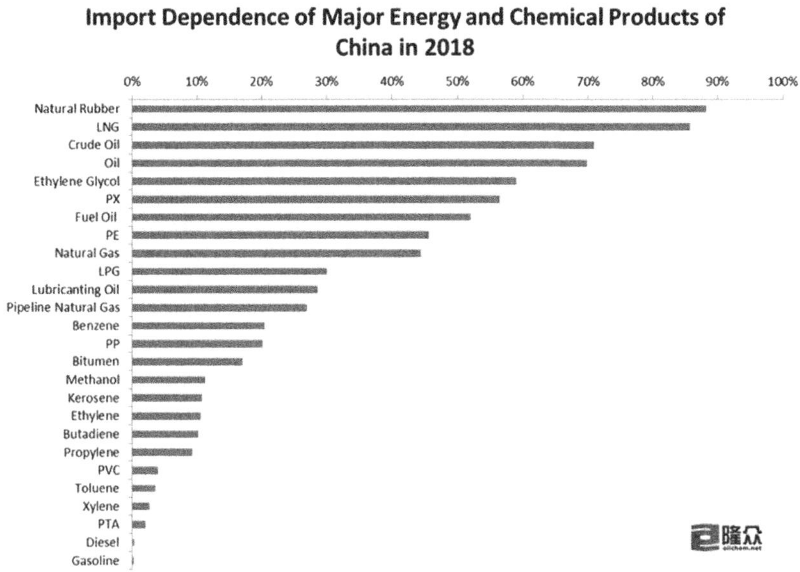

Fig. 5.5 China's Import Dependence on Major Energy and Chemical Products (2018) (*Note* Natural Rubber is ranked first among all major energy and chemical products of China in 2018 in terms of import dependence, followed by LNG and Crude Oil. Commodities in which China was over 30% import-dependent included LPG, Natural Gas, PE, Fuel Oil, PX, Ethylene Glycol, Oil, Crude Oil, LNG and Natural Rubber [OilChem.net]. *Source* https://www.sohu.com/a/290766447_99902541 [February 22, 2019])

[151] MOFCOM, 21/05/2021. http://www.mofcom.gov.cn/article/tongjiziliao/sjtj/jsc/202105/20210503063494.shtml

Table 5.3 Global Coal Consumption (2021) (in million metric tons)

World	*China*	*India*	*United States*	*EU*	*Others*
7,947	4,230	1,053	495	447	1,722
100%	53.2%	13.3%	6.2%	5.6%	21.7%

Source International Energy Agency

China's import dependence will hit 80 percent."[152] According to a Reuters report, China's crude oil imports may rise between 500,000 and 1 million barrels per day (bpd) in 2023, potentially reaching as high as 11.8 million bpd. This would reverse the decline observed in the previous two years and surpass the record of 10.85 million bpd set in 2020, according to analysts from four industry consultancies—Wood Mackenzie, FGE, Energy Aspects, and S&P Global Commodity Insight.[153]

The United States is neither *willing* nor *likely* to "guarantee China's access to sufficient primary products" within a liberal order that can only accommodate "one or two Japans."[154] The peaceful rise of post-1945 Germany and Japan, based on the combination of their population sizes of no more than 200 million, was precisely the result of American Cold War grand strategy. Fearing China's emergence as a technological powerhouse, all industrial nations have a vested interest in keeping China positioned at the low end of the global value chain. This ironic situation has created tensions that the United States and the Western world, which were determined to fully integrate China into the global economy, are unwilling to confront China's insatiable demand for resources to sustain its input-driven growth, which aligns with its extensive industrialization model.

Deputy Premier Wang Qishan emphasized the need for China to switch to a new mode of development in his concern conveyed to U.S.

[152] Radio Free Asia, 04/12/2017. https://www.rfa.org/english/commentaries/energy_watch/chinas-oil-import-dependence-climbs-as-output-falls-12042017102429.html.

[153] "China set for record crude oil imports in 2023, analysts say." *Reuters*, 17/02/2023. https://www.reuters.com/business/energy/china-set-record-crude-oil-imports-2023-analysts-2023-02-17/

[154] Pomeranz, K (2001): "Is there an East Asian Development Path?" *Journal of the Economic and Social History of the Orient*, 44:3, pp. 322–362.

Treasury Secretary Henry Paulson, stating: "If everyone in the world, including big countries like China, India, and Indonesia, wants to live like Americans, four earths won't be enough."[155] President Obama expressed a similar sentiment on April 15, 2010, during an Australian TV interview, when he stated: "If over a billion Chinese citizens have the same living patterns as Australians and Americans do right now, then all of us are in for a very miserable time. The planet just can't sustain it."[156]

However, tensions persist: China's drive for technological advance, aimed at achieving superpower "peer," inevitably escalates competition with the United States. This scenario has raised concerns about the "Thucydides Trap" and the potential for a "tragedy of great power politics," as highlighted by Mearsheimer. Some influential intellectual elites, trusted advisors to the regime, have candidly advocated privately against aggressive industrial upgrading and technological catching up, fearing it could provoke a backlash from the United States.[157] Unfortunately, even if China opts to maintain its semi-peripheral "superpower" status without aggressively pursuing technological parity with leading nations, it will still face conflicts with the international system. This stems from the harsh reality, as noted by renowned energy expert Michael Klare in 2011, that the world confronts an unprecedented resource depletion crisis. The escalating competition for limited resources has significantly increased the likelihood of military confrontations,[158] including the potential for a great power war in the foreseeable future.[159]

The way in which China attempted to industrialize by embracing neoliberal globalization has thus far resulted in a quandary of "growth without development." Unlike South Korea, which earned the moniker "Asia's Next Giant" for its rapid industrialization, China has achieved

[155] Paulson, H. M. (2015), p. 244.

[156] "President Barack Obama Says Prime Minister Kevin Rudd is 'Smart, Humble.'" *Perth Now*, 15/04/2010. https://www.perthnow.com.au/news/nsw/president-barack-obama-says-prime-minister-kevin-rudd-is-smart-humble-ng-fe9b5c28fefd4406de67cef56dd015ed.

[157] The author's several conversations with informed sources in China in the past decade.

[158] Klare, M. T. (2011): *The Race for What's Left: The Global Scramble for the World's Last Resources*. NY: Metropolitan Books.

[159] Rosecrance, R & Miller, S (2015): *The Next Great War? The Roots of World War I and the Risk of U.S.-China Conflict*. Cambridge, Massachusetts: The MIT Press.

impressive economic growth, but has failed to bring about significant structural transformation. The prospect of China catching up with and rivaling advanced countries remains uncertain. The growing risk of China being trapped in dependent development does not symbolize "the most efficient state capitalism," nor does it align with the template of "New Developmentalism" advocated by market skeptics. It is worth emphasizing that China's economic success, even when measured by GDP, is partly fortuitous, considering external events such as 9/11.

The relatively stable and consistent U.S. strategy of engaging with China is self-defeating, not because U.S. policymakers misjudged the politically resistant nature of the Chinese regime (which has, nevertheless, undergone significant institutional changes, rendering Communism or socialism irrelevant in practical terms), or because this strategy has fostered China into a powerful economic, strategic, and possibly military rival. The failure can be attributed to the U.S. government's inability to recognize that its strategy, which focuses on globalizing the Chinese economy through inducement and coercion, ultimately ensnared China in a dependent development model—an outcome contradicting what Rostow's *The Stages of Economic Growth* had suggested. Yet China "sits both inside (economically) and outside (politically and militarily) the post-Cold War liberal international order."[160] Driven by the pursuit of high growth for legitimation purposes at all costs, China would be relegated to the lower end of the global value chain, leading to a premature depletion of its domestic resources due to its empire-sized population. Consequently, the U.S. strategy unintentionally pushes China, lacking sufficient resources, into a scramble for resources worldwide, thereby increasing conflicts with Western democracies. This paradox lies at the heart of "the tragedy of great power politics" in the age of globalization, exemplified by China's specific case.

Elites in China and the United States have rightly recognized the need for structural adjustment in China to achieve economic rebalancing, but they mistakenly insist that more economic globalism, rather than less, is the solution. As Paulson bluntly put it, "I believe it was important to continue to encourage China to integrate its economy with the world's,

[160] Ikenberry, J (2020): *A World Safe for Democracy—Liberal Internationalism and the Crises of Global Order*. New Haven: Yale University Press, p. 273.

to open its markets and endorse free trade."[161] This recommendation persists, even as the United States shifted from "strategic engagement" to "competitive engagement" following Trump's rise to power. However, China's de facto abandonment of the "Made in China 2025" initiative during the trade war and its commitment to further openness are inadequate responses to the developmental challenges and the U.S.-China great power rivalry. China's continued "rise," which the United States has refused to assist, within the semi-peripheral orbit will only exacerbate conflicts with the liberal order, prompting technological decoupling by the West, thereby jeopardizing not only the country's *development* but also its *growth* per se.

[161] Paulson, H. M. (2015), p. 82.

PART III

"Profound Changes Unseen in a Century"

In November 2012, Xi Jinping assumed the position of General Secretary of the Chinese Communist Party (CCP), following a mix of expectations, much like Mikhail Gorbachev did in 1985. Five years earlier, Xi was handpicked by Jiang Zemin's "Shanghai faction" as the heir apparent to General Secretary Hu Jintao in 2007. Jiang's faction outmaneuvered the incumbent "Communist Youth League faction" (CYLF), which was led by then General Secretary Hu Jintao, in deciding the next generation of leadership. Hu Jintao's preferred candidate was Li Keqiang, a member of his CYLF. Despite Li's career advancing more rapidly than Xi's and him receiving a better formal college education after the Cultural Revolution, he was sidelined in the final race for becoming the paramount leader.

Xi Jinping's rapid ascent to power surprised many observers, given his lack of outstanding performance during his tenure in multiple local administrations. The influential "Shanghai faction" threw their support behind Xi primarily due to his princeling status. Although his father, Party veteran Xi Zhongxun, had a positive reputation for supporting reform-minded leaders such as Hu Yaobang and Zhao Ziyang in the 1980s, this factor played a relatively minor role. The selection of a princeling at this crucial juncture represented a significant decision made by Party veterans closely associated with the Shanghai faction. Party veterans harbored skepticism toward non-princeling elites, including senior leaders like Hu Jintao and Premier Wen Jiabao, particularly during times of crisis. They perceived these individuals as mere "servants" or "executive managers" within the CCP's "board of directors." From the perspective of the

Party veterans, the country was their private domain to control at their discretion.

Yet Xi's rise to the top leadership was not without risks and challenges, despite the patronage of Party seniors. When compared to another princeling and emerging political figure, Bo Xilai, whose father ranked among the "eight immortals" with superior political status than Xi's father, Xi Zhongxun, Xi's position as the heir apparent was far less solid than it seemed. Bo Xilai proved to be an ambitious and formidable contender in the intense power struggle leading up to the opening of the Eighteenth National Party Congress in the Fall of 2012. He possessed extraordinary advantages that Xi lacked. Bo's proven record in local economic development was widely acknowledged, and he was well known for his assertive character, greater capabilities, and extensive knowledge, owing to his educational background.

Nevertheless, Bo's "strongman style" proved to be his downfall, costing him dearly. Despite his initial position as Minister of Commerce, he was disliked by many members of the Politburo, leading to his transfer to govern Chongqing, a municipality in southwestern China, in 2007. This move was neither a promotion nor demotion, but rather a de facto "ostracism" due to Chongqing's relative remoteness and underdevelopment.

Discontented with the existing nomenklatura arrangement, Bo Xilai, driven by his ambitions for pivotal positions, if not the paramount leadership, within the forthcoming Politburo Standing Committee, embarked on a profoundly influential yet controversial neo-Maoist political experiment referred to as the "Chongqing model." This endeavor exacerbated the power struggle during the closing stages of the scheduled power transition, ultimately resulting in an unprecedented succession crisis within the Communist nomenklatura system. This crisis posed a significant threat to the established concept of "resilient authoritarianism," a term coined by Cheng Li.[1] This notion had emerged after Deng Xiaoping institutionalized the CCP's power transition system, transforming it into a predictable and procedural process complete with clear term limits.

In April 2012, Bo was relieved of his post as Chongqing Party boss due to allegations of his wife's involvement in the assassination of a British merchant. His downfall removed the threat to Xi's successorship, as it was

[1] Li, Cheng (2012): "The End of the CCP's Resilient Authoritarianism? A Tripartite Assessment of Shifting Power in China." *The China Quarterly*, No. 211, pp. 595–623.

a collective decision by the incumbent leadership, with the endorsement of Jiang Zemin, who still wielded influence from behind the scenes. These Party elites feared the emergence of another Mao Zedong-like dictator. In contrast, Xi was seen as a weak and moderate political figure, easily controlled and unlikely to challenge the vested interests of Party elites.

During the period from 2007 to 2012, the world was abuzz with discussions about China's rise, the decline of the West, the emergence of an illiberal alternative model termed the "Beijing Consensus," and even the notion of "When China Rules the World." However, beneath this narrative, a severe crisis was rapidly building within the "rising" China.

Inequality was expanding, with the Gini coefficient approaching 0.6, placing the country behind only South Africa and Brazil. Despite a massive stimulus package implemented in 2009, the economy was decelerating. Nationwide rights movements, accompanied by approximately 200,000 recorded "mass incidents," were pushing the country toward mass disorders.

Intensive reports from 2012 to 2016 by international media about more than 100 heirs of the CCP's red families, particularly the Deng Xiaoping-led "eight immortals," and incumbent and past Politburo members amassing huge wealth and transferring it overseas stunned the world. These revelations portrayed the People's Republic as a typical kleptocratic state, no less heinous than Putin's Russia,[2] highlighting the doomsday mentality of the Party elites.

[2] "Heirs of Mao's Comrades Rise as New Capitalist Nobility." *Bloomberg*, 26/12/2012. https://www.bloomberg.com/news/articles/2012-12-26/immortals-beget-china-capitalism-from-citic-to-godfather-of-golf?leadSource=uverify%20wall; "Family of Chinese Regulator Profits in Insurance Firm's Rise." *The New York Times*, 30/12/2012. https://www.nytimes.com/2012/12/31/business/global/chinese-regulators-family-profited-from-stake-in-insurer.html; "Leaked Records Reveal Offshore Holdings of China's Elite Files shed light on nearly 22,000 tax haven clients from Hong Kong and mainland China." ICIJ (International Consortium of Investigative Journalists), 21/01/2014. https://www.icij.org/investigations/offshore/leaked-records-reveal-offshore-holdings-of-chinas-elite/; "Panama papers: China leaders' relatives named in leaks." *BBC*, 04/04/2016. https://www.bbc.co.uk/news/world-asia-35962326; "Panama Papers reveal offshore secrets of China's red nobility." *The Guardian*, 06/04/2016. https://www.theguardian.com/news/2016/apr/06/panama-papers-reveal-offshore-secrets-china-red-nobility-big-business; "What Do the Panama Papers Reveal About China?" *The Diplomat*, 09/04/2016. https://thediplomat.com/2016/04/what-do-the-panama-papers-reveal-about-china/

Fearful of a color revolution and determined to maintain "volcanic stability," the Leninist party state staunchly resisted political change and tightened its grip by harshly clamping down on social activists, curbing rights movements, and taking a hard stance against appeals for democracy, such as Charter 08. During this period, China's borderlands, particularly Tibet and Xinjiang, also experienced turbulence. This "restless empire" was fraught with instability, a contrast to the harmony and progress one might expect from a vibrant rising China.

Thus, when Xi Jinping assumed office in late 2012, China was facing a profound socio-political crisis, signaling the limitations of Deng's crony comprador capitalism. This situation compelled within-system elites to recognize the urgency for change, like the atmosphere before Obama's rise to the presidency. However, divisions persisted among these elites regarding the direction and extent of necessary reforms.

The neo-Maoists hoped for Xi to lead China in a revival of Bo Xilai's approach, while moderate reformers sought a return to the brief "New Democracy" era of the early 1950s before the CCP underwent radical Stalinization. The scandal-plagued Premier Wen Jiabao[3] and other liberal-oriented reformers advocated managed political reforms to establish the rule of law and prevent a recurrence of the Cultural Revolution.

On the other hand, powerful vested interests, represented by the "Shanghai faction," sought to shape Xi's mindset, confining his reforming scenarios within the boundaries of Deng Xiaoping's crony comprador capitalism.[4] As a result, Xi Jinping found himself pulled in multiple directions by political forces, facing difficult choices.

Cool-headed comments circulated among senior ranks in Beijing immediately after Xi's rise to power, even questioning his fate and comparing it to a pivotal moment in history: either he would lead China to greatness or risk becoming another "Emperor Chongzhen." This historical reference alluded to the tragic fate of the last Ming emperor who hanged himself before the fall of the imperial capital to a peasant revolt in 1644.

The wide-ranging intra-party consensus for change necessitated some degree of de-Dengification, both politically and economically, making Xi

[3] "Billions in Hidden Riches for Family of Chinese Leader." *The New York Times*, 25/10/2012. https://www.nytimes.com/2012/10/26/business/global/family-of-wen-jiabao-holds-a-hidden-fortune-in-china.html

[4] According to reliable well-informed source. 10/12/2012.

Jinping bound to be a reformer. Sensing the trend of change in China, especially after the "Bo Xilai shock," many Western media labeled him as "a reformer" within a year of Xi's accession to power, expecting him to be China's Gorbachev. However, they misread Xi and the Party, which, as always, dismissed Western democracy as an alternative. This belief was further vindicated by the erosion of Western democracy symbolized by the rise of populism and the election of Donald Trump to the U.S. presidency in 2016.

Meanwhile, despite recognizing that China's economic difficulties were significant and structural, the new leadership was content with the CCP's ability to maintain economic growth, albeit decelerating, while ensuring social stability. In contrast, the weak crisis-management capacity of Western democracies convinced Xi that they were experiencing an irreversible decline. The new leadership seemed to believe that as long as China remained steadfast on its current path through necessary conservative reform scenarios, such as strengthening the party state's governability and reasserting absolute Party dominance over the bureaucracy and society, catching up with and surpassing the West would be only a matter of time. This perception of a greater crisis in the West that eclipsed the one in China fueled not only Xi's hubris but also that of the entire leadership in handling diplomacy. This formed the judgment of Xi Jinping and the entire fifth-generation leadership that the coming of "Profound Changes Unseen in a Century" heralded the rise of a Chinese century.

This section is divided into two chapters. Chapter 6 delves into the origins of the new Cold War, a development influenced by China's deep integration into the global economy and the United States' deliberate "drawing out" strategy. As explored in the preceding chapter, this integration has inevitably given rise to a Sino-U.S. conflict, particularly in terms of its political-economic consequences.

However, it is essential to consider whether this great-power rivalry will inevitably escalate into a new Cold War. Multiple intervening variables promoting great-power cooperation may play a crucial role in preventing such an outcome. To understand this dynamic, this author turns to the power transition theory, which offers valuable insights into the motivations of both powers as they navigate their rivalry.

In Chapter 7, the focus shifts to Xi Jinping's strategy for coping with the impending U.S.-China great-power rivalry. Drawing parallels with the historical context of the Third Reich in the 1930s–1940s, this chapter examines how Xi's China has sought to address the myriad challenges, both domestic and international, that have emerged within the context of the unfolding new Cold War.

Xi's strategy involves strategically reasserting the "primacy of politics" while simultaneously pursuing partial autarky. As part of this endeavor, there has been a noticeable transformation within the Chinese economy, resembling certain aspects of Nazi economic policy. This chapter conducts an in-depth investigation to assess the viability of Xi's strategy and to consider its potential implications for China and the world as global disorder continues to mount.

CHAPTER 6

U.S.-China Great-Power Rivalry: From Trade War to New Cold War

Under Obama's two-term tenure, U.S.-China decoupling began to take shape with the signing of the Trans-Pacific Partnership (TPP) in February 2016. Obama could have taken a tougher stance on trade disputes with China, if not for the need to seek help from China and the EU to address the 2007–2009 economic crisis at home.[1] The U.S.-China trade war did not take place, largely due to significant concessions made by the "rising" China to the "declining" United States on market access. China committed to further trade, investment, and financial liberalization during the eight-round Strategic and Economic Dialogues (S&ED) from 2009 to 2016.

The "Fu Bo Plan" and the Lost Chance of Sino-U.S. Rapprochement

After Trump took office in January 2017, he immediately ordered America's withdrawal from the TPP and adopted a tough stance toward China by terminating the S&ED. Nevertheless, he believed in his ability to persuade North Korea to abandon its nuclear program and saw Beijing's assistance as crucial in bringing the Democratic People's Republic of Korea (DPRK) to the negotiating table. Consequently, he linked China's

[1] Obama, B (2021): *A Promised Land*. NY: Viking, p. 476.

J. Yue, *Crony Comprador Capitalism*,
https://doi.org/10.1007/978-3-031-53154-5_6

cooperation in denuclearizing North Korea with trade disputes, using both threats and incentives.[2]

Given the importance of DPRK's denuclearization in Trump's foreign policy agenda, it is likely that a trade war, which Trump effectively initiated in March 2018 (though he avoided using the term), could have been avoided if China had collaborated in the manner Trump desired. The urgency for North Korea's denuclearization stemmed from the regime's history of conducting five nuclear tests before Trump took office. Furthermore, there were indications that North Korea was rapidly advancing its nuclear weaponization capabilities, including the miniaturization of nuclear warheads in March 2016 to fit on ballistic missiles. This posed an existential threat not only to U.S. allies but also to Guam and even the American mainland in the near future. These developments suggested that Obama's approach of "strategic patience" had failed.

In the immediate aftermath of the positive summit at Mar-a-Lago in early April 2017, Trump became more specific in linking U.S.-China trade policies with cooperation on North Korea. To secure Xi Jinping's support for denuclearizing North Korea, Trump was willing to refrain from engaging in a trade war with China and even avoided labeling China as a "currency manipulator." This approach aimed to ensure China's economic stability that Xi naturally desired before the opening of the Nineteenth National Party Congress, creating the potential for a grand bargain.[3]

Prior to the summit, China appeared to be convinced by the likely U.S. remonstration about a nuclearizing North Korea, which could also threaten China's national security. This might explain why the PLA's chief of general staff, General Fang Fenghui, was present in Xi's delegation during the summit. In the past, the PRC had taken a passive approach

[2] "Trump Says US Will Act Alone on North Korea If China Fails to Help." *The Guardian*, 03/04/2017. https://www.theguardian.com/U.S.-news/2017/apr/02/donald-trump-north-korea-china.

[3] Trump Twitted Twice After His Meeting with Xi Jinping at Mar-a-Lago. On 11 April 2017 (12:59 PM), he twitted: "I explained to the President of China that a trade deal with the U.S. will be far better for them if they solve the North Korean problem!." Four minutes later, he continued: "North Korea is looking for trouble. If China decides to help, that would be great. If not, we will solve the problem without them! U.S.A." See reports: "Trump, Unorthodox as Ever, Offers Grand Bargain to Beijing." *VOAnews*, 12/04/2017. https://www.voanews.com/a/trump-unorthodox-as-ever-offers-grand-bargain-to-beijing/3807245.html.

toward North Korea's nuclearization, viewing a permanently divided Korean peninsula as serving China's geopolitical interests. Resentful of its neighboring "celestial empire," the North Korean regime had frequently managed to outwit China since the Jiang Zemin era, maximizing its economic and strategic interests at China's expense without even a slight likelihood of being controlled by China. Thus, it becomes evident that China's influence over a near-impenetrable North Korea has been greatly overexaggerated.

Beyond the options of advocating direct dialogue between the United States and North Korea or relying on the ineffective "Six-Party Talks," which North Korea had exploited to advance its nuclear program, China found itself without a Plan B to prepare for the possibility of a sudden collapse of the North Korean state. Such a collapse could result from either regime implosion or a DPRK-provoked American-led invasion. In such a scenario, reunification by South Korea with American support and ongoing alliance would be likely, a prospect China would view as a significant geopolitical setback.

Additionally, China shared the concerns voiced by many Western strategists regarding the consequences of a potential influx of tens of thousands of refugees into its northeastern provinces if North Korea were to collapse suddenly. Consequently, unlike the United States, Chinese ruling elites did not possess an alternative strategic vision that involved active intervention for the purpose of denuclearizing North Korea through a bold scenario of armed regime change.

From a counterfactual perspective, akin to the situation in 1994 when Bill Clinton seriously contemplated a military strike on North Korea's nuclear facilities, which at the time had fewer strategic and ecological consequences, there existed a feasible and desirable option for a Chinese military solution. This could have occurred either with or without endorsement from the United States, and it was viable until the last window of opportunity faded away. This window was open before North Korea conducted its fourth nuclear test in January 2016, which detonated the equivalent of 17,000 tons of TNT, just two months before the miniaturization of nuclear warheads.

It is worth noting that certain extra-system elites had such a strategic vision as early as mid-2013, possibly even dating back to 2006 immediately after North Korea's first nuclear test. One scholar of international relations, Fu Bo, proposed an innovative plan that combined military and diplomatic solutions. In his proposal, Fu Bo advocated the implementation of more stringent economic sanctions against North Korea, with the aim of compelling the nation to completely renounce its nuclear program. In exchange, China would provide significant support for DPRK to facilitate economic reform and extend military protection, including the provision of a nuclear umbrella to shield against external threats. Non-compliance with these terms would result in the total cessation of Chinese aid and an elevated risk of a regime collapse.

The "Fu Bo Plan" did not anticipate North Korea's willingness to capitulate. Instead, it accounted for the possibility of North Korea's sustained recalcitrance, which could potentially result in either regime implosion or the North Korean regime provoking a new Korean War. In both scenarios, the involvement of both the United States and China would be justified. Contrary to conventional wisdom, which suggests that China might intervene to support a recalcitrant and dangerous Stalinist regime, China's intervention would, in fact, be aimed at facilitating a regime change.

Amid the process of armed denuclearization, a People's Liberation Army (PLA) intervention into North Korean territory would also serve as a "cordon sanitaire," preventing the influx of refugees into Chinese territory. In the name of humanitarian intervention, China could provide relief to these refugees, safeguarding Chinese border areas from potential disruptions.

Following China's active military intervention, Fu Bo suggested a strategy reminiscent of the "Austriaization" of the newly unified Republic of Korea. Under this plan, permanent neutrality would be guaranteed by the great powers involved, akin to the "Austrian State Treaty" concluded in May 1955. Within this grand design, China's security concerns would find resolution, as the new Republic of Korea would serve as a strategic buffer. This approach would significantly advance China's strategic interests by weakening the U.S.-led triple alliance, with the new Republic of Korea permanently departing from the alliance.[4]

This proposal gained prominence when it was published in the June 2013 issue of "*Leaders*" (《领导者》), a high-profile internally circulated policy journal in China, with a status akin to that of *Foreign Affairs*.

[4] Fu Bo (2013): "China's Interests in the Korean Peninsula." *Leaders* (Hong Kong), No. 52, Issue 3, pp. 61–64.

Its readership included, among others, senior Party cadres at the vice-minister level. Three months later, a RAND report dated September 19, 2013, authored by Bruce W. Bennett and titled "Preparing for the Possibility of a North Korean Collapse," expressed concerns about the potential for Chinese military intervention, aligning broadly with Fu Bo's concept.[5] The United States had a strong incentive to pursue the denuclearization of North Korea with China's cooperation rather than opting for the implementation of the "Fu Bo Plan." The latter outcome would have significantly favored China, granting it a prominent position in Northeast Asia's geopolitical chessboard while undermining U.S. strategic interests.

On March 11, 2014, a proposal for NPRK's denuclearization emerged from within China's political elite. This proposal, known as the "Lantern Plan" (提灯计划), was brought to public attention through Phoenix TV, a media outlet controlled by the CCP based in Hong Kong. It was attributed to Wang Xiang, a strategist within the PLA trusted by Xi Jinping, marking the first instance of a call to prepare for the potential reunification of the Korean Peninsula and China's strategies to address this prospect.

The "Lantern Plan," as outlined by Wang Xiang, laid out six preconditions for China's support of reunification[6]:

1. Signing a permanent peace agreement between China and the reunified Korean state.
2. Resolution of all land and sea territorial disputes.
3. Denuclearization of the Korean Peninsula.
4. Withdrawal of foreign troops.
5. Assurance of China's economic interests in the reconstruction of the peninsula.
6. Conclusion of a China-U.S. agreement and a China-U.S.-Korea tripartite agreement.

However, this approach remains fundamentally passive, contingent on an unexpected U.S.-ROK co-led process for the sudden reunification of

[5] Bruce W. Bennett: "Preparing for the Possibility of a North Korean Collapse." RAND Report issued on Sep 19, 2013. https://www.rand.org/pubs/research_reports/RR331.html.

[6] Phoenix TV report: 11/03/2014. http://phtv.ifeng.com/program/comment/detail_2014_03/11/34646852_0.shtml.

the Korean Peninsula—a scenario that China cannot entirely control. It also hinges on the optimistic assumption that China's economic and strategic interests on the Peninsula would be willingly respected by South Korea and the United States. Furthermore, the "Lantern Plan" falls short in addressing critical aspects such as how to manage the refugee crisis that could arise and how to define the new statehood of the reunified Republic of Korea.

On September 3, 2017, approximately five months after the U.S.-China summit, North Korea conducted its sixth nuclear test, detonating a hydrogen bomb with a force equivalent to 250,000 tons of TNT, surpassing the destructive power of the bomb dropped on Hiroshima during World War II by 16 times. During his 11-day Asia tour in early November, President Trump expressed urgency at his fourth stop in Beijing, stating: "Time is quickly running out. We must act fast, and hopefully China will act faster and more effectively on this problem than anyone."[7] However, Xi's response appeared tepid, as he continued to advocate resolving the issue through diplomatic talks.

Additionally, Premier Li Keqiang's statements about China's growing industrial and technological strength, which seemed to downplay the role of the United States, and China's suggestion of the United States serving as a supplier of "raw materials, agricultural products, and energy" for China's industrial production, enraged Trump and his team,[8] contributing significantly to the deterioration of the bilateral relationship thereafter.

China may have misread the U.S. plea for cooperation and the abnormal "Chimerica," a phenomenon called "dependency-reversed" (where China, albeit a semi-peripheral state, used foreign currency reserves accumulated from trade surpluses with the United States to be lent back to the United States, facilitating its continuous imports from China) as signs of U.S. weakness, which China could exploit to advance its geopolitical interests. Meanwhile, Kim Jong Un, rationally fearful of a U.S.-China collusion that might sacrifice North Korea, shrewdly discerned a schism between the two great powers. He was eager to

[7] Sky News, 09/11/2017. https://news.sky.com/story/trump-china-can-fix-north-korea-problem-easily-11119171.

[8] McMaster. H. R. (2020), p. 126.

exploit this division to mitigate the imminent crisis of a possible U.S. military attack. As a result, secret diplomacy set in, leading to the thawing of relations between the two Communist states in late March 2018, following Kim's surprise visit to Beijing. Kim's intensive visits to China in March (25–28), May (7–8), and June (19–20) ostensibly increased North Korea's bargaining position, leading to the failure of U.S.-DPRK summits on June 12 and the following year, concerning DPRK's denuclearization.

Prior to his meeting with Kim in late May, Trump had sensed the delicate change in North Korea's attitude on denuclearization and condemned what he perceived as China's destructive role. He even called Xi Jinping a "world-class poker player" for prompting Kim's about-face after his second China visit. Surprisingly, it was Kim who managed to keep his nuclear program intact by driving a wedge between the two great powers, intensifying their mutual distrust and pushing the fragile U.S.-China trade relations to devolve into a trade war. In fact, this trade war had been brewing since March 2018, but was by no means a linear progression and could have been averted through U.S.-China cooperation over North Korea's denuclearization. However, the intervening changes in trilateral relations between the U.S., China, and North Korea resulted in North Korea emerging as the real "world-class poker player," positioning the country as the sole victor in this geopolitical game and pushing the U.S. trade war into an inevitability.

Trump's Trade War: Reverse the "Dependency-Reversed"

Before ascending to the presidency during his 2016 election campaign, Donald Trump, a populist and radical economic nationalist, attributed U.S. trade disputes with China to the latter's unfair practices, including currency manipulation, intellectual property theft, and limited access for U.S. companies to the Chinese market. He vowed to reduce the U.S. trade deficit by imposing broad punitive tariffs. However, many U.S. economists questioned the effectiveness of a trade war without addressing the fundamental structural issue of "U.S. overspending and China over-saving." Beyond the trade deficit, the rapid rise of China as the second-largest economy, on track to overtake the United States, and its strides in technological advances became primary concerns for the Republican leader. These concerns fueled his natural realist impulse, as demonstrated in the National Security Strategy (NSS) of 2017, where he aimed to change the course of U.S. policy toward China from engagement to competition.[9]

To gain deeper insights into trade war, a comprehensive timeline should be examined, covering actions and counteractions taken by both sides.

Since March 2018, the Sino-U.S. trade conflict has intensified. On March 6, the United States announced plans to impose additional tariffs on steel and aluminum products from China and other countries. Subsequently, on April 3, the U.S. released a list of 25% tariffs on 1,333 Chinese goods valued at $50 billion, citing findings from the Section 301 investigation. Notably, the list covered numerous high-tech fields that were part of China's "Made in China 2025" initiative. China swiftly responded by announcing a list of retaliatory measures. They imposed 25% tariffs on 106 product categories originating from the United States, including soybeans, automobiles, and chemicals. In an immediate countermove, the United States announced plans on April 6 for additional tariffs on $100 billion worth of Chinese goods.

Amidst the escalating tensions, U.S. Treasury Secretary Steven Mnuchin showed apparent disregard for rumors that China might retaliate by dumping U.S. Treasury bonds, expressing absolute indifference.[10] In response, China clarified that it had no intention of reducing its holdings of U.S. treasury bonds.[11] Despite the threat from PRC's Ministry of Commerce (MOFCOM) on the same day (April 6) that "China will fight to the end and will not hesitate to pay any price," the country refrained from making further responses to the United States' additional tariffs.[12]

Not entirely surprising to the outside world, Xi Jinping delivered a speech at the Boao Forum on April 10, proposing to "significantly

[9] Cox, M (2022), p. 143.

[10] "Mnuchin: Not Worried About China Selling Treasurys, 'Lot of Buyers' for US Debt." *CNBC*, 06/04/2018. https://www.cnbc.com/2018/04/06/mnuchin-not-worried-about-china-selling-treasurys-lot-of-buyers-for-U.S.-debt.html.

[11] "China Boosts Its U.S. Treasuries Holdings by Most in Six Months." *Bloomberg*, 16/04/2018. https://www.bloomberg.com/news/articles/2018-04-16/china-boosts-its-u-s-treasuries holdings by most in six months; "China Holdings of U.S. Debt Rose in 2017 by Most in Seven Years." *Bloomberg*, 15/02/2018. https://www.bloomberg.com/news/articles/2018-02-15/china-2017-holdings-of-u-s-treasuries-rise-most-in-seven-years.

[12] On April 6, the spokesperson of the PRC's Ministry of Commerce made a strong statement, saying: "China Will Fight to the End and Will Not Hesitate to Pay Any Price." http://www.mofcom.gov.cn/article/ae/ag/201804/20180402728771.shtml.

relax market access, especially in the finance and auto industry, create a more attractive investment environment, strengthen protection of intellectual property, and actively expand imports." Xi emphasized that these major market access measures would be implemented as soon as possible, prioritizing a faster rather than slower approach.[13] The next day, China's National Development and Reform Commission (NDRC) published an article titled "Promoting Opening up and Expanding Win–Win Cooperation in the New Era," underlining the need to continue introducing foreign investment and expanding imports.[14] On April 17, NDRC announced that the automobile industry would be fully liberalized within five years, and the shipbuilding and aircraft manufacturing industries would completely remove shareholding restrictions on foreign capital within the year.[15]

The official explanation for this near-complete opening of China's economy is that it has transitioned from "prudent and gradual opening" to "voluntary and proactive opening." This shift is aimed at allowing all countries in the world to benefit from China's economic development expressively. This reflects China's strong determination to promote "reform and opening."[16] The Chinese government intends to emphasize that its wider market access decisions are a natural result of China's successful economic development and not a capitulation to pressure from the United States.

In response to Xi's Boao speech, Trump immediately expressed his appreciation on his personal Twitter.[17] Yet U.S. pressure on China continued unabated. On April 11, the United States warned China not to use the depreciation of the renminbi as a means of retaliation, stating that any such action would be met with a strong response.[18] On April 16, the U.S. Department of Commerce announced severe penalties on ZTE,

[13] *Xinhua*, 10/04/2018. http://www.xinhuanet.com/politics/2018-04/10/c_1122659873.htm.

[14] *China News*, 11/04/2018. http://www.chinanews.com/cj/2018/04-11/8488189.shtml.

[15] *Yicai*, 17/04/2018. http://www.yicai.com/news/5415896.html.

[16] The People's Daily (overseas edition), 10/04/2018. http://paper.people.com.cn/rmrbhwb/html/2018-04/10/content_1846827.htm.

[17] https://twitter.com/realdonaldtrump/status/983774270886236161, 10/04/2018.

[18] VOAnews (Chinese), 11/04/2018. https://www.voachinese.com/a/china-devalue-currency-20180411/4342815.html.

prohibiting all U.S. companies from selling parts and components to ZTE within the next seven years.[19] Three days later (April 19), the U.S.-China Economic and Security Review Commission (USCC), a body that significantly influences the administration's China policy, accused ZTE, Huawei, and Lenovo of engaging in industrial espionage in the United States.[20] On the same day, U.S. officials confirmed that the administration would soon launch the International Economic Emergency Powers Act (IEEPA) as an extension of the Section 301 investigation. This act would comprehensively restrict China's investment activities in sensitive fields, such as semiconductors and robotics.[21] With these developments, the motivation of the United States to launch a trade war with China has become increasingly clear.

Robert Manning maintained that: "This U.S.-China tussle is fundamentally about who dominates the industries of the future. We are on the cusp of a technology revolution more transformational than the rise of the internet in the 1990s, what has been dubbed the 4th industrial revolution. It is the melding of the digital and real economy as AI, robotics, Big Data, 3D printing, new materials, and biotech begin to disrupt the economic and social status quo and become key new drivers of economic growth."[22] Independent analyses suggested that the real objective of the U.S.-waged trade war was to prevent China from achieving global technological leadership. The U.S. Trade Representative's (USTR) office had explicitly stated that the administration's strategic aim was to thwart China's ambition to dominate "key strategic technologies," as exemplified by its "Made in China 2025" initiative.[23]

[19] "U.S. Cuts Off China's ZTE from American Tech for Seven Years." *Bloomberg*, 16/04/2018. https://www.bloomberg.com/news/articles/2018-04-16/commerce-blocks-china-s-zte-from-exporting-technology-from-u-s.

[20] USCC report: "Supply Chain Vulnerabilities from China in U.S. Federal Information and Communications Technology." (April 2018), released on 19/04/2018. https://www.uscc.gov/sites/default/files/Research/Interos_Supply%20Chain%20Vulnerabilities%20from%20China%20in%20U.S.%20Federal%20ICT.pdf.

[21] VOAnews (Chinese), 21/04/2018. https://www.voachinese.com/a/U.S.-china-emergency-act-20180421/4358835.html.

[22] Robert Manning: "Xi Must Follow Words with Deeds." *Nikkei Asian Review*, 12/04/2018. https://asia.nikkei.com/Opinion/Xi-must-follow-words-with-deeds2.

[23] "US Tariffs Target China Industrial Policy, Not Trade Deficit." *The Financial Times*, 23/03/2018. https://www.ft.com/content/bd61c23a-2e62-11e8-9b4b-bc4b9f08f381; "The Real Target Is 'Made in China 2025'; Not the U.S.-China Trade Deficit."

In confidential discussions between Chinese and U.S. officials, the United States forthrightly requested that China discontinue the "Made in China 2025" Initiative.[24] The United States expressed significant concerns regarding China's state-driven technological advances, perceiving them not only as a potential challenge to its economic security but also as a threat to the global expansion efforts of American companies. Brad Setser, a senior fellow at the Council on Foreign Relations (CFR), emphasized that the success of the "Made in China 2025" plan could lead China to achieve technological independence in cutting-edge fields such as microchips, large aircraft, electric vehicles, and artificial intelligence. This potential scenario raised concerns that the United States might be left exporting bulk commodities and energy, like soybeans, oil, and natural gas, to China.[25] White House trade adviser Peter Navarro even went so far as to suggest in his published article that China's emergence in the high-tech industry might eventually lead to a military conflict between the two great powers.[26]

In fact, shortly after Trump assumed office, the United States heightened its concern for economic security, elevating it to the status of national security. In December 2017, with the publication of the NSS report, Trump explicitly equated "economic security" with "national security" for the first time.[27] This differed from the view of some Chinese officials, such as Long Yongtu, who firmly believed that "the more open the economy is, the more secure the country is."[28] In contrast, a senior counterintelligence official from the Office of the Director of National

FIS Group Foresights, April 2018. https://www.xponance.com/wp-content/uploads/2018/04/The-Real-Target-is-%E2%80%9CMade-in-China-2025%E2%80%9D-not-the-U.S.-China-Trade-Deficit-1.pdf.

[24] *Nihon Keizai Shimbun*, 23/04/2018.

[25] VOAnews (Chinese), 11/04/2018. https://www.voachinese.com/a/voanews-20180518-zte-china-U.S.-trade-dispute/4399791.html.

[26] "Team Trump seeks to roll back 'Made in China 2025'." *Nikkei Asian Review*, 02/05/2018. https://asia.nikkei.com/Economy/Trade-tensions/Team-Trump-seeks-to-roll-back-Made-in-China-2025.

[27] "Trump Labels China a Strategic 'Competitor'." *The Financial Times*, 18/12/2017. https://www.ft.com/content/215cf8fa-e3cb-11e7-8b99-0191e45377ec.

[28] New Beijing Daily, 10/12/2006. https://finance.qq.com/a/20061210/000064_2.htm.

Intelligence (ODNI) reaffirmed on April 18, 2018: "Our economic security is our national security, and there is no boundary between the two." From this vantage point, preserving the technological advantages of American companies became a top priority to ensure they would not be "eroded" by their adversaries.[29]

Under such national consensus, on May 7, the Armed Services Committee of the U.S. House of Representatives announced the draft of the new National Defense Authorization Act (NDAA), which prohibits government agencies from using "dangerous" technology products produced by Huawei or ZTE.[30] Earlier, on May 4, Secretary of Defense James N. Mattis sent a letter to members of Congress, urging them to expand the power of the Committee on Foreign Investment (CFIUS) in the bill to strengthen the supervision of foreign investment and prevent China from accessing U.S. sensitive technology. On May 22, the House and Senate overwhelmingly passed an amendment giving CFIUS greater oversight authority to ensure that potential foreign investment does not threaten U.S. national security. The additional provisions of the amendment also specifically limit the relaxation of President Trump's sanctions on ZTE.[31]

The sudden arrival of the trade war far exceeded China's expectations, leaving them entirely unprepared for its intensity. Among Chinese elites, there was a pervasive sense of blind optimism that "China-U.S. relations will be neither too good, nor too bad." They appeared to believe that the United States, despite its bluffing, would not engage in a large-scale or long-lasting trade war. This belief was based on the concept of "Chimerica," a relationship where dependency was reverse, keeping America at bay. As such, from February to early March 2018, the Chinese government sent special envoys to the United States twice within

[29] "Securing the Nation's Secrets, Infrastructure, and Democracy: Counterintelligence in the Digital Age," by William Evanina at the Aspen Institute, Director of the National Counterintelligence and Security Center (NCSC), 18/04/2018. https://www.aspeninstitute.org/events/securing-nations-secrets-infrastructure-democracy-counterintelligence-digital-age/.

[30] Deutsche Welle (DW), 08/05/2018. https://www.dw.com/zh/%E7%BE%8E%E6%94%BF%E5%BA%9C%E6%8B%9F%E7%A6%81%E7%94%A8%E5%8D%8E%E4%B8%BA%E4%B8%AD%E5%85%B4-ndaa%E7%BA%B3%E5%85%A5%E5%8F%8D%E4%B8%AD%E6%8E%AA%E6%96%BD/a-43694489?&zhongwen=simp.

[31] VOAnews (Chinese), 11/04/2018. https://www.voachinese.com/a/U.S.-senate-foreign-investment-20180523/4406580.html.

a month, but they returned empty-handed. On March 27, former Finance Minister Lou Jiwei was still talking about the relationship between China and the United States, resembling that of "destined couples" at a domestic forum, believing that China and the United States were destined to be both rivals and partners.

Indications of China's readiness to make grave concessions were discernible toward the end of April 2018, when domestic media received dictate from the CCP's Propaganda Department, banning the discussion of the U.S.-China trade war.[32] Meanwhile, caught off guard by the unprecedented assertiveness of the Trump administration, China had no other option but to play the great-power card. Since April, China launched an intensive diplomatic offensive, attempting to prompt the EU and Japan into taking "joint action" against the "bad example" of protectionism that the United States "does not abide by world trade rules" in order to "maintain the global free trade system centered on the WTO and build an open world economy."[33]

However, both EU and Japan, being America's strategic allies of the United States, firmly stood on the side of the United States. On April 17, the ambassadors of 27 EU countries to China issued a joint letter, strongly criticizing China's "Belt and Road Initiative."[34]

On May 31, trade representatives from the United States, Japan, and the EU met in Paris to address problems caused by "non-market-oriented policies and practices." Targeting China, although in an unspecified way, the "Joint Statement" issued after the meeting stated that they

[32] Asked by an influential domestic online media to write a 'powerful' article analyzing the U.S.-China trade war in mid-April, I spent two weeks' time completing a 10,000-word manuscript. This article, after having 20% of sensitive contents deleted, was scheduled to go online after the May 1st Labor Day as a blockbuster feature. However, on the last day of April, the publisher received an order from the Propaganda Department, and the publication of this article was forced to be aborted.

[33] "China Calls for EU to Oppose US's Protectionism." *RFI*, 06/04/2018. http://cn.rfi.fr/%E4%B8%AD%E5%9B%BD/20180406-%E4%B8%AD%E5%9B%BD%E5%91%BC%E5%90%81%E6%AC%A7%E7%9B%9F%E5%85%B1%E5%90%8C%E5%8F%8D%E5%AF%B9%E7%BE%8E%E5%9B%BD%E7%9A%84%E4%BF%9D%E6%8A%A4%E4%B8%BB%E4%B9%89; Also, "Prime Minister Shinzo Abe Met with Wang Yi." *Xinhua* (Tokyo), 16/04.2018. http://www.xinhuanet.com/world/2018-04/16/c_129851603.htm.

[34] "EU Ambassadors Band Together Against Silk Road." *Handelsblatt Global*, 17/04/2018. https://global.handelsblatt.com/politics/eu-ambassadors-beijing-china-silk-road-912258.

> concurred on the need to deepen and accelerate discussions regarding possible new rules on industrial subsidies and SOEs ... No country should require or pressure technology transfer from foreign companies to domestic companies, including, for example, through the use of joint venture requirements, foreign equity limitations, administrative review and licensing processes, or other means ...The Ministers further agreed to deepen cooperation and exchange of information, including with other like-minded partners, to find effective means to address trade-distorting policies of third countries, including harmful forced technology transfer policies and practices, and where appropriate, to pursue dispute settlement proceedings at the WTO.[35]

On the following day (June 1), the EU filed a complaint against China for the infringement of the intellectual property rights ("unfair technology transfer") of European companies with the WTO.[36]

As always, when facing pressures from the United States, China attempted to counteract them by leveraging its relationship with Europe, relying on an overrated EU-U.S. divide. Despite the "Joint Statement" issued by the Triad (the United States, EU, and Japan) on May 31, China seemed unaware and continued with its strategy. In early July, during bilateral talks, China offered to open certain industries specifically to European investors, aiming to gain their support in joint action against the United States within the WTO. However, this proposal was categorically rejected by the EU. The EU firmly stated its objections to aligning with Beijing against Washington and openly told Chinese negotiators that it endorsed "almost all the complaints" the United States had made, despite having some reservations about the way in which the United States was handling these complaints.[37]

[35] Joint Statement on Trilateral Meeting of the Trade Ministers of the United States, Japan, and the European Union. USTR Press Release, 31/05/2018. https://ustr.gov/about-us/policy-offices/press-office/press-releases/2018/may/joint-statement-trilateral-meeting.

[36] "EU Launches WTO Case Against China's Unfair Technology Transfers." European Commission Press Release, 01/06/2018. https://ec.europa.eu/commission/presscorner/detail/en/IP_18_4027; "EU Takes China to the WTO Over Technology-Transfer Practices." *Bloomberg*, 01/06/2018. https://www.bloomberg.com/news/articles/2018-06-01/europe-takes-china-to-the-wto-over-technology-transfer-practices.

[37] "China Presses Europe for Anti-U.S. Alliance on Trade." *Reuters*, 03/07/2018. https://www.reuters.com/article/U.S.-usa-trade-china-eu-exclusive/exclusive-china-presses-europe-for-anti-u-s-alliance-on-trade-idUSKBN1JT1KT.

On July 15, European Council President Donald Tusk said in Beijing that it was necessary for the WTO to establish new rules on "compulsory technology transfers and industrial subsidies."[38] Two days later (on July 17), the leaders of the EU and Japan signed the "Economic Partnership Agreement" (EPA) in Tokyo, creating the world's largest open trade zone. This agreement covers nearly a third of global GDP, almost 40% of world trade, and more than 600 million people.[39] On July 25, European Commission President Jean-Claude Juncker, during his visit to the United States, issued a joint statement with Trump, declaring their commitment to "work together toward zero tariffs, zero non-tariff barriers, and zero subsidies on non-auto industrial goods." Juncker also assured Trump that he intended to help him address "the China problem."[40]

While trying to divide the United States and its European and Japanese allies, China also attempted to directly appease the United States. On May 19, Chinese and U.S. negotiators reached a consensus after "constructive consultations" in the second round of talks: China promised to purchase a large number of American products and services to significantly reduce the U.S. trade deficit with China. The Chinese government explained this move in its domestic propaganda as its intention to "meet the growing consumption demand of the Chinese people and the requirements of high-quality economic development."

Despite the trade war seemingly calming down, serious differences over a series of structural issues remained.[41] On May 30, the Chinese government announced that starting from July 1, the import duties on daily consumer goods would be drastically lowered to "meet the people's

[38] "EU's Tusk Says the WTO Needs New Rules on Forced Tech Transfers, Subsidies." *Reuters*, 16/07/2018. https://uk.reuters.com/article/uk-china-eu-wto/eU.S.-tusk-says-the-wto-needs-new-rules-on-forced-tech-transfers-subsidies-idUKKBN1K608M.

[39] "EU and Japan Sign Economic Partnership Agreement." European Commission press release, 17/07/2018. https://ec.europa.eu/commission/presscorner/detail/en/IP_18_4526.

[40] "White House's Kudlow says EU Will Help Trump Confront China." *Reuters*, 26/07/2018. https://www.reuters.com/article/U.S.-usa-trade-eu-kudlow/white-houses-kudlow-says-eu-will-help-trump-confront-china-idUSKBN1KG2FF.

[41] "US, China Release Statement Pledging to Tackle Trade Deficit, Boost Investment." International Centre for Trade and Sustainable Development (ICTSD), 24/05/2018. https://www.ictsd.org/bridges-news/bridges/news/U.S.-china-release-statement-pledging-to-tackle-trade-deficit-boost.

needs for a better life and enhance the people's sense of gain and happiness."[42] Subsequently, during the third round of bilateral negotiations held on June 2–3, China proposed to purchase nearly $70 billion of U.S. agricultural products, manufactured products, and energy products, on the condition that the United States renounce imposing tariffs on $50 billion worth of Chinese products.[43] However, the United States remained unmoved.

On June 15, just three days after the conclusion of the U.S.-DPRK summit in Singapore, Trump issued a presidential statement, announcing a 25% import tariff on $50 billion worth of Chinese goods, including products related to the "Made in China 2025" initiative. The sudden decision to toughen its stance was evidently influenced by the latest developments in Northeast Asia, particularly Trump's perception of China as a spoiler in the North Korean nuclear issue.[44]

In response, the Chinese government swiftly announced retaliatory measures, stating that it would impose 25% tariffs on 659 U.S. goods with a total value of $50 billion. On June 18, the White House issued another statement, threatening additional 10% tariffs on $400 billion worth of Chinese goods if China retaliates further.[45] On the same day, the U.S. Senate passed the National Defense Authorization Act for the Fiscal Year 2019, which initially upheld the Department of Commerce's decision to sanction ZTE. Later, after internal consultations, both houses of

[42] Announcement of the Customs Tariff Commission of the State Council, 31/05/2018. http://gss.mof.gov.cn/zhengwuxinxi/zhengcejiedu/201805/t20180531_2914285.html.

[43] "China Offers to Buy Nearly $70 Billion of U.S. Products to Fend Off Trade Tariffs." *The Wall Street Journal*, 05/06/2018. https://www.wsj.com/articles/china-offers-to-buy-nearly-70-billion-of-u-s-farm-and-energy-products-1528208835.

[44] "Donald Trump Calls Xi a 'World Class Poker Player,' Suggesting He Changed North Korea's Mind about Meeting." *Newsweek*, 05/22/2018. https://www.newsweek.com/trump-calls-xi-world-class-poker-player-suggesting-he-changed-north-koreas-939509.

[45] "White House Is Confident It Has an Edge Over China in Trade Dispute—Behind New Tariff Threats Is a Belief the U.S. Has the Upper Hand in Talks, Administration Officials Say." *The Wall Street Journal*, 19/06/2018. https://www.wsj.com/articles/white-house-sees-an-edge-in-trade-dispute-with-china-1529451511.

Congress accepted the administration's alternative handling of the "ZTE incident."[46]

In light of the escalating situation, China made a strategic decision not to announce further countermeasures. Instead, on June 28, both NDRC and MOFCOM released the "Special Management Measures for Foreign Investment Access (Negative List) (2018 Edition)" on their respective websites. These measures represented a radical shift toward liberalization, aiming to "significantly relax market access." Consequently, items on the Negative List were reduced from 63 to 48,[47] and 22 areas (Table 6.1) saw the introduction of opening-up measures, including several key sectors.[48] Notably, these measures allowed foreign investors unprecedented access to China's manufacturing sector, nearly *fully* opening it up to them.[49]

Despite the conciliatory measures taken by China, the United States remained resolute in its decision to initiate a trade war. As planned, at 00:00 on July 6, 2018, the United States imposed tariff sanctions on China, formally marking the commencement of the Sino-U.S. trade war. During the period from July to August, two U.S. economists, including the former chairman of the White House Council of Economic Advisers, Kevin Hassett, openly advocated China's expulsion from the WTO, without necessitating the United States to withdraw from the organization altogether. Their rationale behind this call was that China was not operating as a market economy and was exploiting loopholes in the WTO, which they deemed to be the fundamental issue.[50]

[46] "Faced With Crippling Sanctions, ZTE Loaded Up on Lobbyists." *The New York Times*, 02/08/2018. https://www.nytimes.com/2018/08/01/us/politics/zte-sanctions-lobbying.html?_ga=2.115826182.1654109200.1533382156-151414152.1526545259.

[47] https://www.ndrc.gov.cn/xxgk/zcfb/fzggwl/201806/W020190905495140644002.pdf (NDRC); http://images.mofcom.gov.cn/wzs/201806/20180628220738627.pdf (MOFCOM).

[48] Yicai, 01/07/2018.

[49] Promoting opening up to the outside world with greater efforts—Relevant person in charge of the National Development and Reform Commission answers reporters' questions on the 2018 special management measures (Negative List) for foreign investment access. Released by NDRC on 29/06/2018. https://www.ndrc.gov.cn/xxgk/jd/jd/201806/t20180629_1182699.html.

[50] "White House Economist Says We may have to Kick China out of WTO." *Breitbart*, 13/08/2018. https://www.breitbart.com/politics/2018/08/13/white-house-economist-says-we-may-have-to-kick-china-out-of-wto/.

Table 6.1 China's Negative List (2018)

1	Remove the restriction that only the Chinese party can control the breeding of new varieties of crops other than wheat and corn and the production of seeds
2	Eliminate the restriction that the exploration and mining of special and scarce coal must be controlled by the Chinese party
3	Lift the restrictions on foreign investment in graphite exploration and mining
4	Abolish the limitations on rare earth smelting and separation, which were previously limited to joint ventures and cooperation, and cancel the restrictions on foreign investment in tungsten smelting
5	By 2018, cancel the restrictions on the proportion of foreign capital in the manufacture of special-purpose vehicles and new energy vehicles. By 2020, remove the restrictions on the proportion of foreign capital in commercial vehicles. By 2022, cancel the restrictions on the proportion of foreign capital in passenger vehicles and the limit of no more than two joint ventures
6	Remove the requirement that the design, manufacture, and repair of ships (including sections) must be controlled by the Chinese party
7	Lift the restriction that the design, manufacture, and maintenance of mainline and regional aircraft, helicopters weighing 3 tons and above, ground and water surface effect aircraft, as well as the design and manufacture of unmanned aerial vehicles and aerostats must be controlled by Chinese parties
8	Remove the restriction that the design, manufacture, and maintenance of general aircraft are limited to joint ventures and cooperation
9	Manufacturing of weapons and ammunition is not subject to the Negative List
10	Cancel the restriction that the construction and operation of the power grid must be controlled by the Chinese party
11	Abolish the restriction that the construction and operation of the main railway network must be controlled by the Chinese party
12	Remove the requirement that railway passenger transportation companies must be controlled by Chinese parties
13	Eliminate the restriction that international maritime transport companies are limited to joint ventures and cooperation
14	Lift the restriction that international shipping agencies must be controlled by the Chinese party
15	Allow foreign investment in the purchase and wholesale of rice, wheat, and corn without restrictions
16	Remove the restriction that the same foreign investor can have no more than 30 branches, and that the construction and operation of chain gas stations selling different types and brands of refined oil from multiple suppliers must be controlled by the Chinese party

(continued)

Table 6.1 (continued)

17	Abolish the shareholding ratio restriction on foreign investors in Chinese-funded banks, allowing single shareholding not exceeding 20%, and total shareholding not exceeding 25%
18	In 2018, securities companies and securities investment fund management companies transitioned from Chinese holdings to foreign-owned shares of no more than 51%. By 2021, the restriction on the proportion of foreign capital will be lifted
19	In 2018, futures companies were changed from Chinese holdings to foreign shareholding ratios of no more than 51%. By 2021, the restriction on the proportion of foreign capital will be lifted
20	In 2018, the foreign ownership ratio in life insurance companies was relaxed from 50 to 51%. By 2021, the restriction on the proportion of foreign capital will be lifted
21	Remove the restriction that surveying and mapping companies must be controlled by Chinese parties
22	Lift the regulations prohibiting foreign investment in Internet access service business premises

Source NDRC website (29/06/2018): https://www.ndrc.gov.cn/fggz/lywzjw/wstz/201806/t20180629_1046379.html

The United States entering into the trade war not only demystified the so-called "dependency-reversed," a phenomenon many people in the West and even in China had taken for granted, but also shattered the semblance of China being an economic superpower capable of inflicting symmetrical damage to the United States. China's substantial weakness in retaliatory capacity highlighted the much greater gap vis-à-vis the United States in hard power, particularly in innovation capabilities. This rendered China's high-tech sectors powerless to withstand U.S. export controls on key high-tech inputs, the denial of which could stymie China's technological development, as already demonstrated in the case of ZTE, which almost went bankrupt under U.S. sanctions. Despite the "paper tiger" exposé by the U.S.-waged trade war, among many good-sensed Chinese citizens, continued underestimation of the U.S. resolve and capacity to force China into submission through the trade war led the Chinese regime to cling to the belief that "China has the conditions, ability, and confidence to win this battle of *defending* free trade."[51]

[51] Ta Kung Pao, 07/07/2018. http://www.takungpao.com/finance/236135/2018/0707/184771.html.

Disregarding the Trump administration's unwavering determination not to back down in the trade war, Beijing would soon feel the intense repercussions. President Trump, along with his White House chief strategist Steve Bannon, vowed to cripple Beijing's delaying tactics and unleash an "unprecedentedly large" and "unbearably painful" trade war on China. Trump's ultimate goal was not merely to address China's "unfair trade practices" but also to "reindustrialize America" by frustrating China's "Made in China 2025" initiative, which aimed to build up the nation's own supply chain.[52] This strategic move was a crucial part of the Trump administration's four-pronged approach to the trade war with China. Firstly, the sheer magnitude of the proposed $500 billion trade war caught Beijing completely off guard. Secondly, the U.S. would employ Section 301 to force Beijing into revising its economic system, which currently required U.S. companies to transfer technology. Thirdly, the United States sought to retain the ability to sever the supply chain with China. And finally, the United States vigilantly monitored China's capital outflows, especially those of high-ranking corrupt officials. These officials, by transferring their assets to Western democracies and circumventing China's strict control over private capital flight, revealed their lack of confidence in China's economy, despite their verbal claims about the nation's economic success.[53]

This strategy appeared to be yielding results as the United States engaged in a series of alternating pauses and resumptions of punitive taxation on China. On May 1, 2019, negotiators from both countries concluded the tenth-round trade talks and reached an agreement in

[52] "Exclusive: 'Trump Won't Back Down': US President Plans to Make Trade War Unbearable for China and Bigger Than Ever, Steve Bannon Says." *South China Morning Post*, 21/09/2018. https://www.scmp.com/news/china/diplomacy/article/2165185/trump-wont-back-down-U.S.-president-plans-make-trade-war.

[53] Sasha Gong's Tweets, 28/08/2018. The full text of Sasha Gong's exclusive interview with Steve Bannon can be found on *Ming Pao* (Hong Kong), 19/09/2018. https://news.mingpao.com/pns/%e5%9c%8b%e9%9a%9b/article/20180919/s00014/1537295686959/%e7%8f%ad%e8%be%b2-%e4%b8%ad%e7%be%8e%e8%b2%bf%e6%98%93%e6%88%b0%e5%bf%85%e7%84%b6%e6%89%93%e5%88%b0%e5%ba%95-%e6%89%ad%e8%bd%89%e9%80%86%e5%b7%ae%e7%82%ba%e6%94%bf%e7%ad%96%e6%a0%b8%e5%bf%83-%e3%80%8c%e7%89%b9%e6%9c%97%e6%99%ae%e5%b0%8d%e8%8f%af%e5%a7%8b%e7%b5%82%e5%a6%82%e4%b8%80%e3%80%8d; https://www.secretchina.com/news/gb/2018/09/21/871498.html.

which, as Michael Pillsbury recalled later, China agreed to "almost everything."[54] The extensive near-150-page document with seven chapters included "binding legal language" that required China to make changes to its domestic laws to ensure verifiable compliance with its commitments. This approach was taken to prevent China from making empty promises, a lesson learned from previous dealings with the country, as stated by U.S. trade representative Robert Lighthizer.[55]

However, two days later, the draft agreement was unexpectedly reversed, reportedly by Chinese President Xi Jinping. A revised text was sent back to Washington, and the United States discovered that China had rescinded its commitments to amend the laws addressing the core issues that had triggered the initiation of the trade war by the United States. These issues included the theft of U.S. intellectual property and trade secrets, forced technology transfer, competition policy, access to financial services, and currency manipulation.[56] In response to this setback, Trump announced on May 6 through his Twitter account that the tariffs on $200 billion worth of Chinese goods would be increased from 10 to 25%, and the new tariff rate would take effect on May 11.[57] This escalation further intensified the trade tensions between the two nations.

On May 13, China's chief negotiator, Vice-Premier Liu He, outlined three core concerns that China believed must be addressed for a successful trade deal. Firstly, China insisted on the complete removal of all additional tariffs. These tariffs were the initial trigger of the ongoing trade dispute between the two countries and would need to be fully revoked for any agreement to be reached. Secondly, China emphasized that the volume of purchases agreed upon during previous negotiations should be realistic and not subject to random changes. Both sides had reached a consensus on purchase volumes during talks in Argentina, and China

[54] "Trump Delays New Tariffs; Expert Claims Secret China Agreement Is Ready to Go." *Fox Business*, 11/09/2019. https://www.foxbusiness.com/politics/secret-150-page-china-trade-agreement-is-ready-to-go-expert-claims.

[55] "Exclusive: China Backtracked on Almost All Aspects of U.S. Trade Deal—Sources." Reuters, 08/05.2019. https://www.reuters.com/article/U.S.-usa-trade-china-backtracking-exclusiv-idINKCN1SE0WJ.

[56] "Exclusive: China Backtracked on Almost All Aspects of U.S. Trade Deal—Sources." *Reuters*, 08/05/2019. https://www.reuters.com/article/U.S.-usa-trade-china-backtracking-exclusiv-idUSKCN1SE0WJ.

[57] Trump's tweet on 05/05/2019. https://twitter.com/realDonaldTrump/status/1125069835044573186.

wanted to maintain that agreement. The third concern raised by China was the need for improved balance in the wording of the text in the trade agreement. China emphasized that each country has its dignity, and the text must be balanced and fair. China sought more discussions on critical issues to achieve this balance.[58]

These points, particularly emphasizing the "balance of text," indicated China's willingness to yield to America's demands but in a face-saving manner. On May 17, the *People's Daily* issued a commentary article vehemently denying the U.S. charges of China's "forced technology transfer" as an "ungrounded accusation." The rebuttal asserted that technological cooperation between U.S. and Chinese corporations was voluntary and autonomous. U.S. firms willingly came to China, driven by the pursuit of maximizing their interests, and there was no evidence of forced technology transfer.[59]

Surprisingly, the commentary made no mention of the fact that forced technology transfer was recognized as *legitimate* policy space under the WTO's TRIMs agreement. China's silence on this matter can be attributed partly to ignorance of WTO rules and, more importantly, to their commitment to abandon this aspect of economic sovereignty in the bilateral agreement with the United States during China's WTO accession in November 1999. Revisiting this fact might damage the image of the Party as a defender of China's national interests. Instead, the commentary chose to underscore China's recent legislation on foreign investment two months earlier, in March, which explicitly prohibits "forced technology transfer by administrative means."

On May 29, the *People's Daily* published an editorial titled "The U.S. Should Not Underestimate China's Countermeasures," employing the diplomatic term "Don't say you haven't been forewarned." In this piece, China issued a warning to the United States, indicating its intention to use rare earths as a weapon to retaliate against what it perceived as unwarranted suppression from the United States. The editorial emphatically stated that the United States had miscalculated its ability to manipulate the global supply chain and cautioned against underestimating China's

[58] "Chinese Vice Premier Urges China-US Cooperation, Vows No Compromise on Major Principles." SCIO (State Council Information Office of the PRC), 13/05/2019. http://english.scio.gov.cn/internationalexchanges/2019-05/13/content_74777535.htm.

[59] The *People's Daily*, 19/05/2019.

resolve to safeguard its developmental interests.[60] However, this editorial failed to adequately elucidate the elements that constitute China's "developmental interests" and the precise methods for their "safeguarding." China's voluntary and significant market concessions, as exemplified by the Negative List (2018), appeared to signal a renunciation of these interests rather than a genuine effort to safeguard them.

One month later, on June 30, NDRC and MOFCOM jointly released the Negative List (2019 Edition), further reducing the number of restricted items from 48 to 40. This involved loosening or removing restrictions on foreign investment in seven major sectors within China. Foreign investment outside the Negative List would be managed in accordance with the principle of "equal treatment" between domestic and foreign investment and granted national treatment. All regions and departments were prohibited from independently setting access restrictions on foreign investment in fields not on the Negative List.[61]

Furthermore, the Negative List on foreign investment in China's free trade zones was also updated, reducing restrictive items from 45 in 2018 to 37.[62] These liberalizing measures were not indicative of China's adherence to the concept of "neomercantilism," but rather marked a continued departure from it. The radical Free Trade Zone experiment in Shanghai was exactly what the United States had hoped for, which, in Michael Pillsbury's words, "behave with an open market the way President Trump wants all of China to do."[63] This stood in sharp contrast to the Trump administration's overt embrace of economic nationalism, ironically echoing a misunderstood image of China.[64]

[60] The *People's Daily*, 29/05/2019. http://world.people.com.cn/n1/2019/0529/c1002-31107670.html.

[61] Xinhua, 30/06/2019. https://m.21jingji.com/article/20190630/herald/07902674ef00eee2589c80509d66ed6e.html; https://www.zhonglun.com/Content/2019/07-01/1511390311.html.

[62] Securities Daily, 11/11/2019. http://finance.people.com.cn/fund/n1/2019/1111/c1004-31447983.html.

[63] "Trump Delays New Tariffs; Expert Claims Secret China Agreement Is Ready to Go." *Fox Business*, 11/09/2019. https://www.foxbusiness.com/politics/secret-150-page-china-trade-agreement-is-ready-to-go-expert-claims.

[64] "Steve Bannon Went to Hong Kong for His First Big Post-White House Speech and Sounded Surprisingly Nice to China." *Business Insider*, 12/09/2017. https://www.businessinsider.com/steve-bannon-hong-kong-speech-china-economy-2017-9?r=US&IR=T.

China took these actions, anticipating that they would divide the Republican and Democrat parties on trade policies toward China. Additionally, China aimed to incentivize U.S. businesses with stakes in China to lobby on its behalf and end the trade war as early as possible. Ironically, despite being depicted as a neomercantilist state, China's elites were true believers in free trade. They sought to leverage this belief to outmaneuver their American adversaries and mitigate the impacts of a trade war that their economy could hardly afford.

During the initial negotiation days in Washington, China's chief negotiator, Deputy Premier Liu He, chose to meet with "free traders" on Capitol Hill instead of the Treasury Department or the White House. Steve Bannon viewed these "free traders" as having a "soft gauzy notion" of Adam Smith's free trade, lacking an understanding of the CCP's nature as "a gangster organization running a totalitarian mercantilist state." As a devout economic nationalist, Bannon ridiculed Liu He for being a "cheerleader of globalization and free trade," believing that such views would please Wall Street corporatists who might act as lobbyists on China's behalf.[65]

However, Chinese elites failed to recognize that these tactics were losing effectiveness as a bipartisan consensus emerged, positioning China as America's most significant long-term strategic challenge, solidified by increasing populism in American politics. China's anticipation of a "friendly White House" during the 2020 campaign year, as Bannon saw it, would prove to be misplaced.[66] Trump's distain for pro-Beijing "global corporatists" also made it difficult for the Chinese regime to influence U.S.-China policy.

U.S. China-hand elites were well aware that "China is not the primary cause of the devastation of the rust belt and rural America, increasing economic inequality, social injustice, the federal deficit, the legitimization of anger as the engine of American politics, or America's declining

65 "Steve Bannon: New Film On Huawei—"Claws of the Red Dragon", Hong Kong Protest & US China Trade War." Steve Bannon interviewed by American Thought Leaders—*The Epoch Time*, 25/09/2019. https://www.youtube.com/watch?v=uCrpSK5r9HY.

66 "Exclusive: Don't Wait for a Friendly White House, Steve Bannon tells China." *SCMP*, 23/05/2019. https://www.scmp.com/news/china/diplomacy/article/3011188/dont-wait-friendly-white-house-steve-bannon-tells-china.

competitiveness. That's on us."[67] However, placing the blame on China for all these misfortunes would not only assist Trump in winning the election but also justify his trade war with China, framing it as a pretext for establishing a "Fortress America," with the belief that doing so would make America great again.

In other words, the raison d'être of "Fortress America" lies in the perceived China's state capitalism that builds up China's strength at the expense of the United States. Therefore, a "Fortress China," as an extension of China's state capitalism, must be dismantled to ensure U.S. absolute national security.

In the realm of U.S.-China experts, whether they aligned with or opposed the trade war and the concept of decoupling from China, few displayed sympathy for the idea of a "Fortress China." Even prior to the ascent of President Trump, renowned China expert Henry Paulson offered advice to China, advocating the persistence of efforts to open up domestic markets, further privatize SOEs, and enable foreign companies to operate unhindered within China's borders. Experts like Henry Paulson, who were well-versed in American economic history, recognized the pivotal role played by the American state in "fostering national industrial development. Paulson argued that nurturing the private sector and attracting foreign investments would foster healthy competition, stimulate demand, and ultimately bolster China's economy."[68]

As a former Wall Street investment banker, it was only natural for Paulson to prescribe a neoliberal approach. His vision of dismantling a virtually non-existent "Fortress China" strongly resonated with numerous Chinese intellectual elites. Their aversion to economic nationalism led them to align not with the pseudo-nationalist, but practically economically globalist Chinese regime, but with the economically nationalist Republican administration led by Trump.

Ironically, many of these elites became ardent Trump supporters, believing he would emerge as a formidable adversary to Xi Jinping and employ all means to counter him. They chose to disregard Trump's various anti-democratic statements and amicable gestures toward autocratic leaders in Russia and China. They stubbornly perceived Trump as the "chief coercer" (*zong daobishi*, 总倒逼师) of much-needed economic

[67] Ibid.

[68] Paulson, H. M. (2015), pp. 82, 313, 348.

reforms in China, guided by neoliberal principles. Consequently, they turned a blind eye to the concept of "Fortress America," accepting it as a rationale solely because it was a product of American democracy, particularly associated with Trump. This phenomenon mirrors the 1980s' trend of "idolizing anything foreign" (*chongyangmeiwai*), with the only difference being that they now idolize anything Trumpian.

They supported Trump's trade war with China as a just cause. An influential liberal intellectual, Bao Tong, who once served as the top secretary to the deposed General Secretary Zhao Ziyang, articulated this viewpoint: "It must be done in accordance with what the United States proposes! Domineering? Not overbearing. What the United States proposes is what the United States itself has actually achieved. The United States does not employ tariff barriers, high subsidies, exchange rate manipulation, intellectual property theft, or forced technology transfer ... The United States simply seeks reciprocity, which implies fairness and mutual benefit."[69]

It is worth noting that Bao Tong appeared to be unaware of or chose not to address a question posed by one of his tweet's followers. This question pointed out that America had, in fact, been the "mother of protectionism," with its industries thriving under protective barriers for nearly a century. Furthermore, the follower referenced Jack Werner's *Foreign Policy* article from three months earlier, which explored true American economic history. This article suggested that in the late 18th and early 19th centuries, America had "enthusiastically engaged in smuggling and theft of cutting-edge production techniques from Great Britain."[70] Bao Tong remained silent and did not provide a response.

In the end, the Chinese regime found itself sandwiched by an assertive American hegemonic power and a substantial array of elites within and outside the nomenklatura system, pressing it to further compradorize the economy.

China's isolation was exacerbated by its unsuccessful diplomatic endeavors to obstruct the "trilateral reform proposal" sponsored by the Triad (the United States, the EU, and Japan). This proposal sought to reshape the rules of the WTO in a manner perceived as more "anti-developmental." It aimed to curtail the already shrinking "policy space"

[69] Bao Tong's tweet: 15/11/2018. https://twitter.com/baotong1932/status/1062900355896242176.

[70] Werner, J (2019): "China Is Cheating at a Rigged Game." *Foreign Policy*, August 8.

available to member countries. On May 23, 2019, amid the complexities of the U.S.-China trade war, the Triad openly announced their intention to propose more stringent regulations concerning industrial subsidies and state-owned enterprises to other members of the WTO.[71] Although not explicitly naming China, this move was primarily directed at China, which was viewed as the "most successful state capitalist" model for the Global South. The objective was to undermine China's "Made in China 2025" initiative, in which state subsidies played a pivotal role.

China's ultimate submission, or yielding, is just a matter of time, facilitated by an ever-decelerating economy, which began in 2014 when the Chinese leadership euphemized it as the "New Normal." Similar to the pre-Gorbachev Soviet Union, genuine economic data was a top secret of the party state, accessible only to Politburo Standing Committee members. In 2018, another gloomy year unfolded, with nominal GDP growth not matching the official statistics' claim of 6.5%, but rather hovering around 1.6% or even negative, as revealed by outspoken economist Professor Xiang Songzuo of the Renmin University of China.[72]

The ongoing trade war with the United States further pressed down the economy, with the official growth rate at 6.1% in 2019. On July 20, the State Council declared 11 financial liberalization measures. In late July, the Chinese leadership's eagerness to end the trade war as soon as possible was unveiled by another Renmin University Professor in International Relations, Jin Canrong, who is well-informed and closely connected with within-system elites, yet infamous for his ultra-pro-regime position. Jin spoke confidently, predicting that a trade agreement might be struck in November. He stated that the Party Center was prepared to make significant concessions to the United States at the forthcoming APEC meeting to reach a trade agreement. The decision was based on three major considerations (below). According to Jin, Trump, a typical businessperson pursuing real interests, was expected to reach a deal in which

[71] "U.S, EU, Japan Seek to Complete Text on Subsidies to Rein in China." *Reuters*, 23/05/2019. https://uk.sports.yahoo.com/news/u-eu-japan-seek-complete-text-subsidies-rein-141708097--finance.html.

[72] Xiang Songzuo: "The Pitiful State of the Chinese Economy." 21/021/2019. https://www.asianews.it/news-en/Xiang-Songzuo:-The-pitiful-state-of-the-Chinese-economy-46023.html.

he would obtain 80% of what he wanted, which also marked the limit of what China could concede[73]:

1. Worries that an unending trade war will lead to the withdrawal of all medium-to-high-end industrial chains from China, which would be detrimental to China's future development.
2. The importance of ending the trade war as soon as possible to restore domestic confidence.
3. The recognition that a general stabilization of Sino-U.S. relations is crucial to China's economic development.

Yet tensions flared up once more following the resumption of trade talks in late June. On August 5, the United States officially labeled China as a "currency manipulator." Subsequently, on August 23, President Trump issued a directive to all U.S. companies, instructing them to explore alternatives to China by relocating their manufacturing operations back to the United States.[74]

By mid-September, there appeared to be a "significant success" as Trump, upon Liu He's request, announced a two-week delay in implementing increased tariffs on China, postponing them from October 1 to October 15. This gesture was made in recognition of China's celebration of National Day on October 1 and as an acknowledgment of concessions made by China. Trump wisely refrained from highlighting these concessions and maintained a discreet stance regarding other negotiation discussions. Both sides took measures to ensure that no leaks occurred during the negotiations. Michael Pillsbury, Trump's most trusted China expert, expressed optimism that a deal could be reached in October, especially since a draft of the 150-page agreement was already in place.[75]

On October 29, MOFCOM reiterated China's commitment to not impose forced technology transfer and announced the removal of all restrictive measures not included in the "Negative List." Additionally,

[73] Jin Canrong's Internal Remarks at a Private Meeting with a Group of Elite Entrepreneurs in Shanghai, 27/07/2019. https://user.guancha.cn/main/content?id=152749&s=fwrmhtycwz.

[74] "Trump Orders US Companies to Find an Alternative to China—Trump Wants Manufacturing Brought Back to the US." *Politico*, 23/08/2019. https://www.politico.eu/article/donald-trump-trade-orders-U.S.-companies-to-find-an-alternative-to-china/.

[75] Fox Business, 11/09/2019.

China pledged to accelerate the opening up of its financial industry by removing business scope restrictions on foreign-funded banks, securities companies, and fund management companies. These measures aimed to ensure stable foreign investment and create a transparent and predictable investment environment. To further demonstrate their commitment to economic liberalization, China released a draft of a new foreign investment law and issued a new rule to streamline the approval process, both of which will take effect next year.[76]

On November 6, Xi Jinping declared 5-point measures to widen China's market access, signaling the government's determination to foster a more open and inclusive business environment. On November 14, the Ministry of Agriculture announced the lifting of poultry import restrictions, further aligning with efforts to promote trade and enhance market access.

By December, "anti-American" propaganda was urgently halted on China's main mouthpieces. The *People's Daily* issued an editorial titled "Rationality is the Basis for Maintaining Sino-US Relations,"[77] emphasizing common interests and signaling China's aversion to further confrontation with the United States. These developments strongly suggest an imminent grand deal in the making. On December 12, Trump tweeted confidently: "Getting VERY close to a BIG DEAL with China. They want it, and so do we!".[78]

The following day (December 13), negotiators from both countries reached an agreement on the proposed text. This news shocked many people in China, who had dismissed the possibility of their country accepting a deal containing so many harsh and humiliating terms, considering it a matter of national dignity. News about the contents of the text swiftly circulated back to China, spreading widely on social media. Wu Qiang, an independent political scientist residing in Beijing, observed that during the week before the agreement was reached, the atmosphere in Beijing indicated that the top leadership had entered a state of "collapse." They appeared shocked and flustered, facing an atmosphere where

[76] VOAnews (Mandarin), 30/10/2019. https://www.voachinese.com/a/china-investment-trade-security-technology/5144429.html.

[77] The People's Daily, 09/12/2019. http://www.xinhuanet.com/world/2019-12/09/c_1125324755.htm.

[78] Trump's Tweet on 12/12/2019. https://twitter.com/realDonaldTrump/status/1205134155853574145.

"great historical compromises" had to be made. Wu Qiang concluded that Beijing had failed to "win" the trade war as they had boasted, only gaining some temporary relief from economic difficulties. Moreover, they had to prepare for a decoupling with the United States in educational, scientific, and military exchanges, and the regime seemed willing to pay any price to avert a trade and economic decoupling.[79]

Wu Qiang's observation resonated with that of Arthur Waldron, a famous conservative China expert at the University of Pennsylvania. After being briefed by one of Xi Jinping's close aides on the failing of the Communist system, Waldron believed that China was in the very stage of disintegration, something that might not be immediately visible.[80]

The Phase One Agreement was eventually signed one month later, on January 15, 2020. In the 91-page agreement, almost unilateral concessions made by China found their expression in 151 places where "China shall…" was stipulated. On the other hand, the United States was stipulated "The United States shall…" in only five places, including two places where both "The United States and China shall…" take specific actions. The Agreement, to be "implemented right down to every detail,"[81] weakens the WTO's dispute settlement mechanism, as disputes under the Agreement would not be submitted to any third party for arbitration, but rather resolved through three-round bilateral talks. If the United States decided to take action, China could not counteract and nor could it sue the United States in the WTO unless China chose to exit from the Agreement.[82]

[79] VOA Program "Dialogue on Hot Topics," 13/12/2019. https://www.voachinese.com/a/voaweishi-20191213-proandcon-trump-reported-to-delay-new-tariffs-on-chinese-goods/5204666.html.

[80] "The Chinese Communist Regime Is on the Brink of 'Disintegration,' Says Leading China Expert." *The Epoch Times*, 11/12/2019 (updated). https://www.theepochtimes.com/china/the-chinese-communist-regime-is-on-the-brink-of-disintegration-says-leading-china-expert-3167543.

[81] "No Date Set for U.S.-China 'Phase Two' Talks, Lighthizer Says." *Bloomberg*, 15/12/2019. https://www.bloomberg.com/news/articles/2019-12-15/no-date-set-for-u-s-china-phase-two-talks-lighthizer-says#xj4y7vzkg.

[82] "U.S.-China Deal Could Upend the Way Nations Settle Disputes—New Approach Is a 'Finger in the Eye' to the World Trade Organization and Its Methods." *The Wall Street Journal*, 16/01/2020. https://www.wsj.com/articles/u-s-china-deal-could-upend-the-way-nations-settle-disputes-11579211598.

The terms sufficed to compel the Chinese regime to adopt a low-key approach to this event, and for the first time, they had to seriously confront the prospect of decoupling after the "relief period." This situation was even more precarious than the post-Tiananmen period in 1989. This "unseen change" ran counter to the optimistic assertions made twice by Xi Jinping in the past two years (December 2017 and June 2018) that "China is currently in the best period of development since modern times, and the world is undergoing profound changes unseen in a century."[83] Xi had envisioned the coming of a multipolar world with power transitioning from the West to non-West, specifically from the United States to China, which he believed was becoming an "irreversible megatrend."

In parallel to the conclusion of the Phase One Agreement, the Triad (the United States, the EU, and Japan) reached a consensus on new rules on the previous day (January 14). These rules stated that "unconditionally prohibited subsidies have to be added to the WTO Agreement on Subsidies and Countervailing Measures," addressing an outstanding issue that had been "left out of the Phase One Agreement."[84] The Triad, seemingly using China as the reference point, also discussed possible core rules to prevent forced technology transfer practices of third countries and emphasized the necessity of "burden-shifting should be reversed."[85] These new rule-makings indicated an illusory deglobalization. Instead, a more radical neoliberal hyperglobalization was underway, primarily due to China's willingness or unwillingness to compromise its critical "developmental interests," which were repeatedly enunciated by the CCP regime and called for respect from the United States.

It is ironic that, in undermining not only its own developmental interests but also those of the entire developing world, China found itself unable to reverse the "irreversible megatrend" where it was being treated

[83] Xinhua, 28/12/2018; Xinhua, 23/06/2018.

[84] "US, EU and Japan Take Aim at China with Proposed WTO Rules Targeting State Subsidies." *SCMP*, 15/01/2020; "Trade Trilateral Targets China's Industrial Subsidies." CSIS (Center for Strategic Studies) report, 22/01/2020. https://www.csis.org/analysis/trade-trilateral-targets-chinas-industrial-subsidies.

[85] "EU, U.S. and Japan Agree on new ways to strengthen global rules on industrial subsidies." Directorate-General for Trade, 14/01/2020. https://policy.trade.ec.europa.eu/news/eu-U.S.-and-japan-agree-new-ways-strengthen-global-rules-industrial-subsidies-2020-01-14_en.

as a "developed country," no longer eligible for the myriad trade privileges accorded only to developing nations. On February 10, the USTR updated its list of developing and least-developed countries under U.S. Countervailing Duties (CVD) law, removing China from the list.[86]

The Phase One Agreement received criticism from the EU, which deemed it as giving U.S. firms an advantage in forcing China to buy more from the United States. This, in turn, had an impact on the competitiveness and jobs of EU countries. EU Trade Commissioner Phil Hogan went so far as to call the trade pact a "managed-trade outcome," and he believed that the deal could violate WTO rules, justifying the prospective EU's legal challenge.[87] Nevertheless, the discord with the United States prompted the EU, much like what had happened in 2000, to reach a similar accord with China known as the Comprehensive Agreement on Investment (CAI) by the end of 2020.[88]

The Trump administration went ahead with its unilateral approach, ignoring even wider skepticism from global institutions, in which the United States has enduringly wielded immense rule-making power. In September, the WTO issued a panel report indicating that the U.S. unilateral actions to "combat China's widespread and damaging theft of American technology and intellectual property" were "inconsistent with WTO rules." The USTR rejected this report, arguing that it failed to stop China's misbehavior and highlighting the necessity for the organization's reform.[89]

[86] "USTR Updates List of Developing and Least-Developed Countries Under U.S. CVD Law." USTR press release, 10/02/2020. https://ustr.gov/about-us/policy-offices/press-office/press-releases/2020/february/ustr-updates-list-developing-and-least-developed-countries-under-U.S.-cvd-law.

[87] "Europe Threatens Legal Challenge to U.S.-China Trade Pact at WTO." *Bloomberg*, 16/01/2020. https://www.bloomberg.com/news/articles/2020-01-16/europe-threatens-legal-challenge-to-u-s-china-trade-pact-at-wto?leadSource=uverify%20wall.

[88] "EU Trade Commissioner Phil Hogan Criticises U.S.-China Phase One Trade Deal." *SCMP*, 17/01/2020. https://www.scmp.com/news/world/europe/article/3046460/eu-review-U.S.-china-deal-any-wto-challenge-says-trade-commissioner.

[89] "WTO Report on US Action Against China Shows Necessity for Reform." USTR press release, 15/09/2020. https://ustr.gov/about-us/policy-offices/press-office/press-releases/2020/september/wto-report-U.S.-action-against-china-shows-necessity-reform.

The Coming of the New Cold War: A Foregone Conclusion?

U.S.-China relations did not improve despite the signing of the trade pact, but instead continued to worsen, especially after the United States removed China from the list of developing countries. The outbreak of the COVID-19 pandemic since late November 2019 and its rapid global spread led to a flurry of accusations exchanged between the United States and China regarding the origin of the deadly virus. China was also accused of intentionally concealing information about the pandemic and providing misinformation about the transmissibility of the virus, which even misled the World Health Organization, resulting in the United States withdrawing from the organization in early July. Furthermore, China's control over the production of medical goods raised concerns among developed countries about the need to recreate supply chains domestically for national security reasons.

A reconfiguration of the global supply chain unnerved the Chinese regime as COVID-19 was set to plunge the global economy into the worst recession since World War II, accompanied by a sharp contraction of merchandise trade. China's GDP declined by 6.8% in the first quarter of 2000, the largest drop since 1978, leading to a surge in unemployment. According to a survey by Peking University, the jobless rate in the first half of the year rose to 15% (with an additional 5% being semi-unemployed), implying that around 100 million people in China's 700-million-strong workforce were jobless.[90] In response, Premier Li Keqiang called for greater economic opening to "stabilize foreign trade and investment."[91] On June 23, NDRC and MOFCOM once again simultaneously issued the Negative List (2020 version), in which restricted items were reduced from 40 to 33; the Negative List for Free Trade Zones decreased from 37 to 30, respectively.[92]

[90] "Unofficial survey shows that there are more than 100 million unemployed people in China due to the epidemic." *RFI*, 19/12/2020. https://www.rfi.fr/cn/%E4%B8%AD%E5%9B%BD/20201219-%E9%9D%9E%E5%AE%98%E6%96%B9%E8%B0%83%E6%9F%A5%E6%8C%87%E4%B8%AD%E5%9B%BD%E7%96%AB%E6%83%85%E4%B8%8B%E6%9C%89%E8%BF%87%E4%BA%BF%E5%A4%B1%E4%B8%9A%E4%BA%BA%E5%8F%A3.

[91] Reuters, 24/04/2020.

[92] https://www.ndrc.gov.cn/xxgk/jd/jd/202006/t20200624_1231942.html (NDRC); http://www.mofcom.gov.cn/article/ae/ai/202006/20200602977244.shtml (MOFCOM).

The emergence of an undiplomatic "wolf warrior diplomacy," despite intermittent friendly gestures,[93] offset their endeavors. Since March, aggressive diplomacy was employed as a mobilizing tool to boost people's sense of national pride and the prestige of the CCP, portraying China as a strong power no longer afraid of foreign bullying. This ultra-nationalist approach involved placing blame on "vicious" Western powers through ungrounded accusations and uncivilized language. It served the purpose of diverting attention from the regime's dereliction of duty, including that of Xi Jinping himself. Unfortunately, this approach backfired fatally, bringing America and its allies closer together and representing a grave foreign policy blunder that the rapidly rising China should have avoided.

In July 2020, both Japan and the United States accused China of seeking territorial expansion in the East and South China Seas. The United States, for the first time, took a position, dismissing China's claims over the South China Sea as "completely unlawful."[94] The EU had developed a tougher approach toward China in 2019, marking a turning point in EU-China relations. For the first time, it rated China as a "systemic rival" in its "strategic reflection paper" in late March and finalized its investment screening mechanism in April to scrutinize investments from China in the EU's critical assets. Furthermore, the EU, along with key Member States Germany and France, decided in December 2019 to retool a Europe-wide industrial policy to protect its technological independence.[95] The EU's position toward China stiffened even further in 2020. Notably, it was the EU, rather than the United States, which first raised the idea in December 2020 of creating a transatlantic body coordinating U.S.-EU policies on export control and investment screening to forge a technological alliance against China's rise. This changing geopolitical landscape posed challenges for China as the EU, despite its distaste for Trump's cowboy diplomacy, viewed reduced cooperation with the United States as detrimental to its "strategic sovereignty agenda," while relieving

[93] For instance, on 28th April 2019, deputy foreign minister Le Yucheng gave an interview to NBC. https://www.fmprc.gov.cn/wjbxw_new/202201/t20220113_10491299.shtml.

[94] "US Toughens Its Stance Against Chinese Aggression in South China Sea." *The World*, 15/07/2020. https://theworld.org/stories/2020-07-15/U.S.-toughens-its-stance-against-chinese-aggression-south-china-sea.

[95] "Europe First: How Brussels Is Retooling Industrial Policy." *FT*, 02/12/2019. https://www.ft.com/content/140e560e-0ba0-11ea-bb52-34c8d9dc6d84.

the U.S. burden would contribute to the joint defense of the multilateral rules-based international order.[96]

Fearing an all-out decoupling, an approach that some CCP-trusted extra-system advisers suggested could be mitigated by China's pursuit of unilateral unrestricted market access, even in the event of a Western blockade[97] (an ultra-anti-nationalist view that was strongly criticized by a famous Chinese liberal intellectual, who called this adviser a "traitor"),[98] the Chinese leadership, facing mounting international hostility partly due to its "wolf warrior diplomacy," had to prepare for the worst-case scenario. The catalyst for this preparation may have been an event on June 15 when China lost a "landmark dispute" with the EU regarding the enforcement of the EU's recognition of China's market-economy status, which had allowed certain benefits to lapse.[99]

This development followed a CCP decision on May 14, 2020 to adopt a new strategy called "internal circulation." This strategy aimed to reduce China's dependence on foreign trade and shift that dependence toward the domestic market. However, amid widespread suspicion about China's new direction, Xi Jinping clarified two months later, on July 21, that "internal circulation" was not intended to shut the door to the world.[100] This clarification was ostensibly made in recognition that China could ill afford such isolation, especially in technological terms.

Yet the worst moment came when U.S. Secretary of State Mike Pompeo delivered a pivotal speech on July 23, 2020 titled "Communist

[96] Leonard, M & Shapiro, J (2020): "Sovereign Europe, Dangerous World: Five Agendas to Protect Europe's Capacity to Act." European Council on Foreign Relations (ECFR) report, December1. https://ecfr.eu/publication/sovereign-europe-dangeroU.S.-world-five-agendas-to-protect-europes-capacity-to-act/

[97] Zheng Yongnian, a pro-Beijing China Expert Based in Singapore, Expressed This Viewpoint on several occasions between April 2018 and 2021. http://www.tsyzm.com/CN/Y2018/V1/I3/46 (2018); http://www.ccg.org.cn/archives/54958 (2020); http://big5.news.cn/gate/big5/www.news.cn/sikepro/20210310/C9335F4B6AD00001A5D4EF404B603D30/c.html (2021). https://user.guancha.cn/main/content?id=454561 (2021).

[98] Rong Jian tweet dated 29/01/2021. https://twitter.com/rongjian1957/status/1354963752253198346.

[99] "China Loses Landmark WTO Dispute Against EU." *Bloomberg*, 16/06/2020. https://www.bloomberg.com/news/articles/2020-06-16/not-with-a-bang-china-loses-landmark-wto-dispute-against-eu#xj4y7vzkg.

[100] Radio Free Asia, 21/07/2020. https://www.rfa.org/mandarin/yataibaodao/jingmao/rc-07212020110004.html.

China and the Free World's Future" at the Richard Nixon Library.[101] Drawing historical parallels, this address can be likened to Winston Churchill's iconic Iron Curtain speech in 1946. During this momentous event, Pompeo, as succinctly summarized by Fred Kaplan, "calls for ending engagement with China, rolling back its fledgling empire, and rallying the Chinese people to overthrow their regime."[102]

Despite being perceived as a "cry for war" by many critics,[103] the ideological impact of this speech, unprecedentedly delivered by a U.S. top official, significantly exacerbated the great-power rivalry between the United States and China, thrusting the world into a new era that was reminiscent of a Cold War. It is worth noting that until Trump's final months in office, U.S. "new containment" (directed not only against China but also Russia and Iran)[104] had little or nothing to do with whether China made itself more democratic.[105] It was the PRC's gross and unrestrained mismanagement of foreign policy, notably exemplified by the infamous "wolf warrior diplomacy" under Xi Jinping and the Communist regime's radical totalitarian turn that justified America's ideological crusade from July 2020.[106]

[101] https://2017-2021.state.gov/communist-china-and-the-free-worlds-future-2/

[102] Fred Kaplan: "Don't Pick a Cold War You Can't Win." *Slate*, 24/07/2020. https://slate.com/news-and-politics/2020/07/pompeo-china-cold-war.html.

[103] Thomas Wright: "Pompeo's Surreal Speech on China." *Brookings Commentary*, 27/07/2020. https://www.brookings.edu/articles/pompeos-surreal-speech-on-china/

[104] Mandelbaum, M (2019): "The New Containment—Handling Russia, China, and Iran." *Foreign Affairs*, Mar/Apr, 98:2, pp. 123–131.

[105] "Trump Trade Chief Wants to Open China, Not Change Its Economic System." *Reuters*, 01/05/2018. https://www.reuters.com/article/U.S.-usa-trade-china/ustr-lighthizer-says-wants-to-open-china-not-change-its-economic-system-idUSKBN1I246K; "15 Times Donald Trump Praised Authoritarian Rulers." *CNN*, 02/07/2019. https://edition.cnn.com/2019/07/02/politics/donald-trump-dictators-kim-jong-un-vladimir-putin/index.html; "Trump Praises Chinese Leader, Not Hong Kong Protesters Seeking Democratic Reforms." *Los Angeles Times*, 15/08/2019. https://www.latimes.com/politics/story/2019-08-15/trump-praises-chinese-leader-not-hong-kong-protesters; "John Bolton: The Scandal of Trump's China Policy." *The Wall Street Journal*, 17/07/2020. https://www.wsj.com/articles/john-bolton-the-scandal-of-trumps-china-policy-115924 19564.

[106] "Robert O'Brien's Phoenix Speech and 'Tough on China'." *National Review*, 26/06/2020. https://www.nationalreview.com/corner/robert-obriens-phoenix-speech-and-tough-on-china/; Speech by Michael R. Pompeo at the Richard Nixon Presidential Library and Museum: "Communist China and the Free World's Future." 23/07/

While debates continue regarding whether it is appropriate to conceptualize the ongoing U.S.-China rivalry as a new Cold War, it is evident that this competition has indeed evolved into a genuine new Cold War, often referred to as Cold War II, particularly concerning the two dimensions of ideology and geopolitics.[107] As Niall Ferguson suggested, this emerging reality "is both inevitable and desirable," given China's assertive foreign policy and domestic repression, alongside the "genuine bipartisan consensus" in the United States for a hawkish policy shift toward China.[108] Pompeo's "distrust and verify" approach toward the increasingly autocratic China, in contrast to Ronald Reagan's "trust but verify" approach toward the democratizing Soviet Union, further vindicated the irreversibility of the new Cold War.

Trump's vagaries may raise doubts about the consistency of U.S.-China policy. However, a bipartisan consensus on adopting a tough stance on China, combined with the competition from Democrat candidate Joe Biden, who displayed no less hawkishness, left little room for Trump to deviate from the objectives stated in his "enlightened realism," as espoused in the NSS of 2017. This strategy demonstrated the administration's determination to "push back against the revisionist powers of China and Russia."

Reportedly, Henry Kissinger proposed a "reverse Nixon strategy" both during and after Trump's election, aiming to engage Putin's Russia to "contain a rising China."[109] This idea was echoed by the renowned Cold War historian Odd Arne Westad, who made a similar policy recommendation in *Foreign Affairs* (September/October 2019). He suggested accommodating Russia over the Ukraine issue to focus on China. Nevertheless, he opposed the concept of decoupling and advocated managing

2020. https://www.state.gov/communist-china-and-the-free-worlds-future/; "Biden Says US Faces Battle to 'Prove Democracy Works'," *CNN*, 26/03/2021. https://edition.cnn.com/2021/03/25/politics/biden-autocracies-versU.S.-democracies/index.html

[107] Garthoff, R (1992): "Why Did the Cold War Arise, and Why Did It End." *Diplomatic History*, Spring, 16:2, pp. 287–293.

[108] Ferguson, N: "America and China Are Entering the Dark Forest." *Bloomberg Opinion*, 05/07/2020. https://www.bloomberg.com/opinion/articles/2020-07-05/is-the-u-s-in-a-new-cold-war-china-has-already-declared-it.

[109] "Henry Kissinger Pushed Trump to Work With Russia to Box In China." *The Daily Beast*, 31/07/2018. https://www.thedailybeast.com/henry-kissinger-pushed-trump-to-work-with-russia-to-box-in-china.

the rivalry with China "within the context of continued economic interdependence," given his recognition that "Overall, China is more of a match for the United States than the Soviet Union was when Kennan wrote down his thoughts."[110]

For many in the West, the rationale for a new Cold War is derived from their realist belief that a risen China has fundamentally challenged the U.S.-dominated hegemonic order. John Mearsheimer viewed past engagement with China as "the worst strategic blunder," actively fostering the rise of a peer competitor. In line with Westad's belief that today's China is likely to be a more powerful competitor than the Soviet Union was in its prime, a Cold War with China has become inevitable, and "it is now too late to do much about it."[111]

However, some scholars, like Beckley and Brands, who subscribe to the power-transition theory, hold different views on China's actual strength. They argue that the dynamic for U.S.-China great-power rivalry comes not from power parity between China and the United States, but from a declining Chinese power. Similar to the pre-World War I German Reich, whose relative decline was highlighted by the Triple Entente, China is inevitably dissatisfied with the status quo and is poised to venture into a war with the United States to overcome its strategic disadvantages. As a result, the United States must "prepare for a major war" in advance.[112] Like Mearsheimer's offensive realism, the power-transition theory assumes that an even distribution of power tends to increase the likelihood of war. The best strategy for the established power is to act preemptively before the revisionist power becomes intractable. Thus, the new Cold War dynamic is shaped not necessarily by a true belief on the part of the United States that China has risen, but more likely by the need of U.S. policymakers to inflate such a "belief" to facilitate U.S. pre-emptions.

The value of pre-emption was equally well understood by practitioner elites, whose assessments of Chinese power were highly accurate. Henry

[110] Westad, O. A. (2019): "The Sources of Chinese Conduct—Are Washington and Beijing Fighting a New Cold War?" *Foreign Affairs*, Sep/Oct, 98:5, pp. 86–95.

[111] Mearsheimer, J (2021): "The Inevitable Rivalry—America, China, and the Tragedy of Great-power Politics." *Foreign Affairs*, Nov-Dec, 100:6, pp. 48–58.

[112] Brands, H & Beckley, M: "China Is a Declining Power—and That's the Problem." *Foreign Policy*, 24/09/2021. https://foreignpolicy.com/2021/09/24/china-great-power-united-states/

Paulson, a former official in the Obama administration, had cautioned against overestimating China's power and advocated continued engagement before Trump's inauguration. Although he did not perceive China as "an unstoppable powerhouse," he emphasized the importance of bolstering U.S. hard power and enhancing deterrence against China.[113] Despite the concern over the "China threat," Secretary of State Pompeo astutely recognized a significant distinction between China and the former Soviet Union. In his "New Cold War" address, he noted that "unlike the Soviet Union, China is deeply integrated into the global economy. However, Beijing is more dependent on us than we are on them."

Former White House chief strategist Steve Bannon held a rather negative view on the so-called "China's rise" thesis. In an interview conducted in August 2018, he contended that China's seemingly impressive economy was built on shaky foundations that harmed the interests of the people and lacked institutional stability and sustainability. He drew a comparison to the Cold War era, when the West had long believed that the planned economy led by the Soviet Union was on the rise while the free economy in the West was in decline. This misconception led to a series of peaceful co-existence policies promoted by Kissinger, based on peaceful negotiations. However, President Reagan's intelligence agencies later found that the real economic strength of the Soviet Union was only half of what was shown in the data and that it was economically vulnerable. As a result, Reagan pursued a strategy of a massive arms race, which eventually led to the Soviet Union's collapse.

Bannon saw parallels between the "rise of China" in 2018 and the Soviet Union's past situation. He pointed to the nervousness of the Xi Jinping government during the U.S.-China trade war, which he believed reflected serious problems within the Chinese economy. Overcapacity and heavy indebtedness had plagued China's state-owned enterprises, forcing the country to rely on dumping goods in the Western market, thus negatively impacting Western industries and threatening the global economy. In Bannon's view, a trade war became a necessity for Trump in the interests of safeguarding American interests, and he believed it was winnable.[114]

[113] Paulson, H. M. (2015), p. 380.

[114] Interview by Sasha Gong with Steve Bannon, 29/09/2018.

With access to precise intelligence-based information regarding China's actual economic and military capabilities, it is highly likely that policymakers within the U.S. administrations during and beyond the Trump era have adopted a strategy reminiscent of the Truman administration's approach when drafting NSC 68. This strategy involved the "conjuring up of an exaggeration of the Soviet threat."[115] History may indeed repeat itself. Present-day America may find every incentive to deliberately overstate the China threat, thereby facilitating preemptive strategies and measures. In fact, discussions regarding preparations for a great power war have been a recurring theme in the U.S. strategic community since 2014.[116] The undeterred risk-taking exhibited by Chinese adventurism, for whatever reason, might be playing directly into America's preferred risk-averse option, thereby enhancing the likelihood of "the Next Great War."

It is worth noting that winning the new Cold War involves adopting an alternative engagement policy. Unlike the strategy of "fencing-in" the Soviet Union during the Cold War, Pompeo's call to end engagement with China by no means implies "no engagement." Instead, it signifies a shift from "strategic engagement" to "competitive engagement," subjecting China to tougher, legally binding constraints within the rules-based liberal international order, forcing China to choose between continued bandwagoning and full isolation.

Lighthizer envisioned the 150-page draft agreement in May 2019, with a view to achieving a near-unrestricted Chinese market access that is "complete, irreversible, and verifiable"—a denuclearization principle previously applied to Iran and North Korea. Trump's national security

[115] Cardwell, C (2011): *NSC 68 and the Political Economy of the Early Cold War*. NJ: Cambridge University Press, p. 262.

[116] For instance: Rod Lyon: "Is major war obsolete?" *The Strategist*, ASPI (Australia Strategic Policy Institute), 19/08/2014. https://www.aspistrategist.org.au/is-major-war-obsolete/; Amitai Etzioni: "Making a U.S.-Sino War 'Thinkable'?" *The Diplomat*, 22/09/2016. https://thediplomat.com/2016/09/making-a-U.S.-sino-war-thinkable/; RAND Report (2016): "War with China: Thinking through the Unthinkable," authored by David C. Gompert, Astrid Stuth Cevallos, Cristina L. Garafala. https://www.rand.org/content/dam/rand/pubs/research_reports/RR1100/RR1140/RAND_RR1140.pdf; RAND Report (2017): "U.S. Military Capabilities and Forces for a Dangerous World—Rethinking the U.S. Approach to Force Planning," https://www.rand.org/pubs/research_reports/RR1782.html; Alan L. Gropman: "America Needs to Prepare for a Great Power War," *The National Interest*, 07/02/2018. http://nationalinterest.org/feature/america-needs-prepare-great-power-war-24392.

adviser, H. R. McMaster, candidly raised the possibility of expelling China from the WTO[117] as part of America's efforts to rein in China's revisionist impulse. He believed that only by pursuing such an approach, along with a natural economic "decoupling" involving reduced investment in the Chinese market and the withdrawal of manufacturing and other industries from China, would they foster China's return to the pre-Xi Jinping era of Deng Xiaoping's "reform and opening."[118]

Chinese elites were stunned by the rapid deterioration of Sino-U.S. relations. In early July, a senior retired official from the CCP's International Liaison Department called for six aspects of preparation to cope with the full escalation of tensions with the United States. These aspects included the following:

1. Preparing for the deterioration of Sino-U.S. relations and the overall escalation of the struggle.
2. Being ready to deal with shrinking external demand and disruptions of industrial and supply chains.
3. Preparing for the normalization of the COVID-19 pandemic and the long-term co-existence of the virus and humans.
4. Getting ready to overcome the hegemony of the U.S. dollar and gradually decoupling the RMB from it.
5. Preparing for the potential outbreak of a global food crisis.
6. Being prepared for the resurgence of international terrorist forces.

These views were, in actuality, reflections of the top leadership.[119]

Pompeo's address served as a reminder to the Chinese elites that the new Cold War had become a *fait accompli*. In response, China extended an olive branch to the Trump administration. On August 7, 2020, Yang Jiechi, former foreign minister and now a Politburo member in charge of foreign affairs, published an article on *Xinhuanet*, refraining from criticizing Trump and calling for the "unswerving maintenance and stabilization of Sino-U.S. relations."[120] Five days later (August 12),

[117] McMaster, H. R. (2020), p. 145.

[118] Ibid, pp. 145–6.

[119] Global Times, 03/07/2020. https://new.qq.com/rain/a/20200703A05VHM00.

[120] Xinhua, 07/08/2020. http://www.xinhuanet.com/politics/2020-08/07/c_1126339837.htm.

Deputy Foreign Minister Le Yucheng expressed his readiness to open dialogue with American counterparts "at any time" on the most difficult and complex issues, stressing that a "radio quiet" must not be allowed between the two countries' foreign ministries.[121] On August 13, MOFCOM declared that the Phase One Agreement had thus far been "seriously implemented."

Shortly after, the Chinese regime changed its tone. On August 17 and 23, the *People's Daily* and the *Economic Daily* issued editorials vehemently condemning America's decoupling attempts, dismissing them as the "unwise choice" of a small number of American politicians. The CCP is clear that notwithstanding the clamor for a "Great War," mainly among China's nationalist elites, the real focus of the new Cold War lies in the unfolding ideologically fueled battle over technological leadership.[122] To put it another way, the new Cold War is quintessentially a unilateral technological decoupling imposed by the United States on a reluctant China, which cannot afford it, given its semi-peripheral "superpower" status. The regime's deep fear of decoupling could hardly juxtapose China with Stalin's USSR that responded with reciprocal counteraction, economically, militarily, and ideologically. To gloss over its weakness and previous appeasement gestures, on August 25, Xinhua news agency issued an extra-long article, a three-full-page, over 30,000-word piece published in the *People's Daily*, titled "Pompeo's China-Related Speech Full of Lies: Truth of Facts," condemning Pompeo by name for his 26-point "anti-China" remarks.[123]

Still underestimating the bipartisan consensus on a tough China policy in the United States, Chinese bureaucratic elites simultaneously placed high hopes on the Democrats, anticipating, as explained by former Chinese ambassador to Washington, Zhou Wenzhong, on August 22, that the new U.S. administration would not treat China in the same way as the

[121] Chinese Foreign Ministry press release, 12/08/2020. https://www.mfa.gov.cn/wjbxw_673019/202008/t20200812_390515.shtml.

[122] "The need for global cooperation on technology goes beyond the hardware or software. It is also about our values, our societies and our democracies." Quoted from *Joint Communication to the European Parliament, the European Council and the Council—A new EU-US agenda for global change*. Issued by The European Commission's High Representative of the Union for Foreign Affairs and Security Policy, Brussels, 02/12/2020. https://ec.europa.eu/info/sites/default/files/joint-communication-eu-U.S.-agenda_en.pdf.

[123] The People's Daily, 25/08/2020.

Soviet Union and would trust China's intentions of not seeking to replace or challenge U.S. supremacy.[124] In late November, when the dust finally settled in the U.S. election campaign, Former Deputy Foreign Minister Fu Ying strove to define the new Sino-U.S. relationship as one characterized by "cooperative competition."[125] This implied, as interpreted by a renowned American historian: "If we can't have Chimerica back, can we at least have détente?".[126]

The U.S.-China trade war might have been averted had China taken a more proactive stance in collaborating with the United States in the critical year of 2018 to denuclearize North Korea. In the absence of this trade war, coupled with a more tactful approach that avoided the pitfalls of "undiplomatic diplomacy" (a euphemism for the infamous "wolf warrior diplomacy"),[127] the onset of the U.S.-China great-power rivalry, which ultimately led to a new Cold War, could have been postponed, if not entirely prevented. This delay would have offered a rare window of opportunity for China to expedite efforts to rebalance its economy and establish itself as an "unstoppable powerhouse."

However, Xi's geopolitical miscalculations strained relations with the Trump administration, resulting in a bipartisan consensus within the U.S. establishment to adopt a more assertive approach toward China. Chinese elites, while recognizing the United States' realist pursuit of *raison d'état* in curbing China's rise, believed that increased economic interdependence and even China's concessions on its developmental interests might dissuade such efforts. They gravely underestimated and were unprepared for the rapid escalation of the trade war into a full-fledged new Cold War, both outcomes tragically undesired and unanticipated by China.

For the United States, the new Cold War is viewed as an imperative, driven by both economic and strategic motivations. This two-pronged

[124] Zhou Wenzhong Talks about 4-decade Sino-US Relations. CCTV (China Central Television), 22/08/2020. http://m.news.cctv.com/2020/08/22/ARTIzoQc9lVM8oFNQ8I388JO200822.shtml.

[125] "Cooperative Competition Is Possible Between China and the U.S.—A former vice foreign minister of China proposes a way forward for the world's two leading powers." *The New York Times*, 24/11/2020. https://www.nytimes.com/2020/11/24/opinion/china-U.S.-biden.html.

[126] Private communication, 27/11/2020.

[127] "Taming the wolf warrior—China's rising aggression." FT, 10/08/2021. https://www.ft.com/content/1b9cba7e-4473-4b27-adb2-67ef63e02717.

strategy encompasses two distinct levels of connotation: "effective push-back from the United States and like-minded nations" to cope with "China's strong combination of insecurity and ambition"[128] in high politics terms; and in low politics terms, engagement where possible, given the symbiotic economic relationship between the two powers, and decoupling where necessary. *Both* aim to "induce China to change in more creative and assertive ways,"[129] thereby "balancing the rise of Chinese power."

[128] McMaster, H. R. (2020) "How China sees the world and how we should see China." *The Atlantic*, May issue.

[129] Speech by Michael R. Pompeo, 23/07/2020.

CHAPTER 7

Xi Jinping's Reverse Course: The Nazification of the Chinese Economy (After 2012)

The year 2012 was a tumultuous one for both Xi Jinping and the Party, characterized by an intense power struggle leading up to the commencement of the Eighteenth National Party Congress in November. This internal conflict brought the party state perilously close to collapse. Contrary to the external perception of a vibrant Chinese model that could potentially be exported to countries in the Global South as a competing illiberal or even a dark alternative to market democracy, a comprehensive economic and sociopolitical crisis was looming. This crisis encompassed a slowing economy triggered by premature deindustrialization, an entrenched kleptocratic state, escalating disturbances across the nation due to widening income disparities and various injustices that remained unaddressed by the corrupt and inept party-state institutions. Incompatible conflicts of interest deeply divided Chinese society, impeding the formation of a social consensus on the way forward. All these factors contributed to significant dissatisfaction, not necessarily directed at the entire regime, but more specifically at the departing "dictator," Hu Jintao, whose purported incompetence was widely criticized. Xi Jinping's "people-centered" inaugural address, delivered immediately after his election as the General Secretary, evoked strong anticipation for a "New China" led by an enlightened and capable leader. This sentiment was vividly reflected in the "Front Words" of the *Phoenix Weekly* (《凤凰周刊》), published on December 5, 2012, which featured a

J. Yue, *Crony Comprador Capitalism*,
https://doi.org/10.1007/978-3-031-53154-5_7

compelling headline: "The Entire Country of China Anticipates Change."[1]

The Shanghai faction, led by former General Secretary Jiang Zemin, assumed the role of kingmaker. They perceived Xi, with his "princeling" background (of utmost importance suggesting his political reliability), unassuming demeanor, as a pliable puppet to be manipulated. This faction acted swiftly after Xi assumed office. Leveraging their controlled media platform, *Caixin Media* (《财新传媒》), one of China's most influential news websites known for its strong market-liberal leaning, they devised a political strategy to influence Xi's views regarding the required reforms for the next stage.

In the December 1 edition, *China Reform* (《中国改革》), a periodical controlled by *Caixin*, published an unusually extensive 20-page cover story, which was notable given its historical publication patterns. In this article, the authors portrayed Deng Xiaoping's market-Leninist reforms in a mystified manner and commended Jiang Zemin's contributions to advancing Deng's legacy. While not overtly linking Deng Xiaoping's "reform and opening" to China's current challenges, they indirectly aimed to cast a shadow on the Hu Jintao and Wen Jiabao era (2002–2012), which was tainted by corruption and perceived ineptitude. They insinuated that Hu and Wen leaned against the market by favoring SOEs.[2] Interestingly, similar tactics were employed in March 2003, when Zhu Rongji was stepping down from the Premiership. The *Southern Weekend* (《南方周末》), a prominent neoliberal media outlet based in Guangzhou, released a 36-page documentary-style story covering Zhu's entire journey from childhood to Premier. The narrative extolled his contributions to the privatization of SOEs and China's accession to the WTO. The coverage exhibited a pronounced bias and lacked objectivity, as it omitted critiques of his policy failures, which had surfaced even before his departure. As a bastion of neoliberal thought, the *Southern Weekend* had ample reason to hold Zhu Rongji in high esteem.

Using these strategies, their intention was to steer Xi toward embracing their plan for enhancing market-oriented reforms rather than veering away from Deng's course of development that had become entrenched along crony comprador capitalist routes. By subtly depicting Xi as a potential

[1] The Phoenix Weekly, 05/12/2012.

[2] *China Reform* (Caixin), 01/12/2012.

faithful heir to the Deng Xiaoping-Jiang Zemin lineage, as implied by the article's title, "How Reform was Relaunched," and by hinting within the article that the reforms initiated two decades ago could "edify tomorrow's (path)," (Fig. 7.1) their aim was to encourage Xi to adopt a more market-fundamentalist approach to reforms.[3]

They gravely underestimated Xi, who, to the astonishment of many, demonstrated exceptional finesse in leveraging his positional authority and the Communist nomenklatura system to orchestrate an anti-graft campaign. This skillful maneuvering allowed him to efficiently centralize power within an impressively brief timespan. Consequently, he attained a level of authority no less significant than that of Chairman Mao, emerging as a de facto dictator equipped with substantial power resources at his disposal. This outcome starkly contradicted the intentions of all factions, notably the Shanghai faction, which had sought to hinder such a trajectory and would eventually come to regret their initial support.

Exploring Xi's ascent to power and his strategies for navigating obstacles, including his patriarch's desire to exert control over him, falls within the purview of historians. Suffice it to say that Xi pursued a distinct agenda of salvaging the crisis-ridden party state and reshaping it as a vehicle to advance his personal objectives. He energetically expedited the party-state's totalitarian turn, a trajectory that had its roots in the Hu Jintao era. This momentum, combined with China's position as the world's second-largest economy, led many realist-oriented observers to draw comparisons between China and Nazi Germany, or even to characterize China as the "most evil regime" since the Third Reich (excluding the Soviet Union).[4] This situation was further compounded by the looming potential of a "Thucydides trap," driving great-power rivalry toward confrontation.

In current discourse, numerous strategists and policymakers often attribute the tension between China and the United States primarily to Xi Jinping's personal actions. A notable exemplar of this viewpoint can be discerned in "The Longer Telegram," which was published on January 27, 2021, on the Atlantic Council website,[5] marking eight years of Xi's

[3] According to a well-informed source, 10/12/2012.

[4] Arthur Waldon on China: https://www.youtube.com/watch?v=w-2cArChw5M&t=2s (released on 27/11/2019).

[5] "The Longer Telegram—Toward a New American China Strategy" (by Anonymous). *The Atlantic Council*, 27/01/2021. https://www.atlanticcouncil.org/content-series/atlantic-council-strategy-paper-series/the-longer-telegram/.

Fig. 7.1 Caixin cover story: "How Reform was Relaunched" (December 1, 2012)

leadership. Such assertions are overly simplistic. As earlier sections have asserted, China's deep integration into the global economy, an outcome influenced by a combination of domestic political dynamics and the U.S. "drawing-out" strategy, has emerged more as a source of conflict than a foundation for enduring peace. It is imperative to emphasize that China, entangled in semi-peripheral development, significantly diverges from the post-1945 trajectories of Germany or Japan. Its susceptibility to external demand has cultivated a predisposition toward economic internationalism. Comparing semi-peripheral China to the pre-1945 autarkic Third Reich or post-1945 "core-state" Germany lacks relevance.

However, even before Xi Jinping assumed office, domestic and international tensions were already apparent, setting in motion elements that were reminiscent of certain aspects of Nazi economic policies in China. This similarity to certain aspects observed during the era of the Third Reich can be distilled into two key components: the reassertion of the "primacy of politics" and the pursuit of partial autarky. These tendencies, which echo the historical Nazification of economic policies and are integral to the unfolding "great struggle," a term coined by Xi Jinping and incorporated into Hu Jintao's political report due to Xi's insistence, were presented at the Eighteenth National Party Congress.[6] These tendencies represent Xi's responses to the crisis, particularly in light of the escalating U.S.-China trade dispute, which subsequently evolved into a new Cold War.

Xi Jinping's Assertion of "Primacy of Politics"

Xi Jinping's rise to power in 2012 occurred amid a profound sense of insecurity within the Chinese regime, which was wary of color revolutions taking place in other parts of the world. These uprisings were often perceived as being instigated by American hegemonic power with the aim to destabilize and disintegrate China. While attributing some blame to the United States, the ruling elites recognized the necessity for change; otherwise, a Chinese version of a color revolution could become imminent. A pivotal choice emerged—"Reform or Revolution," akin to a new Shakespearean question—haunting the Communist rulers.

Ironically, after decades of crony capitalist development, the state has been captured by institutional interests, transforming the Party into an anti-revolutionary right-wing dictatorship. The highest echelons of leadership were acutely aware that a Tocquevillian moment had descended upon an increasingly rigid *old regime* resistant to change.

On November 30, 2012, a mere two weeks after the conclusion of the Eighteenth National Party Congress, Wang Qishan, a member of the Politburo Standing Committee responsible for the influential Central

[6] Xinhuanet, 11/08/2021. http://www.xinhuanet.com/video/2021-08/11/c_1211327587.htm.

Disciplinary and Inspection Committee (CDIC)—the Party's anti-graft watchdog—recommended Alexis de Tocqueville's *The Old Regime and the Revolution* during a CDIC meeting attended by experts.[7] Wang was widely recognized as an erudite, enlightened, and exceptionally insightful leader. His suggestion sparked heightened interest among numerous intellectuals, some of whom had studied the book in the preceding years, prompting them to delve deeper into Tocqueville's warnings: "The regime that a revolution destroys is almost always better than the one that immediately preceded it, and experience teaches that *the most dangerous time for a bad government is usually when it begins to reform.*"[8]

The overseas edition of the *People's Daily* published an article on January 18, 2013, titled "Why Wang Qishan Recommended *The Old Regime and the Revolution*?" In this article, the CCP's urgent need to address challenges while racing against time was candidly acknowledged. However, caution was advised against pursuing radical reforms or engaging in revolution, as such actions could potentially lead the country into chaos and disorder. The article instead advocated bold yet prudent reforms.[9] Exiled political scientist Yan Jiaqi interpreted the mindset of Chinese leaders as a dilemma: either embark on reforms, which would be equivalent to political suicide, or refrain from reforming and await the consequences of an uprising (a revolution). Both options appeared to be dead ends.[10]

Nevertheless, gestures by perceived enlightened leaders like Wang Qishan, who dared to confront reality, ignited hope among many in the intellectual elite for a managed democratization or the establishment of the rule of law at the very least. Regrettably, their hopes were short-lived. Just three months later, in mid-April, the CCP circulated an internal

[7] Jiancha Ribao, 18/12/2012. http://fanfu.people.com.cn/n/2012/1218/c141423-19927025.html.

[8] Alexis de Tocqueville ([1856] 2011): *The Old Regime and the Revolution*, edited by Jon Elsetr. Cambridge: Cambridge University Press, p. 157.

[9] The People's Daily (overseas edition), 18/01/2013. http://www.xinhuanet.com//politics/2013-01/18/c_114410249_3.htm.

[10] RFI, 26/02/2013. https://www.rfi.fr/cn/%E9%A6%96%E9%A1%B5/20130226-%E4%B8%A5%E5%AE%B6%E7%A5%BA%EF%BC%9A%E4%B8%AD%E5%9B%BD%E9%99%B7%E5%85%A5%E2%80%9C%E6%89%98%E5%85%8B%E7%BB%B4%E5%B0%94%E5%9B%B0%E5%A2%83%E2%80%9D.

document referred to as "Document No. 9" (九号文件). This document, titled "Briefing on the Current Situation in the Ideological Field," imposed seven stringent bans ("7 bans"). These included prohibitions on discussing topics such as universal values, press freedom, civil society, civil rights, historical mistakes of the Chinese Communist Party, crony capitalism, and judicial independence.[11]

A dissident scholar, Gao Yu, was arrested for "leaking state secrets" due to her disclosure of the contents of these seven bans overseas. Despite the official denial, the authenticity of the bans' contents was widely believed, as they were corroborated by numerous other sources. On November 8, the *People's Daily* unveiled Xi Jinping's address delivered at the Central Party School to senior cadres in January 2013. In this address, Xi emphasized the eras led by Mao Zedong and Deng Xiaoping must not negate each other, a perspective known as "no mutual negation" (*liangge buneng fouding*, 两个不能否定).[12] This stance was both stunning and highly controversial, revealing Xi's alignment with a neo-Maoist perspective.

Wang Qishan actively responded to Xi's "January 2013 speech" during a CDIC training course meeting on April 13, 2015, explicitly expressing support for Xi's "no mutual negation" position.[13] This alignment was further reinforced by Wang Qishan's conversation with Francis Fukuyama ten days later on April 23. During their discussion, Wang, referencing Xi's views, forcefully rejected Fukuyama's suggestion of establishing an independent judiciary as the fundamental means to combat corruption. Wang argued that the judiciary must operate under the leadership of the CCP.[14]

Xi's embrace of neo-Maoism was not a novel development; rather, it represented a continuity of the Party's stance outlined in January 2011 during Hu Jintao's tenure. At that time, Wu Bangguo,

[11] "Gao Yu Reveals Document 9." *Ming Jing*, 17/04/2015. https://www.chinaaid.net/2015/04/blog-post_19.html.

[12] The People's Daily, 08/11/2013.

[13] The People's Daily, 20/04/2015. http://cpc.people.com.cn/n/2015/0420/c64094-26869875.html. Full video clip of Wang Qishan's remarks can be found at: https://www.youtube.com/watch?v=yWJWCoVYF_Q.

[14] RFI, 12/05/2015. https://www.rfi.fr/cn/%E4%B8%AD%E5%9B%BD/20150512-%E4%B8%AD%E7%BA%AA%E5%A7%94%E4%B9%A6%E8%AE%B0%E7%8E%8B%E5%B2%90%E5%B1%B1%E4%BC%9A%E8%A7%81%E6%97%A5%E8%A3%94%E5%AD%A6%E8%80%85%E9%87%8A%E6%94%BE%E6%A8%A1%E7%B3%8A%E2%80%9C%E4%BF%A1%E5%8F%B7%E2%80%9D.

Chairman of the National People's Congress, introduced the Party's "5 Rejections" (*wu bugao*, 五不搞), which encompassed the rejection of a system involving multiple parties holding office in rotation, the pluralization of guiding ideologies, the separation of powers and the bicameral system, the federal system, and the privatization of SOEs. Both the "5 Rejections" and the "7 Bans" contained elements of insincerity, particularly concerning matters like privatization and crony capitalism, which had long been prevalent. By denying their existence and prohibiting discourse about these issues, the Party aimed to uphold its image of infallibility. This approach also aimed to avert the perception of the CCP as a right-wing party; acknowledging such a characterization would essentially entail self-denial for the Party itself.

Displaying a distinct aversion to Western democracy, Xi Jinping appeared more self-assured—despite his mercurial temperament and gaps in comprehensive knowledge—than his counterparts in the Politburo. His belief in the optimization of the Communist system was conspicuous. His "new thinking" on "no mutual negation" suggested that the *necessary* systemic reforms to address China's Tocquevillian moment would involve degrees of de-Dengification. However, these reforms might bypass addressing the institutional origins of China's crony capitalism, focusing primarily on its outcomes. This approach required a political-ideological reversion, verging on re-Maoification, to render the concept of "no mutual negation" plausible.

In this context, Xi emerged as a "reformer," albeit of a conservative nature, aiming to reinvigorate the party state. In his pursuit of revitalizing China and realizing the "China dream," a term coined by Xi himself, he considered the central role of the Party indispensable. Taking lessons from the mistakes of the CPSU, Xi's administration aimed to sustain economic perestroika while firmly rejecting any glasnost-like openness. To sever the ties between capitalists and political elites, and more broadly, to guide the nation through "great struggles" against both internal and external adversaries, Xi remained steadfast in his mission. His primary objective was to mold himself into a Mao-style Great Helmsman—purging the bureaucracy on the one hand and reaffirming the primacy of politics over private enterprises on the other, reinstating direct Party control.

Xi's attitude toward China's capitalists had a long history. Like his predecessors, and despite his aversion to capitalism, he recognized the resilience of China's capitalist sector. In the period following Mao's death, China's profound poverty and economic underdevelopment compelled

Chinese leaders to maintain openness to private businesses. The swift expansion of these enterprises was supported by Deng Xiaoping, who believed that their growth would not jeopardize the firm control of the CCP over the state apparatus. Nevertheless, the economic liberalization responsible, at least in part, for the Tiananmen movement raised concerns among Party conservatives. They disagreed with Deng's confidence in retaining a monopoly on the state machinery and expressed apprehension regarding the emergence of a new bourgeoisie. These conservatives adhered to the traditional Marxist belief that the economic base shapes the political superstructure. They were concerned that Deng's economic liberalism would inevitably reshape the CCP's ideological framework, potentially altering the Party's character in the foreseeable future.

The Tiananmen incident offered them a pretext to oppose Deng's market reforms. The newly appointed General Secretary, Jiang Zemin, initially sought to curtail private businesses in a bid to appease Party conservatives. Nevertheless, he was eventually compelled to reverse this decision due to the ongoing underperformance of SOEs.

In 1992, Deng, in a strategically calculated move, decisively overcame his adversaries to legitimize China's capitalist development. The objective was to re-establish a legitimacy based on performance for the Communist regime. Despite sharing the same ultimate aim as his opponents—to uphold the Party's absolute control over power—Deng's approach in this endeavor appeared somewhat anti-Marxist. He harnessed market forces that, contrary to expectations, actually reinforced rather than undermined the Communist regime. However, he could neither foresee nor prevent the regime's shift from a left-wing orientation to a right-wing dictatorship, a transition that became evident as crony capitalism proliferated through much of the 1990s.

In contrast to Party elites turned crony capitalists, a significant number of "national capitalists" (private entrepreneurs) emerged who played a crucial role in mitigating the hardships resulting from the decline of SOEs. The massive privatization of SOEs led to extensive layoffs and reduced tax revenues, raising concerns about national stability among the Chinese leadership. Over time, some of these national capitalists transitioned into crony capitalists by forming close ties with Party elites, engaging in unfair competition against other private businesses and remaining SOEs. Their rapid growth could not be ignored as the century turned.

Consequently, in July 2001, Chinese "national capitalists" or private entrepreneurs were officially recognized as "constructors of socialism with Chinese characteristics." This recognition made them eligible for CCP membership. This shift, involving the inclusion of capitalists, aimed to regulate their increasing influence. It also broadened the CCP's power base, empowering the Party to resist democratization on a stronger economic foundation.[15]

In March 2004, the PRC's constitution was amended to recognize private enterprises as "an integral part of China's socialist market economy." This amendment acknowledged the fact that China's private businesses had acquired substantial influence. According to the "Report on the Development of China's Private Enterprises" released by the All-China Federation of Industry and Commerce, the contribution of private enterprises to the national economy exceeded 60% in 2004. These enterprises employed over 100 million people, while the industrial value-added and profits of private industrial enterprises (above a designated scale) constituted more than half of the national totals. Private enterprises accounted for over 70% of China's non-FDI exports and held a share of over 40% in urban-sector fixed asset investment.[16]

The early 2000s marked the emergence of China's high bourgeoisie, which had arisen over more than two decades of reform and opening. These individuals had cultivated close connections with the CCP. Some of these extremely wealthy capitalists were actively engaging with the dissident-minded intelligentsia, drawing inspiration from their insights. Concurrently, they closely monitored foreign commentary on China's political evolution, to which they were particularly sensitive, especially since the late 1990s when the "disintegration thesis" gained prominence and captured their attention. Through the knowledge and information they acquired, they recognized that a post-disintegration China could potentially become an extensively fragmented society. This was primarily due to the decades of Communist totalitarian rule, which had eradicated nearly all integrating forces except its own authority. They harbored concerns about the potential scenario where, following the collapse of

[15] Su Shaozhi: "Where Is the CCP Going?—After Jiang Zemin Allowed Capitalists to Join the Party." BBC (Chinese), 29/08/2001. http://news.bbc.co.uk/chinese/simp/hi/newsid_1510000/newsid_1515200/1515249.stm.

[16] Chinese central government website, 15/08/2005. https://www.gov.cn/ztzl/2005-08/15/content_64699.htm.

Communism, China might either descend into persistent chaos reminiscent of the Warlord Era (1916–1928) or witness the emergence of a new left- or right-wing tyranny—both of which would pose natural threats to their survival.

They realized that preventing such scenarios required some form of self-organizing efforts. In the event of an abrupt collapse of the Communist regime, these civil society-like self-organizing entities would need to step in as the necessary integrating force. This force would help hold the country together and swiftly reinstate order. In their perspective, this post-Communist regime might not necessarily be democratic, but it must support capitalism during the process of reconstituting the state. Their "unconventional" activities were subdued, although not entirely hidden, and were swiftly identified by the Chinese regime, which displayed zero tolerance for any self-organizing endeavors that operated beyond the party state's control.[17] The regime's nearly century-long history of struggles had taught them the unlikelihood of capitalists as potential allies. The purging of these capitalists was merely a matter of time, given the CCP's nature as a totalitarian political organization.

The CCP's mistrust of national capitalists as potential destabilizers shaped the subordinate position of private enterprises, not only in comparison to the SOEs but also in relation to foreign-invested enterprises (FIEs). While the latter entities had a certain level of economic influence in China, as officially recognized, they did not harbor intentions of effecting political change within the country. Instead, they played a significant role in China's comprador capitalistic development. Aligned with the CCP's goals, they engaged in lobbying efforts with their home country governments to maintain normal trading relations with China. This willingness to overlook China's human rights record, particularly demonstrated by Western democracies, most notably the United States, was deemed hypocritical by the Communist regime, which exploited this behavior to bolster its domestic control.

The development of private enterprises, due to its growing significance in job creation, fiscal revenue enhancement, and export earnings, was subject to both encouragement and constraints imposed by the party state. In both 2005 and 2010, the State Council published "Opinions on

[17] This had become an open secret among the upper-echelon Party elites in the early 2000s.

Encouraging and Guiding the Healthy Development of Private Investments," outlining strategies to provide broader access to key economic sectors. However, the phenomenon of state capture by institutional public interests, such as the large SOEs, resulted in the derailment of these encouragement policies. This situation was further exacerbated by the Party's simultaneous intensified efforts to support SOEs, beginning in 2003—an occurrence known as the "advance of the state and the retreat of private enterprises" (*guojin mintui*, 国进民退).

According to surveys conducted in 2010, among 80 major industries, 62 were opened to foreign capital, accounting for 77.5% of the total, while only 41 allowed access to private capital, constituting 51.25%. Private investment in traditional monopoly industries remained relatively limited. For example, private investment represented 13.8% in electricity and heat production and supply, 12.3% in education, 11.8% in health, social security, and social welfare, 9.6% in finance, and 9.6% in transportation and warehousing. In the postal industry, the figure stood at 7.5%, while in water conservancy and environmental management, it was 6.6%, and in public management and social organizations, it was 5.9%.[18]

Discontent among national capitalists steadily increased, paradoxically co-existing with their contentment in collaborating with the Party and benefiting from extensive rent-seeking practices. They were divided on how to influence China's future while engaging with the Communist regime, an act they perceived as "no-choice." Some harbored hopes of instigating positive political change, allegedly aiming to strengthen the rule of law to safeguard their property. These individuals engaged in activities such as supporting NGOs and educational institutions, as well as establishing civic organizations. Indeed, as noted by Desmond Shum, the former crony capitalist "confidant" of the Wen Jiabao family, these efforts led to "an explosion of civic-mindedness."[19]

Nevertheless, some, particularly the high bourgeoisie, held differing perspectives. Jack Ma, Chairman of Alibaba and a CCP member whose identity was later revealed, openly criticized the technocratic incompetence of the party state; however, he endorsed the autocratic rule of the

[18] The *People's Daily*, 24/05/2010. http://finance.sina.com.cn/review/20100524/07537989154.shtml.

[19] Shum, D (2021), p. 189.

CCP. He expressed understanding for Deng Xiaoping's decision to forcefully suppress pro-democracy demonstrators in June 1989, referring to it as the "most correct decision."[20] His commendation of the CCP for the stability and security brought about by its authoritarian governance is worth quoting in its entirety[21]:

> Everyone's got their eye on the Chinese market, and for good reason. China's got two distinctive advantages: First, when it comes to political stability, we've got it better than most. Look at the U.S., you've got the Democrats, then suddenly the Republicans pop up; just when you've wrapped your head around them, the Democrats are back at it. It's a roller-coaster. But here in China, things stay on a steady course. The Chinese Communist Party has really upped its game in the past five years, making big strides and reforms. You won't find another country out there that can match China's crackdown on corruption and its drive for a squeaky-clean government. I've been around the block, and trust me, dealing with corrupt government types is a real headache in many places. Secondly, let's talk safety. China's a safe haven in a topsy-turvy world. The everyday folks here feel secure, and when you've got political stability, social safety nets, and a solid 6% annual economic growth, that brews the best business climate you can find anywhere. (Video clip: https://www.youtube.com/watch?v=YlIdtG2crBg)

Jack Ma's flattering remarks emphasized his preference for authoritarian stability over democratic transformation. Nevertheless, he also displayed an interest in the concept of power-sharing, although not necessarily within a democratic framework. His establishment of Hupan Academy in early 2015, effectively functioning as an association of influential business and intellectual elites, revealed a nascent party-like endeavor. This initiative bore similarities to the Donglin Movement of the late Ming Dynasty and showcased his personal ambition to shape China's future, particularly in the interests of the high bourgeoisie. A perceptive anonymous commentator remarked on the establishment of the Hupan

[20] "'I Made Cruel Decisions,' Said Jack Ma of His Illustrious Career." SCMP, 13/07/2013. https://www.scmp.com/business/china-business/article/1281702/i-made-cruel-decisions-said-jack-ma-his-illustrioU.S.-career.

[21] "Jack Ma Said China Has the Best Business Environment: Political Stability and Social Security Are Important Advantages." *thepaper.CN*, 29/11/2017. https://www.thepaper.cn/newsDetail_forward_1885194.

Academy, noting: "If the previous giants of capital were independently pursuing their own interests, the emergence of the Hupan Academy now sends a politically significant message: the capital giants are displaying a tendency to converge. This can be seen as their fresh response to the evolving situation in China. The academy represents an innovative effort by these prominent elite figures who are reluctant to be controlled by the Party, instead aiming for greater autonomy."[22] As anticipated, Jack Ma's prominent actions raised serious concerns within the CCP, ultimately leading to the cessation of the academy's activities in 2021.

It is indeed accurate that since the mid-2000s, the CCP has progressively tightened its control over private enterprises, associating them with the potential to sponsor color revolutions or to be seen as a "fifth column" for Western "hostile forces"—a term frequently used in relation to Western democracies, particularly the United States. Beginning in 2009, amid the global financial crisis, the Party accelerated the process of "advance of the state and the retreat of private enterprises" (*guojin mintui*), primarily concentrating on sectors like railroad construction, energy, and financial services. Many analysts attribute the CCP's shift away from private enterprises to the belief that the ongoing robustness of the economy and the resurgence of SOEs have diminished the importance of private firms. This sentiment culminated in the notion that "Once we (as private entrepreneurs) were no longer needed, we, too, would become the enemy."[23]

There is no denying the persistent presence of opportunism in the CCP's approach. However, the escalating hostility toward national capitalists primarily originated from deepening political distrust. This distrust was exacerbated by the fact that capitalist forces, often treated with less favor than SOEs and foreign investors, were growing at a quicker pace than the SOEs. The top leadership was acutely aware that the momentum of the Chinese economy had begun to decline after the pivotal year of 2008, signifying the failure of the China model.[24]

Meanwhile, despite undergoing rounds of restructuring and receiving persistent state sponsorship, the SOEs remained uncompetitive. Research conducted by two economists in Hong Kong, as reported by the *South*

[22] Zhihu, 10/05/2020. https://www.zhihu.com/question/29086883.

[23] Shum, D (2021), p. 282.

[24] Yue, J (2018), pp. 281–283.

China Morning Post, revealed that the profits of 250,000 SOEs had been overstated. If these SOEs had encountered the same interest rates as those imposed on private firms, their profits would have been nearly wiped out.[25]

This situation helps clarify why Xi Jinping continues to *openly* express his support for private enterprises. In November 2018, he affirmed: "Our Party's stance on upholding the basic economic system is clear and unwavering." In his capacity as the paramount leader, he emphasized the distinctive characteristics of private enterprises through a structured perspective: contributing to over 50% of tax revenue, accounting for more than 60% of GDP, exceeding 70% of technological innovation achievements, providing employment for over 80% of the urban labor force, and constituting over 90% of the total number of enterprises. Over the years, he observed that China's private enterprises among the world's top 500 companies increased from 1 in 2010 to 28 in 2018.[26]

Xi and the Communist leadership acknowledged that it was neither feasible nor necessary to eradicate private enterprises. Despite the harm caused by Deng's crony capitalism to the party state, Xi, without admitting the existence of entrenched crony capitalism in China, initiated a comprehensive anti-graft campaign shortly after assuming office in late 2012. Paradoxically, this campaign was highly selective, sparing crony capitalists associated with his allies, such as Chairman of the National People's Congress, Li Zhanshu (despite repeated revelations by pro-Beijing media in Hong Kong, like the *South China Morning Post*), or those crony capitalists with princeling backgrounds from severe consequences unless they challenged his authority. The purging of both the bureaucracy and crony capitalists served multiple aims, including curbing the socio-economic burdens of governing the party state. However, its primary function was rooted in power struggles, allowing him to overcome his adversaries.

With no "democratic bone," as Biden depicted him in their interactions, Xi Jinping more closely resembled dynastic emperors who employed anti-corruption measures to control subordinates, rather than addressing the institutional foundations of crony capitalism, which would necessitate

[25] Neil Gough, "What Trade Overhaul?" SCMP, 10/12/2011.

[26] "Xi Jinping: Speech at the Symposium on Private Enterprises." *Xinhua*, 01/11/2018. http://www.xinhuanet.com/politics/2018-11/01/c_1123649488.htm.

introducing democracy and the rule of law. This aligns with Minxin Pei's observation that "it is inconceivable that the CCP can reform the political and economic institutions of crony capitalism, as these are the very foundations of the regime's monopoly on power."[27]

For Xi, preserving a restrained form of crony capitalism was the most convenient way to navigate the Tocquevillian moment and re-establish totalitarian rule. This approach was adopted despite the eventual nullification of his campaign, as exemplified by the adage "power corrupts, and absolute power corrupts absolutely." This suggests the unlikelihood of reversing state capture by institutional interests, whether public or private.

In contrast, national capitalists, no matter how politically docile they might appear, were perceived by Xi and the CCP as potential threats to the Party's monopoly on power. Like his predecessors, Xi tightened his grip on both society and private entrepreneurs, but in a more stringent manner. The proportion of private enterprises setting up party organizations rose from 1.5% in 1999 to 27.42% in 2002, and further increased to 48.31% in 2018.[28] Beginning in November 2020, he initiated a series of campaigns with the aim of purging the ultra-rich privileged oligarchs, primarily in high-tech sectors such as Alibaba and Tencent, which controlled vast amounts of big data, even coveted by the Party. Additionally, he focused on a select group of influential oligarchs who had amassed significant financial and technological power, thereby presenting challenges to the governability of the party state.

To counter alleged monopoly abuses by these industry giants—accusations that had never been directed at the SOEs—regulatory measures were introduced. To further solidify control, state involvement was required as of January 2023 to be represented on the boards of certain giants. Holding 1% golden shares, these entities were granted veto rights over board decisions, thereby ensuring comprehensive compliance.[29] This approach was chosen due to the immense financial scale of these giants, which made a complete takeover unfeasible. As in the case of the Third

[27] Pei, M (2016), p. 268.

[28] China Business Times, 23/05/2019.

[29] "China's Golden Shares Trade Visibility for Stability." *Bloomberg*, 17/01/2023. https://www.bloomberg.com/opinion/articles/2023-01-17/golden-shares-offer-stability-less-visibility-after-china-crackdown?leadSource=uverify%20wall.

Reich, as succinctly conveyed by Timothy Mason, "the essential thing was not the taking over of ownership, but that of control."[30]

Xi's assertion of the "primacy of politics" over national capitalists served a broader purpose in his grand endeavor to rejuvenate China. He embraced a "control but utilize" approach, incorporating private enterprises into his "civil-military fusion" strategy, officially formulated in October 2017 at the Nineteenth National Party Congress. This strategy aimed to propel China into a military superpower by 2049, involving the advance of dual-use technology and facilitating a reciprocal exchange between the military and civilian sectors. Given the remarkable innovative capabilities of private enterprises, they were deemed indispensable participants in this ambitious national project.

Further steps were taken to closely integrate private enterprises with the party state. The implementation of the National Intelligence Law included coercive provisions in Article 7, mandating all organizations and citizens to "support, assist, and cooperate with national intelligence efforts in accordance with the law." This legislation institutionalized private firms' controlled dependence on the party state, raising apprehensions among governments in democratic nations that these enterprises could potentially serve not as autonomous entities, but as instruments of espionage for the Communist regime.

Undoubtedly, in any modern society, exercising control over capital is the norm. Since the era of Deng Xiaoping, the imperative has been to use capitalism to sustain socialism. This implies that the emergence and rise of national capitalists to a certain extent would be inevitable. Paradoxically, even as its elites transformed into crony capitalists, the Communist regime regarded national capitalists as potential threats to the regime's unchallenged monopoly of power. This perception stemmed from their role in fostering the growth of China's civil society or their mere pursuit of greater autonomy from the CCP. National capitalists were allowed to flourish to such a significant extent largely due to the inherent deficiencies of the SOEs in upholding a socialist economic system. The CCP's consistent policy since Jiang Zemin of "controlling capital" has persisted since the early 2000s. Xi Jinping's divergence from his predecessors lay in his heightened emphasis on such control, particularly against the backdrop of

[30] Mason, T (1993): *Social Policy in the Third Reich*. Oxford: Berg; Barkai, A (1990): *Nazi Economics*. New Haven, CT: Yale University, p. 3.

the party state's shift toward totalitarianism, which rendered reasserting the "primacy of politics" an absolute necessity.

Xi's stringent implementation of political control, in conjunction with persistent economic disparities related to sub-national treatment compared to SOEs and FIEs, has led to a gradual erosion of long-term investment confidence within the private sector. This decline has been accentuated during the COVID-19 pandemic due to the Party's active purging and stigmatization of private tycoons, coupled with the introduction of "common prosperity" policies that resonate with a Marxian undercurrent of "expropriating the expropriators." Furthermore, the incorporation of private enterprises into the "civil-military fusion" initiative has rendered them vulnerable to potential sanctions from democratic nations. Significantly, these democratic countries no longer view private enterprises as catalysts for democratic progress, but rather as collaborators with China's autocratic regime. This perception has been further intensified against the backdrop of the unfolding new Cold War.

If Xi Jinping had embodied the qualities of a true nationalist leader, perhaps with a nuanced democratic inclination, he might have formed strong corporatist alliances with national capitalists. Such alliances could strategically guide their investments toward his ambitious goal of shifting the national development strategy from a liberal globalization approach to the proclaimed "internal circulation" approach. In this strategy, priority is given to internal integration through the creation of a unified domestic market. The state's role would involve regulating private enterprises to align with national objectives, thus promoting industrial progress and fostering economies of scale within a sheltered domestic market.

The notion of economic patriotism would also inherently involve the protection of workers' rights, a presumptive socialist aspiration to which the regime is ostensibly committed. This stance would contribute to cultivating sources of consumption. Beyond its economic implications, it holds the potential to engender a collaborative relationship between capitalists and workers, thereby facilitating the cultivation of social democracy and establishing a foundational framework conducive to the eventual transition to a democratic governance structure.

Without a visionary approach, the nominally Communist, right-wing regime struggles to manage its assertion of the "primacy of politics" as an increasingly burdensome liability rather than as a strategic asset.

Xi's Quest for Autarky: A Mission Impossible?

> We must vigorously enhance our indigenous innovation capabilities and expeditiously achieve breakthroughs in critical core technologies. This constitutes a pivotal concern pertaining to our nation's holistic advance and serves as the linchpin for realizing 'internal circulation.' (Xi Jinping's speech at the expert symposium in the economic and social fields, 24/08/2020)

> Within the industrial sector, there exist situations where vital core technologies are under external control, while certain essential components, parts, and raw materials remain reliant on imports. (Xi Jinping's speech at a symposium of scientists, 11/09/2020)

Xi Jinping's repeated call for self-reliance in high-tech development since 2013, shortly after the Eighteenth National Party Congress, serves as a reminder of his preference for reinstating Mao's autarkic import substitution strategy from the pre-reform era. In fact, not limited to China, autarky has become a global trend from 2017 to the present, with major powers such as the United States, China, India, and to a lesser extent the EU, competing to achieve self-sufficiency in high-tech sectors, particularly production of semiconductors. This trend has been catalyzed by the COVID-19 pandemic, the U.S.-China new Cold War, and the war in Ukraine.[31]

The term "autarky" has been vaguely defined, as even economies that have attempted utter autarky, like Nazi Germany and North Korea, could not completely eliminate foreign trade. It is often distinguished from neomercantilism: while autarky involves limited trade, neomercantilism maintains foreign trade links.[32] However, in academic scholarship, the terms "autarky"—referring to a self-reliant approach combined with protectionism in selected sectors—"neomercantilism," and "economic nationalism" are frequently used interchangeably. Given that an absolute autarky does not exist in the real world, the concept of autarky is defined only in a relative sense. As U.S. protectionism can also be categorized

[31] Dieter, H & Biedermann, J (2022): "The New Advocacy for Autarky: Self-Sufficiency Is Now Once Again Becoming Popular for Geopolitical Reasons." *Economists' Voice*, 19:2, pp. 125–145.

[32] Helleiner, E (2021): "The Return of National Sufficiency? Excavating Autarkic Thought in a De-globalizing Era." *International Studies Review*, 23:3, pp. 933–957.

as autarky, the use of the term is not contingent on the extent to which international trade is affected. It is in this context that Xi Jinping's preference for high-tech self-reliance is termed "autarkic," even though a more precise description might be a form of Listian neomercantilism.

China's pursuit of autarky stems from an intrinsic fear of economic and technological dominance by advanced nations, which control the know-how of cutting-edge technologies beyond China's reach. This apprehension was first voiced by Jiang Zemin, who candidly shared his perspective during the National Science Conference in May 1995. He noted that some of the world's most advanced technologies are not commodities that can be purchased. Should the country's capacity for indigenous innovation stagnate, necessitating reliance on imported technologies, China would perpetually find itself at a technological disadvantage.

A decade later, in 2005, indigenous innovation solidified as a new development strategy, aimed at reducing China's reliance on foreign technology. However, this policy trajectory was significantly diverted thanks in large part to China's strong commitments to further liberalize trade and investments following the Strategic and Economic Dialogues with the United States from 2009 to 2016. The final political report delivered by Hu Jintao in November 2012, prior to handing over power to Xi Jinping at the Eighteenth National Party Congress, outlined the concept of "innovation-driven development." This paradigm shift was necessitated by the recognition that while China's economy was growing rapidly, it lacked strength and was characterized by a focus on quantity over quality. This was a consequence of an extensive industrialization model that strained domestic resource supplies.

Upon assuming the leadership, Xi Jinping emphasized multiple times between 2013 and 2016 that China's predicament of technological subjugation to "other nations" remained largely unchanged. As a result, China found itself positioned in the mid- to lower echelons of the value chain. To address this situation, Xi stressed the imperative of resolutely pursuing indigenous innovation, although its implementation has been incoherent since its inception.

In addition to the fear of potential technological coercion by "hostile" foreign powers, particularly the industrial West and notably the United States, the pressing need for economic rebalancing offered an additional rationale for technological self-reliance. Despite the staggering Ricardian growth miracle over the past few decades, China's entrapment in semi-peripheral development becomes evident through persistent under-consumption, as measured by the low proportion of private consumption in the Chinese national economy. This proportion ranked not only the lowest when compared to advanced Global North countries, but also below the BRICS average (Table 7.1). The CCP was unequivocal shortly after the outbreak of the global financial crisis that industrial upgrading was crucially indispensable in order for China to distance itself from the extensive mode of industrialization characterized by the "three lows"—low price, low profit, and low value added. This "low-end pathway" (*diduan zhilu*, 低端之路) of development was unlikely to lead China toward modernization, as highlighted by the *People's Daily* editorial on March 1, 2010.[33]

Henry Paulson correctly noted this fundamental structural weakness of the Chinese economy and recommended that China fully liberalize trade and investment. He argued that removing protective barriers to foreign competition would facilitate China's catching up, thereby rebalancing the economy toward a consumption-driven, high-income model. However, this recommendation is deeply questionable, given that many U.S. policymakers, including Paulson, a former practitioner within the Obama administration, have been reluctant to acknowledge that "despite partial openness, the United States is not a country of free trade."[34] Trump's economic nationalist endeavor to rebuild a "Fortress America," and Biden's extensive support, which includes heavy subsidies for domestic

Table 7.1 Private consumption as a percentage of GDP

Country	*Consumption ratio (%)*
EU	51.9 (December 2022)
Japan	55.2 (March 2023)
United States	68.2 (June 2023)
BRICS (excluding China)	60.6 (December 2022, exc. data for Brazil in June)
BRICS (including China)	56.1 (December 2022, exc. data for Brazil in June)
China	38.2 (December 2021)

Source https://www.ceicdata.com/en/indicator/brazil/private-consumption--of-nominal-gdp

[33] Editorial: "Industrial Upgrading—The Fatal Choice for China's Modernization." *The People's Daily*, 01/03/2010.

[34] Dieter, H & Biedermann, J (2022), pp. 125–145.

industries, can hardly be considered non-market-distorting and compatible with WTO rules.

Should Paulson's notion be feasible, it would nevertheless make little sense, considering that the EU has also begun embracing autarky with no less zeal, particularly in the area of subsidizing semiconductor production, where "there is hardly any difference between China's state economy and OECD countries."[35]

In reality, the Triad (the United States, the EU, and Japan) has a vested interest in constraining China to the lower echelons of the global value chain, thereby hindering its ascent as a technological powerhouse. The Triad pursues this objective through the implementation of equalized market access measures, effectively eroding China's developing-country status. Ironically, these actors have neglected to recognize the intrinsic self-defeating nature of China's global integration strategy—a strategy significantly shaped by the Triad itself. This trajectory, set on a collision course with intense great power rivalry, has contributed to an unparalleled global imbalance, propelling China's unceasing thirst for resources—a pursuit that the West is ill-prepared to satisfy. At present, the Triad shares a mutual strategic apprehension regarding technological competition with China, further amplifying China's pursuit of autarky with a more substantiated rationale.

The anticipated shift toward autarky in China marks a significant departure from the era of hyperglobalization, during which neoliberal and anti-developmental regulations notably curtailed China's policy flexibility. Alternatively, China could leverage its domestic market, which remains relatively underdeveloped due to the persisting institutionalized economic fragmentation inherited from the provincial autarky of the Maoist era. This fragmentation has been further exacerbated by administrative decentralization in the reform era.

A robust central state would take on the responsibility of formulating and ensuring the implementation of industrial policies within a safeguarded and deeply integrated domestic market. Concurrently, the establishment of an efficient NSI would be paramount. These developments would be underpinned by the revitalization of private consumption—the primary driver of domestic demand. Achieving this revitalization necessitates an overhaul of the prevailing system of crony comprador capitalism.

[35] Ibid.

Without substantial restructuring to promote greater economic equality, the persistence of underconsumption could impede China's pursuit of high-tech autarky for industrial advance, rendering the endeavor ineffective.

Nevertheless, substantial barriers persist, both intellectually and institutionally. Foremost among these is Xi Jinping's adherence to a belief in globalization akin to his predecessors. In January 2016, he remarked:

> Economic globalization is the prevailing trend that we must address in our developmental planning ... Marx's exposition on the world market and world trade provides the theoretical foundation for our understanding of present-day economic globalization ... Two decades ago, or even just 15 years ago, the driving force behind economic globalization was the United States and other Western nations. Today, we are seen as the *foremost advocates* of trade and investment liberalization and facilitation worldwide, actively countering various forms of protectionism practiced by Western countries. This position illustrates that aligning ourselves with the world's developmental trajectory not only enhances our own growth and capabilities but also guides the world's path of progress.[36]

Such hollow declarations, which are emblematic of the rhetoric frequently encountered within Communist bureaucracy, reveal a fundamental lack of awareness concerning WTO rules. Some of these regulations were sufficiently counterproductive to put China's national development into jeopardy. Yet, despite this, by persistently upholding globalization as a matter of political correctness, Xi Jinping's uncritical defense of globalization paradoxically clashes with his pursuit of autarky. This pursuit amounts to a proactive step toward deglobalization, diverting from the very "developmental trajectory of the world" that is acclaimed.

Xi's unwavering belief in hyperglobalization, which he perceived as a universal benefit, led to a miscalculation of Trump's determination to engage in a trade war. This misjudgment also caused a delayed shift in the regime's response to subsequent decoupling, as it turned its focus inward toward the domestic market as a novel source of growth. In May 2020, the CCP introduced the concept of "internal circulation" (*neixhunhuan*, 内循环), or internal integration, emphasizing a greater reliance on domestic markets for economic growth.

[36] Xi Jinping on the Governance of China (hereafter, Xi's book) (2017), vol. 2. Waiwen Chubanshe (Beijing), pp. 210–212.

However, it is important to note that this adjustment does not undermine the importance of "external circulation" (*waixunhuan*, 外循环), often referred to as deep integration or external-oriented development. The new strategy aimed to enhance both "circulations" synergistically. Yet they seemed to overlook the fact that expanded market access through increased trade, investment, and financial liberalization ran counter to the autarkic goals of "internal circulation" in the development of advanced technology, rendering it practically dysfunctional.

While the concept of "internal circulation" emerged, an immediate and concerted effort to institutionalize domestic market integration was noticeably absent. It was not until late March 2022—spanning a period of 22 months—that the Party Center and the State Council jointly released the "Opinions on Accelerating the Construction of a Unified National Market."[37] Within this pivotal document, the central government made a resolute commitment to eradicate local protectionism and dismantle inter-regional barriers. The directive aimed to guide each region to effectively harness their comparative advantages, concurrently discouraging redundant construction and excessive industrial isomorphism—strategies intended to decisively deter localities from venturing into isolated autarkic development. Remarkably, these "opinions" addressed issues recognized as early as the 1980s, yet they had languished, trapped in the shadows of a "feudal economy" or economic balkanization (fragmentation), and overlooked for an extended period.[38]

In 1992, the Communist regime, rejecting the path of internal integration, decisively embraced global capitalism. This choice anchored the nation's development strategy in external integration, setting the stage for the emergence of a Ricardian export-led growth miracle. However, when viewed from a long-term perspective, this approach could be considered short-sighted.

As has been discussed in earlier chapters, China was of a substantial size, and had a large scientific community and a diversified economy, making it inherently suitable for advancing import substitution through

[37] Xinhua, 10/04/2022. https://www.gov.cn/zhengce/2022-04/10/content_5684385.htm.

[38] The issue of market fragmentation was acknowledged as early as 1980. In October 2003, Assistant Minister of MOFCOM Huang Hai called for "breaking regional blockade and creating a unified national market." Regrettably, these suggestions largely went unheeded.

market-based economic reintegration within its own borders. This approach, naturally driven by consumption, would reduce dependence on global markets and promote self-sustainability.

Given the enduring effects of administrative decentralization, a strong central government was indispensable for achieving national economic reintegration, especially in the effective implementation of nationwide industrial policies. This decentralization inadvertently fostered influential bureaucratic vested interests at the local level, giving them the ability to challenge central authority and obstruct directives perceived as detrimental to regional interests. This phenomenon was often derided as "executive orders that never leave the confines of Zhongnanhai" (*zhengling buchu Zhongnanhai*, 政令不出中南海), the seat of the highest authority encompassing the Party Center and the State Council.

A notable instance of this is the solar panel development in the early 2010s, which was not overseen by a centralized state apparatus akin to Japan's Ministry of International Trade and Industry (MITI), but rather led by competing local states investing in local interests.[39] This approach resulted in diseconomies of scale, significant waste, and financial losses. Even now, as the necessity for national market integration was belatedly acknowledged in 2022, the critical redefinition of the central-local relationship remains shrouded in ambiguity, casting uncertainty over the concept of "internal circulation."

Moreover, central to the successful economic reintegration into an autarkic framework is alignment with economic nationalism, as opposed to economic internationalism. The latter tendency could potentially tip the competitive advantage scale in favor of foreign firms over domestic counterparts. However, the CCP's insistence on equal weighting for the "two circulations" becomes incongruous when contrasted with its resolute pursuit of autarky rooted in self-reliance.

Xi Jinping takes pride in China's possession of the world's largest scientific community.[40] However, even before he came to power, corruption within the scientific community had proliferated to an astonishing level. Research funds were siphoned off into personal coffers through various means. Over 30% of the allocated 1 trillion-yuan research and

[39] Yue, J (2014), pp. 41–58.

[40] Xi's book, vol. 1, p. 127.

development (R&D) funds were "improperly used" for purposes unrelated to research. College professors were at the forefront of China's "scientific corruption." Only a mere 40% of research funds were directed toward genuine science and technology development, while the remaining 60% were absorbed by assorted unrelated expenses.[41] The state-controlled appropriation of research funds provided ample opportunities for large-scale rent-seeking. Despite Xi Jinping's anti-corruption campaign, without a comprehensive overhaul of China's research incentive system, corruption within the scientific community persisted. Tu Youyou, the first Chinese Nobel Prize Laureate in Physiology or Medicine awarded in 2015 for her discovery of artemisinin, has repeatedly failed to be elected as an academician of the Chinese Academy of Sciences. This failure has caused huge controversy regarding China's academician system, whose evaluation and selection process was riddled with *guanxi* (nepotism) instead of recognizing genuine academic achievements.[42]

In addition to the issue of scientific corruption, which had expanded further to encompass academic corruption involving fraud and plagiarism that was almost omnipresent, Xi Jinping's tightening grip on ideological control within colleges and research institutions led to an even more stringent enforcement of the Great Firewall—a comprehensive blockade that indiscriminately obstructed the flow of information between China and the outside world. This extensive censorship effectively deprived Chinese scientists of access to the latest scientific advances, including vital platforms like Google Scholar. In May 2016, a group of 78 academicians from the Chinese Academy of Sciences penned a petition letter to the Chinese regime, advocating the relaxation of internet restrictions.[43] Unfortunately, their plea went unanswered. The escalating political repression, designed to suppress dissenting voices, consequently fostered a closed society that significantly curtailed China's potential for foundational innovation. This stands in stark contrast to the Third Reich, in which the

41 "'Scientific Corruption' Enraged the Minster of Science and Technology." A series of reports in October 2013. https://www.edu.cn/html/rd/kyjf/.

42 BBC (Chinese), 05/10/2015. https://www.bbc.com/zhongwen/simp/china/2015/10/151005_china_tu_youyou.

43 "Academicians of the Chinese Academy of Sciences Call on Xi Jinping to Treat Them More Leniently in Internet Supervision." *Radio Free Asia* (Mandarin), 02/06/2016. https://www.rfa.org/mandarin/yataibaodao/meiti/nu-06022016100305.html.

education system, in general, yielded results superior to those of the Weimar Republic.[44]

In order to make the autarky strategy effective, addressing the issue of underconsumption was crucial. This requirement necessitated a certain degree of de-Dengification, which involved the reintroduction of socialist principles primarily aimed at combating inequality. Xi Jinping's dedication to preserving the Communist dictatorship was widely regarded in the West as a clear manifestation of his strong commitment to Marxist-Leninist ideology. Indeed, in comparison to the Hu Jintao era, when ideological devotion to Marxism was on the rise, more resources have been allocated to the study of Marxism since Xi assumed power.

Schools of Marxist Studies were established in leading universities, equipped with ample funding, and they attracted a large number of students applying for PhD research. These students were promised promising job prospects after graduation. In late April 2018, the CCP's Propaganda Department aired a five-episode documentary titled "Marx Got It Right" on CCTV (China Central Television). This documentary praised *Das Kapital* and the concept of "human emancipation." This broadcast seemed to confirm the impact of an influential article written by left-wing scholar Professor Zhou Xincheng of the Renmin University of China. Published on January 11, 2018, on the official Weibo of the "Flag" column of "Seeking Truth," a key CCP mouthpiece known for authoritatively interpreting the Party's policies, Zhou's article emphasized the essence of Communism: the elimination of private ownership and the establishment of public ownership of the means of production. According to Zhou, realizing the common ownership of the means of production necessitates the eradication of private ownership. This fundamental principle, Zhou argued, defines the original intention and mission of a Communist and should be kept in mind and never forgotten. Forgetting this principle would constitute betrayal and disqualify an individual from being considered a true member of the Communist Party.

Both Zhou's article and the documentary triggered a wave of unease throughout the country, raising concerns about Xi Jinping's potential shift toward a more fundamentalist Marxism-Leninism. This sentiment was particularly pronounced among private entrepreneurs, who became apprehensive about the potential resurgence of policies advocating the

[44] Fitzgerald, M (2006): *Adolf Hitler—A Portrait*. Chalford: Spellmount, p. 142.

"expropriation of the expropriator," a well-known phrase from the *Communist Manifesto*. Adding to this unease was an article written by Wu Xiaoping, a senior financial professional, on September 12. This article spread across China's social media platforms and was titled "China's Private Economy Has Completed the Task of Assisting the Development of the Public Economy and Should Gradually *Exit* the Market." Within two days, this article garnered over 50 million clicks, further intensifying fears among private entrepreneurs that their assets might be seized by the state, reminiscent of the 1950s during the socialist transformation movement.

However, two weeks later on September 27, Xi Jinping attempted to reassure national capitalists by pledging the unwavering development of the publicly owned economy and expressing unswerving support for the growth of the private economy.[45] Then, on November 1, during a symposium on the development of private enterprises, Xi stressed: "Our country's private economy can only grow, not weaken. Not only can it not '*exit*,' but it must move to a broader stage." He emphasized the inviolability of publicly owned economic property rights, as well as the equal inviolability of non-publicly owned economic property rights.[46] In a separate account from an on-site source, Xi was quoted as saying that private enterprises and private entrepreneurs are "our own people."[47] These two phrases—regarding the inviolability of private property and the reference to private entrepreneurs as "our own people"—were absent in his third volume of *On the Governance of China* (《习近平谈治国理政》), which was published in April 2020.[48]

Whether the regime's approach of alternately threatening and appeasing capitalists is an expediency or not is not the primary concern.

[45] "Unforgettable 50 Days." *News Front*, No. 11, 2019. http://paper.people.com.cn/xwzx/html/2019-11/01/content_1998513.htm.

[46] "Vigorously Support the Development and Growth of Private Enterprises." The *People's Daily*, 14/11/2018. http://theory.people.com.cn/n1/2018/1114/c40531-30399304.html.

[47] "'Private Enterprises and Private Entrepreneurs Are Our Own People'"—Sidelights on Private Enterprise Symposium Presided over by General Secretary Xi Jinping. The *People's Daily*, 02/22/2018. http://politics.people.com.cn/n1/2018/1102/c1001-30377203.html.

[48] Xi's Book (vol. 3), pp. 263–268.

As was discussed in the preceding section of this chapter, the reassertion of the "primacy of politics" was crucial in understanding the CCP's motivation to exert absolute control over all social and economic entities. In this context, the ideology itself becomes less significant. Xi Jinping's overt pro-capitalist statements hardly position him as a steadfast Marxist, despite the broadcasting of "Marx Got It Right." This is further evident in the regime's severe crackdown on college students from several prominent universities who genuinely believed in Marxism and attempted to put anti-capitalist Marxist teachings into practice by organizing independent labor movements. Indoctrinated by the official ideology, these young Marxists, alongside some Maoists, were acutely aware of the disparity between classical Marxism and the concept of "socialism with Chinese characteristics."[49] This "precarious worker-student alliance" had the potential to "rekindle a century-long revolutionary legacy"[50]—a legacy that was largely betrayed by a nominally Marxist party whose ruling elites, including Xi Jinping, exhibited strong elements of "ruling-class consciousness."[51]

The Chinese regime's hypocrisy regarding Marxism was exemplified on another occasion. French political economist Thomas Piketty's first book, *Capital in the 21st Century*, published in 2013, critiquing the shortcomings of modern capitalism, became a bestseller in China and was even cited by Xi Jinping. However, when Piketty extended his critique to address inequality in China in his second book, *Capital and Ideology*, it faced censorship by the Chinese authorities.[52]

While rejecting criticism—a characteristic trait of the CCP—does not necessarily indicate an aversion to problem-solving, Xi's true intentions

[49] Shannon Tiezzi: "Communist China's Crackdown on Labor Protesters—China's Rhetorical Embrace of Marx Hasn't Prevented the Arrests of Activists Supporting an Independent Trade Union." *The Diplomat*, 28/08/2018. https://thediplomat.com/2018/08/communist-chinas-crackdown-on-labor-protesters/.

[50] Chan, J (2020): "A Precarious Worker-Student Alliance in Xi's China." *The China Review*, 20:1, pp. 165–190.

[51] On February 12, 2018, Xi Jinping stated during an inspection that we must protect the Communist Party's "family business." Critics have pointed out that the CCP, which identifies itself as a proletarian party, should not refer to its operations as a "family business," as this metaphor fails to differentiate between public and private property.

[52] "China Censors Thomas Piketty's Book That Touches on Nation's Growing Inequality." *SCMP*, 30/08/2020. https://www.scmp.com/economy/china-economy/article/3099460/china-censors-thomas-pikettys-book-touches-nations-growing.

remain questionable. This is especially evident given his explicit rejection of the kind of populism seen in Latin American countries with high levels of welfare. Xi expressed these views in December 2021 at the Central Economic Work Conference, echoing sentiments from more than six years ago when the *People's Daily* issued a warning in August 2015 that "excessive welfare is the trap of economic development."[53] He also cautioned private capitalists at the Conference against the "barbaric growth of certain capital,"[54] which served as a justification for the regime's recent purge of ultra-rich private tycoons a few months earlier and hinted at the possibility of further such actions in the future.

Contrary to Xi's assertions, the reality is that after decades of crony capitalist development, very little socialism remains in China. Despite this, Xi's regime has resisted both enacting a Chinese sunshine law and abolishing the numerous privileges held by the nomenklatura. This situation is particularly evident in the healthcare sector, where the nomenklatura consumes 80% of the Chinese government's annual medical expenditures.[55] Faced with entrenched bureaucratic interests, the regime's ability to provide essential social security has been significantly hampered. Consequently, ordinary citizens are compelled to reduce spending in anticipation of healthcare and education expenses that ideally should be covered by the state.

Xi seems to be oblivious to the critical importance of "strong welfare states for capitalism" (as highlighted in *The Economist* article),[56] and even to the appeal made by Francis Fukuyama that "socialism ought to come back."[57] This is especially pertinent, given the underconsumption challenges faced by a semi-peripheral China.

[53] The *People's Daily*, 11/08/2015.

[54] Qiushi (Seeking Truth), 15/05/2022. http://www.qstheory.cn/dukan/qs/2022-05/15/c_1128649367.htm.

[55] "Our Government Invests 80% of Medical Expenses to Serve Party and Government Cadres." *Sina News*, 19/09/2006. https://news.sina.cn/sa/2006-09-19/detail-ikknscsk0963191.d.html. There is no evidence to show that things have changed ever since.

[56] "Capitalism Needs a Welfare State to Survive." *The Economist*, 12/07/2018. https://www.economist.com/leaders/2018/07/12/capitalism-needs-a-welfare-state-to-survive?fsrc=scn/tw/te/bl/ed/capitalismneedsawelfarestatetosurvivebacktobasics.

[57] Francis Fukuyama interview: "Socialism Ought to Come Back." *New statesman*, 17/10/2018. https://www.newstatesman.com/politics/2018/10/francis-fukuyama-interview-socialism-ought-come-back.

The recent refusal by the regime—resulting in public outrage—to abolish senior cadre wards was interpreted by Xinhua as a declaration that "Appropriate treatment should be provided for those who have made great contributions." The Xinhua article further suggested that cancelling such privileges might dampen their enthusiasm for work and even impact the nation's stability.[58] It becomes evident that the regime prioritized appeasing bureaucrats over the well-being of the general populace. Furthermore, Xi's crackdown on "certain capital" since late 2020 was intended to strengthen the regime's grip on what it perceived as the unbridled high bourgeoisie. Simultaneously, it aimed to bolster the state's resources to alleviate mounting fiscal challenges rather than prioritize the well-being of the populace. These actions give rise to questions about whether Xi Jinping can indeed be characterized as a devoted socialist.

Hence, China's endeavor to achieve high-tech self-sufficiency rested on unstable intellectual and institutional foundations. However, Xi seemed overconfident in his statecraft, bolstered by his willingness to be adulated, which led to him being surrounded by "yes-men." This vulnerability renders him susceptible to being misled, impairing his ability to make sound judgments. Even prior to his rise to power in 2011, when he was in a succession role, he responded to World Bank President Robert Zoellick's critique of China's economic challenges. He recommended a book he held in high regard, written by Zhang Weiwei, a former professor at the Geneva School of Diplomacy and International Relations, who was later appointed as a professor at Fudan University. Known for his favor with the CCP within China's intellectual community, Zhang was labeled a "propagandist-academic" by the *New York Times*.[59] Rather than a serious academic publication, riddled with fallacies and bias, Zhang's book, titled *The China Wave: Rise of a Civilizational State*, extolled the Party-led state capitalist China model as superior to Western market democracy. The book concluded that China's ascent, coupled with the decline of the West, would usher in "profound changes unseen in a millennium"

[58] "Xinhua News Agency Issued an Article to Set the Tone: Wards for High-Ranking Cadres Cannot Be Cancelled." *Radio Free Asia* (Cantonese), 10/08/2023. https://www.rfa.org/cantonese/news/cn-ward-08102023133454.html.

[59] "China Sees at Least One Winner Emerging from Ukraine War: China." *The New York Times*, 14/03/2022. https://www.nytimes.com/2022/03/14/world/asia/china-russia-ukraine.html.

for the world. This notion may have later served as a theoretical foundation for Xi Jinping's concept of "profound changes unseen in a century," hinting that Xi's robust leadership fundamentally distinguishes him from his predecessors in the task of strengthening China.

This flawed self-confidence left him easily misguided by the notion of "dependency reversed," which suggested that the American "core" depended on a semi-peripheral China no less than vice versa. This altered his earlier judgment when he met Trump at Mar-a-Lago in April 2017 on the subject of China's fatal economic-technological dependency on the United States. In fact, Xi not only underestimated Trump's determination to engage in a trade war but also fatally miscalculated the asymmetrical core-(semi-)peripheral interdependency between the two countries. He believed that such a war would hurt the United States no less than it would hurt China.

Many technocratic elites and academic experts speculated about and influenced Xi's stance on the avoidable trade war. For instance, Chen Ping, an economics professor at Fudan University, dismissed U.S. threats of a trade war as mere bluffing. He argued that the United States could not afford to lose China's market, leading to the decline of its high-tech industries worldwide. Meanwhile, China's high-tech sectors, particularly chipmakers, would rise due to the expanded market scale previously dominated by U.S. firms. As a result, Chen Ping arrived at a "famous" conclusion: China viewed the trade war as advantageous and was not afraid of it. The sooner and on a larger scale it was fought, the better.[60]

In July 2018, as the trade war began, Mei Xinyu, a left-wing researcher affiliated with the Ministry of Commerce (MOFCOM), posted a strongly nationalist article on social media. This article quickly gained hundreds of thousands of views. Mei advocated fighting an "epic" trade war and proposed treating it as a total war—a protracted economic warfare that could extend beyond three to five months. He suggested prolonging the war until the United States' ongoing economic growth was disrupted by this extensive trade war, possibly lasting beyond Trump's term. Mei's strategy implied that China should use war as a means to end the war and inflict economic pain on the Americans.

Mei asserted that as long as the ultimate outcome of the trade war did not hinder China's continuous growth, as long as China's growth rate

[60] Video Clip: Analysis of Chen Ping on China-US Trade War. 17/04/2018. https://www.youtube.com/watch?v=r8USI9ayIgM.

outperformed that of the United States and other Western powers, and as long as its influence in the international economic system continued to grow, China would ultimately emerge victorious in the trade war.[61]

Xi's advisors took note of this influential article and presented it to him for consideration. Xi was particularly pleased with the term "epic," and his optimism led him to be persuaded by Mei's view of winning the trade war.[62]

With or without Xi's subsequent awareness, Mei Xinyu further elaborated on his viewpoint the following year, providing more clarity and logical coherence to his argument, despite potential empirical challenges. He posited that China was undergoing a historical transition from a "Listian era" to a "Smithian era." According to him, the majority of China's industrial sectors had progressed beyond the "infant industry protection" stage and had matured. Mei argued that subjecting these industries to increased foreign competition would further strengthen them and ensure their sustainability.

Within this framework, Mei advocated a timely transition to the "Smithian era," cautioning against excessive protectionism, which could potentially turn mature domestic industries into "parasites" on the national economy.

Mei suggested that as the United States underwent economic deglobalization, the international economic and trade system required a new "free trade advocate," and he believed that China is well-suited for this role.[63]

Similar to the perspectives of "propagandist-academic" Zhang Weiwei, Mei Xinyu, while disregarding various evidence pointing to China's dependent development and the risk of falling into the "middle-income trap," presented an idealized portrayal of China as a de facto developed country. This depiction may align with the preferences of top leaders and provide support to proponents of "New Developmentalism" in the West who consider China as a model for their ideas.

However, the great irony in this self-complacency is that the longstanding marginalization of Listian thought only recently saw some

[61] Mei Xinyu: On the Sino-US Epic Trade War. 12/07/2018. https://www.aisixiang.com/data/110941.html.

[62] According to an informed source. In June 2022.

[63] Mei Xinyu: "From the "Listian Era" to the "Smithian Era"." 28/06/2019.

correction. This is evident in the Chinese translation of Ha-Joon Chang's influential book *Kicking Away the Ladder*, originally published in the West in 2002, in 2020. Additionally, a Chinese scholar's groundbreaking work, a biography titled *Friedrich List: A Pioneer of Catch-Up Development*, was not published until as late as 2022 (Fig. 7.2).

Contrary to Mei's expectations, the trade war ultimately positioned Trump as the victor, with his forceful leadership instrumental in achieving nearly all his objectives with China. Xi, on the other hand, grappled with the discomfort of accepting a humiliating "unequal treaty" (Phase One Agreement) and had to contend with the subsequent push for a "great decoupling" by Trump's administration. This situation was further exacerbated by the rapid spread of the COVID-19 pandemic, which carried the potential for a new "economic split" and the risk of triggering a new Cold War reminiscent of its predecessors—known for sparking two world wars and a crippling depression.[64] However, Xi's confidence steadily revived thanks to China's rapid economic recovery, facilitated by stringent control measures. Remarkably, China became the only nation to sustain positive growth throughout 2020. This starkly contrasted with Trump's mishandling of the pandemic, which plunged the U.S. economy into a severe downturn.

Xi's confidence in the superiority of China's Leninist party-state system became even more resolute as he observed the erosion of liberal democracy, the West's sluggish response to the COVID-19 crisis, and particularly the unsettling "accelerating political decay" under Trump's administration, coupled with the tumultuous presidential election toward the end of his term. These converging factors played a significant role in solidifying Xi's publicly articulated belief in early March 2021, asserting China's capability to engage with the world as equals.[65] His confidence was underscored by his vision of the "rise of the East versus the decline of the West," and the conviction that "time and momentum are on our

[64] "The Great Decoupling—Washington Is Pressing for a Post-pandemic Decoupling from China." *Foreign Policy*, 14/05/2020. https://foreignpolicy.com/2020/05/14/china-U.S.-pandemic-economy-tensions-trump-coronavirU.S.-covid-new-cold-war-economics-the-great-decoupling/.

[65] Xinhua Daily Telegraph, 23/03/2021. http://www.xinhuanet.com/politics/2021-03/23/c_1127242722.htm.

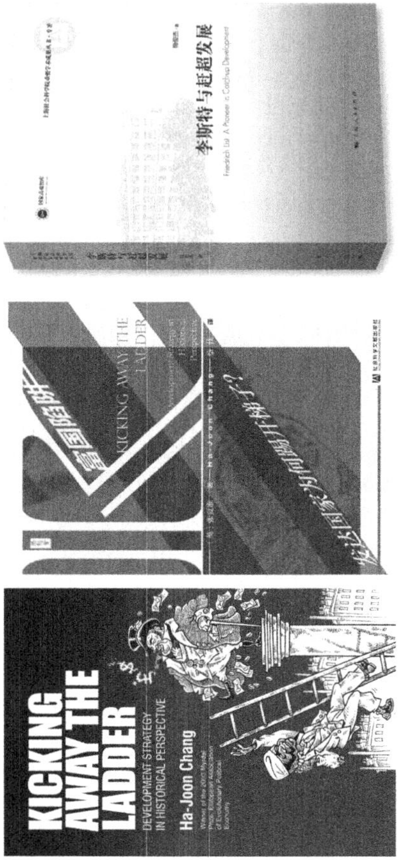

Fig. 7.2 Recent publications in China on anti-free trade ideology (**From left to right**: Ha-Joon Chang's *Kicking Away the Ladder* [2002]; Chinese translation published in May 2020 by the Social Science Literature Press [Beijing]; and Mei Junjie's *List: A Pioneer of Catch-Up Development*, published by the Shanghai People's Publishing House in October 2022)

side."[66] These perspectives encapsulated his earlier observations regarding the seismic shift in global power dynamics—from the Western to the non-West, and from the United States to China—ushering in "profound changes unseen in a century."

That hubris led Xi to "bet that the West was in irreversible decline."[67] His underestimation of the disparity in knowledge and capability between China and the West, particularly the *long-term* efficacy of Western technological decoupling, also spurred his pursuit of a "Great Leap Forward" mentality. This approach aimed to achieve groundbreaking advances in semiconductor manufacturing through a self-assured "all-nation system." Yet China's anticipated "Sputnik moment" failed to materialize. The mobilizing mechanism faltered due to a dearth of decades-long technological accumulation and the pervasive institutional corruption inherent to the market-Leninist regime.

For instance, starting from 2020, the state injected nearly 1 trillion yuan into chip development via the "Big Fund," established in 2014 by MIIT, with the goal of domestic high-end chip manufacturing. An influx of chipmaking firms emerged, benefiting from substantial subsidies provided by both central and local governments. Unfortunately, a multitude of these ventures engaged in fraudulent activities, while several national champions succumbed to severe embezzlement. Consequently, China's endeavor to achieve self-sufficiency in high-end chipmaking ended in disappointment. The aftermath witnessed the arrest of seven high-ranking figures, including leaders of state-owned enterprises and senior MIIT officials, by August 2022, all on charges of corruption.[68]

Xi Jinping could not have foreseen the doomed ineffectiveness of his ambitious "great leap forward" aimed at creating China's own "Sputnik moment" in early 2021. However, he recognized and was apprehensive about the peril of *hasty* Western-imposed decoupling, which would jeopardize his lofty goal of achieving high-tech autarky. For that reason, as early as July 2020, the Chinese government repeatedly voiced opposition

[66] "Time and Momentum are on Our Side." *Red Flag Manuscript* (《红旗文稿》), 11/03/2021. http://www.qstheory.cn/dukan/hqwg/2021-03/11/c_1127198200.htm.

[67] "China Is Betting That the West Is in Irreversible Decline." *The Economist*, 31/03/2021. https://www.economist.com/china/2021/03/31/china-is-betting-that-the-west-is-in-irreversible-decline.

[68] "Chip Anti-corruption Shocked the Industry." *Zhihu*, 01/08/2022. https://zhuanlan.zhihu.com/p/548691055.

to decoupling and called for cooperation with the United States.[69] The Chinese leadership deemed it essential to navigate a delicate path, seeking to appease the United States with the goal of fostering internal divisions within it, particularly after Joe Biden assumed office. This strategy aimed to impede the implementation of intensive decoupling measures and provide Chinese industries with more time to adapt.

As mentioned earlier, in late January 2021, one of his external advisers advocated unrestricted unilateral openness to U.S. investments, even in the face of technological blockades imposed by the United States. Subsequently, on February 7, the Xinhua News Agency issued four editorials extending gestures of goodwill to the United States, emphasizing the importance of maintaining trade and scientific exchanges.[70] Just over two weeks later, on February 24, MOFCOM Minister Wang Wentao expressed China's willingness to "enhance exchanges with the U.S. on trade and economic fronts."[71] On March 3, China's ambassador to Washington, Cui Tiankai, echoed Xi Jinping's remarks from nearly four years

[69] "Deputy Foreign Minister Le Yucheng: The Trend Toward China-US Cooperation Is Unstoppable"—Remarks by Vice Foreign Minister Le Yucheng at the Video Dialogue on Sino-US Relations Co-hosted by the Chinese People's Institute of Foreign Affairs And the Asia Society. *Xinhua*, 08/07/2020. https://www.fmprc.gov.cn/mfa_eng/wjbxw/t1795915.shtml; "Global Times (One of the CCP's Key Mouthpieces) Editorial: Expanding Opening Up Is the Key to China's Response to Challenges." *Global Times*, 27/07/2020. https://opinion.huanqiu.com/article/3zE0JjawRh5; Yang Jiechi, a member of the CCP's politburo, published an article titled "Respect History, Look to the Future and Firmly Safeguard and Stabilize China-US Relations." *Xinhua*, 07/08/2020. http://www.xinhuanet.com/politics/2020-08/07/c_1126339837.htm. The English translation of this article was published on *Global Times*, 07/08/2020. https://www.globaltimes.cn/content/1197044.shtml#.Xy1m_rTFKdg.twitter; Foreign Minister Wang Yi stated in an exclusive interview with Xinhua News Agency, 05/08/2020, "Faced with the most complex situation since the establishment of diplomatic relations in 1979, we need to put in place a clear-cut framework for the relationship: First, steer clear of red lines and avoid confrontation. Second, keep the channels open for candid dialogue. Third, ***reject decoupling and uphold cooperation***. Fourth, abandon the zero-sum mentality and stand up to shared responsibilities." *Xinhua* (Beijing), 06/08/2020. http://www.gov.cn/guowuyuan/2020-08/06/content_5532729.htm (English translation: https://language.chinadaily.com.cn/a/202008/10/WS5f310ac6a31083481725f60a.html); James Palmer: "Xi Jinping Shows His Nerves Over Decoupling." *Foreign Policy*, 27/01/2021. https://foreignpolicy.com/2021/01/27/xi-jinping-davos-world-economic-forum-speech-china-decoupling/.

[70] Xinhua, 07/02/2021. http://www.xinhuanet.com/world/2021-02/07/c_1211015713.htm.

[71] Reuters, 24/02/2021.

earlier, stating that "there are a thousand reasons to make Sino-U.S. relations a success, not a reason to break it."[72]

However, the bipartisan consensus in the United States to contain China remained steadfast, even following Biden's assumption of power. According to former Defense Secretary Robert Gates, it was Chinese leader Xi Jinping who achieved what few others could, resulting in a "rare bipartisan consensus" on adopting a tougher stance toward China. This reversal in approach was something Biden found difficult to change.[73] While the Biden administration avoided explicit discussions of decoupling and trade wars, its foreign policy continued along similar lines to its predecessor, as noted by Henry Kissinger, albeit with a "more liberal rhetoric."[74] Secretary of State Antony Blinken outlined the administration's approach to China as being "competitive when it should be, collaborative when it can be, and adversarial when it must be"[75]—a stance not significantly different from Trump's strategy: simultaneously seeking to contain China while also desiring access to its market.

China's growing frustration became evident as the United States deepened its collaboration with Japan in May 2021 within the high-tech supply chain, with a particular emphasis on sectors like semiconductors and rare earth elements.[76] This expanding partnership raised concerns in China. Likewise, the formal establishment of the EU-US Technology and Trade Council (TTC) on June 15 underscored the extent of Western cooperation. This Council established ten working groups, two of which were dedicated to export controls and investment screening, evoking memories of the functions performed by CoCom (the Coordinating Committee for

[72] Xinhua, 02/03/2021. http://www.xinhuanet.com/politics/2021-03/02/c_1127159441.htm.

[73] "Former senior official of the US Department of Defense: Biden Will Continue His Tough China Policy." *Radio Free Asia*, 29/03/2021. https://www.rfa.org/mandarin/yataibaodao/junshiwaijiao/hc-03292021170451.html.

[74] "A Conversation with Henry Kissinger." *The Economist*, 17/05/2023. https://www.economist.com/kissinger-transcript.

[75] "Blinken Says Only China Can Truly Challenge Global System." *Bloomberg*, 03/03/2021. https://www.bloomberg.com/news/articles/2021-03-03/blinken-calls-china-competition-a-key-challenge-for-the-u-s?leadSource=uverify%20wall.

[76] Oh, M, Hildebrand, and Lee, H. W. (May 2021): "Enhancing U.S.-Japan Cooperation on Global Supply Chains." Atlantic Council issue brief: https://www.atlanticcouncil.org/wp-content/uploads/2021/05/Enhancing-U.S.-Japan-Cooperation-on-Global-Supply-Chains.pdf.

Multilateral Export Controls) during the Cold War. The Council's inaugural formal meeting on September 29 further solidified policy alignment between the United States and the EU. Both committed to upholding "democratic values" and enhancing coordination in foreign investment screening and export control.

Equally concerning for China was the passing of the U.S. Innovation and Competition Act of 2021 on June 8, a clear demonstration of America's wholehearted embrace of an industrial policy that surpassed even the vigor of the Trump era. This comprehensive legislation, which designated China as "the greatest geopolitical and geo-economic challenge for United States foreign policy," had a specific focus on China and stood as proof of the United States' resolute commitment to safeguard its technological supremacy. Notably, the programs financed by this bill bore a close resemblance to those outlined in "Made in China 2025."[77] Interestingly, despite the traditional American reluctance to overtly acknowledge the implementation of industrial policy, as Michael Lind astutely pointed out in his book: "Industrial policy is not alien to the American tradition. It is the American tradition."[78]

It is evident that the Chinese government did heed the recommendation for China to adopt a unilateral market-opening approach in response to the United States' determined efforts to fortify "Fortress America." Commencing in April amid escalating tensions with the United States, China expedited its financial liberalization initiatives. By August, as reported by CCTV, revisions to 34 measures concerning the opening-up of China's banking and insurance sectors were nearing completion.[79] This proactive effort primarily aimed to bolster foreign investors' confidence, a pivotal factor for China's economic recovery. Concurrently, it was a strategic response to counteract America's decoupling momentum by engaging Wall Street finance in China's financial market.

China's eagerness to stabilize its investment environment signaled a sluggish demand at home. Despite the facade of inflated growth rate data, the reality of unemployment painted a different picture. Following the

[77] "Senate Poised to Pass Huge Industrial Policy Bill to Counter China." *The New York Times*, 08/06/2021. https://www.nytimes.com/2021/06/07/us/politics/senate-china-semiconductors.html.

[78] Lind, M (2012), p. 465.

[79] CCTV news, 13/08/2021. https://www.gov.cn/xinwen/2021-08/13/content_5631247.htm.

trend of soaring unemployment in 2020, official sources revealed in May 2021 that China's "flexible employment"—a euphemism for the semi-employed or fully unemployed—had reached a staggering 200 million.[80] By July 2021, the unemployment rate for young people aged 16–24 had climbed to 16%,[81] underscoring a pronounced economic downturn. This contrasted starkly with the remarkable economic rebound in the United States, which had driven the jobless rate down to 5.4% during the same period.[82]

Positioned as a semi-peripheral economy on the precipice of the "middle-income trap," China's archaic growth model, centered on extensive industrialization, faces a critical juncture. The nation's growth potential now hinges on its capacity for innovation, a necessity due to the aging population and changing work ethos of the once pliable young labor force. However, shortsighted Chinese policymakers have consistently underinvested in human capital over the past few decades, resulting in a scarcity and decline of a well-paid, highly skilled labor force.[83] This, combined with China's flawed national innovation system, has hindered the development of dynamic comparative advantages essential for the transition to a high-income industrial economy and crucial for China's ascent to economic superpower status.

The trade war, despite its contentious nature, ultimately compelled Chinese leadership to confront the nation's vulnerability amid U.S.-led technological decoupling. As achieving technological self-sufficiency is a time-consuming endeavor, maintaining uninterrupted trade relations with the United States and its allies became a top priority. However, the denial of access to technological products, let alone the know-how of cutting-edge technologies, poses a significant threat to China's potential for import substitution and technological self-sufficiency through reverse engineering.

[80] The PRC government website, 20/05/2021. https://www.gov.cn/xinwen/2021-05/20/content_5609599.htm.

[81] Radio Free Asia, 14/02/2022. https://www.rfa.org/mandarin/yataibaodao/jingmao/hx1-02142022094652.html.

[82] "Unemployment Rates Were Lower in 17 States and DC in July 2021." BLS, released on 25/08/2021. https://www.bls.gov/opub/ted/2021/unemployment-rates-were-lower-in-17-states-and-the-district-of-columbia-in-july-2021.htm.

[83] Beijing Daily, 25/05/2015. http://theory.people.com.cn/n/2015/0525/c49154-27049754.html.

Confidence in the U.S. decoupling strategy to slow China's ascent has notably strengthened. This growing conviction is fueled by mounting evidence of a "peak China," a term coined by Michael Beckley in 2018[84] and that gained traction in 2023,[85] suggesting that China's rise may not be irreversible. A noteworthy report by *Bloomberg*, released on July 5, 2021 and titled "When Will China Rule the World? Maybe Never," outlined three crucial factors—reform failures, international isolation, and financial crises—that could potentially halt China's rise. This marks a shift from the previous perception that China's ascent was unstoppable. While acknowledging concerns about the reliability of Chinese statistical data, the report suggested that U.S. decoupling, whether partial or comprehensive, could lead to a 5–13% reduction in China's GDP.[86]

The phenomenon of "peak China" casts doubt not only on the once-dominant notion of a power shift but also on arguments presented by some influential voices against aggressive decoupling. These individuals insist that such a strategy might push China toward self-reliant technological leapfrogging. The strong indications of a "peak China" seem to have rendered their recommendations on "managing the rivalry with China within the context of continued economic interdependence"[87] unnecessary.

Despite leaders' concerns about decoupling, China's "wolf-warrior" approach continued to gain strength following Xi Jinping's "China's rise versus the West's decline" address in March 2021. The Sino-U.S. talks held in late March in Alaska, the first major meeting aimed at détente after the Trump era, showcased China's "public theatrics," as exemplified by Politburo member Yang Jiechi's 16-minute opening remarks. These remarks strongly condemned American hegemonism. Behind closed doors, however, the two-day meetings proved to be more "productive" than the public tensions suggested. American negotiators understood

[84] Beckley, M: "The Power of Nations: Measuring What Matters." *International Security*, 43:2, pp. 7–44.

[85] For instance: "Peak China?" *The Economist*, 13/05/2023. https://www.economist.com/weeklyedition/2023-05-13; https://www.economist.com/leaders/2023/05/11/is-chinese-power-about-to-peak.

[86] "When Will China Rule the World? Maybe Never." *Bloomberg*, 05/07/2021. https://www.bloomberg.com/news/features/2021-07-05/when-will-china-s-economy-beat-the-u-s-to-become-no-1-why-it-may-never-happen.

[87] Westad, O. A. (2019): "The Sources of Chinese Conduct."

that this often involved an exaggeration of diplomatic presentation, often tailored for a domestic audience.[88]

In a way, "wolf warrior diplomacy" was ignited by the deteriorating geopolitical situation in the Indo-Pacific. China's heightened awareness was sparked by Biden's united front approach, aimed at rallying alliances in China's periphery. Despite agreeing to maintain dialogue and communication, significant divisions persisted. Whether the "productive" closed-door talks involved secret protocols remains to be seen; only time and the declassification of foreign policy archives in the decades ahead may reveal the truth. Geopolitical tensions continued after the meeting, with Sino-Russian rapprochement gaining further ground. The United States pressed ahead with diplomatic and military alliance-building to confront China's growing challenges. Ironically, China's prominently showcased "wolf warrior diplomacy" inadvertently played into the hands of the United States, which strategically leveraged it to advance its goal of deterring China.

The geopolitical pressures that China quickly discerned soon began to cast a shadow on its economic prospects. The signing of AUKUS on September 15, intended to create substantial deterrence against China, stirred significant apprehension among Chinese leaders. The swift and resolute U.S. move toward preemptive deterrence underscored potential economic repercussions in the unfolding new Cold War, further reinforcing the notion that decoupling was becoming an inevitable reality. This mounting sense of urgency led to a hasty decision. On the following day, September 16, MOFCOM declared its intention to seek membership in the Comprehensive and Progressive Agreement for Trans-Pacific Partnership (CPTPP). This pivotal decision was of significant importance, given that the CPTPP was formed with the specific objective of preventing China's inclusion, ultimately undercutting its export-led growth potential.

However, should China's application succeed, it could inevitably lead to a substantial loss of its developmental interests—interests that the Chinese regime has identified as the nation's third core national interest. The "to join or not to join" dilemma, akin to another Shakespearean question, has placed China at a crossroads. The choice presented is

[88] Reuters, 19/03/2021. https://www.reuters.com/world/us/U.S.-china-set-broach-icy-relations-alaska-talks-2021-03-18/.

a difficult one, as its critical economic transformation faces a pivotal juncture.

China's willingness to jeopardize its core national interests in an effort to stave off decoupling underscores the regime's deep-seated fear that even its semi-peripheral development could be derailed. In this challenging context, the regime finds itself with limited options, essentially choosing among the "least worst" alternatives.

On December 27, MOFCOM unveiled a new nationwide Negative List that also applies to the Free Trade Zone. In this updated list, the number of prohibited items was further reduced from 33 to 31 for the nationwide application, and from 30 to 27 for the Free Trade Zone.[89]

As the year 2021 drew to a close, it became increasingly evident that full decoupling is unlikely, at least in the short term (Table 7.2). The real focus has remained centered on partial decoupling, particularly in high-tech sectors where the United States is making forceful advances—an approach that even the renowned nationalist figurehead Wang Xiaodong found deeply concerning.

In a Weibo post on December 21, 2021, Wang disclosed his recent meeting with two prominent senior technocratic figures. He dismissed the notion of pure self-reliance as unrealistic. Acknowledging the substantial gap between China and the United States in scientific and technological development, he cautioned against the risk of China's exclusion from the U.S.-dominated international system. Such exclusion could make it exceedingly challenging for China to catch up in less-advanced sectors and potentially lag even further behind in more advanced areas.

Table 7.2 U.S.-China trade (2018–2022) (in US$ billions)

Year	*US EX*	*US IM*	*Total*	*Balance*
2022	153.8	536.8	690.6	−383
2021	151.1	506.4	657.5	−355.3
2020	124.5	434.8	559.3	−310.3
2019	106.5	450.8	557.3	−344.3
2018	120.3	538.5	658.8	−418.2

Source https://www.bis.doc.gov/index.php/smart-search?searchword=china&searchphrase=all

[89] http://www.mofcom.gov.cn/article/syxwfb/202112/20211203232113.shtml.

Wang argued that the cost of preventing China's exclusion, even if it involved sacrifices and perhaps even some humiliation, would be worthwhile. He believed that thwarting the global consensus on decoupling from China could achieve this goal. However, Wang did not delve into the specifics of the price China should pay. Paradoxically, he expressed a lack of concern about China's exclusion—a politically correct gesture—despite recognizing the significant economic toll such an outcome would impose.[90]

China was compelled to pay this price eight months later when, on August 26, 2022, it reached an agreement with the U.S. Securities and Exchange Commission (SEC)—a deal more comprehensive than any other country had agreed. This decision was made under the looming enactment of the CHIPS and Science Act on August 9, was aimed primarily at countering China's "Made in China 2025" initiative. As a result of this agreement, the Public Company Accounting Oversight Board (PCAOB) was granted an unprecedented level of access to audit work papers of over 200 Chinese companies trading in the United States, all of which were facing the risk of delisting from the U.S. stock market.

The SEC remained steadfast, refusing to compromise with China. Under the terms of the agreement, the PCAOB obtained complete access through three significant provisions:

1. The PCAOB was granted sole discretion in selecting firms, audit engagements, and potential violations to inspect and investigate, without requiring consultation with or input from Chinese authorities.
2. Procedures were established for PCAOB inspectors and investigators to view complete audit work papers, including all information, and for the PCAOB to retain information as needed.
3. The PCAOB was granted direct access to interview the audits it inspects or investigates.

In essence, this agreement granted the PCAOB unrestricted access to audit work papers, audit personnel, and all pertinent information,

[90] Wang Xiaodong Weibo post: "China's Current Grand Strategy Is to Employ All Available Means to Prevent Its Exclusion from the U.S.-Led Global Economic Order." 21/12/2021. https://weibo.com/5505421209/L785Cvlef.

without any loopholes or exceptions.[91] China was apprehensive about the potential delisting of these firms, as their combined market value had reached a staggering $1.3 trillion—a sum too significant to be redirected to Chinese mainland or Hong Kong stock markets. This left China with limited bargaining leverage in its negotiations with the United States, a predicament that was exacerbated by a severe economic contraction since the beginning of 2022. This contraction was brought about by stringent lockdown measures implemented in several Chinese cities, including metropolitan Shanghai, as a response to the pandemic's resurgence.

Nevertheless, downplaying the role of values in solidifying Western unity and still overestimating China's strength, coupled with Russia's military power, led Xi Jinping to misjudge the global balance of power once again. He believed that it was shifting in China's favor. This miscalculation not only played a role in the ongoing prevalence of "wolf warrior diplomacy" worldwide but also helped prompt the revival of a "brain-dead" NATO. Additionally, it reinforced the consensus among the United States and its allies regarding decoupling from China or adopting derisking measures (the latter initiated by the EU since January 2023). These factors accelerated the diversification of supply chains toward safer alternatives within the developing world, a situation that had raised deep concerns voiced by Wang Xiaodong toward the end of the previous year.

Putin's invasion of Ukraine on February 24, 2022, ostensibly under the cover of signing the Sino-Russian Joint Declaration expressing mutual collaboration to challenge the liberal international order, further strained U.S.-China relations in high politics. The escalating domestic instability due to lockdown weariness and the looming threat of secondary sanctions imposed by the West, given China's alignment with Russia, significantly heightened the regime's sense of insecurity. This pressure pushed China to focus inward, leading to the decision in April 2022 to establish a unified domestic market—a belated initiative aimed at implementing its "internal circulation" strategy. Simultaneously, China accelerated its efforts to construct a "Fortress China," encompassing self-sufficiency in

[91] "US, China Reach Preliminary Deal in Push to Avoid Delistings." *Bloomberg*, 26/08/2022. https://www.bloomberg.com/news/articles/2022-08-26/U.S.-and-china-reach-preliminary-deal-on-audit-reviews-sec-says?leadSource=uverify%20wall.

technology, energy, and food supply, as well as the internationalization of the renminbi.[92]

Russia's self-inflicted entrapment in a war of attrition, particularly due to the significant disparity in military technology, caught its strategic partner China off guard. This compelled China to reassess the feasibility of a swift military intervention in Taiwan—a region whose defense has now become a critical U.S. national interest, safeguarding advanced chip manufacturing and supply chains. Additionally, the West's imposition of sanctions on Russia, including its expulsion from SWIFT, FDI exits, and trade embargoes, served as a poignant reminder to China of John Ikenberry's famous observation about the nature of the liberal international order established by the United States after World War II: "easy to join but hard to overturn."[93]

Putin's military actions and China's substantial foreign policy mismanagement, which led to the alienation of American allies in Europe and East Asia, hardly improved the position of the two revisionist powers vis-à-vis a divided and weakened West. Instead, it potentially marked a "return of the Pax Americana," bolstered by a fortified democratic alliance.[94] This outcome amounted to a strategic debacle, signifying a significant shift in the high-politics landscape that had maintained China's peaceful development over recent decades.

The resurgence of mutual enmity between China and the United States reignited China's historical resentment toward Western imperialism, which had compelled it into the Westphalian state system over a century and a half ago. A highly controversial dissertation, posted on its WeChat official account on August 24 by the Chinese Academy of History under the Chinese Academy of Social Sciences, contended that China's self-exclusion policy during the Ming and Qing Dynasties was a

[92] "Fortress China: Xi Jinping's Plan for Economic Independence." *The Financial Times*, 15/09/2022. https://www.ft.com/content/0496b125-7760-41ba-8895-8358a7f24685.

[93] Ikenberry, J (2011): *Liberal Levithan: The Origins, Crisis, and Transformation of the American World Order*. Princeton, NJ: Princeton University Press, p. 9.

[94] "The Return of Pax Americana? Putin's War Is Fortifying the Democratic Alliance." *Foreign Affairs*. https://www.foreignaffairs.com/articles/russia-fsu/2022-03-14/return-pax-americana.

just act of autonomous self-defense.[95] This perspective contradicted previously held notions of Ming and Qing China being economically backward and politically conservative, factors at the root of its inability to resist Western military encroachment. This article sparked widespread discussion about the regime's motivations for potentially "North Koreanizing" China in the name of defending China's national security. Ostensibly, this potential new "self-exclusion" seems to serve the purpose of protecting not so much national security, but rather mirroring the practices of old imperial regimes, safeguarding the regime's security from external threats.

Regime stability, veiled under the term "political security," involving "regime security, systemic security, and ideological security," has been consistently emphasized by Xi Jinping since 2017. This emphasis intensified as the Twentieth National Party Congress approached in October 2022. In this Congress, Xi achieved a resounding victory, quelling all opposing factions and solidifying his position as an undisputed leader with no term limits. In the political report delivered to the Congress, while Xi maintained the customary rhetoric of highlighting the importance of economic development, his primary focus became evident: "security," a term mentioned 50 times more frequently than "economic," which was cited only 22 times. This signaled a shift in priority from economic growth to regime stability.

This shift became even more pronounced in early November when a draft amendment to the Legislation Law, previously deliberated by the Standing Committee of the National People's Congress (the equivalent to the U.S. Senate or the UK's Upper House), was made available for public comments online. Notably, in Article 3 of the "General Principle," the previously included terms "focusing on economic development" and "adhering to reform and opening up" were conspicuously absent.[96]

Biden's 2022 NSS, unveiled on October 12, affirmed Xi Jinping's emphasis on security over economics. This strategy represented a significant departure, shifting toward a "renewed focus on great-power rivalry,"

[95] Research Group of the Chinese Academy of History (2022): "A New Exploration on the Issue of 'Self-Exclusion' in the Ming and Qing Dynasties." *History Research*, No. 3, pp. 4–21.

[96] RTHK news, 10/11/2022. https://gbcode.rthk.hk/TuniS/news.rthk.hk/rthk/ch/component/k2/1674971-20221110.htm?spTabChangeable=0.

aligning more closely with former President Trump's approach rather than that of President Obama.[97]

The NSS document identified China as the "most consequential geopolitical challenge," recognizing China as the sole rival with the intent and increasingly convergent economic, diplomatic, military, and technological power to reshape the global order. The 2022 NSS emphasized that the United States is actively engaged in a "strategic competition to shape the future of the international order." It stressed the commitment to "prioritize maintaining a lasting competitive advantage over China," while also addressing concerns about Russia's influence.[98]

On the same day, President Biden stated that the primary challenge in the coming years would be to "outcompete China and constrain Russia."[99] Biden's commitment to "rapid decoupling, whatever the consequences"[100] appears to be influenced by observed outcomes of Xi Jinping's policies, which have seemingly weakened China's competitive position against the United States and made China's rise less certain. Increasingly, to the relief of American elites, the longer President Xi Jinping remains in power, the more favorable the circumstances may become for the United States to "enhance its global standing."[101]

Xi Jinping could not have anticipated the contents of Biden's 2022 NSS, which coincided with the Twentieth National Party Congress held October 16–22. Nevertheless, discernible trends signaling a "sea change" in U.S. thinking about the "return of great power rivalry" were evident. This shift in U.S. perspective also contributed to a transformation in Xi's thinking, leading to the removal of the archaic "Peace and Development

[97] "Biden's New National Security Strategy: A Lot of Trump, Very Little Obama." *Foreign Policy*, 17/10/2022. https://foreignpolicy.com/2022/10/17/national-security-strategy-nss-biden-trump-obama-china-russia-geopolitics/.

[98] NSS 2022 (October): https://www.whitehouse.gov/wp-content/uploads/2022/10/Biden-Harris-Administrations-National-Security-Strategy-10.2022.pdf.

[99] "Biden's National Security Strategy Focuses on China, Russia and Democracy at Home." *The New York Times*, 12/10/2022. https://www.nytimes.com/2022/10/12/us/politics/biden-china-russia-national-security.html.

[100] "Biden Is Now All-In on Taking Out China." *Foreign Policy*, 12/10/2022. https://foreignpolicy.com/2022/10/12/biden-china-semiconductor-chips-exports-decouple/.

[101] "China's Mistakes Can Be America's Gain." *The Atlantic*, 26/09/2022. https://www.theatlantic.com/international/archive/2022/09/xi-jinping-china-U.S.-mistakes/671544/.

is the main theme of the contemporary world" (the "two-theme" thesis) from his political report. This notion had been reiterated since the Thirteenth National Party Congress in 1987 until the preceding Nineteenth Congress held in 2017. Simultaneously, there was the abandonment of the "period of strategic opportunity," which had signified the end of Xi's previous acceptance of pacific idealism that had permeated the Party elites. The "period of strategic opportunity," as used in this context, referred to a period without imminent war threats. In contrast to the Sixteenth National Party Congress held in 2002, during which Jiang Zemin removed "opposing hegemonism" from the foreign policy section, Xi Jinping reinstated it in 2022.

In this latest Congress, Xi elaborated extensively on his vision of "Chinese-style modernization," defining it as a "socialist modernization led by the Chinese Communist Party." This, combined with the stance of "opposing hegemonism," appears to signal the Party's return to its anti-imperialist tradition and a determination to break with the West amid the backdrop of an intensifying new Cold War. According to Xi's narrative, this party-state-led modernization fundamentally diverges from Western modernization and is not merely a pursuit of Westernization. Xi outlined five major characteristics: a vast population, common prosperity for all, material and cultural-ethical advance, harmony between humanity and nature, and, finally, peaceful development. However, this depiction is marked by contradictions that blur the line between vision and reality.

First and foremost, inequality in China has surpassed that of virtually all countries in the Global North, and the level of welfare provision is so inadequate as to disqualify China from being classified as a socialist state. Can the party leadership be held accountable for China's crony capitalist development, which has institutionalized the astonishing wealth gap? In what way can the pursuit of common prosperity be guaranteed under the leadership of the same Communist Party that has siphoned wealth from the people to benefit itself—a defining characteristic not of socialism, but of crony capitalism?

Secondly, rather than nurturing co-development between material and culture and achieving harmony between humanity and nature, the relentless pursuit of materialism and consumerism—both products of Western civilization—has corroded ethical values and contributed to the decadence of Chinese society. As the world's largest emitter of pollution, the concept of harmony remains elusive, as evidenced by the spread of cancer villages across the country, to say the least.

Last but not least, the mention of "peaceful development" could be interpreted as a reaffirmation of China's past approach to modernization. However, the removal of the "two-theme" thesis from Xi's political report contradicts this characteristic, possibly implying an intention to sustain China's rising trajectory through less than peaceful means.

Nevertheless, Xi's response to such skepticism has been to persistently maintain his commitment to China's global integration. He has strongly opposed the protectionism and decoupling imposed by the United States, promising the continued broader market access that China's "internal circulation" strategy would naturally entail due to the country's super-large domestic market. While rejecting Western-style modernization, Xi's anti-imperialist approach to modernization paradoxically does not involve a rejection of liberal globalization—an international public good (or evil) propelled by Western market democracy. Rather, as he had acknowledged in earlier years, without globalization Chinese-style modernization would lead nowhere.

Xi's apprehension regarding decoupling and his steadfast belief in globalization imply that his pursuit of autarky has its limits. Apart from the intellectual shortcomings of not only Xi but also the ruling elites, the failure to boost demand stood out as a primary cause. Since 1998, attempts to enhance consumption have been undertaken, starting with Zhu Rongji in the Jiang Zemin era and continuing through Li Keqiang in the Xi Jinping era, aimed at steering the economy in the right direction for rebalancing. However, these attempts achieved little success, primarily due to the persistently unreformed party-state institutions that fostered crony capitalist development.

Following China's swift containment of the pandemic and the subsequent initiation of economic recovery, a Politburo meeting on April 17, 2020 determined to "resolutely implement the strategy of expanding domestic demand." Marred by monopolized authentic economic data, Premier Li Keqiang's groundbreaking revelation on May 28 during the "Two-Session" Conference exemplified that apprehension. He mentioned that 600 million Chinese citizens lived on less than 1,000 yuan per month. However, the more accurate figure, as cited by Li Keqiang, should be 1,090 yuan, equivalent to US$163, which is approximately $5.42 per day per person (pdpp). Given this challenging economic situation, the strategy of expanding domestic demand becomes a near-impossible mission, at least in the short term.

On December 11, 2020, during a Politburo meeting, the inadequacy of the supply-side reforms that had been initiated since 2015 was acknowledged. This marked the first instance when a call was made to give equal importance to demand-side reform. This strategic shift aimed to propel the Chinese economy forward, transitioning it from an investment-driven model to one centered on consumption.

Faced with a noticeable slowdown in economic momentum, which threatened to push GDP growth well below the pre-set target of 5.5% (the actual figure being 3%, as disclosed in January 2023), the Central Economic Work Conference convened on December 15–16, 2022. During this conference, the significance of both supply-side and demand-side reforms was reaffirmed. It underscored the imperative to exert greater efforts in expanding consumption, attracting FDI, and *accelerating China's negotiations for accession to the CPTPP*.

Before the commencement of the Central Economic Work Conference, a significant development occurred on December 7 when the State Council abruptly announced the abandonment of the zero-COVID-19 policy that had been in effect since the start of the year. The decision to lift this policy primarily stemmed from the deteriorating fiscal conditions prevalent throughout the nation. Across all provinces and municipalities, there had been a continuous escalation in fiscal deficits for three consecutive years, spanning from 2020 to 2022 (as indicated in Table 7.3, data for 2022). This financial predicament compelled certain sub-national administrations, commencing in 2022, to take the unprecedented step of reducing the salaries of civil servants and other public sector employees—an occurrence seldom witnessed in the post-Mao era. In addition to these fiscal challenges, spontaneous demonstrations erupted in various Chinese cities, which further contributed to the determination to discontinue the zero-COVID-19 policy.

The sudden and severe economic downturn sent shockwaves throughout the world, prompting increasingly pessimistic assessments of China's economic future. On December 14, 2022, Japan's Center for Economic Research revised its earlier projections, which had previously predicted that China would surpass the United States as the world's largest economy in 2028 and 2033, according to its 2020 and 2021 forecasts. The Center now contended that "China's GDP is unlikely

Table 7.3 Fiscal conditions in provinces and municipalities (2022) (in hundred million yuan)

Province/ municipality	*Fiscal revenue*	*Fiscal expenditure*	*Fiscal balance*	*Province/ municipality*	*Fiscal revenue*	*Fiscal expenditure*	*Fiscal balance*
Guangdong	13,279.7	18,509.9	−5,230.2	Inner M	2,824.4	5,885.1	−3,060.7
Jiangsu	9,258.9	14,903.2	−5,644.3	Liaoning	2,524.3	6,253.0	−3,728.7
Zhejiang	8,039.4	12,017.7	−3,978.3	Chongqing	2,103.0	4,893.0	−2,790.0
Shanghai	7,608.2	9,393.2	−1,785.0	Yunnan	1,949.3	6,699.7	−4,750.4
Shandong	7,104.4	12,131.5	−5,027.5	Xinjiang	1,889.2	5,726.1	−3,836.9
Beijing	5,714.3	7,156.0	−1,441.7	Guizhou	1,886.4	5,849.2	−3,962.8
Sichuan	4,882.2	11,914.7	−7,032.5	Tianjin	1,846.6	2,751.5	−904.9
Henan	4,614.9	10,644.6	−6,029.7	Guangxi	1,687.7	5,893.9	−4,206.2
Hebei	4,084.4	9,336.5	−5,252.5	Heilongjiang	1,290.6	5,452.0	−4,161.4
Anhui	3,589.1	8,378.9	−4,789.8	Gansu	907.6	4,263.5	−3,355.9
Shanxi	3,453.9	5,872.6	−2,418.7	Jilin	851.0	4,044.0	−3,193.0
Fujian	3,339.1	5,702.9	−2,363.8	Hainan	832.4	2,095.5	−1,261.1
Shaanxi	3,311.6	6,766.3	−3,454.7	Ningxia	460.1	1,583.5	−1,123.4
Hubei	3,281.0	8,626.0	−5,345.0	Qinghai	329.1	1,975.1	−1,646.0
Hunan	3,101.8	9,005.3	−5,903.5	Tibet	179.6	2,593.8	−2,414.2
Jiangxi	2,948.3	7,288.3	−4,340.0				

Note In 2019, nine provinces and municipalities made a net fiscal contribution to the state's finances. The remaining provinces had to rely on receiving subsidies from the central government. *Yicai*, 18/08/2022. https://m.yicai.com/news/101510170.html

Source Jinri Toutiao, 03/03/2023. https://www.toutiao.com/article/7206212081975607823/?source=seo_tt_juhe

to surpass that of the United States in the coming decades."[102] These already cautious forecasts were to be overshadowed by even bleaker assessments from *Bloomberg* nearly nine months later in early September 2023. *Bloomberg* argued that "China's economic slowdown means it may never overtake the US economy."[103] On January 3, 2024, Wells Fargo released its latest report, acknowledging the inevitable ascent of China to surpass the United States as the world's largest economy. However, the report posited a revised timeline, projecting China's achievement of this milestone in 2042—ten years later than previously estimated.[104]

As 2023 unfolded, contrary to extensive speculation about a robust economic rebound following China's unexpected lifting of pandemic control measures in December 2022 and thanks to unprecedented fiscal difficulties across the country, a significant economic contraction took place instead. FDI declined by 9.8% from January to July, while both exports and imports declined by 14.5% and 12.4%, respectively. The RMB depreciated by 2.73% against the U.S. dollar. Consequently, unemployment surged, with the official jobless rate for individuals aged 16–24 reaching a record high of 21.3% by the end of June. This figure was notably lower than the 46.5% reported in March, as indicated by an independent survey conducted by an economics professor at Peking University.[105] The situation was so dire that the State Bureau of Statistics (SBS) ceased to disclose unemployment data thereafter.

This situation contradicted the SBS's reported GDP growth rate of 5.5% for the first half of the year. Additionally, it challenged the conclusion reached during the Politburo meeting held on July 24, which asserted

[102] Nikkei (Asia), 14/12/2022. https://asia.nikkei.com/Economy/China-s-GDP-unlikely-to-surpass-U.S.-in-next-few-decades-JCER.

[103] "China Slowdown Means It May Never Overtake US Economy, Forecast Shows." *Bloomberg*, 04/09/2023. https://www.bloomberg.com/news/articles/2023-09-05/china-slowdown-means-it-may-never-overtake-U.S.-economy-be-says?leadSource=uverify%20wall.

[104] Wells Fargo's report, issued on 03/01/2024. https://externalcontent.blob.core.windows.net/pdfs/pdfs/WellsFargo01032024(1).pdf.

[105] Caixin, 17/07/2023. https://opinion.caixin.com/2023-07-17/102076568.html.

that the economy was continuing to recover and exhibit overall improvement. The meeting attributed the economic sluggishness primarily to a demand shortfall and external challenges.[106]

In an effort to restore the confidence of private entrepreneurs, who had not fully recovered from the purge of high-tech tycoons in the preceding years, the Party Center and the State Council introduced a set of 31 guidelines across eight different aspects on July 19. These guidelines were designed to reassure private enterprises.[107]

However, whether these measures were sincere or not, they encountered significant challenges in restoring confidence. This difficulty arises within the context of the regime's growing political-ideological North Koreanization, reinforced by advances in digital technologies. Additionally, rising geopolitical tensions led to an accelerated exodus of FDI from China, as companies sought to diversify their supply chains.

Despite China's persistent opposition to "decoupling and confrontation" and its appeal for "finding a correct way of coping with each other,"[108] the Americans appeared unimpressed. They seemed to view all of Beijing's attempts at returning to a strategy of "hide and bide," an example of which was Foreign Minister Qin Gang's "effusive praise of Americans" in early January,[109] as strategic deception. On August 9, President Biden signed an executive order that heightened concerns within the Chinese regime. This executive order prohibited specific U.S. investments in sensitive technologies, including quantum computing, advanced semiconductors, and specific domains of artificial intelligence within China.[110]

[106] The People's Daily, 25/07/2023. http://politics.people.com.cn/n1/2023/0725/c1024-40042590.html.

[107] Xinhua, 19/07/2023. https://www.gov.cn/zhengce/202307/content_6893055.htm.

[108] Zaobao, 04/02/2023. https://www.zaobao.com.sg/realtime/china/story20230204-1359581.

[109] "China's Foreign Minister Says 'Deeply Impressed' with Americans." *Bloomberg*. https://www.bloomberg.com/news/articles/2023-01-03/china-s-foreign-minister-says-deeply-impressed-with-americans?leadSource=uverify%20wall03/01/2023.

[110] "US Senate Panel Approves Measure to Strip China of 'Developing' Status." *Reuters*, 09/06/2023. https://www.reuters.com/world/us/U.S.-senate-panel-approves-measure-strip-china-developing-statU.S.-2023-06-08/; "US to Ban American Investments in China Tech Sector." *BBC*, 09/08/2023. https://www.bbc.co.uk/news/business-66454313.

This new ban effectively closed the last remaining loophole in previous restrictions that limited the sale of sensitive technology by U.S. firms and scrutinized Chinese investments in American companies. The possibility that the United Kingdom and the EU might adopt similar measures shortly thereafter was almost equally ominous. If these measures were to be rigorously enforced, they would undermine Xi's vision of early-stage high-tech self-sufficiency by denying access to essential technology, and significantly impede China's aspirations for self-reliance in its high-tech industries.

Fearing the acceleration of the West's decoupling, which was exacerbating its economic challenges, on August 14, 2023, the State Council issued the "Opinions on Further Optimizing the Foreign Investment Environment and Increasing the Attraction of Foreign Investment." The document outlined 24 policy measures across six key areas. Among these measures was a commitment to further reduce the Negative List, thereby expanding market access for foreign investors. The State Council also vowed to revise the government procurement law to ensure that foreign investors producing goods in China would receive national treatment.[111]

On September 2, Xi Jinping personally announced China's new initiatives to open up service trade in sectors such as telecommunications, tourism, legal services, and vocational examinations.[112] On September 27, Xi reconfirmed the infallible "momentous decision making" during the Politburo meeting regarding China's accession to the WTO. He underscored China's determination to stand on the "right side of history" by upholding the "general direction of economic globalization" and "defending free trade and genuine multilateralism." Emphasizing the necessity of active participation in the forthcoming WTO reforms, Xi stressed the importance of "proactively aligning with high-standard international trade and economic rules" to enhance China's ability to use these rules in safeguarding its "developmental rights and interests."[113]

On October 18, during his keynote speech at the opening ceremony of the "One Belt, One Road" International Cooperation Summit Forum, Xi

[111] Xinhua, 14/08/2023. http://www.news.cn/fortune/2023-08/14/c_1129803010.htm.

[112] Zaobao, 02/09/2023. https://www.zaobao.com.sg/news/china/story20230902-1429762.

[113] Xinhua, 29/09/2023. http://politics.people.com.cn/n1/2023/0927/c1024-40086720.html.

Jinping announced the "comprehensive lifting of restrictions on foreign investment access in the manufacturing sector."[114] This move was clearly aimed at addressing the decline in FDI during the first eight months of 2023. However, it is worth noting that this announcement stands more as a gesture than a new move toward investment liberalization, as access restrictions to FDI have virtually been non-existent after five consecutive years of updating the Negative Lists since 2017.[115]

Despite these ongoing and *ex post* liberalization commitments and declarations, the prospect of China losing its "developing country" status at international organizations due to legislation approved on June 8 by the U.S. Senate Foreign Relations Committee, following the unanimous passage in the House of Representatives in March (with a vote of 415–0), has the potential to turn globalization—something in which China has been deeply engaged—against the country's efforts to sustain economic growth. Meanwhile, despite diplomatic efforts made by China in mid-July to sway Japan and South Korea away from the United States, these endeavors backfired. The two countries' strategic calculations prioritized their national interests over China's outreach, eclipsing any allure of alignment based on a shared Asian identity.[116] The trilateral Camp David meeting on August 18 further solidified the U.S.-led alliance. The alliance is motivated by concerns about China and North Korea's "aggressive rhetoric and behavior, as well as their increasing cooperation with

[114] Xinhua, 18/10/2023. https://www.gov.cn/yaowen/liebiao/202310/content_6910132.htm.

[115] Yicai, 19/10/2023. https://www.yicai.com/epaper/pc/202310/19/content_32920.html.

[116] The CCP's mouthpiece *Global Times* twitted on 12/07/2023: "Europeans and Americans can't distinguish between Chinese, Japanese, and South Korean individuals. No matter how much we dye our hair yellow or how sharp we make our noses, we can't become Westerners. We should always remember our roots. Senior Chinese diplomat Wang Yi emphasized the importance of cooperation between these three countries in revitalizing Asia and benefiting the world during the 2023 International Forum for Trilateral Cooperation on Monday." https://twitter.com/globaltimesnews/status/1676051698064977920?ref_src=twsrc%5Etfw%7Ctwcamp%5Etweetembed%7Ctwterm%5E1676265570986074130%7Ctwgr%5E0437949a73347154abd47fa4962425950ff94ba6%7Ctwcon%5Es3_&ref_url=https%3A%2F%2Fwww.voachinese.com%2Fa%2Fchina-on-twitter-wang-yi-20230704%2F7167090.html.

Russia."[117] These external constraints serve to amplify the pressure on China's inward-looking tendencies.

To outcompete the United States and emerge victorious in the new Cold War, reviving the economy is of utmost importance and an urgent need. Yet to the surprise of the world, this ostensibly robust party state has shown significant reluctance thus far to stimulate the economy as it has usually done in past decades. A groundbreaking report from the *Wall Street Journal*, dated August 27, 2023 and citing informed sources in China, attributed this delay to Xi having changed his mind. He has apparently relinquished the option of consumption-led growth, a Party policy previously agreed upon for rebalancing the economy and presumed to be a core component of the "internal circulation" strategy. Instead, emphasis has shifted toward armament-related industrial investment.

Quoting Xi's criticism of welfarism as a flaw in the Western consumption-driven model that encourages laziness and leads to resource wastage, the report referenced a *Study Times* article dated August 16. This date was carefully chosen to convey a specific signal. The article reaffirmed the Party's previous stance favoring investment-led growth. It referred to Xi's thinking dating back to 2016, when he did not even acknowledge the existence of insufficient demand in China. Instead, he favored supply-side measures aimed at building more industrial capacity to reduce dependence on Western products.[118]

This revelation contradicts many of Xi's previous statements in which he explicitly supported the Party's strategy of expanding demand. However, it is worth noting that the *People's Daily* issued an editorial on August 11, 2015—earlier than the 2016 date mentioned by the *Wall Street Journal*—arguing against the "excessive welfare" seen in many Latin American countries. This suggests that divisions within the Party persisted, and when other factions opposing Xi's views held sway, he was unable to impose his preferred alternative.

[117] "Experts React: The U.S.-Japan-South Korea Summit Was 'Historic.' But What Did It Accomplish?" Atlantic Council experts, 18/08/2023. https://www.atlanticcouncil.org/blogs/new-atlanticist/experts-react/experts-react-the-U.S.-japan-south-korea-summit-was-historic-but-what-did-it-accomplish/.

[118] "Communist Party Priorities Complicate Plans to Revive China's Economy—Western Experts Say More Stimulus Is Needed, but Xi Jinping Resists Handouts to Consumers, Fearing They Could Lead to 'Welfarism'." *The Wall Street Journal*, 27/08/2023. https://www.wsj.com/world/china/communist-party-priorities-complicate-plans-to-revive-chinas-economy-84a156d7.

Furthermore, the consumption-focused strategy's lack of success cannot be directly attributed to the party-state system itself, as it serves as a breeding ground for crony capitalism. The ongoing failed attempt, as Xi saw it, has underscored its impracticality, making it unworthy of further investment—particularly considering the financial stress that has reached a tipping point, with the debt crisis pushing the country toward the brink of bankruptcy. This situation has severely curtailed the state's ability to further stimulate demand through rapid campaigns.

Xi's resounding victory over the Communist Youth League faction, loosely led by Premier Li Keqiang at the Twentieth National Party Congress, removed the last barrier to implementing his preferred policies. The sustained emphasis on demand-side management during the initial months following the Congress, under the leadership of Premier-in-waiting Li Qiang, only served to justify its eventual abandonment when the timing was right. Xi's belief in adapting tactics as necessary is evident in his approach to the original strictness of the zero-COVID-19 measures and their sudden discontinuation, despite the damage inflicted on the credibility of his strong leadership.

Finally, as a member of the princeling and Red Guard generation, Xi is unburdened by the same quest for regime legitimacy as his non-princeling predecessors, who pursued economic growth at any cost. Regardless of performance, Xi's deep-rooted belief in "L'état, c'est moi" (The state, that is me), or the holding of the "mandate of heaven" as imperial Chinese sovereigns did, suffices to serve as the source of legitimacy for both himself and the party state.

Xi's decision to abandon economic rebalancing in favor of emphasizing autarky underscores the regime's profound insecurity. This is evident in the 2023 budget, which allocates a 7.2% increase for national defense spending and a 6.4% increase for public security—both figures exceeding the 5% GDP growth target and the modest 2% increase designated for education. The journey toward digital totalitarianism initiated during the Hu Jintao era has now evolved into an increasingly repressive Orwellian surveillant state that is solidly entrenched.

However, unlike Adolf Hitler, who pursued war to create a Mitteleuropa with the aim of emulating the consumer affluence of the United States and "countering America's seemingly inevitable economic and military dominance,"[119] Xi Jinping's China lacks the vision, statecraft, and capacity to build an exclusive and self-sufficient imperial bloc for a potential conflict with a militarily preponderant United States. Similar to its imperial predecessors, China aspires to international respectability—seeking respect rather than overseas hegemony, as Henry Kissinger recently put it.[120] Matthew Kroenig's assertion that "when the CCP worries about domestic stability, it seeks external accommodation" holds true in this context.[121] This illiberal semi-peripheral "superpower" more closely resembles a reverse-fascist state, primarily focused on deterring its own people rather than the United States.

Regarding the United States, while an immediate regime change in China may not be feasible, there is a notion that removing Xi Jinping from office and returning to the pre-2013 "reform and opening era," as suggested in "The Longer Telegram" in January 2021, could pave the way for U.S.-China reconciliation.[122] Similarly, the concept of decoupling, a core element of the new Cold War, does not aim to permanently "fence-in" China as in the old Cold War. The idea of "natural decoupling" proposed by McMaster aims to coerce China into submission rather than complete isolation. As Adam Tooze persuasively asserts, the United States has been "dictating its economic peace terms" to China: "China must accept America's demarcation of the status quo. If it fails to respect the boundaries set by Washington between harmless prosperity and historically significant technological development, it should anticipate massive sanctions."[123] The message is clear: the hegemonic American empire could tolerate a China, with or without Xi's removal, that fully embraces compradorization.

"What is to be done?"—the Leninist question—now confronts Xi Jinping, who finds himself at a critical historical juncture, facing a difficult

[119] Tooze, A (2006), p. 658.

[120] The Economist, 17/05/2023.

[121] Kroenig, M (2020): *The Return of Great Power Rivalry. Democracy Versus Autocracy from the Ancient World to the U.S. and China*. Oxford University Press, p. 194.

[122] The Longer Telegram (by Anonymous): Toward A New American China Strategy. *Atlantic Council*, 27/01/2021. https://www.atlanticcouncil.org/content-series/atlantic-council-strategy-paper-series/the-longer-telegram/.

[123] Tooze, A: "America Has Dictated Its Economic Peace Terms to China." *Foreign Policy*, 24/04/2023. https://foreignpolicy.com/2023/04/24/america-has-dictated-its-economic-peace-terms-to-china/.

choice and having to make decisions with far-reaching consequences for an ancient civilization state.

Xi Jinping's response to the "Tocquevillian moment" involves a reassertion of the "primacy of politics" through heightened social control measures. These efforts have accelerated the trajectory toward a more totalitarian state, building on trends that were already present during the Hu Jintao era. Additionally, Xi's aversion to liberal democracy and deep-seated insecurity prompted a pursuit of high-tech autarky. He aimed to achieve technological independence as a means to compete with the established American power that sought to curb China's rise. His overconfidence drove him to bet on "an irreversible decline of the West." Paradoxically, this pursuit of autarky contradicts his disregard for the welfare state, his unwavering belief in anti-developmental globalization, and his fixation on "wolf warrior diplomacy"—aspects that a semi-peripheral developing "great power" should have avoided. These conflicting choices counteract potential efforts to cultivate a highly integrated and safeguarded domestic market, and to prevent a Western coalition from pursuing decoupling, both of which are pivotal for China's autarkic success.

Xi's failure lies in his inability to recognize that succeeding in the new Cold War necessitates not a reduction, but an augmentation of socialism; a thorough reassessment of globalization instead of a blind embrace; and a mastery of the art of diplomacy to effectively engage in "great power diplomacy." The absence of these pivotal elements underscores not only the cognitive limitations of his generation's leadership but also the influence of entrenched vested interests capable of continuing to obstruct attempts to overhaul the institutional foundations of China's crony comprador capitalism. This endgame could potentially present Xi's China with more of a crisis than an opportunity when navigating an unwinnable war against the hegemonic American power.

PART IV

Conclusion

CHAPTER 8

Conclusion

Crony comprador capitalism, a direct product of China's market-Leninist reforms combined with an intimate embrace of global capitalism, laid the institutional foundation for its rapid ascent within a semi-peripheral orbit and its subsequent decline.

In contrast to Mikhail Gorbachev, whose idealistic reform agenda unraveled in just a few years, Deng Xiaoping was a revolutionary reformer who would not tolerate political disorder under any circumstances. His ultimate goal was neither the achievement of liberal democracy nor democratic socialism, but the permanent retention of power for the CCP. To achieve this, he initially utilized capitalism to "develop socialism" in the 1980s, and later to "salvage socialism" from 1992 onward, adapting to changing political conditions.

Deng's market-socialist reforms, from the very beginning, sowed the seeds for China's crony capitalism. His ambiguous definition of socialism, particularly the vaguely defined policy of "allowing some people to get rich first," primarily benefited the princelings—his own family was also involved. This undermined his socialist promises, despite his sincere vision of "common prosperity" in the distant future. Chen Yun played a pivotal role in facilitating the princelings' transition into the new bourgeoisie. Their adoption of ruling-class consciousness convinced him of their political loyalty. Their embourgeoisement paved the way for the events at Tiananmen Square during the summer of 1989.

J. Yue, *Crony Comprador Capitalism*,
https://doi.org/10.1007/978-3-031-53154-5_8

However, it was not the Tiananmen incident itself, but Deng Xiaoping's opportunistic approach to drawing lessons from it against the backdrop of global events in 1989—the collapse of Soviet Communism in Central and Eastern Europe and the conclusion of the Cold War, known as the *Global 1989*—that reshaped the path-dependent market-socialist reforms of the 1980s. Deng interpreted from the *Global 1989* the triumph of global capitalism as an institution. In his view, the paradoxical way to "salvage socialism" was to relinquish socialism in practical terms, while subtly sidestepping the rigid interpretation of socialism, a term that could be discreetly redefined within the confines of the Party's authority. This concept, held in his mind and put into action, redirected China's path of marketizing reform toward market Leninism, driving China's institutional transition to capitalism since 1992.

The princelings significantly contributed to this transformative process. Emerging in the 1980s under the auspices of their New Class parents, they were among the earliest crony capitalists. Their policy recommendations after the abortive August coup attempt in the Soviet Union in 1991—no longer appeasing the public to promote radical marketizing reform and privatizing state assets for the exclusive benefit of nomenklatura elites in exchange for loyalty—had a substantial impact on decision-makers.

Equally significant, Deng's link between regime legitimacy and GDP led to the reconfiguration of the party-state, transforming it into a kleptocracy. Pressured by the demands of "forced growth" within the new context of radicalizing marketizing reforms, the nomenklatura now had strong incentives to relentlessly pursue an exclusive model of economic growth at all costs, favoring efficiency while sacrificing social justice and the socialist principle of egalitarianism. Without checks and balances to restrict them, they effectively privatized the state to enrich themselves through rent-seeking and the expansion of the economic pie. Alongside the princelings, they emerged as the primary beneficiaries of China's market-Leninist reforms, driving the flourishing of the country's crony capitalist development during most of the 1990s and beyond.

Chinese comprador capitalism can be traced back to the early years of reform in the 1980s. The erosion of national pride due to Mao's backward socialism left the country vulnerable to foreign influence, particularly the emerging paradigm of neoliberalism that gained prominence in China since the late 1980s. Systemic pressures for greater trade and investment liberalization from the triumphant West and the Bretton Woods institutions after the *Global 1989* translated into a compelling incentive for "growth by invitation." Late developers were enticed to trade economic nationalism for externally focused export-led growth, pursuant to the principle of comparative advantage.

Driven by the flawed doctrine of neoliberal economics and influenced by figures from the U.S. administration, Bretton Woods institutions, and "Chicago boy" economists, the Chinese elites enthusiastically embraced neoliberal reforms in a spirit that resembled the Washington Consensus throughout much of the 1990s.

A particularly significant aspect of this era was the privatization of numerous small and medium-sized SOEs. This period marked the convergence of China's crony capitalism and comprador capitalism. These two modes of capitalism mutually reinforced each other: the extensive trade and investment liberalization that began in 1992 further destabilized SOEs that were already struggling, accelerating their decline and ultimately justifying their subsequent privatization.

The widespread looting of state assets, a characteristic of China's crony capitalism, led to extensive layoffs of SOE employees without adequate safety nets, resulting in significant underconsumption. This increased China's dependence on exports and FDI, thereby justifying further liberalization of trade and investment.

This sustained a deflationary growth, a phenomenon rarely witnessed in economic history, ensuring a continued economic boom and achieving a "soft landing." In other words, the existence of China's crony capitalism, marked by inevitable acute inequality and underconsumption, provided ample justification for the flourishing of comprador capitalism. This, in turn, further enriched China's crony capitalists, strengthening their alliance with global capitalists in industrial democracies, particularly within Wall Street finance.

The evolving landscape of the CCP—now composed of and dominated by crony capitalists—ceased to adhere to its anti-capitalist and anti-imperialist stance by the turn of the millennium, following China's accession to the WTO. This shift culminated in the complete institutionalization of China's crony comprador capitalism, effectively causing the party to morph into a "major right-wing dictatorship" on the global stage. This unbridled form of capitalism has resulted in an unparalleled Ricardian export-led growth miracle, yet it has come at a substantial social, environmental, and institutional cost. Most significantly, this transformation has been significantly detrimental to China's autonomous national development, placing the nation on a trajectory of semi-peripheral dependent development. This trajectory has been further confirmed by the continued narrowing of China's "policy space" under further American pressure after its WTO accession, which has heightened the nation's vulnerability to the "middle-income trap."

The United States played a crucial role in shaping China's pathway of development along comprador capitalistic lines. Believing that the "end of history" had arrived and seeking to prevent the emergence of peer superpower rivals in the post-Cold War era, the United States resolved to integrate China into the global economy, hoping to induce positive political change and transform China into "a responsible stakeholder in the fundamental order of the international system"—a status quo power subservient to American hegemonic influence.

However, this grand strategy has been self-defeating in the long term—not because it misjudged the Chinese regime's determination to resist changes in its superstructure, or because China's capabilities could one day pose a threat to the rules-based liberal international order, but because China is an "empire" in terms of its size. Its deep integration would inevitably create unprecedented global imbalances that must be addressed sooner or later. Moreover, as a price paid for this deep integration, China had to lower its protective barriers, opening up market access. As a consequence, the country found itself positioned at the lower end of the global value chain, engaging in an extensive mode of industrialization.

Given China's sheer size, this approach could lead to a premature depletion of domestic resources, prompting China to scramble for natural resources all over the world to sustain high growth. This would necessitate efforts to enhance its global power projection capabilities to address the strategic vulnerability of resource scarcity, ensuring a safe and uninterrupted supply of resources. Such a scenario is ostensibly susceptible to straining great power relations in high politics terms. "Chimerica," a term coined by Niall Ferguson to depict the phenomenon of an entrenched interdependent economic relationship between China and the United States, is by no means a relationship that is structurally peace-oriented; rather, it is poised for conflicts, both geoeconomically and geopolitically, regardless of political and ideological divides. Therefore, China's deep integration, shaped both by political imperatives at home and by the U.S. liberal integrationist grand strategy, is more of a potential source of conflict than a conduit for lasting world peace.

China's pursuit of peaceful development appears unwarranted within this grand context. Regardless of whether it seeks autonomous national development, China seems inevitably headed toward a confrontational stance with the United States; this outcome is merely a matter of time.

Nevertheless, the most formidable developmental challenge that China faces is that, despite its remarkable growth miracle, its deep integration has fallen short of turning it into another post-1945 Germany or Japan. Instead, breaking free from the trap of dependent development demands economic rebalancing to rectify the structural weaknesses of the Chinese economy, such as enduring underconsumption and an excessive reliance on investment and exports. Achieving this necessitates the implementation of proactive industrial policies aimed at facilitating technological upgrading.

Advocates of New Developmentalism emerging after the 2007–2009 global financial crisis wrongly idealized China as a template for achieving economic success by strategically rejecting the Washington Consensus neoliberal paradigm. They misunderstood the nature of the Chinese state, which had become entwined with institutional interests supporting a crony comprador capitalistic development model. The CCP's conservative tendencies in the political-ideological sphere were a strong affirmation not of China's economic success, but rather of a partial success at best, one that overshadowed more fundamental concerns such as an as-yet incomplete structural transformation. This transformation, which is crucial for China's modernization based on an autonomous rather than dependent foundation of national development, is still in progress.

Indeed, on a trajectory of dependent development, China found its extensive industrialization model already approaching its limits in the final years of Hu Jintao's tenure. Escalating tensions that needed management arose from social disturbances triggered by the kleptocratic state on the one hand and the growing geopolitical and geoeconomic conflicts abroad resulting from China's deep integration on the other. Such crises are emblematic of crony comprador capitalism. Far from being an exportable development model, the country was mired in a severe sociopolitical crisis, teetering on the "brink of revolutionary turmoil." It was precisely within this pivotal moment that Xi Jinping assumed power, stepping into an atmosphere of disappointment, despair, and conflicting expectations.

While his selection was orchestrated by the Shanghai faction, the most potent and corrupt clique within the party state, Xi's rise infused hope for change due to his distinctive princeling background and his father's reputation as a morally upright reform-minded Communist. Yet uncertainties lingered about his capacity to steer China toward greatness or whether he would merely echo the tragedy of Emperor Chongzhen, whose futile efforts to salvage a hopeless, moribund empire ended in failure.

Xi's remarkable maneuvers in the realm of power dynamics, achieved through an extensive anti-corruption campaign, positioned him as a strongman with authority rivaling that of Chairman Mao. With this authority, he held the key to instigating change. Even before assuming office, Xi and his Politburo colleagues recognized the advent of a Chinese "Tocquevillian moment"—a signal that "even modest reform efforts could unleash a revolution." While addressing the crisis spawned by China's crony comprador capitalist development would inevitably necessitate a certain level of de-Dengification, this should not be misconstrued as an intention to overhaul the party-state system, particularly in light of the lessons drawn from Gorbachev's experience. In this context, he shares similarities with Deng, both pivotal in rescuing the party state from profound crises.

Nevertheless, Xi's paramount objective is to cleanse the party-state apparatus, thereby rejuvenating the Chinese nation—an aspiration encapsulated in the term he coined: the "Chinese dream." Consequently, Xi's aim is not to eradicate crony capitalism, which has become intricately intertwined with the party-state system and, as Minxin Pei has noted, constitutes the "very foundations of the regime's monopoly of power,"[1] but rather to harness and regulate its influence.

Hence, to safeguard the "old regime" from the looming specter of a "[color] revolution" that deeply unsettled the CCP, the leadership of the red-guard generation, guided by Xi Jinping, embarked on a comprehensive endeavor to reinstate absolute control across all facets of society. As part of this effort, Xi launched a campaign from late 2020 to mid-2023 to purge the high bourgeoisie—the increasingly unyielding cohort of ultra-rich privileged oligarchs. These oligarchs had once been targeted for co-option as part of former General Secretary Jiang Zemin's influential "Three Represents" concept, introduced in 2001. This conceptual framework aimed to placate national capitalists, who played a pivotal role in the party-state's strategy to generate employment following the bankruptcy

[1] Pei, M (2016), p. 268.

of SOEs. Xi's decisive actions marked a clear fracture within the elite coalition that "Three Represents" had painstakingly cultivated.

Contrary to Jiang Zemin's approach, which aimed to broaden the Party's ruling foundation, Xi's party state embraced a resolute stance of total dominance, even at the potential cost of economic development. Drawing parallels with Hitler's Third Reich, Xi was aware of the inherent limitations in the state's ability to exercise control over the "commanding heights" of the economy—essentially, strategically crucial sectors that required state oversight. In the expansive landscape of the economy, where private enterprises held overwhelming influence, the state lacked the capacity to enforce nationalization and was compelled to tolerate their existence, despite any reservations. Yet Xi's objective was to assert the "primacy of politics," a concept coined by Timothy Mason to depict Hitler's Third Reich. Xi employed similar phrases inherited from Mao, such as "politics in command" or "the Party predominates everything," emphasizing an identical belief in the value of controlling assets rather than merely owning them.

In addition to domestic crises, China's accelerating turn toward totalitarianism under Xi Jinping was influenced by impending conflicts with the United States, a challenge also faced by his predecessor, Hu Jintao. Both leaderships were marked by a mix of insecurity and hubris. The fear of a Western-instigated color revolution heightened the sense of vulnerability among Communist rulers from the early 2000s onward. Simultaneously, the aftermath of the global financial crisis, which exposed the vulnerabilities of industrial capitalism and market democracy, bolstered the Chinese leadership's confidence in the superiority of their repressive Leninist party-state system. This complex psychological landscape led China to make significant miscalculations about the United States, believing it had passed the point of no return in an accelerating decline, on two pivotal occasions.

During Hu Jintao's era, the first misjudgment unfolded, resulting in a brief period of assertive foreign policy between 2008 and 2010. This stance prompted a response from the Obama administration, leading to its "rebalancing to Asia" strategy. The second, even more assertive shift in foreign policy occurred during Xi Jinping's tenure, starting in 2013. This shift, combined with Xi's mishandling of North Korea's nuclearization, played a pivotal role in triggering the trade war, which subsequently escalated into a new Cold War between the two great powers.

Xi's approach to managing the challenges posed by the trade war and the new Cold War was built around advancing his high-tech autarky strategy. This concept emerged in 2013 shortly after he took office and is justified by both "wars." It forms the foundation of the regime's "internal circulation" strategy, developed in May 2020. This strategy, coupled with the reaffirmation of the "primacy of politics," raises questions about a potential trend toward some degree of Nazification in China's economy.

Drawing parallels with Hitler's Third Reich, the pursuit of autarky in the latter's context was driven by the goals of achieving full employment and a more equitable distribution of wealth. In Hitler's vision, the nation's preference for "guns" (armament) over "butter" (consumption) was meant to be temporary, with the focus shifting to the latter only after acquiring *Lebensraum* in Mitteleuropa. This strategic sequence would have allowed an autarkic Germany to attain a level of consumer affluence similar to that of the United States.[2]

An autarkic strategy would typically involve deepening internal integration by consolidating a tariff-protected domestic market to enable economies of scale. This approach would encompass efforts to improve the well-being of the population, thereby facilitating a transition to a consumption-driven economy. Moreover, a pivotal aspect of this strategy would involve establishing a robust national system of innovation (NSI), a plan that would align well with the imperative of rebalancing the economy.

However, no such strategy materialized as a meticulously formulated and coordinated plan aimed at constructing a "Fortress China" through the utilization of its "all-nation system." Instead, it gained prominence only in response to the eruption of the trade war, a development that caught the Chinese elites wholly unprepared. Emphasis on internal integration ("internal circulation" strategy) was belatedly raised in May 2020, while the concept of market integration to support this strategy wasn't proposed until even later, in April 2022.

Unlike National Socialist Germany's pursuit of territorial expansion to secure the resources of western Eurasia so that Germany could confront Britain and the United States with the prospect of success, China, under Xi's leadership, does not require Lebensraum in the pursuit of its "peaceful rise." China already possesses an inherently vast market, which is still undergoing integration through the concerted efforts of a strong central state. As a *semi-peripheral* "superpower," China qualitatively

[2] Tooze, A (2006): *The Wages of Destruction: The Making and Breaking of the Nazi Economy*. London: Penguin Books, p. 512.

differs from both resource-rich America and resource-poor Germany—both before and after 1945. Despite the potential to access resources through trade rather than war in the era of liberal globalization, China's insatiable demand would instead be curtailed through an intensive, rather than extensive, industrialization model. This paradoxically involves a rethinking of China's existing devotion to neoliberal hyperglobalization.

Xi's apparent hostility to "welfarism" distinguishes his approach from Hitler-style national socialism. This distinction is further underscored by his persistent focus on liberal globalization and close alignment with economic internationalism rather than economic nationalism. However, the relatively limited authority of the central state in unifying its fragmented domestic market, coupled with the existence of a corrupt and inherently flawed NSI, compounds the challenges to Xi's pursuit of autarky. These factors collectively contribute to the regime's anxieties about decoupling, as evidenced by China's bizarre eagerness to join the CPTPP, an institution specifically designed to counteract China's ascent.

Xi Jinping's position as neither a true socialist nor a genuine economic nationalist, despite his seemingly paradoxical pursuit of autarky, underscores the enduring presence of China's crony comprador capitalism. This reality, in turn, sheds light on the significant irony underlying the new Cold War. Unlike the original Cold War, this contemporary geopolitical rivalry is not waged between equals of superpower status; rather, it unfolds between an established economic superpower and a rising semi-peripheral economic juggernaut, a determined rule-maker vis-à-vis an aspirant rule-maker in the international system that is perhaps hopelessly condemned to be a rule-taker. Nor is it an ideological struggle between capitalism and Communism. Instead, it represents a clash between two forms of capitalism—democratic capitalism versus totalitarian capitalism adorned with a pseudo-Marxist façade, a sort of Orwellian dictatorship with distinct legalist attributes.[3]

This new Cold War is fundamentally characterized by an ideologically fueled battle for technological leadership in the coming decades. China's pursuit of technological self-sufficiency faces significant challenges and is unlikely to succeed without a greater infusion of socialist principles and a commitment to clean governance favoring autonomous development. Zhang Chunqiao's predictions about China's trajectory toward

[3] Yue, J (2022), pp. 91–106.

semi-peripheral status, ensnared in the trap of dependent development as long as self-reliance is abandoned, may seem to have been vindicated. Xi's professed support for self-reliance is juxtaposed with his concurrent emphasis on broader market access. As such, his autarkism diverges fundamentally from that of the Mao era. The current Chinese Communist leadership, instead of strictly adhering to self-reliance, remains preoccupied with the mythology of globalization and apprehensive about decoupling. Amidst an almost unstoppable economic meltdown in 2023 and into 2024, this apprehension compels them to sustain an even stronger commitment to economic internationalism. For this purpose, commencing from late October 2023, they have, as always, resorted to obsequiously courting the United States (Fig. 8.1),[4] promising not

[4] On October 31, 2023, the *People's Daily* sent out the inaugural signal of China's overture to the U.S. through its editorial. The highly anticipated 24-episode anti-American propagandist TV drama, "The Battle of Shangganling" (known as the "Battle of Triangle Hill" in the U.S.), originally slated to air during prime time on November 13, was postponed. This delay, orchestrated to foster improved relations with the Americans, preceded President Xi Jinping's meeting with Biden on November 15 (*Singtao*, 18/11/2023. https://std.stheadline.com/sc/daily/article/2556997/%E6%97%A5%E5%A0%B1-%E4%B8%AD%E5%9C%8B-%E6%8A%97%E7%BE%8E%E6%8F%B4%E6%9C%9D%E5%8A%87-%E4%B8%8A%E7%94%98%E5%B6%BA-%E5%BB%B6%E6%92%AD). Concurrently, there was an abrupt softening of anti-American propaganda. From November 11 to 15, the official Xinhua News Agency issued five editorials advocating the normalization of bilateral relations. However, analysts in the U.S. dismissed these gestures as China's attempt at "strategic deception" (RFA, 13/11/2023. https://www.rfa.org/mandarin/yataibaodao/junshiwaijiao/hx-11132023091252.html). During his address to the American audience in San Francisco, Xi Jinping asserted that China "never bets against the United States." Arguing that China "will not fight a cold war or a hot war with anyone," Xi expressed a desire for friendship with the U.S. (Bloomberg, 16/11/2023. https://www.bloomberg.com/news/articles/2023-11-16/xi-says-china-seeks-to-be-friends-with-us-wants-peaceful-ties?leadSource=uverify%20wall). On November 16, U.S. Ambassador to Japan, Rahm Emanuel, candidly explained Xi's "desperate" need for U.S. investment amid an economic slowdown caused by his mistaken policies (*BNN-Bloomberg*, 16/11/2023. https://www.bnnbloomberg.ca/xi-is-desperate-for-us-capital-amid-a-slowdown-rahm-emanuel-says-1.1999705). The following day (November 17), the Chinese Foreign Ministry claimed that China-U.S. relations, once opened up, would not be closed again. On December 31, Xinhua issued a commentary urging a "relaunch" of China-U.S. relations in commemoration of the 45-year establishment of diplomatic ties. However, Americans remained lukewarm to this commemoration. On January 6, 2024, Foreign Minister Wang Yi emphasized that "Sino-U.S. cooperation is a necessity, not a matter of choice" (*Zaobao*, 06/01/2024. https://www.zaobao.com.sg/realtime/china/story20240106-1460346).

(a)

(b)

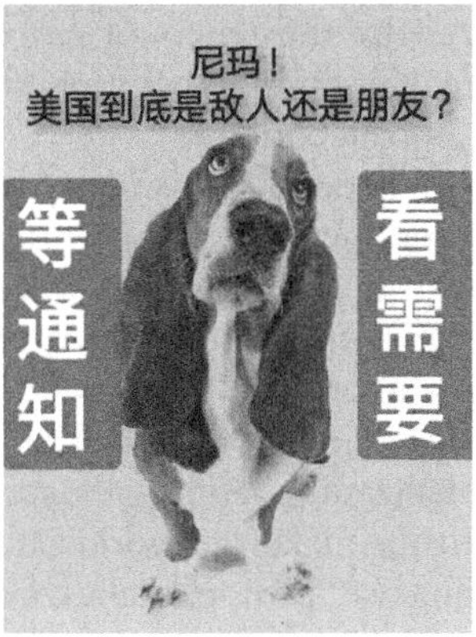

Fig. 8.1 (a) U.S.-China relations—A honeymoon, once again?: (b) Perplexed and eager Chinese youth patriots *Note* Text in above image (in English): *Horizontal* What on earth! America: friend or foe? *Vertical* Just wait for (the Party's) instructions, depending on needs!

to upend the "current international order,"[5] *lest the country's ongoing trajectory of dependent development be derailed.*

Caricatures circulated on China's social media ahead of President Xi Jinping's scheduled meeting with Biden in San Francisco during the APEC meeting in mid-November 2023.

China's "rise" in a semi-peripheral orbit strongly aligns with the concept of "Capitalism 3.0," as articulated by the development economist Dani Rodrik of Harvard University. The era of neoliberal globalization

[5] "Official: China won't upend global order." *China Daily*, 10/01/2024. https://www.chinadailyhk.com/article/370780.

has diminished the state's role in managing the "instabilities and insecurities of industrial capitalism," leading to a global rise in populist sentiments and undermining the foundations of democracy. In light of these pressing concerns, a re-evaluation of globalization has become imperative. According to Rodrik, the prevailing sentiment now leans toward favoring less globalization rather than more in order to safeguard democracy and uphold national sovereignty. This core idea is encapsulated in his notable concept of the "globalization trilemma."[6] This paradigm shift advocates a creative reversion to the era of post-World War II mild globalization, characterized by the tenets of embedded liberalism. This approach aims to restore equilibrium between the principles of social democracy and an open global economy.

China's full embrace of hyperglobalization, owing to its substantial size and influence, has significantly contributed to the global regression of democratic norms on a global scale and complicated the country's own transition to a democratic system. Accurately assessing China's development is now an urgent task for Western policymakers, as the "against democracy" implications of globalization have reverberated worldwide.[7] To make globalization better—*pro-developmental* rather than *anti-developmental*—and thus make the world safe for democracy rather than autocracy, decoupling (at least partially) from the China, whose conduct has inspired the United States and perhaps the entire Western world to "distrust and verify,"[8] is vitally necessary, and might ultimately turn China toward inclusive growth and democratic transformation in the long term.

It is essential to clarify that advocating decoupling between the West and China should not aim to force complete compradorization of China, as some U.S. elites suggest. Instead, it should serve as a catalyst for political transformation within China. A combination of decoupling and a renewed focus on democracy promotion is needed to potentially create an environment conducive to global democracy.

[6] Frieden, J. A. (2020): *Global Capitalism—Its Fall and Rise in the Twentieth Century, and Its Stumbles in the Twenty-First*. New York: W. W. Norton & Company, p. 503.

[7] Wu, G (2017): *Globalization against Democracy: A Political Economy of Capitalism after its Global Triumph.*

[8] "Distrust and verify: Pompeo refits Cold War slogan for China." *Nikkei Asia*, 24/07/2020. https://asia.nikkei.com/Politics/International-relations/Distrust-and-verify-Pompeo-refits-Cold-War-slogan-for-China.

Amidst the evolving landscape of the global political economy, China's continued rise—which is nevertheless reversible—depends in large part on the efforts the country's elites might make to seek alternative paths of development to replace the existing liberal globalization approach. Such a path would of necessity be predicated upon belatedly realizing Francis Fukuyama's extravagant 1992 prophecy about the future of humanity, by introducing the rule of law and democracy at home and relying in international affairs on diplomacy rather than propaganda, disinformation, and force.

Lacking a visionary perspective and effective statecraft, Xi's China now seems poised to strive in the coming decades for a Cold Peace with the United States and the world of democracies—not necessarily to "rejuvenate the Chinese nation," but first and foremost to ensure the survival of its decrepit Leninist Leviathan.[9]

Faced with concerns about decoupling and displaying resistance to liberal democracy, Xi Jinping appears both unprepared and unwilling to initiate a comprehensive overhaul of the party-state institutions necessary for establishing a "democratic developmental state." This transformation is the most pragmatic option in the post-Cold War era to free the country from dependent development. Instead, Xi continues to solidify China's crony comprador capitalism—a system now marked by totalitarianism and kleptocracy. This approach not only fulfills the prophecy of a new Cold War but also lays the groundwork for a foreseeable future characterized by China's "imperial decline," as its peaceful ascent reaches its limits and stagnates.

[9] Yue, J. (2021): "The Limits to China's Peaceful Rise—Deep Integration and a New Cold War." *Global Policy*, 00, e13040. Available from: https://doi.org/10.1111/1758-5899.13040

References

A New Great Game—China, the U.S. and Technology—A Report by the China Senior Analyst Group, 13/10/2020. https://www.spglobal.com/_division_assets/images/special-editorial/a-new-great-game-china-the-u.s.-and-technology/2019_05_csag_uschina.pdf

A Record of Zhu Rongji's Remarks (2011): Beijing: Renmin Chubanshe, vols. 2–3.

Amsden, A. H. (1989): *Asia's Next Giant—South Korea and Late Industrialization*. New York: Oxford University Press.

Amsden, A. H. (2007): *Escape from Empire—The Developing World's Journey Through Heaven and Hell*. Cambridge: MIT Press.

(Anonymous): "The Longer Telegram—Toward a New American China Strategy." *The Atlantic Council*, 27/01/2021. https://www.atlanticcouncil.org/content-series/atlantic-council-strategy-paper-series/the-longer-telegram/

Barkai, A (1990): *Nazi Economics*. New Haven, CT: Yale University.

Bartel, F (2022): *The Triumph of Broken Promises—The End of the Cold War and the Rise of Neoliberalism*. Cambridge: Harvard University Press.

Beckley, M (2018): "The Power of Nations: Measuring What Matters." *International Security*, 43:2, pp. 7–44.

Beckley, M & Brands, H (2022): "The Return of Pax Americana? Putin's War Is Fortifying the Democratic Alliance." *Foreign Affairs*. https://www.foreignaffairs.com/articles/russia-fsu/2022-03-14/return-pax-americana

Bennett, Bruce W.: "Preparing for the Possibility of a North Korean Collapse." RAND Report Issued on Sep 19, 2013. https://www.rand.org/pubs/research_reports/RR331.html

J. Yue, *Crony Comprador Capitalism*,
https://doi.org/10.1007/978-3-031-53154-5

Black, J. S. & Morrison, A. J. (2021): "The Strategic Challenges of Decoupling." *Harvard Business Review* (May–June), 99:3, pp. 49–54.

Blackwill, R. D. & Tellis, A. J. (2015): "Revising U.S. Grand Strategy Toward China." *Council on Foreign Relations* Special Report released in April. https://www.cfr.org/report/revising-U.S.-grand-strategy-toward-china

Brands, H & Beckley, M: "China Is a Declining Power—and That's the Problem." *Foreign Policy*, 24/09/2021. https://foreignpolicy.com/2021/09/24/china-great-power-united-states/

Brown, A (2020): *The Human Factor—Gorbachev, Reagan, and Thatcher, and the End of the Cold War*. Oxford: Oxford University Press.

Buzan, B (2010): "China in International Society: Is 'Peaceful Rise' Possible?" *The Chinese Journal of International Politics*, 3:1, pp. 5–36.

Cardwell, C (2011): *NSC 68 and the Political Economy of the Early Cold War*. Cambridge, NJ: Cambridge University Press.

CGPSE Report (2015): "*Is the Private Sector More Efficient? A Cautionary Tale*," by UNDP Global Center for Public Service Excellence (GCPSE).

Chan, C. L. (2015): "Fallen Behind: Science, Technology, and Soviet Statism." *Intersect*, 8:3, pp. 1–11.

Chan, J (2020): "A Precarious Worker-Student Alliance in Xi's China." *The China Review*, 20:1, pp. 165–190.

Chang, H. J. (2003): *Kicking Away the Ladder—Development Strategy in Historical Perspectives*. London: Anthem Press.

Chang, H. J. (2010): "Hamlet Without the Prince of Denmark: How Development Has Disappeared from the 'Development' Discourse?" in Khan, S. R. and Christiansen (2011) (ed.), *Towards New Developmentalism—Markets as Means Rather than Master*. London: Routledge, pp. 65–76.

Chang, H. J. & Grabel, I (2004): *Reclaiming Development—An Alternative Economic Policy Manual*. London: Zed Book.

Chen, F (1997): *The Wrath of Heaven*. Hohhot: Yuanfang Chubanshe.

Chen, M (2001): "A Cost-Effect Analysis of FDI in China." *Strategy and Management*, No. 3, pp. 93–103.

Chen, M and Yue, J (2002): "Exchange Market Share for Technology? An Analysis of China's Strategy in Absorbing FDI." *Modern China Studies*, No. 4, pp. 93–100.

Chen, X: "Lessons from Sino-Soviet Territorial Negotiations in the Mao Zedong Era." *Mirror-History*, 05/07/2012. http://www.mingjinglishi.com/2012/07/blog-post_2890.html

Chen, Y (2013): *A Memoire*. Hong Kong: New Century Publisher.

Cheng, X (2003): "Reinterpreting China's Miracle: Dynamism and Consequences of Economic Growth." *Modern China Studies*, No. 1, pp. 25–46.

Cheng, Y (2011): "From Campus Racism to Cyber Racism: Discourse of Race and Chinese Nationalism." *The China Quarterly*, No. 201, pp. 561–579.

Ching Cheong: “How the CCP’s Crony Capitalism Came into Being?” *HK: ejinsight*, 29/05/2014. http://forum.hkej.com/nodel/113277
Chow, C. K. (2016): “How the United States Uses the Trans-Pacific Partnership to Contain China in International Trade.” *Chicago Journal of International Law*, 17:2, pp. 370–402.
Chwieroth, J (2007): “Neoliberal Economists and Capital Account Liberalization in Emerging Markets.” *International Organization*, 61:2, pp. 443–463.
Clarivate Top 100 Global Innovators 2023 Report (Released on 16/02/2023): https://clarivate.com/wp-content/uploads/dlm_uploads/2023/02/XBU975564118_Top-100-Innovators_Report_V7.2_singlepages.pdf
Communist Manifesto: https://www.marxists.org/archive/marx/works/1848/communist-manifesto/ch02.htm
Cox, M (2022): *Agonies of Empire—American Power from Clinton to Biden*. Bristol: Bristol University Press.
Deng Xiaoping Nianpu (1975–1997) (II), Zhongyang Wenxian Yanjiushi (Beijing), 2004. http://news.china.com/history/all/11025807/20120301/17066016.html
“Deng Xiaoping’s Southern Tour Remarks” [Original]. *zhongwaiguanli* (《中外管理》), 20/07/2016. https://k.sina.cn/article_1790671321_6abb79d9022001lah.html
Dieter, H & Biedermann, J (2022): “The New Advocacy for Autarky: Self-sufficiency Is Now Once Again Becoming Popular for Geopolitical Reasons.” *Economists’ Voice*, 19:2, pp. 125–145.
Dikötter, F (2022): *China After Mao—The Rise of a Superpower*. London: Bloomsbury.
Ding Dong: “The Archive Incident Concerning Zeng Shan During the Cultural Revolution.” http://www.hybsl.cn/beijingcankao/beijingfenxi/2013-05-15/37151.html
Djilas, M (1957): *The New Class—An Analysis of the Communist System*. Orlando: Harcourt Brace Jovanovich Publishers.
Dosh, R: “The Chinese Communist Party Has Always Been Nationalist—China’s Quest for Rejuvenation Dates Back More Than a Century.” *Foreign Policy*, 01/07/2021. https://foreignpolicy.com/2021/07/01/chinese-communist-party-nationalist-centennial/
(Economist) “China’s Industrial Policy: Plan v Market.” *The Economist*, 05/11/2016. https://www.economist.com/finance-and-economics/2016/11/05/plan-v-market
(Economist) “Capitalism Needs a Welfare State to Survive.” *The Economist*, 12/07/2018. https://www.economist.com/leaders/2018/07/12/capitalism-needs-a-welfare-state-to-survive?fsrc=scn/tw/te/bl/ed/capitalismneedsawelfarestatetosurvivebacktobasics

(Economist) "China Is Betting That the West Is in Irreversible Decline." *The Economist*, 31/03/2021. https://www.economist.com/china/2021/03/31/china-is-betting-that-the-west-is-in-irreversible-decline

(Economist) "Peak China?" *The Economist*, 13/05/2023. https://www.economist.com/weeklyedition/2023-05-13;//www.economist.com/leaders/2023/05/11/is-chinese-power-about-to-peak

(Economist) "A Conversation with Henry Kissinger." *The Economist*, 17/05/2023. https://www.economist.com/kissinger-transcript

Elleman, B. A. (2021): *International Rivalry and Secret Diplomacy in East Asia, 1896–1950*. London: Routledge. Preface.

Endo, H (2015): *Mao Zedong—The Man Who Conspired with the Japanese Army*. The Chinese Version of this Book Was Published by Mirror Books Based in New York.

Etzioni, A: "Making a U.S.-Sino War 'Thinkable'?" *The Diplomat*, 22/09/2016. https://thediplomat.com/2016/09/making-a-U.S.-sino-war-thinkable/

Evans, P (1979): *Dependent Development: The Alliance of Multinational, State, and Local Capital in Brazil*. NJ: Princeton University Press.

Fahnbulleh, M (2020): "The Neoliberal Collapse—Markets Are Not the Answer." *Foreign Affairs*, Jan/Feb, 99:1, pp. 38–43.

Farley, R: "How Does Industrial Espionage Affect Economic Growth?" *The Diplomat*, 15/1/2017. https://thediplomat.com/2017/01/how-does-industrial-espionage-affect-economic-growth/

Ferguson, N: "America and China Are Entering the Dark Forest." *Bloomberg Opinion*, 05/07/2020. https://www.bloomberg.com/opinion/articles/2020-07-05/is-the-u-s-in-a-new-cold-war-china-has-already-declared-it

Ferraro, V (2008): "Dependency Theory: An Introduction," in Secondi, G. (ed.), *The Development Economics Reader*. London: Routledge.

Fitzgerald, M (2006): *Adolf Hitler—A Portrait*. Chalford: Spellmount, p. 142.

Frieden, J. A. (2020): *Global Capitalism—Its Fall and Rise in the Twentieth Century, and Its Stumbles in the Twenty-First*. New York, NY: W. W. Norton.

Frum, D: "China Is a Paper Dragon." *The Atlantic*, 03/05/2021. https://www.theatlantic.com/ideas/archive/2021/05/china-paper-dragon/618778/

Fu, Bo (2013): "China's Interests in the Korean Peninsula." *Leaders* (Hong Kong), 52:3, pp. 61–64.

Fukuyama Interview: "Socialism Ought to Come Back." *NEW Statesman*, 17/10/2018. https://www.newstatesman.com/politics/2018/10/francis-fukuyama-interview-socialism-ought-come-back

Garthoff, R (1992): "Why Did the Cold War Arise, and Why Did It End." *Diplomatic History*, Spring, 16:2, pp. 287–293.

Gewirtz, J (2017): "The Little-Known Story of Milton Friedman in Chin." Policy Report of CATO Institute, September/October. https://www.cato.org/policy-report/september/october-2017/little-known-story-milton-friedman-china

Gilboy, G. J. (2004): "The Myth Behind China's Miracle." *Foreign Affairs*, July/Aug, 83:4, pp. 33–48.

Goncharov, Sergey N. and Li Danhui (2002): "'Territorial Claims' and 'Unequal Treaties' in Russia-China Relations." *Twenty-First Century*, No. 85 (October), pp. 110–117.

Gong, S (2018): Interview with Steve Bannon, 29/09/. https://news.mingpao.com/pns/%e5%9c%8b%e9%9a%9b/article/20180919/s00014/1537295686959/%e7%8f%ad%e8%be%b2-%e4%b8%ad%e7%be%8e%e8%b2%bf%e6%98%93%e6%88%b0%e5%bf%85%e7%84%b6%e6%89%93%e5%88%b0%e5%ba%95-%e6%89%ad%e8%bd%89%e9%80%86%e5%b7%ae%e7%82%ba%e6%94%bf%e7%ad%96%e6%a0%b8%e5%bf%83-%e3%80%8c%e7%89%b9%e6%9c%97%e6%99%ae%e5%b0%8d%e8%8f%af%e5%a7%8b%e7%b5%82%e5%a6%82%e4%b8%80%e3%80%8d

Grabas, C & Nutzenadel, A (2014): *Industrial Policy in Europe After 1945—Wealth, Power and Economic Development in the Cold War*. London: Palgrave Macmillan.

Greenfield, G & Leong, A (1997): "China's Communist Capitalism: The Real World of Market Socialism." *Socialist Register*, Mar 18. https://socialistregister.com/index.php/srv/article/view/5684

Gropman, Alan L: "America Needs to Prepare for a Great Power War," *The National Interest*, 07/02/2018. http://nationalinterest.org/feature/america-needs-prepare-great-power-war-24392

Gutmann, E (2005): *Losing the New China: A Story of American Commerce, Desire and Betrayal*. New York: Encounter Books.

Haggard, S (2018): *Developmental States*. Cambridge: Cambridge University Press.

Harvey, D (2007): *A History of Neoliberalism*. New York: Oxford University Press.

He, A (CIGI Senior Fellow): "What Do China's High Patent Numbers Really Mean?" 20/04/2021. https://www.cigionline.org/articles/what-do-chinas-high-patent-numbers-really-mean/

He, Q (1998): *The Pitfalls of Modernization*. Beijing Jingji Zhongguo Chubanshe.

He, Qinglian: "30 Years of Reform: The Abnormal Development of State Capacity and Its Consequences." *Modern China Studies*, No. 4, 2008.

Helleiner, E (2021): "The Return of National Sufficiency? Excavating Autarkic Thought in a De-globalizing Era." *International Studies Review*, 23:3, pp. 933–957.

Ho, W. C. (2013): "The New 'Comprador Class': The Re-emergence of Bureaucratic Capitalists in Post-Deng China." *Journal of Contemporary China*, 22:83, pp. 812–827.

Hsiao, F, Lawrence, R, Sullivan, L. R. (1979): "The Chinese Communist Party and the Status of Taiwan, 1928–1943." *Public Affairs*, 52:3, pp. 446–467.

Huang, Y (2003): *Selling China—Foreign Direct Investment During the Reform Era*. New York: Cambridge University Press.

Huang, Y (2008): *Capitalism with Chinese Characteristics—Entrepreneurship and the State*. New York: Cambridge University Press.

Huang, Yifeng, et al (1982): *The Comprador Class in Old China*. Shanghai: Shanghai People's Press.

Ikenberry, J (2011): *Liberal Levithan: The Origins, Crisis, and Transformation of the American World Order*. Princeton, NJ: Princeton University Press.

Ikenberry, J (2020): *A World Safe for Democracy—Liberal Internationalism and the Crises of Global Order*. New Haven: Yale University Press.

Jain-Chandra, S, et al (2018): "Inequality in China—Trends, Drivers and Policy Remedies." *IMF Working Paper* (WP/18/127), June. https://www.imf.org/~/media/Files/Publications/WP/2018/wp18127.ashx

Jepson, N (2019): *In China's Wake—How the Commodity Boom Transformed Development Strategies in the Global South*. New York: Columbia University Press.

Johnson, C (1999): "The Developmental State: Odyssey of a Concept," in Meredith Woo-Cuming (ed.), *The Developmental State*. Ithaca and London: Cornell University Press.

Kang, See-Way (2008): "The Root Cause of East-Turkistan Issue: A Study of Xinjiang's 'Three Regions' Revolution'." *Prospect & Exploration* (Taiwan), 6:10, p. 59.

Kaplan, Fred: "Don't Pick a Cold War You Can't Win." *Slate*, 24/07/2020. https://slate.com/news-and-politics/2020/07/pompeo-china-cold-war.html

Kennedy, S: "China's Uneven High-Tech Drive: Implications for the United States." *CSIS*, 27/02/2020. https://www.csis.org/analysis/chinas-uneven-high-tech-drive-implications-united-states

Khan, S. R. & Christiansen, J (2011): *Towards New Developmentalism—Markets Are Means Rather Than Master*. Routledge.

Kiely, R (2006): *New Political Economy of Development: Globalization, Imperialism, Hegemony*. Oxon: Palgrave.

Kitchen, N (2020): "Why American Grand Strategy Has Changed." *Global Affairs*, 6:1, pp. 87–104.

Kitchen, N and Cox, M (2019): "Power, Structural Power, and American Decline." *Cambridge Review of International Affairs*, 32:6, pp. 734–752.

Klare, M. T.: "'Congagement' with China?—GOP Hawks Want Containment; Others Favor More Trade and More Toughness." *The Nation*, 12/04/2001. https://www.thenation.com/article/archive/congagement-china/

Klare, M. T. (2011): *The Race for What's Left: The Global Scramble for the World's Last Resources*. New York: Metropolitan Books.

Kornai, J (1992): *The Socialist System: The Political Economy of Communism*. Oxford: Clarendon Press.

Kroenig, M (2020): *The Return of Great Power Rivalry, Democracy Versus Autocracy from the Ancient World to the U.S. and China*. Oxford: Oxford University Press.

Krugman, P: "What Happened to Japan?—What Japan's Economy Can Tell Us About China?" *The New York Times*, 25/07/2023. https://www.nytimes.com/2023/07/25/opinion/japan-china-economy.html

Kurlantzick, J (2016): *State Capitalism—How the Return of Statism Is Transforming the World*. Oxford: Oxford University Press.

Kvangraven, I. H. (2017): "The Relevance of Dependent Development—Then and Now: Peter Evans," in Kvangraven, et al (ed.), *Dialogues on Development Volume 1: Dependency* (eBook). NY: Institute for New Economic Thinking.

Kwong, P (2006): "The Chinese Face of Neoliberalism," Oct. 7. https://www.counterpunch.org/2006/10/07/the-chinese-face-of-neoliberalism/

Lamy, P (2013): *The Geneva Consensus—Making Trade Works for All*. Cambridge University Press.

Lardy, N (1995): "The Role of Foreign Trade and Investment in China's Economic Transformation." *The China Quarterly* 144 (Dec.): 1065–1082.

Lardy, N (2002): *Integrating China into the Global Economy*. Washington: Brookings Institution Press.

Leonard, M & Shapiro, J (2020): "Sovereign Europe, Dangerous World: Five Agendas to Protect Europe's Capacity to Act." European Council on Foreign Relations (ECFR) Report, Dec. 1. https://ecfr.eu/publication/sovereign-europe-dangeroU.S.-world-five-agendas-to-protect-europes-capacity-to-act/

Li, Cheng (2012): "The End of the CCP's Resilient Authoritarianism? A Tripartite Assessment of Shifting Power in China." *The China Quarterly*, 211, pp. 595–623.

Li, C & Xu, L: "Chinese Enthusiasm and American Cynicism over the 'New Concept of Great Power Relations." *Brookings Commentary*, 04/12/2014. https://www.brookings.edu/articles/chinese-enthusiasm-and-american-cynicism-over-the-new-type-of-great-power-relations/

Li Danhui: "The Truth of the Zhenbao (Damansky) Island—An Investigation into Sino—Soviet Border Relations." 10/04/2010. https://www.aisixiang.com/data/36173.html

Li, Jiagu (1998): "On the Signing of 'Soviet-Japanese Neutrality Treaty' and Its Actual Influence on China's War of Resistance." *The Journal of Studies of China's Resistance War Against Japan*, No. 1, pp. 56–75.
Li Rui (1989): *A True Record of Lushan Conference*. Beijing: Chunqiu Chubanshe.
Lin, C (2008): "China: Changing the Rules of the Game." *Soundings*, 39:1, 7–19.
Lind, M (2012): *Land of Promise: An Economic History of the United States*. New York: Harper Collins.
Liu, Ji (1997): "Who Is the Marshall Today? The Choice of Sino-U.S. Relations in the 21st Century." *Zaobao*, 23/10/1997.
Lord, W (1989): "China and America: Beyond the Big Chill," *Foreign Affairs*, Fall, 68:4, pp. 1–26.
Luo, Y (2015): *Bidding Farewell to the General Staff*. Hong Kong: Open Books.
Lyman, P. Van Slyke (ed.) (1968): *The Chinese Communist Movement—A Report to U.S. War Department*. Redwood: Stanford University Press, pp. 101–102.
Lyon, R: "Is Major War Obsolete?" *The Strategist*, ASPI (Australia Strategic Policy Institute), 19/08/2014. https://www.aspistrategist.org.au/is-major-war-obsolete/
Mandelbaum, M (2019): "The New Containment—Handling Russia, China, and Iran." *Foreign Affairs*, Mar/Apr, 98:2, pp. 123–131.
"Mao Apologised to Yugoslavian Delegates, Told Stalin Blocked Our Revolution." *Other Aspect*, posted on 11/08/2015. https://otheraspect.org/category/revisionism-of-mao/
Mao Zedong's Manuscripts Since the Founding of the People's Republic of China. Beijing: Zhongyang Wenxian Chubanshe, 1998, 13, p. 32.
Mason, T (1993): *Social Policy in the Third Reich*. Oxford: Berg.
Mastanduno, M (1997): "Preserving the Unipolar Moment: Realist Theories and U.S. Grand Strategy After the Cold War." *International Security*, 21:4, pp. 49–88.
Maxell, N (1970): *India's China War*. London: Pelican.
McMaster, H. R. (2020a): "How China Sees the World and How We Should See China." *The Atlantic*, May issue.
McMaster, H. R. (2020b): *Battlegrounds: The Fight to Defend the Free World*. London: William Collins.
Mearsheimer, J (2021): "The Inevitable Rivalry—America, China, and the Tragedy of Great-power Politics." *Foreign Affairs*, Nov–Dec, 100:6, pp. 48–58
Medeiros, Evan S & Fravel, M. Taylor (2003): "China's New Diplomacy." *Foreign Affairs*, Nov/Dec, 82:6, pp. 22–35.
Meisner, M (1996): *The Deng Xiaoping Era: An Inquiry into the Fate of Chinese Socialism, 1978–1994*. New York: Hill & Wang

Myrdal, G (1968): *Asian Drama—An Inquiry into the Poverty of Nations*. London: Allen Lane The Penguin Press.
Nathan, A. J. (2003): "China's Changing of the Guard: Authoritarian Resilience." *Journal of Democracy*, 14:1, pp. 6–17.
Nealer, K. G.: "*Trading Iron Curtain for Chinese Walls: Is It Different This Time?*" in CSIS Report: "China's Uneven High-tech Drive." 27/02/2020, pp. 47–50. https://www.csis.org/analysis/chinas-uneven-high-tech-drive-implications-united-states
Nixon, Richard (1989): "Crisis in Sino-American Relations." *Times*, Nov. 20, pp. 45–49.
Nolan, P (2001a): "China, the U.S. and the WTO: Battle of the Giants or Defeat of the Pygmies" (Manuscript).
Nolan, P (2001b): *China and Global Economy: National Champions, Industrial Policy, and the Big Business Revolution*. London: Palgrave.
Nye, J (2015): *Is the American Century Over?* Cambridge: Polity Press.
Obama, B (2021): *A Promised Land*. New York: Viking.
OECD Data: Income Inequality. https://data.oecd.org/inequality/income-inequality.htm
Olson, M (1982): *The Rise and Decline of Nations: Economic Growth, Stagflation, and Social Rigidities*. New Haven: Yale University Press.
Overholt, W (2005): China and Globalization—Testimony Before the U.S.-China economic and Security Commission, RAND, released on 19/05/2005.
Palmer, J: "Xi Jinping Shows His Nerves Over Decoupling." *Foreign Policy*, 27/01/2021. https://foreignpolicy.com/2021/01/27/xi-jinping-davos-world-economic-forum-speech-china-decoupling/
Paulson, H. M. (2015): *Dealing with China—An Insider Unmasks the New Economic Superpower*. New York: Headline.
Pei, M (2016): *China's Crony Capitalism—The Dynamics of Regime Decay*. Cambridge: Harvard University Press.
Pilsbury, M (2015): *The Hundred-Year Marathon: China's Secret Strategy to Replace America as the Global Superpower*. New York: Henry Holt and Co.
Pomeranz, K (2001): "Is there an East Asian Development Path?" *Journal of the Economic and Social History of the Orient*, 44:3, pp. 322–362.
Qi, B (2016): *A Memoir of Qi Benyu*. Hong Kong: 中国文革历史出版社, pp. 669–670.
Quah, D. (2011): "The Global Economy's Shifting Centre of Gravity." *Global Policy*, 2:1, pp. 3–9.
Rachman, M. (2011): "Think Again—This Time, It's for Real." *Foreign Policy*, 03/01/2011. Available at: https://foreignpolicy.com/2011/01/03/think-again-american-decline/

RAND Report (2016): "War with China: Thinking through the Unthinkable." https://www.rand.org/content/dam/rand/pubs/research_reports/RR1100/RR1140/RAND_RR1140.pdf

RAND Report (2017): "U.S. Military Capabilities and Forces for a Dangerous World—Rethinking the U.S. Approach to Force Planning." https://www.rand.org/pubs/research_reports/RR1782.html

Red Flag Manuscript (<红旗文稿>): "Time and Momentum are on Our Side." 11/03/2021. http://www.qstheory.cn/dukan/hqwg/2021-03/11/c_1127198200.htm

Reeve, C's Review on Yiching Wu's The Cultural Revolution at the Margins: Chinese Socialism in Crisis, published on H-Socialisms (October 2015). https://www.h-net.org/reviews/showrev.php?id=43036

Renato Cruz De Castro (2013): "The Obama Administration's Strategic Pivot to Asia: From a Diplomatic to a Strategic Constrainment of an Emergent China?" *The Korean Journal of Defense Analysis*, September, 25:3, pp. 331–349.

Research Group of the Chinese Academy of History (2022): "A New Exploration on the Issue of 'Self-exclusion' in the Ming and Qing Dynasties." *History Research*, No. 3, pp. 4–21.

Rodrik, D (2011): *The Globalization Paradox: Why Global Markets, States and Democracy Can't Co-exist*. Oxford: Oxford University Press.

Rosecrance, R & Miller, S (2015): *The Next Great War? The Roots of World War I and the Risk of U.S.-China Conflict*. Cambridge, MA: The MIT Press.

Sally, R (1998): *Classical Liberalism and International Economic Order—Studies in Theory and Intellectual History*. London: Routledge, pp. 38–39.

Sarotte, M. E. (2021): *Not One Inch—America, Russia and the Making of Post-Cold War Stalemate*. New Haven: Yale University Press.

Saussy, H (2001): *Great Walls of Discourse and Other Adventures in Cultural China*. 1st ed., vol. 212, Harvard University Asia Center.

Schuman, M: "Don't Believe the China Hype." *The Atlantic*, 16/06/2020. https://www.theatlantic.com/international/archive/2020/06/united-states-china-power-influence/612961/

Segal, G (1999): "Does China Matter?" *Foreign Affairs*, 78:5, pp. 24–36.

Selected Works of Deng Xiaoping, Vol. 3, Beijing: Renmin Chubanshe, 1993.

Shen Zhihua (2017): *The Last "Celestial Empire"—Mao Zedong, Kim Il-Sung and Sino-North Korean Relations (1945-76)*. Hong Kong: The Chinese University Press.

Shum, D (2021): *Red Roulette—An Insider's Story of Wealth, Power, Corruption and Vengeance in Today's China*. London: Simon & Schuster.

Søndergaard, R. S. (2015): "Bill Clinton's 'Democratic Enlargement' and the Securitisation of Democracy Promotion." *Diplomacy & Statecraft*, 26:3, pp. 534–551.

Song, Yongyi (ed.) (2018): *Newly Discovered Talks of Mao Zedong in Confidential Archives*. New York: Guoshi Chubanshe.
Starrs, S (2013): "American Economic Power Hasn't Declined—It Globalized! Summoning the Data and Taking Globalization Seriously." *International Studies Quarterly*, 57, pp. 817–830.
Steinfeld, E (2010): *Playing Our Game—Why China's Rise Doesn't Threaten the West*. Oxford, NY: Oxford University Press.
Stiglitz, J (2003): *Making Globalization Work: The Next Step to Global Justice*. London: Penguin Books.
Su, Nan (2021): "How to Break the 'Disadvantage of Backwardness' of China's Upgrading of Machine Tool Industry." *China's Science and Technology*, No. 4, pp. 1–4.
Sutton, A. C. (1972): *National Suicide: Military Aid to the Soviet Union*. LV: Dauphin Publications Inc.
Thun, E (2006): *Changing Lanes in China: Foreign Direct Investment, Local Governments, and Auto Sector Development*. New York: Cambridge University Press.
Tocqueville, Alexis de ([1856] 2011): *The Old Regime and the Revolution*, edited by Jon Elsetr. Cambridge: Cambridge University Press.
Tooze, A (2006): *The Wages of Destruction: The Making and Breaking of the Nazi Economy*. London: Penguin Books, p. 512.
Tooze, A: "America Has Dictated Its Economic Peace Terms to China." *Foreign Policy*, 24/04/2023. https://foreignpolicy.com/2023/04/24/america-has-dictated-its-economic-peace-terms-to-china/
Tsai, J. F. (1981): "The Predicament of the Comprador Ideologists: He Qi (Ho Kai, 1859–1914) and Hu Liyuan (1847–1916)." *Modern China*, 7:2, pp. 191–225.
USCC Report: "Supply Chain Vulnerabilities from China in U.S. Federal Information and Communications Technology." (April 2018), released on 19/04/2018. https://www.uscc.gov/sites/default/files/Research/Interos_Supply%20Chain%20Vulnerabilities%20from%20China%20in%20U.S.%20Federal%20ICT.pdf
USTR's 2021 National Trade Estimate Report on Foreign Trade Barriers (NTE), released on 31/03/2021. https://ustr.gov/sites/default/files/files/reports/2021/2021NTE.pdf; USTR: Rebalancing U.S.-China Trade: https://ustr.gov/phase-one
Wade, R (2003a): "What Strategies Are Viable for Developing Countries Today? The World Trade Organization and the Shrinking of 'Development Space.'" *Review of International Political Economy*, 10:4, pp. 621–644.
Wade, R (2003b): *Governing the Market—Economic Theory and the Role of Government in East Asian Industrialization* (2nd ed.). NJ: Princeton University Press.

Wallerstein, I (1992): "The Concept of National Development." *The American Behavioral Scientist*, 35:4, pp. 517–529.

Walter, A and Sen, G (2003): *Analyzing the Global Political Economy*. New York: Princeton University Press.

Wang, J (2005): "China's Search for Stability with America." *Foreign Affairs*, Sept/Oct, 84:5, pp. 39–48.

Wang, L (1998): *Sky Burial: The Fate of Tibet*. New York: Mirror Books.

Wang, L (2000): "The 'Mao Zedong Complex' at the Bottom of Chinese Society and Undercurrents." *Modern China Studies*, Issue 3.

Wang Xiaodong (in penname Shi Zhong) (1995): "We Should Not Push the Logic of Comparative Advantage to the Extreme." *Strategy and Management*, No. 3, pp. 11–15.

Wang, Xiaodong, et al (1999): *China's Road Under the Shadow of Globalization*. Beijing: Zhongguo Shehui Kexue Chubanshe.

Wang Xiaodong Revealed this Inside Story When Addressing the Audience in a Public Lecture at the London School of Economics, titled "Chinese Nationalism under the Shadow of Globalization," dated 07/02/2005. https://digital.library.lse.ac.uk/objects/lse:mih335foy

Wang, Xizhe: "China's Bureaucratic Bourgeoisie and the Insights of Chen Yun—An Interview with Yan Huai." *Mingjing News*, 07/07/2018. https://www.mingjingnews.com/article/91551-80

Watkins, P: "Introduction: A Three-Pillar Strategic Framework for Competing with China," in "*Protect, Constrain, Contest Approaches for Coordinated Transatlantic Economic And Technological Competition with China*." LSE IDEAS China Foresight Project (hereafter called "LSE-IDEAS Report 2021"), Jan, 2021. https://www.lse.ac.uk/ideas/Assets/Documents/reports/LSE-IDEAS-Protect-Constrain-Contest.pdf

Wei Jinqiao: "A Failed 'Market for Technology' Strategy." *The Financial Times* (Chinese version), 20/04/2011. http://www.ftchinese.com/story/001038180?full=y&archive

Wellington Koo Memoirs (Chinese Version), vol. 2. Beijing: Chunghwa Book.

Werner, J: "China Is Cheating at a Rigged Game." *Foreign Policy*, 08/08/2018. Available at: https://foreignpolicy.com/2018/08/08/china-is-cheating-at-a-rigged-game/

Westad, O. A. (2019): "The Sources of Chinese Conduct—Are Washington and Beijing Fighting a New Cold War?" *Foreign Affairs*, Sep/Oct, 98:5, pp. 86–95.

Westad, O. A.: "Identity Politics with Chinese Characteristics—How the CCP's Quest to Define 'China' Shapes Beijing's Agenda." *Foreign Affairs*, 01/06/2021. https://www.foreignaffairs.com/reviews/review-essay/identity-politics-chinese-characteristics

Wolf, M: "How China Can Avoid the Japan Trap?" *The Financial Times*, 26/09/2023. https://www.ft.com/content/156c092a-4313-48cc-8103-79bb26c0faaa

World Development Report 2012: https://doi.org/10.1596/978-0-8213-8810-5

Wright, T: "Pompeo's Surreal Speech on China." *Brookings Commentary*, 27/07/2020. https://www.brookings.edu/articles/pompeos-surreal-speech-on-china/

Wu, G (2017): *Globalization Against Democracy—A Political Economy of Capitalism After Its Global Triumph*. Cambridge: Cambridge University Press.

Wu Haoyang and Li Ping (2021): "Analyzing China's Industrial Structure—Does China Really Have 'All the Industrial Categories Listed in the United Nations Industry Classification System'?" *Ceibs Business Review*, No. 6, pp. 76–82.

Wu, J & Ma, G (2012): *Twenty Issue on China's Economic Reform*. Beijing: Sanlian Bookstore.

Wu, Jinglian, et al (1989): *Corruption: An Exchange Between Currency and Power*. Beijing: China Outlook Publishing House. The second edition of this book was renamed *Corruption: An Exchange Between Power and Money*, published by Chinese Economics Publishing House in 1993. The third edition was published by the same publisher in 1999 and renamed *In Search of Roots for Corruption: Will China Become a Rent-seeking Society?*

Wu, Y (2014): *The Cultural Revolution at the Margins: Chinese Socialism in Crisis*. Cambridge: Harvard University Press.

Xu, Z (David Tsui) (2015): *China's Military Intervention in Korea: Its Origins and Objectives*. Bloomington: Trafford Publishing.

Yan, H (2017): *In and Out of the Central Organization Department*. New York: Mirror.

Yang, Degang: "The Ultimate Investigation on the Sino-Indian Border Issue." 19/04/2019. https://www.aisixiang.com/data/74079.html

Yang, J (2016): *The World Turned Upside Down?* Hong Kong: Cosmos Books.

Yang, Kuisong (2000): "The Initial Collision of National Interests and Emotions Between China and the Soviet Union—with the Signing of the 'Sino-Soviet Treaty of Friendship, Alliance and Mutual Assistance' as the Background." *Journal of Historical Research*, No. 6. https://xinguancha.net/?p=4214

Yu, A. L.: "*China: Bureaucratic Capitalist?*" An interview by Terry Conway with Yu, A. L., 07/11/2012. https://socialistresistance.org/china-bureaucratic-capitalist/4188

Yu, A. L.: (2014): "What Is the Nature of Capitalism in China? On the Rise of China and Its Inherent Contradictions," in Yu, A. L. et al., *China's Rise: Strength and Fragility*. Merlin: Resistance Book.

Yu, Luoke: "On Class Origins." 18/01/1967. https://www.marxists.org/chinese/reference-books/minjian-1966-1976/05.htm

Yue, J (2004): "A Bleak Prospect of China's Industrialization." *Dushu* (Beijing), July.
Yue, J (2008): "Peaceful Rise of China: Myth or Reality?" *International Politics*, 6:1, pp. 439–456.
Yue, J (2012): "What Does Globalisation Mean for China's Economic Development?" blog article on *Global Policy* Journal on May 24, 2012. You Can Access the Article Here: http://www.globalpolicyjournal.com/blog/24/05/2012/what-does-globalization-mean-china%e2%80%99s-economic-development
Yue, J (2014): "Has Globalization Led to China's Rise?" *Leaders*, No. 8, pp. 41–58.
Yue, J (2016): "China, Global Capitalism, and the Quest for Legitimacy." *International Politics*, 53:6, pp. 752–774.
Yue, J (2018): *China's Rise in the Age of Globalization: Myth or Reality?* London: Palgrave Macmillan.
Yue, J (2022): "The Limits to China's Rise—Deep Integration and a New Cold War." *Global Policy*, 13:1, pp. 91–106.
Zhang, Chunqiao (1976): "Why Must the Chinese People Oppose the Slavish Comprador Philosophy?" *Red Flag*, No. 4.
Zhang, Niangen (2011): "On the Changes of Chinese Legal System for Implementing the WTO Laws." *The Legist* (faxuejia), No. 1, pp. 9–18.
Zhang, Sheng (2008): *Coming out of the War—A Dialogue Between Two Generations of Soldiers*. Beijing: China Youth Press.
Zhang, W (1997): "Corruption: The Second Best If Not the First Best." In: *China's Economic Debate*. Beijing: Jingji Guanli Chubanshe.
Zhen-Gang Ji: "The South China Sea Island China Gave Away—Bach Long Vi Island and Its Secret Transfer from China to Vietnam." *The Diplomat*, 14/08/2019. https://thediplomat.com/2019/08/the-south-china-sea-island-china-gave-away/
Zheng, B (2005): "China's 'Peaceful Rise' to Great-Power Status." *Foreign Affairs*, September/October, 84:5, pp. 18–24.
Zong, F (2007): *Zhao Ziyang: Captive Conversation*. Hong Kong: Open Press.
Zou, J (2015): "The Debate on the Issue of 'Armed to Defend the Soviet Union' Between the Communist International and the Communist Party of China." *Advances in Social Sciences*, 4:4, pp. 225–229.
生活读书新知三联书店香港分店:《走资派就是党内的资产阶级》, 1976年。

Index

J. Yue, *Crony Comprador Capitalism*,
https://doi.org/10.1007/978-3-031-53154-5

D

H

M

T

SPRINGER NATURE

GPSR Compliance

The European Union's (EU) General Product Safety Regulation (GPSR) is a set of rules that requires consumer products to be safe and our obligations to ensure this.

If you have any concerns about our products, you can contact us on ProductSafety@springernature.com

In case Publisher is established outside the EU, the EU authorized representative is:

Springer Nature Customer Service Center GmbH
Europaplatz 3
69115 Heidelberg, Germany

The manufacturer's authorised representative in the EU is Springer Nature Customer Service Centre GmbH, Europaplatz 3, 69115 Heidelberg, Germany. If you have any concerns regarding our products, please contact ProductSafety@springernature.com

Printed and bound by CPI Group (UK) Ltd, Croydon, CR0 4YY

28/09/2026

02224062-0001